Turbocharging MS-DOS®

Caroline M. Halliday

que®

Turbocharging MS-DOS®

Copyright© 1991 by Que® Corporation.

All rights reserved. Printed in the United States of America. No part of this book may be used or reproduced in any form or by any means, or stored in a database or retrieval system, without prior written permission of the publisher except in the case of brief quotations embodied in critical articles and reviews. Making copies of any part of this book for any purpose other than your own personal use is a violation of United States copyright laws. For information, address Que Corporation, 11711 N. College Ave., Carmel, IN 46032.

Library of Congress Catalog No.: 91-61343

ISBN 0-88022-729X

This book is sold *as is*, without warranty of any kind, either express or implied, respecting the contents of this book, including but not limited to implied warranties for the book's quality, performance, merchantability, or fitness for any particular purpose. Neither Que Corporation nor its dealers or distributors shall be liable to the purchaser or any other person or entity with respect to any liability, loss, or damage caused or alleged to be caused directly or indirectly by this book.

94 93 92 91   4 3 2 1

Interpretation of the printing code: the rightmost double-digit number is the year of the book's printing; the rightmost single-digit number, the number of the book's printing. For example, a printing code of 91-1 shows that the first printing of the book occurred in 1991.

Turbocharging MS-DOS is based on MS-DOS through Version 5.0.

Publisher: Lloyd J. Short

Associate Publisher: Karen A. Bluestein

Acquisitions Manager: Terrie Lynn Solomon

Product Development Manager: Mary Bednarek

Managing Editor: Paul Boger

Book Designer: Scott Cook

Production Team: Martin Coleman, Sandy Grieshop, Betty Kish, Bob LaRoche, Sarah Leatherman, Howard Peirce, Tad Ringo, Suzanne Tully, Johnna VanHoose, Christine Young

For Ed Kidera, George Taylor, George Lemon, and Jon Wilson: who showed me the true potential of users' groups.

Product Director
David Solomon

Senior Editor
Sandra Blackthorn

Editors
Kelly Currie
Barbara K. Koenig
Mike La Bonne
Rob Lawson
Lori A. Lyons
Daniel Schnake
Susan Shaw

Technical Editor
David Knispel

*Composed in Garamond and Macmillan
by Que Corporation*

About the Author

Caroline M. Halliday

Caroline M. Halliday is an electrical engineer with High Tech Aid in the Chicago area. Her company specializes in technical documentation and teaching for the PC environment. She has a Bachelor of Science (Hons) degree from the University of Manchester, England, and is a former technical editor for *PC Tech Journal*. She is a contributing author of *MS-DOS User's Guide, Special Edition*, and *MS-DOS PC Tutor*, and she is the principal author of *Using OS/2*, all published by Que Corporation. She now contributes articles to various magazines, including *InfoWorld* and *Design Management*.

Trademark Acknowledgments

Que Corporation has made every effort to supply trademark information about company names, products, and services mentioned in this book. Trademarks indicated below were derived from various sources. Que Corporation cannot attest to the accuracy of this information.

1-2-3 and Lotus are registered trademarks of Lotus Development Corporation.

386-MAX and 386-to-the-MAX are trademarks of Qualitas, Inc.

AutoCAD is a registered trademark of Autodesk, Inc.

COMPAQ is a registered trademark of COMPAQ Computer Corporation.

dBASE IV is a trademark of Ashton-Tate Corporation.

DESQview is a trademark of Quarterdeck Office Systems.

HardCard is a trademark of Plus Development Corporation.

IBM is a registered trademark and Micro Channel and PS/2 are trademarks of International Business Machines Corporation.

Microsoft, Microsoft Windows, and MS-DOS are registered trademarks of Microsoft Corporation.

Norton Utilities is a trademark of Peter Norton Computing.

Paradox is a registered trademark of Ansa-Borland.

PC Tools Deluxe is a trademark of Central Point Software, Inc.

Quadram is a registered trademark of Quadram Corporation.

SideKick is a registered trademark of Borland International.

SpinRite is a trademark of Gibson Research Corporation.

Super PC-Kwik is a trademark of Multisoft Corporation.

WordPerfect is a registered trademark of WordPerfect Corporation.

WordStar is a registered trademark of WordStar International Incorporated.

Acknowledgments

I would like to thank the following people:

David Solomon, for continuing to believe in this book's viability and fighting for the cause. His technical assistance made the writing far easier.

My husband, Steve, and Jim Shields, for their advice, support, and expert knowledge.

Terrie Lynn Solomon and Stacey Beheler, for handling the administrative side with compassion and humor.

All the Que staff involved in this book's production, including Sandy Blackthorn, David Ewing, and Lloyd Short.

Contents at a Glance

Introduction 1

Part I Examining PC and DOS Basics

Chapter 1	Understanding the Personal Computer 11
Chapter 2	Understanding DOS 35
Chapter 3	Extending the Basic Standard 59

Part II Enhancing Disk Performance

Chapter 4	Examining Disk Architecture 97
Chapter 5	Employing Routine Maintenance 137
Chapter 6	Examining Disk Performance 191
Chapter 7	Improving Disk Performance 219

Part III Managing Memory Resources

Chapter 8	Using Device Drivers 249
Chapter 9	Stretching Your Resources 279
Chapter 10	Regaining Base Memory 309
Chapter 11	Using the Processor's Power 345
Chapter 12	Improving the Operating System 377

| Appendix A | Comparing DOS Versions .... 403 |
| Appendix B | Using Hexadecimal and Memory Addresses .... 415 |

Index 419

TABLE OF CONTENTS

Introduction 1
   Who Should Use This Book 2
   How To Use This Book 2
   What Is in This Book 3
   What Is Not in This Book 6
   What Are the Conventions in This Book 6
      Special Typefaces and Representations 6
      Command Syntax 7
      Mandatory vs. Optional Parts of Commands 8

Part I   Examining PC and DOS Basics

1   Understanding the Personal Computer 11
   Enhancing Computer Technology 12
   Understanding the Microprocessor 14
   Using Microprocessors in PCs 16
      Intel 8086 and 8088 17
      Intel 80286 18
      Intel 80386SX 18
      Intel 80386 19
      Intel 80486 19
   Addressing Memory Space 20
      Local Memory and I/O Bus Memory 21
      System Memory 21
   Using Basic Hardware Components 22
      Central Processing Unit 22
      Peripheral Devices 23
      Expansion Bus 24
      Video Subsystem 27
      Keyboard 29
   Chapter Summary 34

2   Understanding DOS 35
   Understanding the Operating System 36
   Using Variations of DOS 36
   Changing Versions of DOS 37
   Understanding the Parts of DOS 38
      The Command Interpreter 39
      The System Files 40

The BIOS	40
The DOS Utilities	41
Understanding the DOS Environment	41
Understanding DOS Functions	42
Booting DOS and Memory	43
Initializing the POST	44
Examining Common POST Errors	45
Analyzing POST Problems	47
Loading System Files	47
Examining DOS's Position in Memory	48
Starting Applications Programs	51
Device Drivers	53
Memory-Resident Programs	54
Chapter Summary	57

3 Extending the Basic Standard 59

Understanding Device Drivers	60
Dividing Device Drivers into Groups	62
Character Device Drivers	62
Block Device Drivers	63
Examining Resident and Installable Device Drivers	63
Resident Device Drivers	64
Installable Device Drivers	65
Adding Extended and Expanded Memory	68
Extended Memory	70
Expanded Memory	72
Keeping Up with Memory Expansion Boards	74
Selecting the Right Cache	75
Access Times	76
Disk Caching	76
Cache Controllers	78
Shadow RAM	79
386 Memory Managers	80
Keeping Track of Your System	80
Taking Small Steps	80
Breaking Down the Major Elements	81
Using Tools To Assist	82
Control Room	83
System Sleuth	89
Chapter Summary	92

Part II Enhancing Disk Performance

4 Examining Disk Architecture **97**
   Examining the Disk's Magnetic Storage Technique 98
   Understanding Disk Drives 99
      Hard Disk Drives 99
      Floppy Disk Drives 100
   Understanding Disk Drive Dynamics 101
      Disk Drive Heads 101
      Disk Tracks 102
      Disk Cylinders 103
      Seek Time 104
      Disk Drive Alignment 105
   Applying Drive Dynamics to Data Storage 105
      Track Density 106
      Data Density 107
      Disk Sectors 108
   Understanding Disk Formats 110
      Floppy Drive Formats 110
      Raw Capacity and Usable Capacity 112
      Hard Drive Formats 113
   Understanding Disk Partitions 116
   Examining How DOS Manages Disks and Files 119
      Understanding Storage Allocation Logging 120
      Understanding Coordinates and Logical Sectors 125
   Knowing What DOS Stores—The Directory 127
      Understanding the Root Directory and its Subdiretories 132
      Examining Subdirectories as Files 134
   Looking at DOS's File System from the Ground Up 134
   Chapter Summary 136

5 Employing Routine Maintenance **137**
   Examining Fragmentation of Files 138
   Analyzing a Disk with CHKDSK 139
      Understanding the Operation of CHKDSK 140
      Finding Lost Clusters with CHKDSK 142
      Using CHKDSK To Find Fragmented Files 144
      Using Third-Party Software To Defragment 146
         PC Tools' Compress Program 146
         Norton's Speed Disk Program 151
   Choosing Benchmarks 153

Assessing Hard Disk Performance	155
Changing a Hard Disk's Interleave	156
Low-Level Formatting with a ROM-Based Formatter	159
Low-Level Formatting with Disk Manager	164
Partitioning the Hard Disk	172
Using FDISK with DOS 3.2 and Earlier Versions	172
Using FDISK with DOS 3.3 and 4	174
Using FORMAT To Prepare the Hard Disk	177
Using SpinRite	179
Choosing the Best Interleave	179
Performing Routine Maintenance	188
Chapter Summary	190

6 Examining Disk Performance 191

Understanding the DOS Environment	192
Optimizing the PATH Sequence	194
Changing the Environment Size	196
Using Multiple PATH Settings	198
Comparing Disk Drive Types	200
Typical Hard Disks	201
ST-506	202
IDE	203
ESDI	203
SCSI	204
Other Large Capacity Disk Types	204
Hardcard	205
Removable Media Disks	208
RAM Disks	209
Understanding the RAMDRIVE Options	210
Learning More about RAM Disks	212
A RAM Disk in 640K of Memory	212
A RAM Disk in Expanded or Extended Memory	214
Chapter Summary	216

7 Improving Disk Performance 219

Using BUFFERS	220
Understanding How DOS Uses Disk Buffers	221
Fine-Tuning with BUFFERS	222
Understanding DOS 4 BUFFERS Options	224
Understanding DOS 5 BUFFERS Options	225
Gaining Speed with FASTOPEN	226
Understanding Disk Caches	230

Installing IBMCACHE.SYS 232
    Changing Cache Location 235
    Changing Cache Size 235
    Changing Cache Page Size 235
    Changing IBMCACHE Settings in CONFIG.SYS 237
Using SMARTDRV.SYS 238
Applying Your Knowledge 239
"Caching In" with Control Room 241
Chapter Summary 245

Part III Managing Memory Resources

8 Using Device Drivers 249
DEVICE Directives in CONFIG.SYS 250
    Ordering of Character Device Drivers 251
    Ordering of Block Device Drivers 253
    Ordering Approaches in General 254
Interaction between CONFIG.SYS Directives 257
    Understanding DRIVPARM and DRIVER.SYS 258
    Using DRIVPARM with Floppy Disk Drives 260
    Using DRIVER.SYS with Floppy Disk Drives 264
    Exploring Expanded Memory Device Drivers 268
Display and Keyboard Enhancements with ANSI.SYS 273
PS/2 and Other MCA Computers 274
Device Drivers at the Command Prompt 276
Chapter Summary 277

9 Stretching Your Resources 279
Assessing Your Needs 280
Making Do with the Bare Minimum of Memory 282
Expanding Memory with Little Expense 286
Using Expanded Memory Emulators 287
    Emulating Expanded Memory with Extended Memory 288
    Emulating Expanded Memory with Magnetic Storage 289
    Using All Your Resources 289
    Keeping Purposes Straight 290
Being Organized with Your Storage 291
    Organizing Your Floppy Disks 291
        Labeling Disks 291
        Reducing Disk Swapping 292

	Reserving Enough Room 294
	Backing Up Your Floppy Disks 295
	Partitioning Your Hard Disk 296
	Planning Partitions with Your Programs in Mind 296
	Considering Partition Size 297
	Organizing Your Files for Optimal Access Time 298
	Considering Your Hardware 299
	Using Subdirectories 300
	Using SUBST for Efficiency 302
	Using Alternative Microprocessors 303
	Using the V20 and V30 Microprocessors 303
	Using Math Coprocessors 304
	Using Accelerator Boards 305
	Chapter Summary 307

10 Regaining Base Memory 309

Examining 8088 Architecture 311
Examining 80286 Architecture 311
Examining DOS Memory 312
Using Expanded Memory 314
    Expanded Memory Boards 315
    MOVE'EM 316
        Example: Using MOVE'EM To Regain Low DOS Memory ... 317
        Measuring Program Size with MOVE'EM 318
        Rearranging CONFIG.SYS and AUTOEXEC.BAT for
          MOVE'EM 322
        Making the Best Use of Memory 324
    QRAM 326
        Example: Using QRAM To Regain Low DOS Memory 327
        Using QRAM to Regain Low DOS Memory 329
    ALL CHARGECARD for ATs 331
        Installing ALL CHARGECARD 333
        Example: Using ALL CHARGECARD To Regain Low DOS
          Memory 334
        Rearranging CONFIG.SYS and AUTOEXEC.BAT for ALL
          CHARGECARD 337
Using DOS's HIMEM.SYS Feature 339
    Examining the HIMEM.SYS Syntax 340
    Loading Part of DOS into High DOS Memory 343
Chapter Summary 343

11 Using the Processor's Power 345

- 386 Architecture 346
- 386 Memory Managers and Loaders: An Overview 346
- 386-to-the-MAX 347
  - Installing 386-to-the-MAX 348
  - Example: Using 386LOAD To Regain Low DOS Memory 353
  - Running MAXIMIZE To Configure 386LOAD 356
- QEMM 357
  - Installing QEMM 358
  - Example: Running OPTIMIZE To Configure LOADHI 361
- All Charge 386 362
  - Using ALLOAD for 386- and 486-Based Computers 365
  - Example: Using ALLOAD To Regain Low DOS Memory 366
  - Improving Performance with All Charge 386 368
- EMM386 371
- DEVICEHIGH 375
- LOADHIGH 376
- Chapter Summary 376

12 Improving the Operating System 377

- Examining DOS's Functional Sections 379
- Replacing Individual DOS Commands 380
- Replacing the Command Interpreter 381
- Making Use of Machine Architecture 381
  - Understanding the Steps to Creating a Program 383
  - Using DOS Extenders 384
- Exploring Multitasking Products 387
  - Using Multitasking Environments 390
    - DESQview 390
    - Windows 392
  - Using Multitasking Multiuser Operating Systems 395
    - VM/386 395
    - Concurrent DOS 386 397
    - PC-MOS 398
    - 386/MultiWare 399
- Exploring the Network Alternative 400
- Chapter Summary 401

A Comparing DOS Versions 403

- Changes between DOS 2.x and DOS 3.0 403
  - New CONFIG.SYS Features 403

    New Commands 404
    Changed Commands 404
    Changed Features 405
Changes between DOS 3.0 and 3.1 405
    New Commands 405
    Changed Commands 405
Changes between DOS 3.1 and 3.2 406
    New CONFIG.SYS Features 406
    New Feature 406
    New Commands 406
    Changed Commands/Directives 406
Changes between DOS 3.2 and 3.3 407
    New CONFIG.SYS Features 407
    New Features 407
    New Commands 407
    Changed Commands/Directives 408
Changes between DOS 3.3 and 4 409
    New CONFIG.SYS Features 409
    New Features 409
    New Commands 409
    Changed Commands/Directives 410
Changes between DOS 4 and 5 411
    New CONFIG.SYS Features 411
    New Commands 412
    Changed Commands 412

B Using Hexadecimal and Memory Addresses 415

Binary and Hexadecimal Numbering Systems 416
Memory Addresses 417

Index 419

Introduction

Millions of people use PCs daily, but everyone uses the PC in different ways. The versatility of the PC is a major reason for its popularity. DOS can be adjusted to suit a particular need, but a computer's performance often is not optimized. Only when a program doesn't work does the user examine the computer's configuration. By stepping back and assessing how you use the computer, you can make your computer work best for you.

You don't have to be a hardware expert to improve your performance. Even if you are frightened to take the cover off your computer, you can make many adjustments through software that you probably use already on a daily basis. The main requirement for using this book is a willingness to be methodical and to relate your specific situation to the examples given in this book.

Turbocharging MS-DOS is written so that you can make more efficient use of your computer. If you are a complete beginner with PCs, this book is not the place to start. If you are inquisitive about your computer, however, *Turbocharging MS-DOS* can help you alter your computer's configuration to work best for you.

Who Should Use This Book?

Turbocharging MS-DOS is designed for intermediate and advanced DOS users who are comfortable with their PCs and can assess their computer use. These types of users can assess, for example, that they use mostly two applications programs—such as WordPerfect and 1-2-3—and occasionally a communications program. By assessing your computer use and by gaining an understanding of what is actually happening when you use your computer, you can ensure that your computer is working at peak efficiency. This book enables you to optimize your computer's performance.

Beginning DOS users have trouble remembering how to use the COPY command, for example, but after they become familiar with the command, its use is automatic. Many users reach a level of comfort with their computers after they have learned a central core of DOS commands, such as COPY, REN, BACKUP, and RESTORE. The idea of learning an additional command doesn't seem overwhelming to them, provided that they can see its purpose. These types of users are intermediate users.

Having learned the basics, intermediate users can assess their computer's performance and can begin to tailor DOS settings and hardware to improve their productivity. At the most basic level, improving productivity may involve better hard disk organization or streamlining the CONFIG.SYS and AUTOEXEC.BAT files. You already may own utility programs, however, that can further enhance your computer's performance.

Even advanced users will find information of value in this book. Most advanced users have specialized in an applications program's use and have an intimate knowledge of their computer's performance. For example, a word processing expert knows that invoking the spell checker involves a delay of several seconds before spell checking occurs. This book offers ways to reduce this type of delay by showing how you can optimize your computer for your particular use.

How To Use This Book

As a learning tool, *Turbocharging MS-DOS* can be read at will. Part I is the introductory section, but advanced users also should read through this section quickly. Less-advanced users should read each chapter carefully and, before progressing to the next chapter, should try to relate what they learned to their own computers.

Parts II and III are full of practical suggestions of how you can improve your computer's performance. Part II focuses on disk performance, and Part III focuses on making the best use of memory and taking advantage of your microprocessor.

Remember two important items when trying to improve your computer's performance. First, know how good your current configuration is and keep a backup copy of all your current settings before making changes. Second, change only one thing at a time so that you really know whether the change has improved performance. If you juggle with all the settings in CONFIG.SYS and your computer doesn't boot, for example, tracking down a problem is much harder than if only one change was made.

What Is in This Book?

This book builds on basic DOS knowledge to give insights into the PC and its operation. Starting in Part I, "Examining PC and DOS Basics," you are introduced to the PC hardware and DOS operating system. You learn the fundamentals necessary to make intelligent choices in optimizing your computer. The terms introduced in this part are used extensively throughout the book.

Chapter 1, "Understanding the Personal Computer," introduces the various hardware components that make up the PC. This chapter also covers how each section of the computer, such as the CPU, memory, and devices, have to work together to make a fully functional computer.

Chapter 2, "Understanding DOS," gives an overview of DOS. The chapter examines the role of an operating system and the way DOS interfaces with the computer. All versions of DOS, including DOS 5, are covered. The functions of DOS and the role of device drivers, memory-resident programs, and applications programs are included.

Chapter 3, "Extending the Basic Standard," shows how the basic standard has been extended. This chapter includes information on DOS's modularity. This flexible interface enables device drivers to alter the computer's component parts without needing customized DOS versions. This chapter examines expanded and extended memory as well as how these memory management techniques add to the DOS standard. Techniques used by computer manufacturers to improve performance by the use of RAM are discussed. These techniques include disk caches and hardware cache controllers, shadow RAM, and memory managers. This chapter examines how you can assess your computer configuration and arm yourself with the tools to optimize your productivity by evaluating your computer's performance.

Part II, "Enhancing Disk Performance," gives detailed, practical information on how your disks work and how you can optimize their performance.

Chapter 4, "Examining Disk Architecture," gives an overview of disk structure. This chapter introduces magnetic media and how disks are arranged to accept data. Information on how DOS uses the disk space to store files, directories, and boot data is included. By understanding disk interleave and why a floppy disk is much slower than a hard disk at retrieving data, you can make intelligent use of your magnetic media resources.

Chapter 5, "Employing Routine Maintenance," covers routine disk maintenance. By using the tools supplied with your computer and DOS, you can ensure that your disk is working at its optimum performance. You should check your disks regularly to improve your disks' access time. Defragmenting of files and interleave checking are covered in detail. This chapter also examines alternatives to using DOS that are faster and more efficient. Third-party software, such as SpinRite and PC Tools Deluxe, are introduced.

Chapter 6, "Examining Disk Performance," covers apparent disk performance. Your computer may appear to have a sluggish disk performance due to your DOS settings. Techniques such as streamlining your path can have significant performance effects. Alternative disk drive types are covered, along with the relative benefits of each type. This chapter also examines the fastest disk drive type: a RAM disk.

Chapter 7, "Improving Disk Performance," covers improving disk performance by using memory. Several programs supplied with certain DOS versions enable you to improve your disk's responsiveness. This chapter covers in detail DOS's BUFFERS command, as well as disk caching programs such as IBMCACHE and SMARTDRV. The interaction of different caching techniques is covered with explanations of how more disk caching is not necessarily a good thing. Control Room, a diagnostic utility program, is used for vividly demonstrating the advantages of disk caches when they are set up correctly.

Part III, "Managing Memory Resources," gives practical information on how to improve your memory use and assess where additional purchases may prove worthwhile. This section includes chapters that are microprocessor-specific and shows how your AT or 386-based computer increases your alternatives for better memory management. Alternatives to DOS that still enable you to run DOS applications also are covered in Part III.

Chapter 8, "Using Device Drivers," shows how to best use the device drivers supplied with DOS and your computer. You can use device drivers supplied with DOS to enhance your display and keyboard.

Chapter 9, "Stretching Your Resources," shows how to use your limited resources. For those who use PCs with limited memory and perhaps only an 8088 microprocessor, this chapter shows how to make the best use of what you have. This chapter is aimed mainly at PC owners rather than AT and 386-based computer owners. You learn how to assess your needs, expand memory with little expense, and even create expanded memory using a disk rather than RAM. This chapter examines organization tips that enable you to make the best of your PC. Lower cost alternatives to purchasing new computers are suggested, and the benefits and drawbacks of installing math coprocessors and accelerator boards are presented.

Chapter 10, "Regaining Base Memory," discusses using base memory to improve applications program performance. This chapter is aimed mainly at AT owners because the discussed programs take advantage of the 80286 microprocessor. This chapter reviews the architecture of the 8088 and 80286 microprocessors, to allow discussion of how you can enhance DOS by using high DOS memory. DOS 5 is supplied with HIMEM, which enables you to regain high DOS memory. Other third-party alternatives, such as MOVE'EM and QRAM, for use with earlier DOS versions, are covered. The ALL CHARGECARD, a hardware rather than software alternative, also is examined.

Chapter 11, "Using the Processor's Power," discusses memory management on 386- and 486-based computers. This chapter reviews the architecture of the 80386, to show the unique microprocessor features that can be exploited by both DOS 5 and third-party products such as 386-to-the-MAX, All Charge 386, and QEMM. This chapter also covers the new features of DOS 5, which perform memory management and enable programs to be loaded into high DOS memory.

Chapter 12, "Improving the Operating System," introduces look-alike alternatives to DOS. These third-party products range from a replacement command processor, such as 4DOS, to multitasking multiuser operating systems. You may choose to replace a single DOS command, such as FORMAT, with a preferable third-party alternative. You may choose to write batch files that can automate your computer's use. A replacement command processor gives you DOS-like commands but doesn't alter the underlying operating system. Programmers use DOS extenders to produce products such as AutoCAD/386, which—although processor-specific—have greatly enhanced functionality. Multitasking products, such as Windows and

DESQview, enhance DOS's functionality. Finally, multitasking multiuser products give DOS compatibility (in most cases), yet additional functionality.

This book also contains two appendixes. Appendix A compares DOS versions, and Appendix B examines how to use hexadecimal and memory addresses.

What Is Not in This Book?

Turbocharging MS-DOS is not designed as a command reference manual. This book includes some commands and their syntax but is not intended to be a comprehensive command reference. If you want to learn about DOS commands, you should read *Using MS-DOS 5*, published by Que Corporation.

Turbocharging MS-DOS also is not a substitute for the manuals supplied with your computer and software. This book examines how to use the information in the hardware manuals in conjunction with DOS and other software you own in order to make the best of your computer. After you are able to assess your own computer by understanding Part I, you can use the subsequent parts of *Turbocharging MS-DOS* to make informed purchasing decisions that will improve your computer's performance.

What Are the Conventions in This Book?

Certain conventions are followed in this book to help you more easily understand the discussions, use of commands, and syntax lines.

Special Typefaces and Representations

In most cases, the keys on the keyboard are represented as they appear on your keyboard—with the exception of the arrow keys. Arrow symbols and their corresponding terms, such as *up arrow* or *up-arrow key*, have been used.

Ctrl-Home indicates that you press the Ctrl key and hold it down while you also press the Home key. Other hyphenated key combinations, such as Ctrl-Z or Alt-F1, are performed in the same manner.

Words or phrases defined for the first time appear in *italic* characters. Words or phrases you are to type appear in **boldface** characters.

Uppercase letters are used for distinguishing file names and DOS commands. Uppercase letters usually are used in the examples for what you type, but you can type commands in either upper- or lowercase letters. For a few commands, the case of the letters makes a difference. When the case is significant, the difference is specifically mentioned in the discussion of the command.

All screen displays and on-screen messages appear in the following special typeface:

```
This is a screen message.
```

Command Syntax

The notation for issuing commands and running programs appears, in fullest form, in lines such as the following:

*dc:pathc***CHKDSK** *filename.ext /switches*

In any syntax line, not all elements of the syntax can be represented in a literal manner. For example, *filename.ext* can represent any file name with any extension. It also can represent any file name with no extension at all.

To activate the command CHKDSK.COM, for example, you must type the word **CHKDSK**. To use the CHKDSK command with the /V (verbose) switch, you can type the following:

CHKDSK /V

Any literal text that you type in a syntax line is shown in uppercase letters. Any text that you can replace with other text (variable text) is shown in lowercase letters.

As another example, note the following syntax line:

FORMAT d:

This representation means that you must type **FORMAT** to format a disk. You also must type the drive represented by **d:**. However, **d:** can be replaced by any disk drive and therefore is in lowercase.

If **d:** is to be drive A, you would type the following:

    FORMAT A:

Mandatory vs. Optional Parts of Commands

Not all parts of a syntax line are essential when you type a command. You must be able to distinguish mandatory parts of the syntax line from optional parts. Any portion of a syntax line that you see in **boldface** letters is mandatory; you always must give this part of a command. In the preceding example, to issue the FORMAT command, you must type the word **FORMAT** as well as substitute the drive letter you want for **d:**.

Not all items in a command line are always mandatory. Portions of a syntax line that you see in *italic* characters are optional; you supply these items only when needed. In the CHKDSK example, you substitute for *dc:pathc* the appropriate disk drive and path name. You substitute for *filename.ext* a file name or other item. You use the appropriate character or characters for */switches*. If you do not type an optional item, DOS uses its default value or setting for the item.

In most cases, the text also helps you distinguish between optional and mandatory items, as well as those mandatory items that are variable.

Part I

Examining PC and DOS Basics

Includes

Understanding the Personal Computer
Understanding DOS
Extending the Basic Standard

Understanding the Personal Computer

1

To fine-tune your computer's performance, you need to understand the basic components of the computer. Understanding the software is essential, of course, but you also need to know about the hardware. With an understanding of the hardware elements, you can better tailor your software (including the operating system) to take advantage of your system's features.

Part I of this book introduces the basic components of the PC and DOS operating systems and explains PC hardware, operating system software, and memory. The first three chapters also define such terms as *expanded* and *extended memory*, *logical devices*, and *BIOS*. Knowledge of these terms is assumed in Parts II and III of the book.

This chapter gives you an overview of PC technology, explains the logical components of the PC, and defines such terms as *RAM*, *ROM*, and *bus memory*.

Enhancing Computer Technology

Personal computer systems based on the IBM PC are functionally the same, despite the wide variety of configurations available. The basic design of the personal computer hasn't changed since the IBM PC debuted in 1981. However, the standard hasn't been static. New technology, such as more advanced microprocessors, disk drives, and other peripheral hardware, has enhanced the standard rather than changed it.

The term *hardware* refers to the system unit, keyboard, screen display, disk drives, and printer. Figure 1.1 shows three common configurations for PCs. Each configuration includes a display, keyboard, disk drive, and system unit.

Software refers to the programs you can run on the computer and falls under two headings: *system software* with operating systems such as DOS, UNIX, or OS/2 and *applications software*, such as word processors, spreadsheets, and databases. Hardware and software work together to create the whole system known as the personal computer.

If you want to use the computer for simple programs, this basic understanding of the computer system may be adequate. However, if you want to use the computer to its full potential, you need more detailed knowledge of hardware and the operating system.

The heart of the personal computer is the microprocessor chip. This chip is used in association with other electronic components to link with the other parts of the PC. For example, when the microprocessor performs a calculation, other components are necessary to get the numbers for the calculation and then store or transfer the information.

A block diagram of the PC is shown in figure 1.2. The microprocessor and the math coprocessor make up the central processing unit (CPU). The microprocessor is connected to memory and to the peripheral devices. Any device used for input or output of data is a *peripheral*. These devices include the video subsystem (video board and screen display), disk drives, keyboard, and ports.

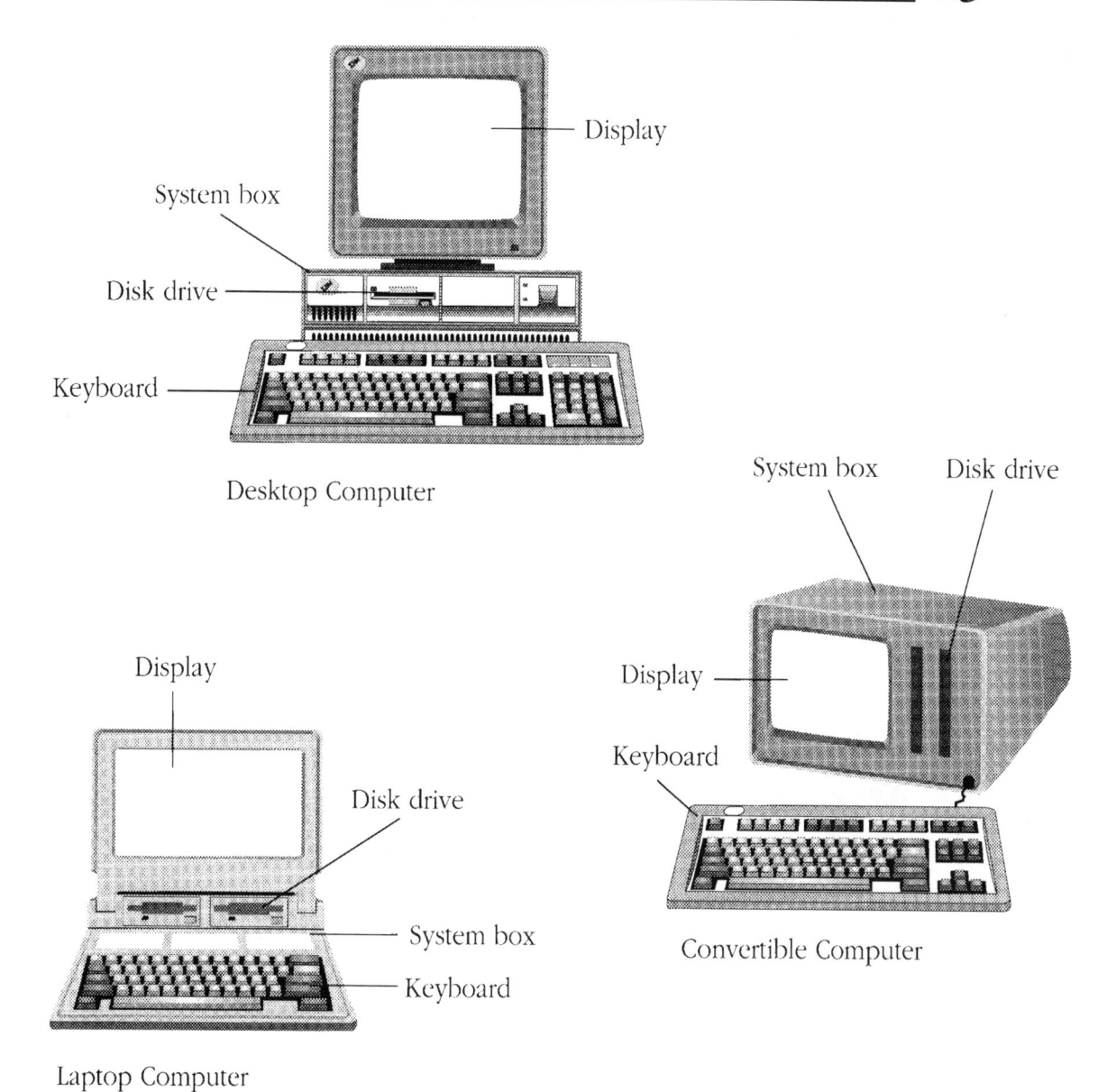

Chapter 1: Understanding the Personal Computer   **13**

Fig. 1.1. Various PC configurations.

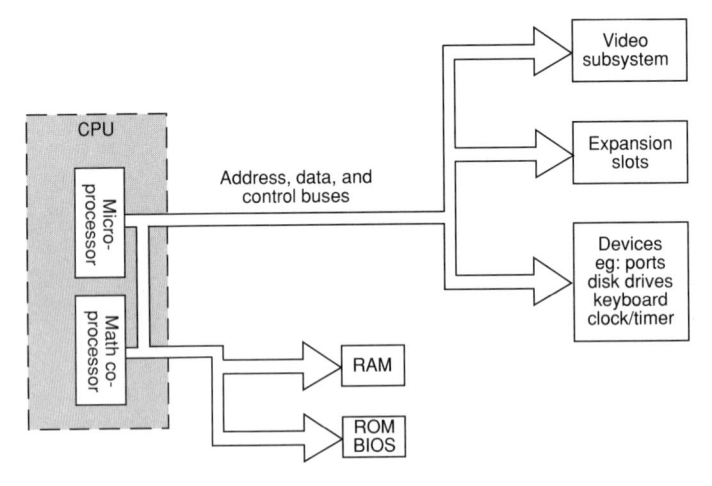

Fig. 1.2. Block diagram of the PC.

Some of these devices, such as the keyboard, supply input for the computer to operate; others, such as the video subsystem, supply output; and the rest, such as disk drives, supplies both input and output.

Understanding the Microprocessor

Microprocessors compute by loading a series of instructions and executing each instruction in turn. The instructions are bytes or multiples of bytes that form a pattern of on-and-off signal levels (logical 0s and 1s) that are meaningful to CPUs of the same family. The binary-level instructions are *machine instructions* or *machine codes* because they exist at a level the PC understands. You can think of machine code as a language spoken in the CPU's native tongue. The microprocessor executes a program by using this machine language. The signal driving the microprocessor dictates the time for each cycle of operation. This regular cycle time is known as the *system clock*. Some instructions can be completed in a single cycle, but others may take several cycles. Even at the slowest speed (4.77 MHz), thousands of instructions can be executed in a single second.

The components in the computer keep in step with the system clock, which comes from the signal that drives the microprocessor. At regular intervals, the system clock sends pulses that synchronize the work cycles of the components as well as the work cycles of the microprocessor. To work in harmony, system hardware must step through its tasks by using as a timing cue the "beat" of the system clock.

Tasks occurring outside the synchronized environment of the system hardware, such as pressing a key, have no way of "falling into step" with the smooth flow of clock-controlled activity. Outside events happen in their own time frames, not in the time frame of the system clock. Outside events are *asynchronous* to the system clock.

To service an outside event, the CPU must interrupt what it is doing and give immediate attention to that event. For example, when an outside event occurs, the CPU executes an interrupt-service routine. Under this routine, a special control component called the *interrupt controller* detects external events and informs the CPU that the current series of instructions must be "put on hold." The interrupt controller then informs the CPU where to find the instructions that process the outside event. The CPU then can begin executing the interrupt-service routine to clear the interrupt condition. After the outside event has been cleared, the CPU picks up where it left off and continues processing. In effect, the interrupt controller has taken an asynchronous outside event and made possible the handling of that event by the synchronized system hardware. When more than one outside event needs CPU attention, the interrupt controller determines the order in which the CPU handles each event.

In a series of events, the CPU executes instructions in an orderly fashion by keeping track of its location through its internal program counter.

Initially, when the CPU starts a program, the internal program counter is set to 1. The CPU gets instruction number 1 from memory location 1, executes the instruction, adds 1 to the program counter, and gets the next instruction from the memory location that matches the new value of the program counter (in this case, location 2). As the CPU executes each instruction and retrieves the next higher numbered instruction from memory, the CPU "steps" its way through—or executes—a program.

The CPU usually executes the next higher instruction number. However, depending on the outcome of the current instruction, the CPU can execute instructions elsewhere in the series of numbered instructions. If the CPU executes elsewhere, it in effect "jumps" from one series of instructions to another series. Perhaps the computed result of the most recent instruction marks a condition, meaning that a sequence of instructions has successfully been completed. From the computed result, or from information encoded into the instruction itself, the CPU sets its program counter to a new number of a new sequence and begins to execute that new sequence of instructions.

Using Microprocessors in PCs

Most microprocessors contain similar building blocks: a bus interface unit (BIU), arithmetic logic unit, execution-control system, instruction queue, and registers.

The *BIU* is responsible for linking the internal parts of the microprocessor to the rest of the computer. The *arithmetic logic unit* performs the actual calculations on the data. The *execution-control system* controls which part of the microprocessor does what and when. The *instruction queue* holds instructions (or commands) until the arithmetic logic unit can take an instruction and perform a calculation (such as adding two numbers). *Registers* are small areas of memory where data can be stored. Some registers are used for general purposes, and others are used for specific purposes such as addressing external memory or controlling the microprocessor.

The microprocessor is linked to the rest of the computer by pins on the chip. Data is transferred onto these pins, and the microprocessor reads the data for internal use. The microprocessor then places the resulting data onto the pins so the other components can read the information.

Data is taken on and off the microprocessor through the BIU. As instructions are received, they are placed in the instruction queue. The instructions tell the arithmetic logic unit which registers contain the data for calculation and where to put the result of the process. The execution-control system determines the sequence of operations.

Different microprocessors implement this basic system in different ways. For example, the number of registers may vary, with some microprocessors housing more and larger registers than others. The number of instructions that can be held in the queue may vary also. Finally, the actual pattern of bits making up the instructions and the way data is entered in and taken from main memory may vary also with the microprocessor.

IBM-compatible PCs use Intel microprocessors. Each Intel microprocessor is downwardly compatible with its predecessor. For example, the 80386 has modes that make it identical to an 8086, although the 80386 has extra modes that increase its capabilities.

The 80X86 microprocessors are considered general-purpose microprocessors and are often used with math coprocessors. For example, the 8086 and 8088 microprocessors can use the 8087 math coprocessor; the 80286 can use the 80287; the 80386SX can use the 80387SX; and the 80386 can use the 80387. A *math coprocessor* is designed for mathematical functions rather than general-purpose functions. Consequently, when performing mathematical computations, the coprocessor can be a hundred times faster than its corresponding main microprocessor.

For example, using the main microprocessor to calculate the square root of a number takes many steps involving dividing numbers and creating approximations that come closer and closer to the required value. However, the math coprocessor can perform this function much faster than the main processor. The programmer issues a single instruction, and the math coprocessor does the rest.

The math coprocessor and main microprocessor use different instruction sets. Consequently, a math coprocessor may improve your computer's performance only when it runs programs (such as spreadsheets) that require intensive amounts of calculations and that were written specifically to use instructions the math coprocessor can use.

Intel 8086 and 8088

The original IBM PC contained an Intel 8088 microprocessor. Although internally the 8088 microprocessor is a 16-bit device, the BIU, which is responsible for getting data onto and off the microprocessor, can collect and send out data only 8 bits at a time.

The 8088 contains fourteen 16-bit registers that fall into one of four types: general, addressing, segment, and control. The four general registers can be used either as four 16-bit registers or as eight 8-bit registers. These registers typically are used for holding the data for calculation. For example, if you need to add two numbers, the two numbers and their sum would be placed into the general-purpose registers.

The three addressing registers, combined with the four segment registers, point to a particular area in main memory where data is to be placed or read. These registers tell the BIU where to get or place its data.

The three control registers are the instruction counter, flags, and stack pointer. The instruction counter shows the number of the instruction being executed. The flags are set and reset by the arithmetic logic unit and can affect the flow of instructions. For example, the arithmetic logic unit sets a flag to indicate that a sequence of instructions has been successfully completed. The stack pointer tracks the position of data. The 8086 is used in some PCs instead of the 8088. The 8086 microprocessor is almost the same as the 8088, but it has a 16-bit data path—the BIU can get data 16 bits at a time. The internal arrangement of registers is the same, so all software written for the 8088 works on the 8086. However, because of the 16-bit interface, the software may run faster on an 8086 PC.

Intel 80286

The 80286 is used in the IBM Personal Computer AT. This 16-bit microprocessor is more advanced than the 8088 and 8086. The 80286 has two operating modes: *real mode* and *protected mode*. In real mode, the processor operates as if it were an 8088. Because DOS is designed to work on an 8088, ATs run with the 80286 in real mode when running DOS. When the processor is in protected mode, more advanced features are available. OS/2 is the first major operating system to use the 80286 protected mode in ATs.

The 80286 uses the same registers as the 8088 but has one additional segment register that it uses when operating in protected mode. Although the 80286 executes some instructions faster than the 8088, most of the performance improvement among DOS applications running on PCs and ATs is due to the faster clock speed of the AT's microprocessor. Remember that when you run identical programs on the 8088 and the 80286, the programs must contain the same instructions. The programs designed for the PC will not use the more advanced instructions the 80286 can handle.

Intel 80386SX

The 80386SX is an 80386 microprocessor that has only a 16-bit data path. The BIU therefore must put information onto and take information off the chip 16 bits at a time. This arrangement enables computer manufacturers to build less expensive computers that can run software designed for the 80386. Support circuitry, such as RAM chips, costs less if it is a 16-bit, rather than a 32-bit, device.

The internal architecture of the 80386SX is similar to that of the 80386. Both microprocessors have the same registers, execution units, and execution-control circuitry. The only difference is in the BIU and how it gets data onto and off the chip.

In terms of performance, the 80386SX is approximately equivalent to the 80286. Software written specifically for the 80386 does not run on 80286-based computers but does run on 80386SX systems. In the next few years, more applications programs, such as AutoCAD/386 and Paradox/386, may be available. Consequently, the 80386SX systems may be a better investment for the future than an AT.

Intel 80386

For many DOS users, the 80386 is only a faster 8088. This 32-bit microprocessor is a superset of both the 8088 and the 80286. The additional features include a 32-bit data bus and improved memory architecture.

Like the 80286, the 80386 has two operating modes: real and protected. Real mode enables programs written for the 8088 to run. Protected mode can be used for running operating systems such as OS/2, which can make use of protected mode.

Virtual 8086 mode, available when operating in protected mode, also is available to DOS users. Memory-manager programs, such as 386-to-the-MAX by Qualitas and QEMM by Quarterdeck, operate in virtual 8086 mode. Memory-manager programs serve as an additional link in the chain between the hardware and applications software. The programs interface between the hardware and DOS. If you have a memory manager (usually supplied by the computer manufacturer) installed on your computer, you actually are running DOS on top of the memory manager on your system. Virtual 8086 mode has advantages over real mode, as described later in the book, but to the end user, the modes are identical. Consequently, DOS appears unchanged, but you may be able to tailor your computer's performance by adjusting the memory manager or DOS settings.

The 80386 has 32 registers, which include all those found on the 8088 and 80286. Additional registers are used for debugging and testing as well as for extending the capability of the registers found in the other microprocessors (8088 and 80286).

Intel 80486

The 80486 microprocessor is a superset of the 80386. All the features of the 80386 are included as well as the features of the 80387 math coprocessor. Applications programs that use the math coprocessor run faster on the 80486 than on the 80386 and 80387. In a computer with 80386 and 80387 chips, control is transferred between the 80386 and 80387 for the execution of relevant math-specific instructions. On the 80486 computer, the relevant part of the microprocessor is used without any delay.

If and when an operating system is written specifically for the 80486, the additional features of this advanced microprocessor can be exploited. For DOS users, the downward compatibility with the 8086 enables all DOS applications to run on 80486-based systems. Because of the increased clock speed, applications run many times faster on the 80486 than on a PC using the 8088 microprocessor.

The data and instructions used in a computer are stored as 0s and 1s in memory. Each portion of memory can be accessed by the microprocessor because each memory location has a reference number, an *address*. When an address is placed on the pins of the microprocessor, the microprocessor can examine or alter the contents of that position. The range of positions is *address space*, the topic of the next section.

Addressing Memory Space

Memory gets its name from its capacity to retain values placed in individual memory locations. Memory is used for storing programs, easing interaction among system devices, and containing data on a more permanent basis. The CPU gets its instructions from memory. In all cases, the values that memory "remembers" are binary values (patterns of ons and offs). For convenience and design efficiency, memory retains binary values in patterns of 8-bit (binary digit) or 1-byte locations. Each byte location is individually addressable by the CPU. Because each memory byte location has its own unique address, the CPU can access program instructions as a series of addresses. When the CPU develops values or data as a by-product of processing, the CPU can store in memory for access later the values in addresses.

The CPU can store values in any location within its address range. To the CPU, the memory is randomly accessible. The CPU reads instructions from some randomly addressable memory locations and writes data to others.

The 8088 can address up to 1 megabyte (M) of memory, because it has 20 address lines. This capability means that the microprocessor can use 1,048,576 direct bytes (2^{20}) of information. The largest binary number that can be expressed with 20 bits is 11111111111111111111_2 (1,048,575 decimal), and the lowest is 0. Because the AT and 386-based systems emulate the 8088 when they run DOS as the operating system, they, too, can address 1 megabyte of memory. This megabyte of memory is divided into two main areas: *base* or *user memory,* and *high memory.* The lower 640K is random-access memory (RAM) and is called base or user memory, which can be used for storing programs or data. The upper 384K of memory, called high memory, consists of both RAM and read-only memory (ROM) and is used by the operating system itself. Each device, such as the video system and the disk drives, has its own area in this upper 384K.

Local Memory and I/O Bus Memory

From a hardware viewpoint, RAM and ROM are the only types of memory in a PC. However, a fully functioning PC needs software. How the memory is accessed by software and where in the address space memory is accessed make further definitions in the forms of memory in a PC.

The memory in a PC, whether it is RAM or ROM, is either written to or read from by the microprocessor. The physical location of the memory in the computer doesn't affect the method used to access it, but the location does affect the time needed to perform the read or write.

The computers that separate the memory onto its own bus, instead of locating it in the I/O expansion slot, use different terminology for referring to RAM. Memory on its own bus is *local memory*, and memory located in the I/O channel slots is *I/O memory*.

The microprocessor reads and writes to local memory at the full processor speed. Because these reads and writes occur frequently, you can achieve significantly better computer performance by using the full complement of local memory before you use expanded memory on the I/O bus.

System Memory

As discussed earlier, PCs use RAM and ROM memory. Random-access memory can be read from or written to when power is supplied to the computer. When power is removed, however, the contents of the RAM chips are lost. Read-only memory, as its name suggests, can be read only. The data in ROM is programmed into the chips before they are installed in the PC. When power is removed, the data is not lost. The next time the computer is turned on, the ROM data is still there. Both forms of memory are randomly addressable by the CPU.

Most PCs house various sets of ROM. Any device in the PC may have associated ROM. For example, the EGA (enhanced graphics adapter) video board contains ROM. The stored information in ROM also is called *firmware* because it falls between hardware and software. The physical components cannot be changed the way software can, but you can replace the existing ROMs with ones containing different data.

All PCs have a set of ROM chips known as *system ROM*. The system ROM contains the programs used for starting the computer and interface with the various devices, such as the disk drive and I/O ports. The programs stored in the system ROM are the *BIOS* (basic input/output system).

ROM BIOS is what makes any given model PC unique. For example, although both an IBM PC and a COMPAQ PC perform similar functions, the contents of their system ROMs are different. Two computers may use the same type of microprocessor, disk drive, and video system, but the two systems are unique because of the different program information in their BIOS.

Using Basic Hardware Components

The microprocessor and memory are only part of a PC. For you to actually make use of the computer, other components such as a disk, display, and keyboard also are needed. Each of these devices interacts with the central processing unit in different ways and provides the means for entering, storing, and displaying data.

Central Processing Unit

The microprocessor is the computer's central controller. Driven by a signal oscillating at a high frequency—4.77 MHz in PCs and up to 33 MHz in 386-based systems—the microprocessor controls each part of the computer. For example, if information stored on the disk is to be printed, the microprocessor instructs the disk controller to read the information on the disk. When the information is available, the microprocessor transfers it to the appropriate input/output (I/O) port for printing.

In a PC, the microprocessor is an Intel 8086 or 8088; in an AT, the microprocessor is an 80286; and in a 386-based system, the microprocessor is an 80386. The 80286 functions as a superset of the 8088 and can look, to software, exactly like an 8088. The 80386 is a superset of both the 8088 and the 80286 and also can function in the same way as the 8088. Similarly, the 80486 in 486-based systems is a superset of the 8088, 80286, and 80386 microprocessors. Intel has said that all microprocessors in the 80X86 family also will have operating modes that allow software written for earlier microprocessors to run.

The AT systems operate faster than the 8088 systems for several reasons, but the basic system architecture is the same in both PCs and ATs. The signal used to drive an 80286 has a higher frequency than the signal used to drive the less powerful 8088. The time taken for the 80286 to perform an action—for example, adding two numbers—is less than the time taken for an equivalent action with an 8088. As a result, your programs on an 80286 computer run faster.

Peripheral Devices

PC peripheral devices include disk drives, keyboards, printers, and modems. These devices interact with the CPU to perform tasks. For example, the keyboard is the most common method of supplying input to the computer, and the display is the most common device for showing output from the CPU.

Each device is located in the 1M of address space and can be addressed by the CPU. Many of these positions are defined, so although two computers may use devices from different manufacturers, the CPU still addresses them in the same way. Figure 1.3 shows the memory address map for the PC.

The method of interaction between devices, such as what goes on after you press a key and before the result is displayed on-screen, is a function of the operating system installed on the computer.

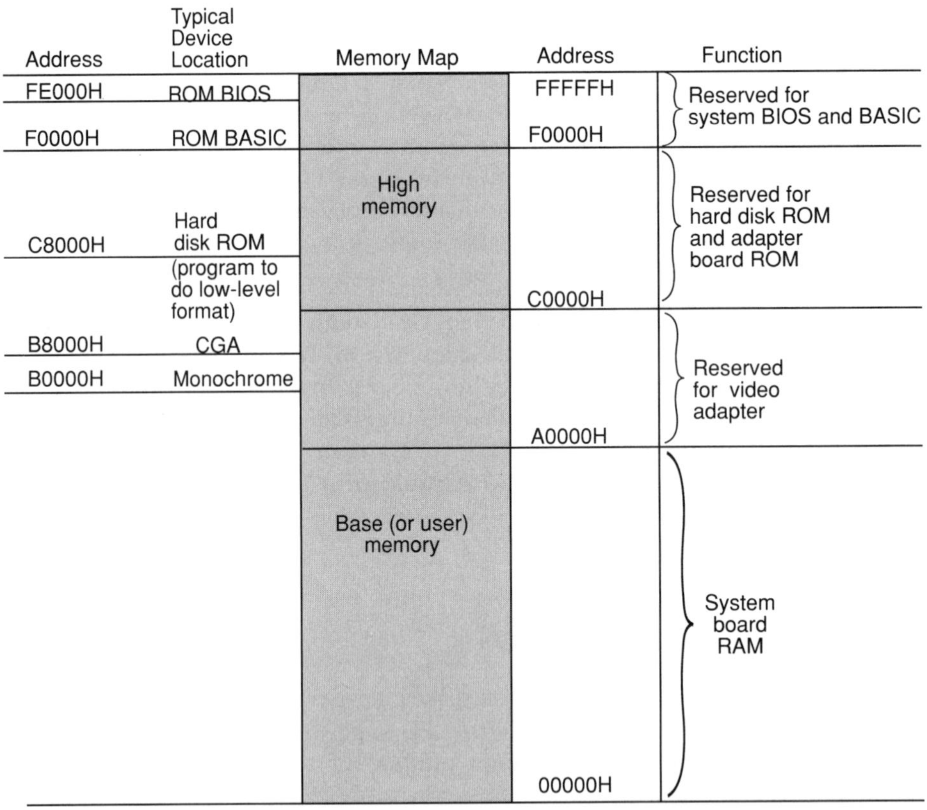

Address	Typical Device Location	Memory Map	Address	Function
FE000H	ROM BIOS		FFFFFH	Reserved for system BIOS and BASIC
F0000H	ROM BASIC		F0000H	
C8000H	Hard disk ROM (program to do low-level format)	High memory	C0000H	Reserved for hard disk ROM and adapter board ROM
B8000H	CGA			Reserved for video adapter
B0000H	Monochrome		A0000H	
		Base (or user) memory		System board RAM
			00000H	

Fig. 1.3. Memory map for PC address space.

Expansion Bus

The modular nature of the PC enables a variety of devices (such as the disk drive and the video display) to be attached to the computer. The connection between these devices is identical. The connector for a disk drive is similar to the connector for a video board. The series of connectors on the motherboard that connects the devices inside a PC is the *expansion bus*. Each connector is basically the same and contains three parts: data bus, address bus, and control bus. The data bus moves data between the CPU and the devices, the address bus shows where the data is located in RAM, and the control bus determines when and how the data is moved.

By plugging a circuit board into one of these connectors, you can expand the computer's capabilities. The disk controller and video adapter are commonly found plugged into expansion slots. Some newer systems incorporate this video and disk controller capability into the main system board instead of using a slot. However, these items are still referred to as devices, even if they cannot be separated physically from the system board.

Other devices may be added to a PC, such as additional ports for connecting printers, modems, joysticks, or mice. Alternatively, an adapter may be added to drive an additional hard disk or a tape drive.

The CPU coordinates all computer activities and asserts its control by signaling the buses. The support circuitry around the buses ensures that the correct device is the recipient or sender of internal information.

The devices attached to the PC are often asynchronous and signal to the interrupt controller when they need attention. For example, the microprocessor may instruct the hard-disk controller to read information from the disk. When the controller has the information, it signals to the interrupt controller that the data is ready. The CPU then can collect it by using the interrupt-service routine that services the hard-disk controller.

Expansion slots are commonly used for adding extra memory to PCs. This arrangement is less common, however, in faster systems. The faster computers often have a separate and different expansion slot for memory, or the system board itself accepts memory. The reasons for this separation are compatibility and speed.

On faster PCs and ATs, the expansion bus, which is driven by the system clock, also is faster. Older expansion boards, although they work fine at slower bus speeds, cannot cope with the higher bus speed of faster systems. To compensate, computer manufacturers run the bus at a speed slower than that of the main CPU's.

One disadvantage of this compromise in speed is that any memory located on the bus also operates slowly. To lessen the problem, several manufacturers, most notably COMPAQ Computer Corporation, make two separate buses: one for memory and one for all other devices

Apart from memory boards, most devices would not benefit from higher bus speeds. For example, the length of a single cycle in a PC running at 4.77 MHz is 210 nanoseconds (billionths of a second). A typical PC disk drive has an access time of 85 milliseconds (thousandths of a second). So a request for data from the hard disk is insignificant in time when you consider the time taken to remove the data from the disk. A faster bus cycle time does not make the drive operate noticeably faster. The CPU requests the data more quickly, but the hard disk still takes about 85 milliseconds before setting its interrupt. Only then does the interrupt controller signal to the CPU that it can collect the data. The faster bus cycle reduces only the system's cycle time, not the access time.

The expansion bus in a PC is an 8-bit I/O bus. Data can be transferred to and from devices on the bus 8 bits at a time. The bus is referred to as being 8 bits wide. The AT and 386-based systems have a 16-bit I/O bus. (Data can be transferred to and from devices on the bus 16 bits at a time.) This increase in speed has a dramatic effect on performance. A disk controller, for example, can transfer twice as much data at a time on a 16-bit bus.

The AT bus accepts 8-bit or 16-bit adapters. The AT bus is a superset of the PC bus. You can use PC-style expansion boards in the AT, but you will not gain the advantage of the 16-bit-at-a-time transfers. If you buy new devices for AT or 386-based computers, you should select 16-bit rather than 8-bit adapters to improve performance.

Most PS/2 computers, except Models 25, 30, and 30/286, have a different expansion bus from the PC, AT, and 386-based systems from other manufacturers. This bus is Micro Channel or MCA (Micro Channel Architecture). As with the PC and AT bus, known as the Industry Standard Architecture (ISA) bus, the MCA is composed of three parts: the data bus, the control bus, and the address bus. The electrical parameters for ISA and MCA are different, and the physical connectors used to plug boards into the computer are different. Both buses' software, however, use the same method to communicate with devices.

The 80286-based PS/2s—Models 50, 50Z, 55, and 60—have a Micro Channel bus that is 16 bits wide. (Data can be transferred 16 bits at a time.) Models 70, P70, and 80 have 32-bit buses and can transfer data 32 bits at a time. With an upward compatibility similar to that of the PC and AT, 16-bit Micro Channel expansion boards can be used in computers with the 32-bit MCA. Obviously, the 16-bit board transfers data only 16 bits at a time, regardless of the type of computer in which it is installed. To achieve optimum use of your computer, you should use expansion boards designed for the maximum bus width of your computer.

As an alternative to the 32-bit Micro Channel, some computer manufacturers, such as COMPAQ and AST, have released a 32-bit bus called Extended Industry Standard Architecture (EISA). This bus is downwardly compatible with the AT bus, and you can use PC and AT expansion boards in the slots in the same way as you can use PC expansion boards in the AT. However, to make use of the 32-bit architecture, you must use an EISA board in the EISA slots. As with the 32-bit Micro Channel, EISA slots are found only in 80386- and 80486-based systems.

Table 1.1 shows the bus widths and types for many popular computers.

Table 1.1
Bus Widths and Types for Popular Computers

Computer Type	Bus Type	Bus Width	Suitable Adapters
IBM PC	ISA	8-bit	8-bit PC adapters
PC compatible	ISA	8-bit	8-bit PC adapters
IBM AT	ISA	16-bit	8-bit PC and 16-bit AT adapters
AT compatible	ISA	16-bit	8-bit PC and 16-bit AT adapters
COMPAQ 386	ISA	16-bit	8-bit PC and 16-bit AT adapters
386-based COMPAQ compatible	ISA	16-bit	8-bit PC and 16-bit adapters
PS/2 Models 25 and 30	ISA	8-bit	8-bit PC adapters
Model 30/286	ISA	16-bit	8-bit PC and 16-bit AT adapters
Models 50, 50Z, 55, and 60	MCA	16-bit	16-bit MCA adapters
Models 70, P70, and 80	MCA	32-bit	16- and 32-bit MCA adapters
EISA compatible	EISA	32-bit	8-bit PC, 16-bit AT, and 32-bit EISA adapters

Video Subsystem

The video subsystem is another PC device, along with the keyboard, that makes the user interface significantly better than that of earlier computers. Before PCs had keyboards, users programmed computers by flicking switches and watching red lights on consoles or by using punched cards or punched tape with codes on them.

The video subsystem has two parts: the adapter board and the display screen itself. The CPU interacts with the video adapter, which in turn drives the display. The video adapter may be a circuit board plugged into an expansion slot on the system board, or the video circuitry may be incorporated into the system board itself.

Most display adapters are one of the following standards: monochrome display and printer adapter (MDA), Hercules monographics controller (HGC), color graphics adapter (CGA), enhanced graphics adapter (EGA), multicolor graphics array (MCGA), or video graphics array (VGA). For certain situations, such as running desktop publishing programs or computer-aided design (CAD) programs, a higher resolution video adapter may be installed.

With the exception of the MDA, all the commonly used video adapters can display text and graphics. All the adapters need a display screen matched to the display adapter. For example, you cannot use a monochrome display with a CGA.

Text images consist only of text characters, such as letters of the alphabet or punctuation. Each character displayed is a series of pixels in a particular pattern that fits in a box. For example, on a CGA the characters are series of dots that fit into a grid eight dots wide by eight dots high. The shapes of these characters are stored in ROM on the system board. When the computer is set into text mode by software, the character to be displayed is looked up in the ROM table, and the correct dots for the character appear on-screen.

Graphics images consist of dots rather than characters. Each dot on-screen can be turned on or off by the software. The different video adapters have different numbers of dots available for display. The *resolution* of a video adapter is defined as the number of dots that can be displayed on-screen. The number given, such as 640 by 200, refers to the number of horizontal and vertical dots that can be displayed on-screen.

The various video adapters display a different number of colors. For example, the CGA can display only four colors, whereas the VGA can display 256 at a time. Table 1.2 shows the resolution and colors for the most common display adapters.

Although many applications programs operate in graphics mode, DOS operates only in text mode. The type of video adapter supported by an applications program usually is marked on the packaging.

Video boards from different manufacturers can have different performances even if they are made for the same type of computer. For example, the IBM Personal System/2 Display Adapter is a VGA board for PCs and ATs. However, it has only an 8-bit bus. Many other manufacturers, including COMPAQ, supply VGA-compatible boards in the ATs and 386-based systems that have a better performance. This improvement is due primarily to a 16-bit bus interface, which permits the display information to be given to the adapter twice as fast.

**Table 1.2
Resolution and Colors for Display Adapters**

Adapter Type	Graphics Mode	Pixel Resolution	Colors Available
CGA	Medium resolution	320 x 200	4
CGA	High resolution	640 x 200	2
EGA	All CGA modes		
EGA	CGA high resolution	640 x 200	16
EGA	EGA high resolution	40 x 350	16
HGC	Monochrome graphics	720 x 348	2
MDA	Text only	N/A	N/A
VGA	All CGA and EGA modes		
VGA	Monochrome	640 x 480	2
VGA	VGA high resolution	640 x 480	16
VGA	VGA medium resolution	320 x 200	256

Keyboard

The keyboard is the normal input device used on personal computers. The IBM PC and many PC compatibles use a standard keyboard. The IBM AT and a few AT compatibles use Personal Computer AT keyboards. Other systems, such as the 8 MHz IBM AT, many AT compatibles, and all PS/2 computers, use the 101-key Enhanced Keyboard. The standard keyboard and the Personal Computer AT keyboard furnish 10 function keys along the left side of the keyboard. The Enhanced Keyboard provides 12 function keys located along the top.

Just like a typewriter, the computer keyboard contains all the letters of the alphabet, and the numbers, symbols, and punctuation characters are virtually the same. The computer keyboard also has the familiar QWERTY layout, but a computer keyboard is different from a typewriter keyboard in several important ways.

The most notable difference is the "extra" keys—the keys that do not appear on a typewriter. These keys include Enter, cursor-movement keys, Del, Ins, Ctrl, Alt, Esc, Num Lock, PrtSc, Print Screen, Scroll Lock, Pause, and Break. (Table 1.3 lists the purpose of each of these keys.)

Table 1.3
Special Keyboard Keys

Key	Function
Alt	The Alternate key. When pressed in combination with another key, changes the standard function of that key.
Break	Stops a program in progress.
Ctrl	The Control key. When pressed in combination with another key, changes the standard function of that key.
Cursor keys	Changes the cursor location on the screen. Included are the arrows, PgUp, PgDn, Home, and End. Del deletes, or erases, any character at the location of the cursor.
Enter	Signals the computer to respond to the command you type. Also functions as a carriage return in programs that simulate the operations of a typewriter.
Esc	In some situations, enables you to "escape" from a current operation to a previous one. Sometimes Esc has no effect on the current operation.
Ins	Inserts a character at the location of the cursor.
Num Lock	Changes the numeric pad from cursor-movement to numeric-function mode.
Pause	Suspends display output until another key is pressed. (Not provided with standard keyboards.)
PrtSc	Used to send the characters on the screen to the printer.
Print Screen	Found on Enhanced Keyboards. Same as PrtSc.
Scroll Lock	Locks the scrolling function. Instead of moving the cursor, the cursor-control keys scroll the screen.

Many of these extra keys are used in combination with other keys. For example, on a standard or AT keyboard, pressing Shift and PrtSc in combination causes DOS to print the contents of the current screen. Pressing Ctrl and PrtSc simultaneously causes DOS to print continuously what you type and what DOS sends to the screen. On the Enhanced Keyboard, pressing only Print Screen causes the contents of the screen to be printed. Pressing Ctrl-PrtSc a second time turns off the printing. The Print Screen and PrtSc keys on the different keyboards are similar, but on the standard and AT keyboards, the PrtSc function is in the "shifted" position. Consider the colon and semicolon key. The colon is in the "shifted" position because you activate it by pressing the Shift key in combination with the colon and semicolon key.

To improve your efficiency with DOS commands, you should learn the DOS editing keys that enable you to recall parts or all of the last command typed at the keyboard. For example, pressing F3 at the DOS prompt displays the whole of the last command line, whereas typing F1 displays the last command line one character at a time. When you type a line and press Enter, DOS copies the line into an input buffer. Using the editing keys recalls the information in the buffer. Table 1.4 shows the DOS editing keys.

Table 1.4
DOS Editing Keys

Key	Function
Tab	Moves the cursor to the next tab stop
Esc	Cancels the current line and does not change the buffer
Ins	Enables you to insert characters into the line
Del	Deletes a character from the line
F1 or right arrow	Copies one character from the preceding command line
F2	Copies all characters from the preceding command line up to but not including the next character you type
F3	Copies all remaining characters from the preceding command line
F4	Deletes all characters from the preceding command line up to but not including the next character you type (opposite of F2)
F5	Moves the line you are typing into the buffer but does not allow DOS to execute the line
F6	Produces an end-of-file marker when you copy from the console to a disk file

A comprehensive file manager is a standard feature with DOS Version 5. The Shell program can be used in place of many existing DOS shell programs from third-party manufacturers. DOS Version 4 also was supplied with a Shell program, but it is not as advanced as the one supplied with DOS 5.

You can use the Shell program to perform most standard file-maintenance procedures that previously had to be performed individually at the command prompt. For example, you can select several files from a list and copy all those files to a new directory.

In the same way that applications programs, such as WordPerfect and 1-2-3, use special keys for different functions, Shell takes advantage of special keys on the keyboard. Many special keys and key combinations are available. You can use the function keys, for example, to perform various editing tasks (see table 1.5).

Table 1.5
DOS 5 Shell Function Keys

Key	Function
F1	Displays the on-line help system.
F2	Copies programs in the program list.
F3 or Alt-F4	Exits the DOS Shell and returns you to the DOS command prompt.
F5	Redisplays the directory tree and file list.
F7	Moves selected file(s) to another directory.
F8	Copies selected file(s) to another directory.
F9	Displays a file's contents. Pressing F9 again switches between ASCII and hexadecimal display in the file viewer.
F10 or Alt	Selects the main menu bar.
Shift-F8	Turns add mode on and off. Used for adding files to a selection.
Shift-F9	Leaves the DOS Shell temporarily and returns you to the DOS command prompt. Typing **EXIT** at the DOS prompt returns you to the Shell.

Each character you type is converted by the keyboard electronics into a code (called a *scan code*) that the computer can process. A key's code—not the key's position or the legend on the key itself—is significant to DOS. Similar keys on the different-style keyboards have similar scan codes, which enable DOS and applications programs to look for a particular scan code. Some programs, particularly older ones, may not respond or may respond incorrectly to keystrokes. For example, the Enhanced Keyboard contains two left-arrow keys. Some programs may not respond to both keys because the programs are not looking for all the possible scan codes.

Some new keyboards enable you to change key caps and to switch key definitions for the Caps Lock, Ctrl, Esc, and ~ keys. The various keyboards available have not standardized the positions for these keys. If you use more than one type of keyboard, you may want to change the key definitions of the keys that are in different positions. Northgate Computer Systems, Inc., for example, not only offers these options but also its own version of the Enhanced Keyboard. The first 10 function keys of the Northgate version are to the left of, instead of across the top of, the keyboard.

Small computers, such as portables and laptops, may use nonstandard keyboards, usually to conserve space. Some of these keyboards include an additional key to the Shift key that gives a single key more capability or use the keys in an unconventional way. For example, the Toshiba 3100 puts the semicolon, colon, and plus keys on a single key. Pressing the key on its own is the same as pressing the semicolon; pressing the key while holding down Shift results in a colon; and pressing the same key when Num Lock is turned on produces a plus sign.

DOS acts on combination keys in predefined ways. Table 1.6 lists the key combinations and the action that DOS takes when you use a key combination.

Table 1.6
DOS Key Combinations

Key	Function
Ctrl-Num Lock or Ctrl-S	Freezes the display; pressing any other key restarts the display.
PrtSc or Print Screen	Prints the contents of the video display (print-screen feature).
Ctrl-PrtSc	Sends lines to both the screen and the printer; giving this sequence a second time turns this function off.
Ctrl-C or Ctrl-Break	Stops the execution of a program.
Ctrl-Alt-Del	Restarts DOS (warm boot).

Chapter Summary

This chapter provided an overview of personal computer hardware. You learned that the PC is a modular system with a CPU, memory, and devices, and that software works in association with the hardware to make the PC a whole system. In addition, you learned the following terms: *Hardware* is all the components that make up the PC. These components include the system unit, disk drives, and display. Any program is known as *software*. Also, software may be an operating system, such as DOS, or an applications program, such as a word processor. *Programs* are sets of instructions that produce a desired result.

The *microprocessor*, either an 8088, 8086, 80286, 80386SX, 80386, or 80486, is the central processing unit (CPU) of the computer. The microprocessor controls everything that operates in the PC.

Memory is used for storing data in the computer as the computer is being used. *RAM* is memory that can be written to and read from, and *ROM* is read-only memory. The data in RAM is lost when the computer is turned off, but the data in ROM is preserved when the power is removed.

The system ROM contains the *BIOS*, which is used for initializing the computer and helping the CPU interact with the attached devices.

Memory located on the expansion bus is known as *I/O bus memory*; memory on the system board, or in a dedicated memory expansion slot, is known as *local memory*. Local memory typically runs at the full microprocessor speed, whereas the expansion bus memory may run slower to provide compatibility with PC and AT adapter boards.

The *expansion bus* in the PC is a series of connectors that accepts expansion boards. These boards contain circuitry linking the CPU with such devices as video boards and disk drives.

Any device used for input or output is a *peripheral device*. These devices typically are connected to the computer through expansion boards.

The *video subsystem* consists of the video adapter and display. On some computers, this device is an integral part of the system board; on others an expansion board is used.

Understanding DOS 2

Chapter 1 described the hardware portions of a personal computer. This chapter introduces the software common to all IBM and compatible PCs—DOS. Also covered are applications programs and terminate-and-stay-resident (TSR) programs (also known as memory-resident programs) and how they interact with DOS and the hardware.

Chapter 1 defined *software* as any program, or list of instructions, that can be run on a computer. This chapter goes beyond that definition by identifying and discussing the major classifications of software.

The two main software classifications are operating systems and applications programs. Applications programs include word processors, spreadsheets, and databases. An operating system provides the link between the applications programs and the hardware. Examples of operating systems are DOS, OS/2, and UNIX.

Understanding the Operating System

An *operating system* is a collection of computer programs that provides recurring services to other programs or to the computer user. These services consist of disk and file management, memory management, and device management. When an applications program needs information from the disk, the program asks the operating system for the information, and the operating system runs the appropriate portions of its programs to activate the disk and retrieve the information.

Without an operating system, every applications program would have to contain instructions telling the hardware each step the hardware should take to do its job, such as storing a file on a disk.

The purpose of an operating system is to provide a standard interface between the applications programs or the user and the computer hardware. This interface reduces the complexity of applications programs because the programmer can use this interface for many portions of the program and because the interface provides a consistent method for programs to operate the hardware. This interface also has produced thousands of applications programs for the marketplace that work on all IBM and compatible personal computers.

The operating system commonly used on IBM and compatible PCs is called DOS (disk operating system) because many of the programs, such as the XCOPY or FORMAT command programs, are stored on disk instead of in the computer's memory.

Using Variations of DOS

IBM-compatible personal computers use MS-DOS as an operating system. MS-DOS is the disk operating system developed by Microsoft Corporation to provide a foundation of services for operating an IBM PC or compatible computer. Manufacturers of personal computers, such as IBM, COMPAQ, and Zenith, tailor MS-DOS for use on their computers. In fact, hundreds of types of PCs use some form of MS-DOS. The manufacturers may put their own names on the disks and include different manuals with the DOS packages they provide, but all these types of DOS are similar when they operate on a PC. When you read about DOS in this book, you can assume that what you read applies to the version of DOS used by most manufacturers. In special cases, differences may be noted.

The variations in MS-DOS implementations among PC manufacturers appear to users as subtle differences, usually limited to the names of a few commands or the way parameters are given. Some manufacturers include in their MS-DOS packages additional utilities that work with a feature of that manufacturer's model of PC. As a general rule, if you are proficient at using one variation of MS-DOS, you are proficient with all variations of MS-DOS. In a practical sense, the terms MS-DOS, PC DOS, and DOS are interchangeable. You may be able to use just about any compatible computer that runs DOS as its operating system by using what you know about DOS from working with another PC.

The versions of DOS may interact with the hardware in different ways. As mentioned in Chapter 1, the BIOS makes a PC from a particular manufacturer unique. The BIOS, stored in the system ROM, is different in every type of PC compatible. This set of programs can be considered part of the operating system. The result of these variations in disk operating systems is that the interface between the user and the applications programs can be the same on all types of PCs. The interaction between DOS and the hardware, however, may vary from manufacturer to manufacturer. This difference is transparent but may enable you to tailor DOS with its various settings to work more efficiently for your particular configuration.

Note that the BIOS, which interacts with DOS to make up a whole operating system, is not part of DOS. When you purchase DOS, you do not purchase the BIOS, but you purchase programs that work in association with the BIOS to provide all the services the user or applications program needs.

Changing Versions of DOS

Just as personal computer hardware has evolved from PCs to ATs to 386- and 486-based systems, the operating system also has evolved. Some of the improvements were necessary to accommodate the new hardware, such as bigger hard disks, but additional features also have been added at each new release. Table 2.1 lists the important differences among versions of DOS (see Appendix A for more detailed coverage of these changes).

Table 2.1
Quick Reference to Versions of DOS

Version	Significant Change
1.0	Original version of DOS
1.25	Accommodates double-sided disks
2.0	Includes hierarchical directories needed to organize hard disks
3.0	Uses high-capacity floppy disks, the RAM disk, volume names, and the ATTRIB command
3.1	Includes provisions for networking
3.2	Accommodates 3 1/2-inch drives
3.3	Accommodates high-capacity 3 1/2-inch drives; includes new commands
4.0	Introduces the DOS Shell and the MEM command; accommodates larger files and disk capacities
5.0	Memory-saving features for 286 and 386 systems, additional on-line help feature, safe format command, better support for high-capacity disks

DOS consists of a variety of programs that you usually store in a subdirectory on the hard disk. Some commands are called internal commands because they are loaded into memory when the computer is booted. Others, such as FORMAT, are in individual files on the disk. When you execute the FORMAT command, you actually are running a program named FORMAT.COM. To understand DOS better and be able to tailor it for your individual situation, consider the various components of DOS.

Understanding the Parts of DOS

DOS can be viewed as having four main functional components:

- The BIOS (basic input/output system)
- The system files
- The command interpreter
- The DOS utilities

You can think of DOS as a layering system over your hardware. The layer of software immediately above the hardware is the BIOS. Above the BIOS in the hierarchy are the DOS system files and then the command interpreter. Figure 2.1 shows this layering concept.

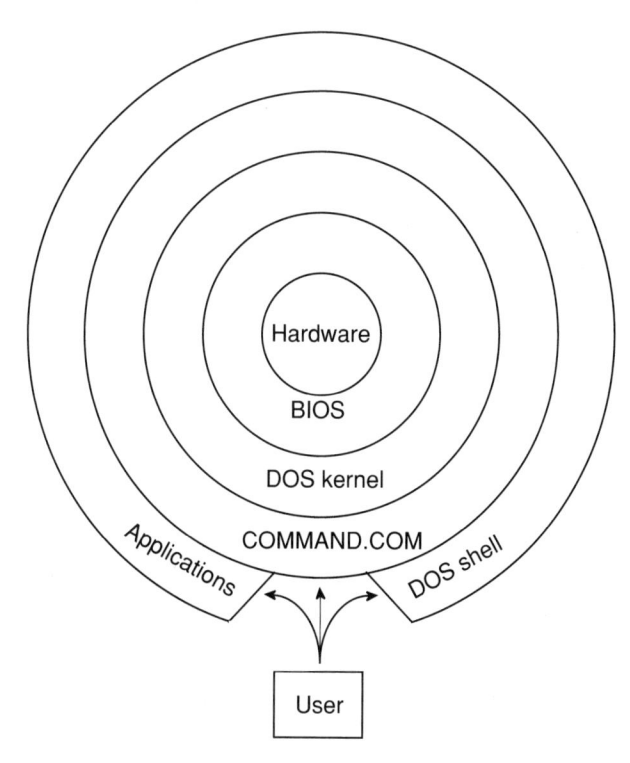

Fig. 2.1. The "layers" of DOS.

The Command Interpreter

The command interpreter is DOS's interface with you, the user, and interacts with you through the keyboard and screen when you operate your computer. The command interpreter also is called the command processor and often is referred to simply as COMMAND.COM (pronounced *command dot com*). COMMAND.COM accepts your DOS command and sees that the command is carried out.

COMMAND.COM prints on the display the DOS prompt (C>, A>, and so on). The DOS prompt is a request for input. When you enter a command, you are communicating with COMMAND.COM, which then interprets what you type and processes your input so that DOS can take the appropriate action. COMMAND.COM, through DOS commands, handles the technical details of such command tasks as displaying a directory listing, copying files, and starting your applications programs.

COMMAND.COM is loaded into memory when the computer is booted. The internal DOS commands, including COPY, REN, and DEL (for copying, renaming, and deleting files) are a part of the command processor and consequently are loaded into memory when the computer is booted. COMMAND.COM not only can complete these commands but also can send error messages to the display when commands cannot be executed.

The System Files

When DOS is installed on a disk, two or three system files also are installed. The number of files depends on your computer, and the names of the files depend on the manufacturer of the DOS version. These files, hidden from view, are the files that make the computer bootable. If you format a disk using the /S parameter, the files are placed automatically on the disk and hidden from view. For example, PC DOS Version 3.3 places on my Personal Computer AT two system files called IBMBIO.COM and IBMDOS.COM, whereas the version of MS-DOS 3.3 supplied with my Gateway 2000 386-based computer places on the disk two system files called IO.SYS and MSDOS.SYS.

These system files are the go-between files for COMMAND.COM and the BIOS itself. Although the BIOS is the basic input/output system, providing the more fundamental control of input and output, the system files also are the input/output system, providing the next level of control.

The BIOS

The BIOS consists of a collection of small programs and routines that are accessed by the system files. These programs deal directly with the hardware. For example, selecting a text mode on the video adapter involves, among other things, the BIOS instructing the microprocessor to set the video adapter mode.

If an operating system different from DOS is used—UNIX, for example—the BIOS is available for interaction with that system. The other system may provide different commands and features than DOS. When the microprocessor selects a different video mode, however, the actual method used is the same when the program in the BIOS is the same.

The IBM PC is considered the standard that all the other manufacturers of personal computers try to emulate. As IBM has copyrighted its BIOS, the other manufacturers implement their BIOS in a different manner. The degree of compatibility of these other systems is, in part, determined by the BIOS.

The internal file system and input/output aspects of DOS are often as invisible to DOS users as interaction with COMMAND.COM is obvious. When considered as a whole, however, DOS is a collection of services offered in the form of built-in groups of related instructions. Understanding which part of the DOS structure is involved in executing a command generally is unimportant. When you are trying to fine-tune the performance of your computer, however, understanding where the various elements fit in, and therefore how you can adjust these elements, is a great benefit.

The DOS Utilities

External commands, such as XCOPY and FORMAT, which are stored on the disk as separate files, are considered the DOS utilities. The DOS utilities provide a collection of commands less commonly used than the internal commands included in COMMAND.COM. You load these utilities into memory only as required. You can compare the external commands with small applications programs.

Some external commands, such as FORMAT, are loaded into memory for use and are removed from memory when the command is completed. Other commands, however, remain in memory until the computer is rebooted. The PRINT command, for example, remains in memory after it is loaded. This program enables you to print files as you are working on other programs. The program can use the spare time when you are just looking at your computer—between keystrokes, for example—to print parts of a file.

Understanding the DOS Environment

Among the duties COMMAND.COM carries out in the working PC are loading and executing programs. COMMAND.COM, as well as other specialized programs, can load additional programs into memory. Only one program can run at one time, however, because DOS is a single-tasking operating system. When a program is loaded into memory, the program is given a set of values that DOS stores in reserved memory locations. The name for the storage area is the *environment*. Some DOS commands, such as PATH and PROMPT, place values in the environment when you issue the command. Other values are assigned with the SET command. Consider the following sample SET command:

SET FINDIT=C:\DOS

The variable name FINDIT is assigned the character value of C:\DOS; both the variable and the variable's value become part of the environment. The word environment has the connotation "surroundings." To a program and to some DOS commands, the values that are part of the surroundings tell the programs how to perform certain aspects of the programs' jobs. Collectively, all the variables and their values are called the *environment string*. You don't arbitrarily put variables in the environment. You put values in the environment so that they are available to any program operating on the PC.

A database program, for example, may need to know in which directory its data files are located. The program can search the environment string, looking for the predetermined variable FINDIT. When FINDIT is located, the program can extract FINDIT's value. The program then can use the variable's value as the directory to search.

Understanding DOS Functions

You use DOS for a variety of functions that fall into one of six general categories. DOS is used for managing files, managing disks, running applications programs, running batch files, redirecting input and output, and handing miscellaneous tasks, such as setting the computer's date and time.

The file management facilities enable you to keep control of large numbers of files. For example, the directory command, DIR, lists your files, the hierarchical directory system enables you to segregate files into separate sections of the same disk, and the COPY and DELETE commands enable you to duplicate or remove files as needed.

Disk management features include such commands as FORMAT, for preparing disks for data; CHKDSK, for checking the data integrity of your disk; and BACKUP and RESTORE, for safety purposes. The method of storing the data on a disk or transferring information from one position to another is not visible to the user. DOS takes care of the details and enables you to use a simple command for a complicated purpose.

Most people use their PCs to run applications programs, such as word processors, spreadsheets, or databases. DOS is really only a support program; the applications programs produce the work. However, the applications programs make use of the DOS facilities wherever possible. Applications programs generally don't control the hardware directly but instruct DOS to perform tasks for them. A word processor can instruct DOS to display the words typed on the keyboard, for example, instead of having to handle that instruction itself.

Although batch files often are only a list of DOS commands saved in a file, they are programs. A *program* is a list of instructions that can be run automatically, and a batch file fits this definition. In a manner similar to the way large applications programs operate, you don't need to define the details of manipulating the hardware directly to run a batch file. You use typical DOS commands, with a few special batch commands, if necessary, and let DOS take care of the details.

The modular nature of DOS, which treats everything it interacts with as a device, has advantages for users. DOS has the capacity to redirect input and output. For example, the standard input device is the keyboard, and the standard output device is the screen. If you want to take input from a file on disk rather than from the keyboard, you direct DOS to take the input from the disk rather than from the standard input device. Screen output can be redirected to a printer to get a hard copy version of the information on-screen.

The DOS Shell program supplied with DOS 5 is a windowed user interface that enables the user to execute DOS functions by selecting an item from a menu. The Shell program does not actually contain instructions for running the commands. If you select the Format Disk option, for example, the Shell program starts the DOS FORMAT command. When the format is completed, DOS returns control to the Shell program, and you again see the list of options in the Shell program.

Booting DOS and Memory

When you turn on the computer, a sequence of events called *booting* is initiated. The expression "booting" has been used for many years in computers and refers to the term "pulling himself up by his bootstraps."

Booting means that without any external help, the computer can get itself ready to run your programs. In this process the PC tests itself, initializes the various devices, and then loads the system files and COMMAND.COM.

Initializing the POST

The ROM chip that contains the BIOS starts the initialization process, the power-on self test (POST). POST checks devices such as the video adapter and serial port and any memory installed in the system. The sequence of testing the various parts of the computer tends to vary with the manufacturer of the computer, but each element is tested in turn.

The BIOS contains instructions that the CPU uses to write to the RAM memory. The testing starts with the memory that has the lowest address. Data is written to the RAM, and then the CPU reads the data back, checking that what is read is the same as what was written. With most PCs, you see the current address of RAM memory being checked on-screen. Other devices are tested in a similar sequential fashion. Most of these tests produce no on-screen display. If you have a keyboard with lights on, however, the lights flash when the keyboard is checked during the boot process.

After POST has successfully tested each part of the computer, the initialization can continue. On most computers, you hear a single beep, indicating that the POST operation was successful. COMPAQ computers beep twice for a successful boot. Some computers that can be started at different speeds depending on a switch setting, such as Gateway 2000's 25 MHz 386, give a beep with a different tone for different speeds.

POST serves two related purposes. POST ensures that the computer is working properly before the full operating system is loaded, and POST also is a useful troubleshooting tool when things are not working. If a RAM chip is defective and POST doesn't check the chip, for example, you may have strange problems. Suppose that you run a program that writes to that area of memory. You may get strange data, or, if instructions were stored in the defective chips, you may crash your computer. POST checking the RAM before you load the programs results in a much more reliable system.

POST can inform you of problems in two different ways. The familiar beep you hear when the computer boots successfully may be replaced with a series of beeps, and/or you may get error messages. This error information is an excellent starting place for troubleshooting problems.

Examining Common POST Errors

The most common time you see a POST error message is when you have moved the computer or taken the cover off to install something. If you add an extra disk drive on an AT, for example, you get a POST error message until you run the Setup program. Replacing the battery is another innocent instance in which the computer complains, and there's nothing to repair.

The different tones you hear and error messages you see when POST detects an error consist of a series of short and long beeps or an error-code number on-screen. In some instances, you get a number and a combination of beeps. POST tries to give the clearest message possible to indicate the problem but cannot always be precise. If your display adapter has failed, for example, POST may not be capable of displaying a message; in this case, the beeps are the best POST can do.

Table 2.2 lists some of the audible beeps you may hear when the system is booting, and table 2.3 lists some of the error-code numbers that may appear. POST tries to complete itself, even if it finds an error, so you may see more than one code. In table 2.3, a number range is listed—for example, 200 range—which means that you may see an error code beginning with a 2 and two digits appearing after the 2.

Table 2.2
POST Error Beeps

Audible Sound	Probable Area of Problem
Continuous beeps or repeating short beeps	Power supply or system board
One long and one short beep	System board, display adapter, or power supply
One long and two short beeps	System board or power supply
One short beep and blank display	System board or power supply
One short beep and prompt for disk	Disk drive, system board, power supply, disk controller, or cable

Table 2.3
POST Error Codes

POST Error Number	Probable Area of Problem
100 range	System board
161	Battery error
162	Configuration error
163	Time and date error
165	System options not set
200 range (exact location sometimes listed)	Memory error
301, 303, or 304	Keyboard
305	Keyboard fuse
401	Parallel port
600 range (except 602)	Floppy disk drive
602	Reference disk
701	Math coprocessor
1100 or 1200 range	Serial port(s)
1700 range and 10400 range	Hard disk drive
2400 range	System board video
8600	Pointing device

You shouldn't panic when you hear or see a POST error. In many cases a cable simply may have come unplugged, or your battery is failing and needs replacing.

To see one of these error codes, try unplugging your keyboard before turning on your computer. If you're using a COMPAQ, you get a 304 error and a single beep rather than the successful COMPAQ boot signal of two beeps. Provided that you insert or remove the connector only when the computer is switched off, you will not damage the computer with this experiment.

A defective RAM chip can play havoc with your programs and data and should be replaced promptly. If you're lucky, the actual memory location where the error occurred may be displayed in the POST code, and by referring to the documentation that came with your system or memory boards, you should be able to isolate the problem. If you don't know the actual location but regularly get memory errors, several public domain programs exist that exercise the RAM and enable you to locate the problem precisely.

Analyzing POST Problems

If you get a POST error when you aren't expecting one, note the numbers displayed and the beeps you hear. Try turning off and restarting the computer. Consider whether anything has changed since you last used the system. Perhaps you moved the computer forward yesterday to reach something behind it and knocked a cable loose.

The error codes are accurate but not definitive. For example, if you get a code in the 600 range, you know that the hard-disk system didn't pass POST. If nothing actually is broken, however, this error code may be caused by a loose power supply connector on the disk drive, by a disk controller not fully seated in the expansion slot, or by loose cables between the controller and disk drive. Check these items and try again before you start counting the money in your piggy bank.

The error codes are not exhaustive, and not all errors can be detected by POST. For example, POST cannot tell if you don't have your monitor plugged into the display adapter. POST is an integral part of the computer itself and can check only the items it interacts with directly. Remember that the CPU interacts with devices but doesn't determine how the devices themselves work. The CPU may request data from the hard-disk controller but doesn't supply instructions on how to actually retrieve the data on the disk.

Even if you are not the type to get out solder and pliers when your computer fails, you can make good use of the error codes given by POST. Saying to a repair company that you get a 10481 error code is likely to get them to bring a new system board and hard disk drive, whereas saying that your computer doesn't work isn't as constructive.

Loading System Files

After the POST procedure is completed, booting continues. The BIOS instructs the PC to access track 0 of the boot disk and read the boot sector into RAM. The boot sector contains a short assembly language program that finds and loads the two DOS system files. The boot program then looks for the CONFIG.SYS file in the root directory of the boot disk. If CONFIG.SYS is found, the boot program opens the file and installs into memory any device drivers to which CONFIG.SYS refers.

Through the device drivers loaded at the time of booting, the computer can operate in a configuration tailored to its hardware and running requirements. Whereas most device drivers are built into DOS's BIOS extensions, CONFIG.SYS device drivers are selectable and under your control. CONFIG.SYS even has a provision to tell the boot program where to look for COMMAND.COM in the directory structure. The boot program locates COMMAND.COM in the disk location designated by CONFIG.SYS or in the boot disk's root directory. When COMMAND.COM is found, it is loaded into memory.

When COMMAND.COM is loaded into RAM, the boot program turns control over to COMMAND.COM by putting COMMAND.COM's first instruction location into the CPU's program counter. COMMAND.COM does not immediately display the system prompt and await your input, however. First, COMMAND.COM relocates part of its own instructions to another location in memory. In effect, COMMAND.COM splits itself into two parts. One part remains in memory at all times. Another part, a transient part, is overwritten by incoming programs as they need the memory space occupied by the transient part. The part of COMMAND.COM that stays in memory has the capability of reloading the transient part from the disk to become a whole program again.

COMMAND.COM searches the root directory of the boot disk for a file named AUTOEXEC.BAT. If the AUTOEXEC.BAT file is found, its contents are executed as a series of DOS commands. By providing for this special batch file to be executed when booting, DOS can tailor the start-up of every PC to meet the specific needs of the user. AUTOEXEC.BAT can contain any DOS command but normally contains such commands as PROMPT, PATH, TIME, and DATE.

When COMMAND.COM has executed AUTOEXEC.BAT, you see the command prompt (assuming that one of the commands in AUTOEXEC.BAT does not start a program). COMMAND.COM then is ready to receive your command.

Examining DOS's Position in Memory

If you are using DOS 4.0 or a later version, you can see where the various parts of DOS load into memory. The MEM command with the /DEBUG parameter lists the various positions. If you use DOS 4.0 on a system with 512K of base memory and no CONFIG.SYS or AUTOEXEC.BAT file, you may see the following display when you type **MEM /DEBUG** at the DOS prompt:

```
Address         Name            Size            Type
-------         --------        ------          ------
000000                          000400          Interrupt Vector
000400                          000100          ROM Communication Area
000500                          000200          DOS Communication Area

000700          IBMBIO          002540          System Program
                CON                                 System Device Driver
                AUX                                 System Device Driver
                PRN                                 System Device Driver
                CLOCK$                              System Device Driver
                A: - E:                             System Device Driver
                COM1                                System Device Driver
                LPT1                                System Device Driver
                LPT2                                System Device Driver
                LPT3                                System Device Driver
                COM2                                System Device Driver
                COM3                                System Device Driver
                COM4                                System Device Driver

002C40          IBMDOS          0088D0          System Program

00B510          IBMBIO          002580          System Data
                                0000C0              FILES=
                                000100              FCBS=
                                0014E0              BUFFERS=
                                0001C0              LASTDRIVE=
                                000CD0              STACKS=
00DAA0          COMMAND         001640          Program
00F0F0          MEM             000030          Environment
00F130          COMMAND         0000A0          Environment
00F1E0          MEM             012F60          Program
022150          IBMDOS          05DEA0          -- Free --

    524288 bytes total memory
    524288 bytes available
    462352 largest executable program size
```

The locations of the various elements are similar in earlier versions of DOS, which do not have a MEM command to display this information. However, the absolute positions are different because the file sizes are different. For example, COMMAND.COM in 4.0 is larger than in any of the earlier versions. DOS 5 also includes a MEM command. Because of better memory management features, however, COMMAND.COM can occupy less space in memory than in earlier versions.

The left column of this listing contains the starting address for the item. The second column contains the name, such as COMMAND, the third column contains the length of the item, and the fourth column contains the item's type. The address and the length of the program are shown in bytes. The actual number given is in hexadecimal (base 16). Appendix B explains hexadecimal and memory addressing.

The first item in the display is the interrupt vector table, which is the list of addresses for the various devices in the computer. When the interrupt controller detects an interrupt, it signals to the CPU that the device needs attention and gives a location in the interrupt vector table. The CPU looks at the memory address found in the particular location in the interrupt vector table and jumps to the address given to service the interrupting device.

This seemingly indirect approach is, in fact, logical. By listing only the starting addresses for the device's interrupt routine, the interrupt controller does not have to keep track of the size of the various interrupt routines or their respective locations in memory. A PC can be configured with different types of devices without the necessity of changing the fundamental interrupt controller routine.

Consider, for example, two different hard disks that may be installed into a system at different times. Because DOS uses this indirect method of pointing to an address, each hard disk can have an interrupt routine that is any size or in different locations in memory. The only value for the starting address must be in a specific location in the interrupt vector table.

The next two items shown in the MEM listing are used by the BIOS and by DOS, respectively, for communication. At address 0700H is the beginning of the system program IBMBIO, the first of the system files read from the boot sector of the disk. Within IBMBIO are the internal devices that DOS always uses. (Additional devices are added by the CONFIG.SYS file.) Some devices you probably recognize; others generally are used only internally by DOS. For example, the PRN and LPT1 devices are the printer ports, and CON refers to the console, which consists of the keyboard and display. When you copy a file to PRN or LPT1 by using the DOS COPY command, you are accessing the devices that have their device drivers located in IBMBIO.

The next area of memory contains the second system file, IBMDOS. This item is followed by a data area used by IBMBIO to store system data. The values for the configuration subcommands are kept in this area of memory. These values can be set in the CONFIG.SYS file. FILES and BUFFERS are the items most commonly set, because many applications programs require a larger number of files or buffers open than the DOS default values.

In the area of memory immediately after the IBMDOS program is the COMMAND.COM program. In the listing, the MEM program environment follows; then comes the COMMAND.COM environment and the MEM program itself. As mentioned earlier, the environment is a reserved area of memory used for storing variables used by a program.

The MEM listing includes its own environment and program, which shows its position in memory. If an applications program were running instead of the MEM program, the applications program would start at an address in memory similar to the start position of MEM (F1E0H).

This listing shows that, with MEM running, the memory is free from address 22150H on. The first 136K of memory is taken up by DOS and MEM. The next listing shows that the system contains 512K of memory (524,288 bytes) and that the maximum size of a program you can run is 451K (462,352 bytes). MEM has subtracted its own size from the used memory to give you this value.

Figure 2.2 shows the address map for a personal computer with DOS loaded. The absolute values are for a system with 512K of memory and no CONFIG.SYS or AUTOEXEC.BAT file running DOS 4.0.

Starting Applications Programs

After DOS is loaded into memory at the end of the boot process, you can use DOS commands or you can run an applications program. The amount of memory available to the program is the amount of memory left in the base 640K of memory. In the example, a program can occupy 451K of memory. This is the memory available for the program, its environment, and any data that needs to be in memory.

When you start an applications program, it loads itself into memory directly above DOS and reserves an area for the environment. As you work in the applications program—by typing a document in a word processor, for example—the applications program takes up more memory as necessary to hold the additional data.

When you exit from the applications program and return to DOS, the memory used by the data, environment, and program are returned to the general pool for another applications program to use.

Part I: Examining PC and DOS Basics

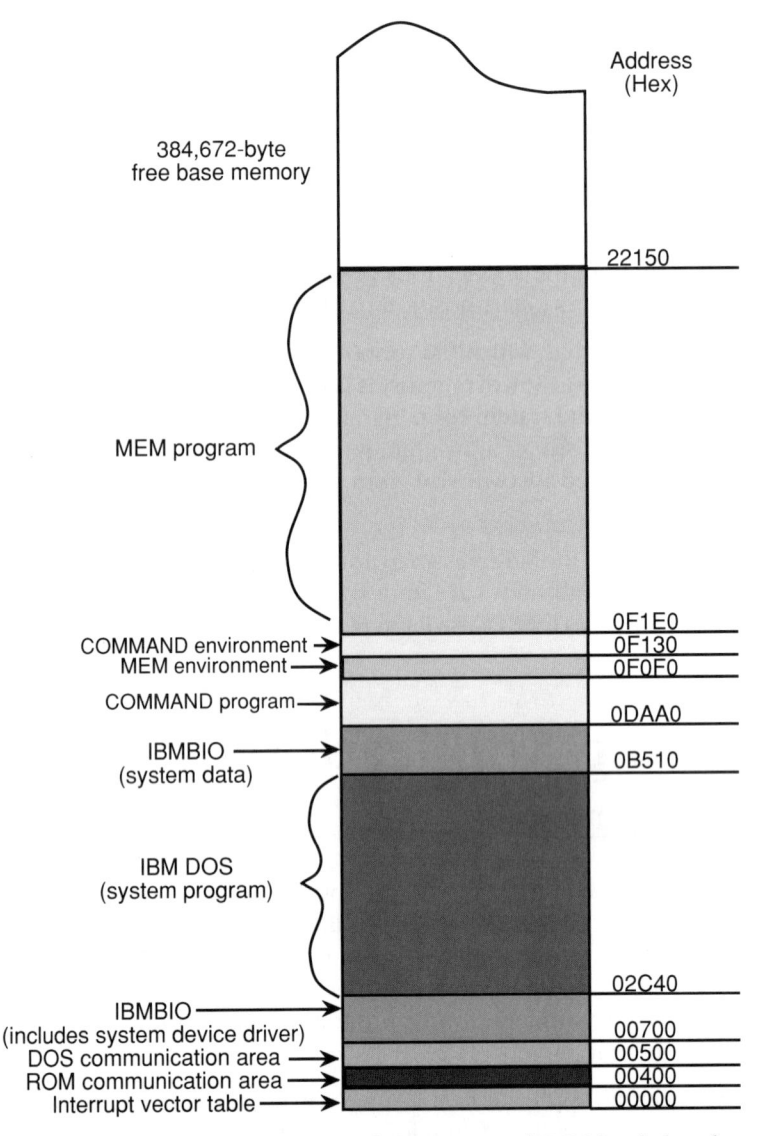

```
                                      Address
                                       (Hex)

      384,672-byte
      free base memory

                                       22150

      MEM program

                                       0F1E0
COMMAND environment →                  0F130
    MEM environment →                  0F0F0
   COMMAND program →                   0DAA0
           IBMBIO →                    0B510
      (system data)

         IBM DOS
      (system program)

                                       02C40
           IBMBIO →                    00700
(includes system device driver)
  DOS communication area →             00500
  ROM communication area →             00400
    Interrupt vector table →           00000
```

Fig. 2.2. An address map for a personal computer with DOS loaded and MEM running.

While an applications program is running, the program needs to communicate with various devices in the computer, such as the hard disk or display. This communication is done most often by DOS, which the applications program asks to perform the function.

In certain instances, however, programs do not follow the "rules" and are considered ill-behaved. Instead of asking DOS to perform a function, the applications program may communicate directly with a device. A common example is an applications program that writes to the screen. The BIOS routines (programs) that are responsible for transferring data from the applications program to DOS and then to the screen work more slowly than an applications program that writes directly to the video device. Because you, the user, are acutely aware of how fast things are written to the screen, the applications program is written to give the best possible video performance.

This technique has advantages in that programs appear to run fast. The severe disadvantage, however, is that such a program is not device-independent. The method used to write to each video adapter is different. Consequently, the applications program needs to have different programming code for each video board it supports. If you own a device that is not supported by that particular applications program, you cannot run the program. Also, if your version of the particular device, say a Brand A VGA, is not fully compatible with the standard IBM VGA device, you may not be able to use the program either.

DOS can run only one program at a time. However, some operating systems, such as UNIX, are multitasking and allow more than one program to operate at once. As new multitasking operating systems, such as OS/2, become more widely used, the importance of having applications programs follow the rules increases. The computer may have more things to keep track of at any time, and programs must be willing to share computer resources, such as devices, equitably. Circumventing the operating system and communicating directly with the hardware is not acceptable in the new applications programs written to work with the operating system.

Device Drivers

Remember that DOS communicates with the devices in a system through the interrupt vector table. You can add or change device drivers with the CONFIG.SYS file. When CONFIG.SYS is loaded, new devices—such as a different keyboard handler to support a foreign keyboard—are incorporated into the interrupt vector table. The old address for the keyboard handler listed in the interrupt vector table is discarded, and the new value is inserted. Device drivers installed in the interrupt vector table by DOS are known as *resident device drivers*, and device drivers listed in CONFIG.SYS that replace the resident device drivers are known as *installable device drivers*.

For example, when you press a key on the keyboard, the keyboard signals to the interrupt controller that it requires attention. The interrupt controller signals to DOS that an interrupt requires attention. When DOS services the interrupt, as described earlier, DOS is directed to a point in the interrupt vector table that contains the address for the keyboard handler. DOS is unaware whether an address is the same as when it originally booted the computer; DOS simply loads the address into the program counter. If a new keyboard handler's address is in the interrupt vector table, the new handler then translates the keyboard's scan code.

An applications program that supplies its own device handler also can change the devices listed in the interrupt vector table. Because the device driver is required only when the applications program runs, the replacement is done as part of the applications program's loading procedure. When you exit from the applications program, the address for the original device driver is reinserted into the interrupt vector table. Other programs, including DOS, are unaware that the device was changed as the applications program was running. Some applications programs, however, circumvent the interrupt vector table completely and, by controlling the hardware directly, avoid using the DOS functions at any level.

DOS's flexibility in handling a variety of different devices is one of the biggest strengths of the personal computer. That flexibility has allowed the standard to evolve over the years, instead of making the original PC a static system. For example, as new video boards have become available, only the device driver has changed. The same is true for hard and floppy disks and drives. The size of the device driver is relatively unimportant, because only its starting address is stored in the beginning of memory.

Memory-Resident Programs

Not all applications programs operate in isolation in memory. Many utility programs, and even some external DOS commands, operate in a different way than that described previously. When you activate the program—the DOS PRINT command, for example—the program is loaded into memory, the command is processed, and the command prompt returns. However, a portion of the program remains in memory. Hence, the term memory-resident program. These programs also are known as TSRs, *terminate-and-stay-resident programs.*

A portion of a TSR remains in memory for one of two reasons: The TSR is a background task, or it is waiting for a particular event to occur. If the program is operating as PRINT does, the program runs while you run another program. PRINT can use the spare time between your keystrokes to send files to the printer and therefore is a background task. The DOS MODE command also is memory resident. One of DOS MODE's capabilities is to enhance the features of the existing serial port device driver. Like PRINT, DOS MODE is a background task.

The second type of memory-resident program is dormant until a particular event occurs: pressing a particular key combination, for example, or accessing a particular device. The program detects the occurrence of the event and then activates itself. You can use the activated program. When you exit from the program, the applications program or DOS is reactivated, and the memory-resident program waits to be activated again.

A good illustration of this second type of TSR is the PC Tools Desktop Manager program, which can be made memory resident. To do so, you type **DESKTOP /R** at the command prompt. This command loads the program and returns the command prompt so that you can run other programs. The memory-resident portion of Desktop Manager does two things. It looks at every keystroke and waits for the key combination Ctrl-Space. When that key combination is detected, the memory-resident portion takes control, unloading any applications currently running and loading Desktop Manager into memory.

The memory-resident program in the example needs to examine each keystroke to watch for its "hot key" to occur. When you make it resident, the TSR replaces with its own address the address for the keyboard handler in the interrupt vector table. Now, every time a key is pressed, the address for the start of the TSR's keyboard handler—instead of the original keyboard handler's address—is loaded into the program counter. The TSR examines the scan code and determines whether the key pressed is its hot key. If not, the scan code is passed on without alteration to the original keyboard handler. The TSR loads the value it found in the interrupt vector table into the program counter. The keyboard handler then translates the scan code and passes it on to DOS, which in turn passes it on to any applications program running in the computer. Figure 2.3 shows the flow of control with and without a memory-resident program loaded.

No TSR

Interrupt controller → Interrupt vector table → Device driver (device's interrupt handler)

TSR

Interrupt controller → Interrupt vector table → TSR's interrupt controller → Device driver (device's interrupt handler)

Multiple TSRs

Interrupt controller → Interrupt vector table → TSR #1's interrupt controller → TSR #2's interrrupt controller → Device driver (device's interrupt handler)

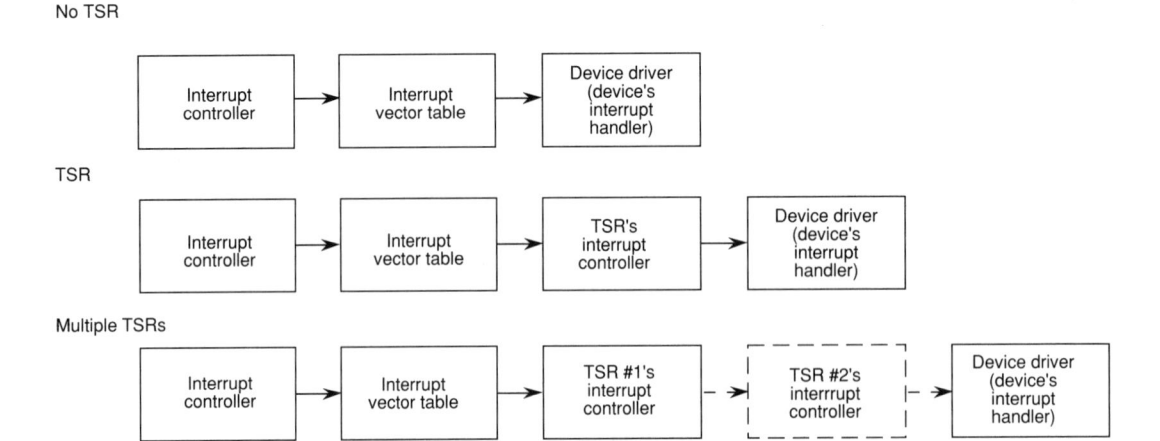

Fig. 2.3. Memory-resident programs alter the interrupt vector table.

If you consider the sequence of events to interpret a keystroke into a character as a chain of events, the memory-resident program inserts itself into the chain to operate. Of course, the memory-resident program does not have to change the keyboard interrupt vector, nor is it restricted to only intercepting a single interrupt. However, the keyboard interrupt vector is commonly intercepted by memory-resident programs so that they can activate and deactivate themselves as required.

Multiple memory-resident programs can be installed, and they insert themselves into the chain in the same manner as the first program. Many TSRs are very possessive about interrupts, however, and do not always complete the chain properly. Most notable of these programs are previous versions of Borland International's SideKick program.

The sequence in which memory-resident programs are loaded may affect their capacity to work together. Although some memory-resident programs do not work with each other at all, sometimes only the loading sequence causes the problem. In some arrangements, the chain may be logical and link each section to the correct locations. In others, however, the chain may be broken. The effect of a broken chain can be merely strange behavior or can lock up your computer completely.

Although memory-resident programs are convenient, you should exercise restraint in using them. Every memory-resident program takes up valuable memory and may not leave you with enough memory to run your applications programs; in addition, TSRs have the reputation for not working with each other and with applications programs. If you experience problems with an applications program, remove all the TSRs and then try to replicate the problem. The various chains of communication between the devices may not be working correctly.

Chapter Summary

This chapter introduced the personal computer operating system, DOS.

Although different manufacturers supply different implementations of DOS, all DOS programs function in a similar manner, with only small differences between them. DOS has evolved over time, and the newer versions have additional features, support more devices, and occupy more base memory.

Using a hierarchical system, the four parts of DOS work with each other to make up the whole operating system. The four parts are the command interpreter, system files, BIOS, and utility programs. DOS is used for managing files, managing disks, running applications programs, running batch files, redirecting input and output, and handling miscellaneous tasks, such as setting the date and time.

The initialization process for DOS includes a power on self test (POST) that gives important information regarding your computer's integrity. The beeps and error codes help pinpoint faults without requiring any test equipment.

After POST is completed, DOS loads itself into memory in a predefined way. The organization enables other programs to alter the computer's configuration. Alternative devices can be added through the CONFIG.SYS file, an applications program can change devices as it is running, or a memory-resident program can put itself between DOS and a device.

Every time you add a new device or program—in particular, memory-resident programs—you should be aware that you are altering the computer's configuration. You should test the various parts to ensure that they work together. The chain of device drivers possibly may have missing links, which can result in unpredictable computer behavior.

Chapter 3 shows how the basic PC standard has been extended over time. Terms such as extended and expanded memory are introduced, as well as disk caches, cache controllers, and device drivers supplied with DOS.

Extending the Basic Standard

3

The popularity of the PC has revolutionized business. If the PC had remained a static standard, it would not be so popular today. As new microprocessors become available, the PC incorporates them without destroying the existing standards. The same has been true of software. Each version of DOS enhances the standard, increasing both its functionality and flexibility.

Chapter 3 explains the variety of device drivers now available for the PC with DOS and defines expanded and extended memory. Commonly used techniques for improving performance, such as disk caches and cache controllers, also are discussed. Two diagnostic programs that analyze your computer's configuration are used in examples, demonstrating features covered in Part I.

Understanding Device Drivers

The layers of DOS, introduced in Chapter 2, interact with each other in a hierarchical manner. When you run your programs, you are interacting with a higher layer of the PC. In this higher layer, you see computing as spreadsheet cells, word processor function keys, and modem links to on-line data services. This surface activity of manipulating information using the keyboard and screen is quite an abstraction from the logical and electromechanical activity going on at lower layers of the PC. Perhaps you are interested in creating an accurate financial model of next year's sales or in reformatting a block of text for a manual. Just the fact that you can use a personal computer as a tool to do useful work without worrying about how the computer operates is a tribute to how far computers have come in the past decade.

The internal processes of the system are hidden from view. When you issue DOS commands at the DOS prompt to manage your disks, directories, files, and devices, you are at a slightly lower and slightly less abstract layer of the computer. While working with COMMAND.COM, you are more aware of the file system and the devices connected to your PC. At the DOS prompt, you maintain the PC so that it is more orderly and useful for your computing work. Tailoring your configuration to suit your particular needs is a natural extension of your current understanding of DOS.

DOS maintains order in your PC below the visible surface of COMMAND.COM. This core layer of the operating system is the DOS kernel, which is less abstract than COMMAND.COM. The *kernel*, IBMDOS.COM for PC DOS and MSDOS.SYS for MS-DOS, deals with requests from COMMAND.COM and manages data from files and devices. The kernel sends requests from you or the program to logical sectors, starting clusters, and RAM buffer locations. The kernel translates input or output requests from the higher layers into uniform requests of a predetermined form for lower layers. Thanks to the kernel, a program can be totally independent of the burden of managing the file system and can count on requests, such as file input or printer output, to be fulfilled in a constant and reliable fashion.

Below the kernel layer, a system of basic input/output services is built into the hardware itself. Called *BIOS*, or basic input/output system, this least-abstract layer of the PC deals with peripheral hardware at the binary level. You can think of BIOS as the PC's device-dependent layer. The responsibility for getting input from and output to the peripheral hardware rests on the BIOS. Because the BIOS processes kernel requests through uniform service routines, the kernel is device-independent. Any new peripheral hardware that the BIOS supports is available for kernel requests. BIOS routines are the glue that attaches hardware to the basic computer in a fashion that disguises the seams.

As discussed in Chapter 2, *device drivers* are specialized program modules or routines that accommodate the attachment of peripheral hardware to DOS. Most peripheral hardware, such as disk drives, serial printers or modems, parallel printers, video displays, and mice, connect to the PC's bus system through adapters or controllers.

Adapters, introduced in Chapter 1, are electronic circuit boards that contain the necessary support logic to control a physical device. Adapters often are called *controllers* because their primary function is to control devices. Device drivers are written to manage the activities of the controllers.

Display adapters are examples of controllers. A PC may have one or more display adapters, such as a monochrome display adapter (MDA), color graphics adapter (CGA), enhanced graphics adapter (EGA), or video graphics array (VGA). Each display adapter has its own supporting device driver.

When any one of these adapters is in text mode, the adapter can display characters, numbers, and symbols all based in ROM. The characters, numbers, and symbols are encoded into ROM as patterns of bits that correspond to points of light, or *pixels*, on the display screen. Each character is composed of a rectangular grid of possible pixels, with the pixels that form the character illuminated. The number of possible pixels in each character grid varies among adapters.

The driver for each adapter enables the DOS kernel (and therefore a program) to request a character for placement on the screen. When you press a key and see the character echoed on the screen, you are seeing the work of the driver and the adapter. If you press the A key, you see an A on the screen even though the pixel density of the A may not be the same as that of another display adapter. The drivers for display adapters shield the kernel from the details of how the A is produced on the screen.

Disk controllers are another example of adapters. Whereas the disk drive has a limited electronic function, the disk controller supplies much of the underlying logic or intelligence of disk operations. Although disk drives are fundamentally alike, each type of drive has its own electromechanical personality. When the kernel requests a logical sector number from the disk device driver, the driver manages the controller to ensure that the drive is ready for transfer and has been given the correct head, track, and sector number. When the drive controller returns the data, the device driver supervises the placement of the returned data into memory. The kernel is unaware of the nature and the number of individual tasks that the driver carries out to make the sector available. When the kernel calls on a disk device driver, the kernel can make a generic request for sectors and count on the driver to deal with its specific disk drive.

If a programmer is sufficiently familiar with how a new peripheral works, the programmer can write a device driver for the hardware (or for its adapter). DOS clearly defines the programmed interface between the kernel and the device driver. If a programmer strictly follows the definition, DOS can use the device.

Dividing Device Drivers into Groups

Physical devices as diverse as disk drives and keyboards tax the definition of a single type of device driver interface to the kernel. DOS provides for device drivers to fall into one of two groups: *Character* device drivers are designed for devices such as the keyboard and printer; *block* device drivers are designed for devices such as disk drives and tape drives.

Character Device Drivers

Character devices perform input or output one character or byte at a time. Typical character devices in PCs are the keyboard, display, serial ports, and parallel ports. Usually, one device driver controls one character device. The device driver for a character device supplies a one-character to eight-character device name to the DOS kernel. The character device name is quite similar to a root file name in that both can have as many as eight characters in the root name. Character device names do not include extensions, however. Programs that use character devices treat the devices as though they are files.

The DOS kernel transfers characters to or from the character device driver by using RAM to store or buffer the characters temporarily. In some cases, the kernel checks the character stream for a Ctrl-Break or an Enter character. In other cases, the kernel passes a stream of serial characters to or from the character device driver and does not look at the actual characters. The kernel also can echo to the screen each character received from the character device driver. The actual behavior of the kernel-to-device-driver interface during character input/output is determined by the program initiating the requests for input/output.

Character device drivers support the less complex peripheral hardware. Although the character-oriented peripheral may not be complex, character-oriented devices are too numerous and difficult to supervise for the DOS kernel to see to their detailed requirements. Yet the more complex device drivers that move massive amounts of data to and from such devices as disk drives are not well served by character device drivers.

Block Device Drivers

To deal with the movement of massive amounts of I/O data, DOS incorporates block device drivers. Like character device drivers, block device drivers are well-defined program routines. But unlike character device drivers, block device drivers transfer data to and from the kernel in large units called *blocks*—hence the term *block device driver*.

Block device drivers interface peripheral hardware with the kernel by handling blocks of addressable data. The most common type of block device driver is the disk device driver. On the disk, the addressable blocks of data are the data sectors. Block devices are given one-letter names, such as A, B, and C. These letter names are the same kinds of names DOS gives to your disk drives.

Unlike character devices, which DOS treats like logical files, block devices are considered logical disks by DOS. In fact, through the magic of the device driver, you can address one physical disk drive as several logical disk devices. Even a nondisk emulation of a disk's function can be incorporated into a block device driver. DOS is supplied with RAMDRIVE, a virtual disk device driver that uses RAM to simulate a disk drive. The RAMDRIVE device driver, for example, uses a portion of system RAM that appears to the DOS kernel as a disk drive complete with sectors. Thanks to the special RAMDRIVE block device driver, a program can access a file from the virtual disk unaware that the requested file is actually a block of RAM.

Character and block device drivers form the backbone of the PC's input/output system. By hiding the hardware detail from the kernel and at the same time interfacing with the kernel in a uniform fashion, device drivers make the hardware modular or uniform. Modularity is why the same program can run on an IBM Personal Computer PS/2 Model 80 or a Dell 310. Uniformity of driver design is why, for example, an optical-character-recognition device can transfer characters to a program through a serial port. In an hour, the same serial port may be downloading a file through a modem.

Examining Resident and Installable Device Drivers

The DOS system disks contain files that collectively make up the device drivers for a PC. Not all device drivers are supplied with the DOS package. DOS cannot possibly anticipate all the hardware that you have or will have. Additional device drivers can be added at any time, however, to the ones that come with DOS. On the DOS disk, the hidden system file IO.SYS

(IBMBIO.COM in PC DOS) contains the device drivers that always load into memory at boot time. Because IO.SYS is part of the DOS-supplied software, the device drivers included in IO.SYS are called the *resident drivers*. In Version 2.0 and later, the DOS package contains other device driver files with SYS extensions such as ANSI.SYS, VDISK.SYS, PRINTER.SYS, and others. Not every version of DOS has all these driver files. The SYS files load into memory as part of the boot processing of the CONFIG.SYS file. The controlled way the PC loads drivers into memory is called *driver installation*. The device drivers with SYS extensions therefore are called *installable device drivers*. In a DOS environment, device drivers are either resident or installable.

Resident Device Drivers

Each version of DOS has its own selection of resident device drivers in the hidden system file IO.SYS (IBMBIO.COM). PC vendors may modify the list of IO.SYS device drivers to include a particular hardware feature.

A program accesses the resident device drivers as a standard set of devices below the kernel. The kernel views these device drivers as logical devices capable of providing input, supplying output, or doing both.

The disk block-device-driver routines support the standard PC disk devices. As higher capacity floppy drives become standard equipment, new versions of DOS-included drivers are added to support these disk drives. If you are running Version 3.1 and want to install a 720K 3 1/2-inch disk drive, for example, you discover that your version of DOS does not support the added drive. Your PC is not the problem; the older version of DOS is most likely the problem. As newer devices are added to PCs, the resident drivers are modified to keep pace.

DOS provides many resident character device drivers. As is the rule with character device drivers, the resident character device drivers reserve names for the devices they control. Table 3.1 lists the resident character device drivers for PC DOS 4.0. Other versions and implementations have most of these resident device drivers.

Because these resident device drivers are defined by DOS, their names are reserved. DOS first tests file parameters to see whether the parameters are device names. If you use a file name, even with an extension that has the root name of a reserved device, DOS assumes that you are referring to the device, not to a file. To avoid such naming conflicts, don't provide file names that are similar to reserved device names. The file name DON is just one keystroke away from the device name CON. In a COPY command line, pressing **C** rather than **D** can send file output to your screen, not to DON.

Table 3.1
PC DOS 4.0
Resident Character Device Drivers

Device Name	Meaning
CLOCK$	The system clock device driver
CON	The keyboard as input and the display as output
AUX or COM1	The first serial communications port
COM*n*	The *n*th serial communications port up to 4
LPT1 or PRN	The first parallel port (output only)
LPT*n*	The *n*th parallel printer port up to 3
NUL	A nonexistent (dummy) device used for discarding output when device output is unwanted; often used in batch files to suppress (throw away) screen output

Installable Device Drivers

Ever since Version 2.0 of DOS, your PC's device complement does not have to be limited to those devices supported by IO.SYS. Because DOS provides for additional device support to be added at boot time, the installed device drivers are an extension to the kernel. DOS inspects the contents of the special file CONFIG.SYS in the boot disk's root. If CONFIG.SYS contains any device installation directives, DOS installs the indicated device driver from the proper disk. You can consider CONFIG.SYS as a pathway from the disk file to the installed location in the system. The number of installed device drivers varies based on CONFIG.SYS. By providing a means to load additional device support at boot time, DOS produces a kernel interface with the hardware that is much more versatile than the one provided by IO.SYS. After boot time, the device drivers, regardless of whether they are resident or installable, are accessed.

DOS provides some installable device drivers on the master DOS disks. Again, different versions supply different numbers of device driver files. Table 3.2 lists the installable device drivers that come with DOS 5.0.

**Table 3.2
PC DOS 5.0
Installable Device Drivers**

Device Driver	Action
ANSI.SYS	Replaces the standard console device driver with a device driver that incorporates ANSI terminal control sequences
DISPLAY.SYS	Enables code-page switching on an EGA display and on the IBM PC Convertible LCD display
DRIVER.SYS	Operates an external disk drive through a block device letter name
EMM386.EXE	Uses extended memory on 80386- and 80486- based PCs to simulate an expanded-memory adapter device; provides access to the reserved memory area of high DOS memory; provides support for the Weitek math coprocessor
HIMEM.SYS	Helps with memory management when used with applications programs that use high DOS memory areas and extended memory
PRINTER.SYS	Enables code-page switching for parallel ports LPT1, LPT2, LPT3, and PRN
RAMDRIVE.SYS	Installs and operates a virtual (RAM) disk device as a simulated disk drive
SMARTDRV.SYS	Creates a disk cache in expanded or extended memory
XMA2EMS.SYS	Supports the LIM Expanded Memory Specification (EMS) with DOS 4.0

If you look at the action of each installable device driver, you will notice that only DRIVER.SYS is capable of supporting additional hardware on the PC. You can configure DRIVER.SYS to support an additional disk device—a disk device different in design from the disk devices supported by the resident disk driver routines.

The other installable device drivers in table 3.2 don't add any new devices to the computer. Instead, the rest of the device drivers modify or enhance certain resident drivers and add logical devices created from existing system resources. Users who don't need a standard device enhanced obviously don't need to install a device driver that enhances. Because device drivers are an integral part of DOS's kernel, they can be added or removed only at boot time. Changing CONFIG.SYS and rebooting the computer enables you to change the device drivers currently available. Some of the installable device drivers are for special purposes.

EMM386.EXE, for example, is useful for owners of 80386- and 80486-based computers. Through the addressing mode of the CPU and the device driver translation, RAM that is located above the one-megabyte (1M) addressing range of DOS appears to be an expanded-memory adapter board. Expanded and extended memory are covered later in this chapter. Some implementations of DOS 4—most notably IBM PC DOS—call the EMM386.EXE file XMAEM.SYS. Although some installable device drivers included with DOS are for special purposes, others have a more general appeal to users.

XMA2EMS.SYS is another special-purpose device driver that makes an expanded-memory adapter usable with your computer so that DOS or an application may access expanded memory. On a 386-based computer with EMM386.EXE installed, XMA2EMS.SYS enables DOS or an application to access the memory that is acting as expanded memory. This is an example of two device drivers working together.

ANSI.SYS, for example, replaces the resident keyboard device and display device driver. ANSI.SYS enables the device's character stream to encode device control sequences that position the cursor, change the screen colors, give keys new definitions, and more. Many third-party programs are available that give even more functionality to the keyboard and display. Products such as Fansi-Console from Hersey Computing and NANSI.SYS make even ANSI.SYS's features seem mundane.

RAMDRIVE.SYS and PC DOS's VDISK.SYS add one or more virtual drives or RAM disks to a system. Because a *RAM disk* is actually system memory that emulates but is not a disk drive, a RAM disk is very fast. Many users create RAM disks to speed operations involving heavy file searching, such as the spell-checking of a document from a dictionary file.

DISPLAY.SYS and PRINTER.SYS accommodate the international character set configurability of DOS. Versions 3.3, 4.0, and 5.0 have extensive provisions for international configuration.

Third-party software vendors and hardware manufacturers offer a wide variety of installable device drivers that either enhance existing hardware or accommodate new peripheral hardware. DOS also can install these device drivers at boot time. The key to installing device drivers is in CONFIG.SYS.

Pointing devices such as mice and digitizer pads often include device driver files. MOUSE.SYS and KOALA.SYS are examples of pointing device drivers. External add-on disk drives often come with special block device drivers. The 5 1/4-inch add-on floppy driver from Sysgen for IBM PS/2 systems is delivered with a driver named BRIDGE.DRV. Note that the DRV extension is used for the disk drive's driver file name. DOS 3 or later can use other driver file extensions besides SYS. IBMCACHE.SYS is a disk-caching driver that uses extended memory in PS/2 computers to speed disk operations. Disk caches are introduced later in this chapter. IBM supplies IBMCACHE.SYS with some of IBM's computers. The variety of third-party installable device drivers is large. Chances are good that you use or will use a third-party installable device driver in your system. Thanks to DOS's use of CONFIG.SYS, installing a device driver is easy.

Judicious use of device drivers can enhance your productivity with DOS and help you to make full use of your PC. Fansi-Console, for example, can increase the speed that characters are written to the screen more than four times, and you can create professional-looking menuing systems with little effort. Using a mouse in certain word processing programs makes editing far faster than using cursor-movement keys to move around the screen. Products such as Isogon's Fontspace, which is a *terminate-and-stay-resident (TSR)* program that works with downloadable LaserJet fonts, may remove your need to upgrade your hard disk when you run out of space. Fontspace automatically compresses LaserJet soft fonts on your hard disk, saving typically more than 70 percent of the disk space. Fontspace expands files to their full size before passing them along for transmission to the printer through the parallel port device driver. (A TSR is a memory-resident program that, after loaded into memory, remains in memory and monitors your use of the PC. When a particular action occurs—in this case, when a LaserJet font file is accessed—the TSR becomes active and performs its function—in this case, uncompressing the file.)

On the other hand, too many device drivers can create problems. You shouldn't use more than one device driver for the same job, for example. One device driver may conflict with the other, or you may think that you are using features of one when the other is actually the installed driver. The end result is unpredictable behavior.

Adding Extended and Expanded Memory

The presence of the DOS 4 and 5 EMM386.EXE and XMA2EMS.SYS device drivers shows that DOS is "modernizing" to keep up with the developments in memory-addressing capabilities of the 80286, 80386, and 80486 members of the Intel 8086 microprocessor family. Third-party companies have supplied device drivers for a similar purpose for several years. The device drivers typically are distributed on a floppy disk supplied with an adapter board.

DOS normally can address only 1 megabyte of memory. This 1M limit is because of the number of address lines available on the 8086 microprocessor. The 8086 has 20 binary address lines. The highest binary number that can be addressed with 20 address lines is 11111111111111111111_2 (2^{20}), or more familiarly, 1,048,576 (1 megabyte) in decimal notation. To address just one byte more of data than the 1 megabyte of data that 20 address lines support, a microprocessor must have 21 or more address lines. When DOS was designed, the Intel microprocessors didn't have 21 or more address lines. The newer 80286 and 80386 do have more than 20 address lines and can address far more memory than 1 megabyte.

Programs and data reside in memory. The more memory a PC has, the larger the program size and data the PC should be capable of accommodating. Without some electronic intervention, this larger memory, larger capacity axiom turns out to be not true for DOS. When DOS was designed, the 80286 and 80386 processor chips were not used in PCs. The 8086 and 8088 chips with their memory limit of 1M were the top Intel microprocessors of the era. DOS designers placed DOS routines at specific locations within the 1M of memory space available. DOS's internal tables could be used to manipulate addresses within 1M.

When the 80286 and 80386 microprocessors began to appear in PCs, DOS already had a huge installed base. In order to accommodate the larger memory capacity of the newer CPUs, DOS would have had to abandon the installed base of users and program developers. DOS designers chose not to change the basic arrangement of DOS and to keep DOS uniform. Still, the lure of larger memory capacities gave third-party vendors the incentive to find a way for DOS to break the 1M memory barrier.

Two basic methods are used for giving programs access to more memory. The first method is the use of extended-memory addressing. The name given to the memory involved in this technique is, not surprisingly, *extended memory*. The second method uses memory through a device driver. Instead of being an extension of the existing memory, the device-accessed memory is actually an expansion of the memory below 1M. The memory involved in this second method is called *expanded memory*. Expanded memory follows the Expanded Memory Specification, or EMS. Because *extended* and *expanded memory* are similar terms, they are confused easily. Because these two types of memory are a significant part of today's PC environment, you should understand the difference between them.

Extended Memory

The Intel 80286 has 24 address lines and can address 16,777,216 bytes, or 16M, of memory. The newer 80386 and 80486 have 32 address lines and can address 4,294,967,296 locations, or 4 gigabytes, of memory. The first 1 megabyte of this address range is called the system's *conventional memory* because the 8086 chip uses only 1M and DOS is designed around this 1M convention. Addresses above the 1M point are called *extended-memory addresses*. Figure 3.1 shows the addressable memory of the various Intel 8086 family members. This figure shows that the 80286 and 80386 can address a significant number of extended addresses.

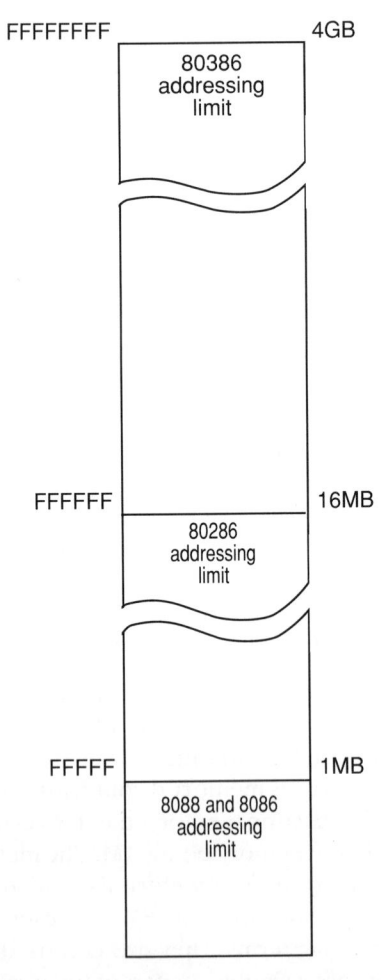

Fig. 3.1. Addressable memory of Intel 8086 family members.

Any memory at these extended addresses is called extended memory. You can think of *ex*tended memory as memory "stuck on *t*op" of the 1M of conventional memory (*exp*anded memory is "*p*aged"). Only the 80286, 80386, and 80486 can use extended memory. The 8086 and 8088 cannot.

The 80286, 80386, and 80486 address conventional memory like an 8086 by using an internal operating mode called *real* mode. In real mode, the microprocessors are restricted to the same 1M address range as the 8086. Unlike the 8086, however, the newer microprocessors can enter another mode to address the extended-memory locations. This extended-memory mode is called *protected* mode. DOS became a standard before the advent of protected mode and cannot effectively take advantage of protected mode's extensive address range. Figure 3.2 shows how conventional memory is divided. DOS addresses the first 640K of memory as conventional low memory. DOS addresses the remaining 384K of conventional memory as conventional high memory.

Some DOS utility programs and drivers can use extended memory, however. The programs switch the CPU from real mode to protected mode. The DOS kernel has nothing to do with the switch. Because the kernel is DOS's administrative bookkeeper and does not do the switching, the kernel is unaware of how the extended memory is being used or what programs are using it. The programs that use extended memory in protected mode must indicate to each other—through memory-based tables—which program is using which memory. Unless the programs agree to "cooperate," any program can "steal" the extended-address range of another program. The result is an extended-memory conflict. The DOS device drivers, such as RAMDRIVE.SYS, that can use extended memory cooperate in memory use, but "outside" programs that use extended memory may not.

Protected mode and extended memory have some operational disadvantages when used with a real-mode operating system such as DOS. The switch from real to protected mode is not easy for a programmer to code. The DOS kernel and the BIOS offer little functional support for protected mode. Programs that use extended memory must do some careful checking in set-aside memory locations to determine which programs are using which extended memory. Unfortunately, not all extended-memory programs check thoroughly, and memory conflicts arise. Some memory conflicts simply make a program work erratically. Some conflicts "crash" a program so badly that you have to reboot. Still, the lure of additional memory beyond the limits of 1M keeps programmers trying the extended-memory protected-mode method.

Another method of accessing more memory—the expanded-memory method—enables even the 8086 to take advantage of more RAM.

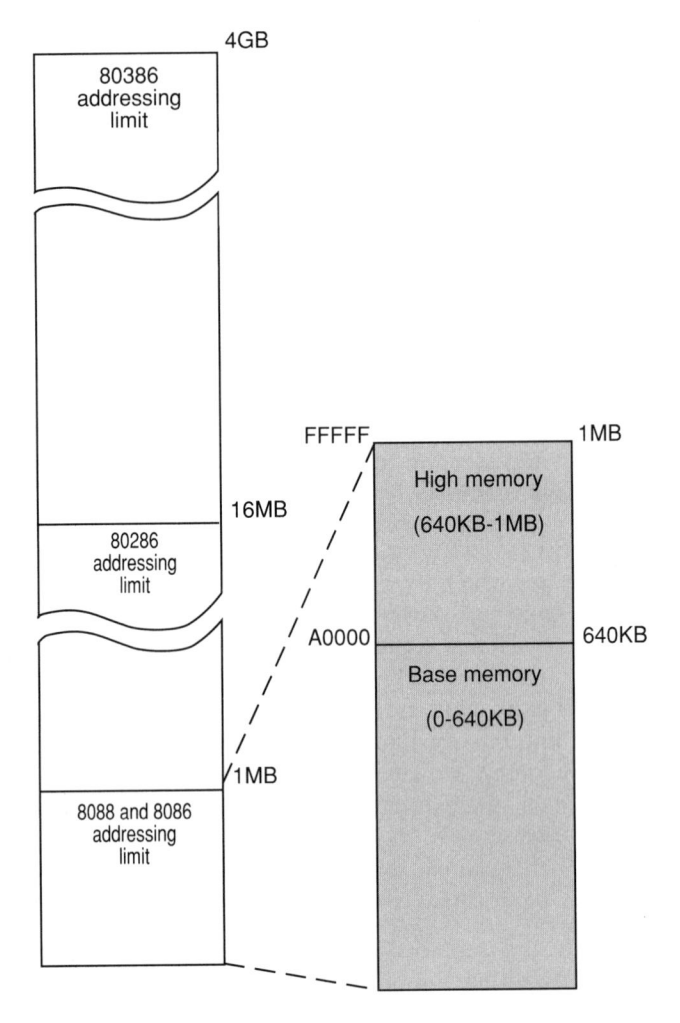

Fig. 3.2. Limit of DOS's addressability.

Expanded Memory

Although the term *expanded* sounds much like *extended*, expanded memory is not extended memory. Programs, including some DOS programs, access the contents of expanded memory, or *EMS*, in real mode as addresses within the first 1M of memory. Using expanded memory, any CPU in the 8086 family can break the 1M conventional-memory barrier. The way expanded memory provides access to additional memory marks the true difference between expanded and extended memory.

Expanded memory is accessed through a device driver as though the expanded memory were a device. A defined portion of the expanded memory, called a *page*, temporarily is assigned to a predefined portion of conventional memory, called a *page frame*. Figure 3.3 shows the paged-memory concept. Notice that more than one memory page is associated with a page frame.

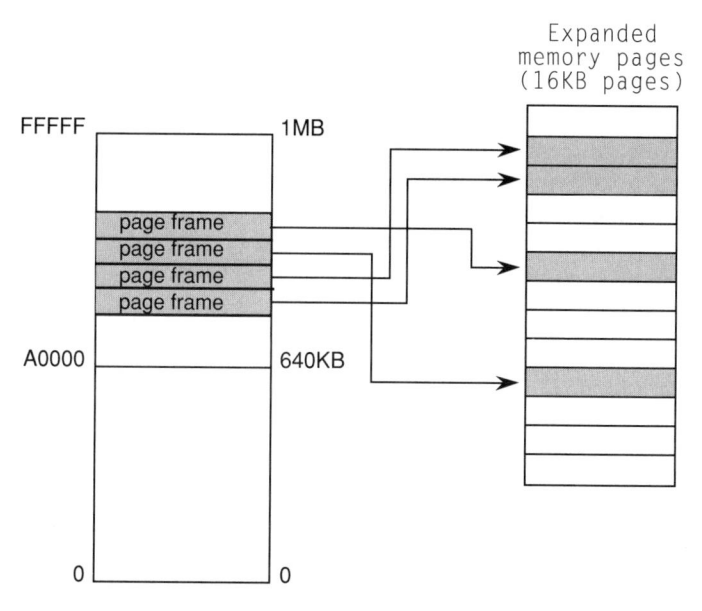

Fig. 3.3. Paged-memory concept of expanded memory.

Chapter 2 explained the address map for DOS's 1M of conventional memory. Device drivers are located in high memory, between 640K and 1M. However, not every position in high memory is occupied on a specific system. In particular, the E000H segment of memory is usually empty, leaving room for expanded memory page frames. Although the 1M of addressability is unaffected, you—or your program—can access other memory through a page frame and look at more memory. At any given time, DOS is addressing a total of 1M of memory only. The position and size of the page frame installed on your computer varies with the particular hardware configuration. The device driver that manages the expanded memory can operate properly only where room is available. By default DOS installs four contiguous 16K page frames into a 64K area of high memory.

Consider for a moment a single page frame. Although the page frame is a fixed size (16K), the total amount of expanded memory that can be accessed through the page frame is limited only by the amount of expanded memory in your computer. You can see only one page frame's worth (16K) of the expanded memory at a time. It's like looking through a periscope in a submarine. Although you can scan the whole horizon with the periscope, you can see only a small section of the horizon at one time. You are located below sea level in conventional memory, and the expanded memory is above the horizon, located above the 1M address range. The page frame is the periscope or instrument that enables conventional memory to have access to a small amount of expanded memory. Having multiple page frames is like having multiple periscopes. Any memory that you are not currently looking at is still there; you just cannot see it all at once.

When the CPU addresses the page frame, the CPU actually is accessing the values in a page of expanded memory. The expanded-memory device driver locates unused portions of conventional memory in 16K blocks and uses the blocks for page frames. Normally, the number of 16K pages of expanded memory on the expanded-memory adapter far exceeds the number of page frames established in conventional memory by the driver. To access all the pages of expanded memory, the driver must swap pages of memory in and out of the available page frames.

When a program needs to access a page of expanded memory that is not in the page frame, the device driver establishes the new page in the page frame. This "swapping" of page frames is a processing overhead that extended-mode addressing does not have. Still, expanded-memory operation offers the capability for specially designed programs to have access to more than 1M of memory through pages frames. Expanded memory also has the advantage of following recognized standards that make memory conflicts rare.

Keeping Up with Memory Expansion Boards

As with DOS, expanded memory standards evolve over the years. Originally, two standards existed. Lotus Development Corporation, Intel Corporation, and Microsoft Corporation created the LIM Expanded Memory Specification (EMS), and AST Research, Quadram, and Ashton-Tate created a superset called the Enhanced Expanded Memory Specification (EEMS). The current EMS standard evolved from both standards into LIM Version 3.2 and LIM Version 4.0. If you have used expanded memory boards for some time or are using old versions of applications software, you may not be using the current standards.

The early AT boards came as either an extended memory board or an expanded memory board. Extended memory boards could not be used as expanded memory. You used a device driver with the expanded memory boards in the same way you do now with memory boards, but some of the actual paging manipulation was done by the hardware rather than in the device driver. Consequently, the hardware couldn't be removed to enable you to use the expanded memory board as extended memory. Additionally, boards that were designed to support the original LIM EMS could not support the newer standards. Now many AT-style memory boards enable you to select how much memory is assigned to extended and how much to expanded memory. You do this procedure by changing jumpers or switches on the expansion board. If possible, choose a board that offers this flexibility, even if you currently anticipate using only expanded or extended memory. On 386-based systems, the memory manager program, which is a sophisticated device driver and usually is supplied with the computer, can do the assigning of extended and expanded memory from settings within CONFIG.SYS. Old versions of applications software can be used on these new boards. However, you will not see the full benefit of the latest EMS standards.

Today, two different versions of EMS exist. LIM 3.2 and LIM 4.0 both use the paged switching of expanded memory. LIM 4.0 provides for more flexible page-frame location and greater expanded-memory access. If you have expanded memory on your system, check your system documentation to determine whether it is LIM 3.2 or LIM 4.0. Applications software that uses expanded memory usually is configurable to either type. Because of the additional flexibility, LIM 4.0 is more desirable.

Computers that have the 80386 or 80486 processor can take advantage of the advanced memory management features of the processor and thus can emulate an expanded-memory adapter board. DOS 4 and 5 provide EMM386.EXE and XMA2EMS.SYS to "trick" extended memory into following the EMS convention. These two device drivers create a logical bridge between the extended memory and programs that make use of expanded memory.

Selecting the Right Cache

Hardware and software manufacturers always find new ways to improve the performance of computers while not significantly increasing the cost. Newer computers often include disk caching software, cache controllers, and/or shadow RAM in an attempt to squeeze the last ounce of performance from the hardware. Some versions of DOS itself include disk caching software and settings such as BUFFERS and FILES to improve performance. 386-based computers with memory management software give you extra speed. Although each of these features used in isolation improves performance, more of a good thing is not necessarily better. An understanding of the speed-improving mechanisms enables you to select intelligently the best combination for your particular needs.

Access Times

The mixture of components in a computer results in different actions taking different lengths of time to complete. Reading RAM locations, for example, is much faster than getting the same information from a disk drive. If every action could be done with RAM rather than with other devices, computers would be many times faster than they actually are.

However, RAM has two disadvantages: cost and volatility. A memory board with 4M of RAM costs as much as an 80M hard disk, and when you turn the power off, the hard disk keeps the stored data but RAM loses its contents.

As discussed in Chapter 1, you should use a memory board designed for your computer's expansion bus. If you have an AT, for example, you should use a 16-bit memory board rather than an 8-bit board; the computer works faster because the 16-bit board transfers 16 bits of data at a time whereas the 8-bit board transfers only 8 bits at a time. Additionally, the types of RAM used on the 8-bit board may have a slower access time and consequently take longer to fetch data than the RAM on the 16-bit board.

The other memory type in a personal computer, ROM, can be a performance bottleneck. Fetching information from ROM takes about seven times longer than reading the same information from RAM. Using various methods, however, you can use tools supplied by both hardware and software manufacturers to overcome many of the performance shortcomings of these devices.

Disk Caching

Programs such as IBMCACHE.SYS, supplied with PC DOS 4, or SMARTDRV.SYS, supplied with some implementations of MS-DOS, are disk caches. You set aside part of the RAM in your computer to be used as a temporary storage area for data from the disk. Usually, you select extended memory for this purpose. However, low memory can be used.

When a program or DOS requests data from a disk, the disk's device driver (a block-device) translates the request into a head, sector, and track position, and then instructs the hard disk to read the information. Because of the nature of a block device and the way the data is arranged on the disk, a whole track is read at a time—even if only a single byte of information is requested by the program.

Even though a program often requests only a portion of a track—a sector, for example—the next piece of data requested from the disk probably will be the next sector of information. By placing the read track into memory instead of ignoring the unrequested parts, the data is ready for the next request. Instead of the track being reread on the disk, with its associated slow access time, the second piece of information is taken quickly from the cache because of RAM's short access time.

The disk cache, a device driver installed through CONFIG.SYS, manages the memory that you set aside it and intercepts any program requests for data from the disk. If the data already is stored in the cache, the disk caching software takes the information from the cache rather than from the disk. Only when information is not in the cache does the disk get reread.

Most disk caches have several settings that affect the way they work. For example, parameters typically control the size of the whole cache, the amount of data that is read at a time, and the particular data to be overwritten when data is not available in the cache. Using a poor disk cache or using inappropriate settings can affect your computer's performance dramatically. Chapter 7 discusses how to choose the settings for a disk cache.

At first glance you may think that the larger the disk cache the faster your computer operates, but other factors are involved. If you are running a large spreadsheet in 1-2-3, for example, the disk rarely is accessed except for initial loading, and the disk cache therefore is not used. But because 1-2-3 can make use of expanded memory, you may be better off assigning a large portion of memory to expanded memory rather than to a disk cache.

If your version of DOS doesn't have a cache program, you may want to purchase Windows to get SMARTDRV.SYS. Alternatively, many excellent third-party caching programs, such as Multisoft's Super PC-Kwik, are available.

Although a DOS *disk buffer* (a certain amount of RAM set aside through BUFFERS in CONFIG.SYS) is a form of a disk cache, a good caching program outperforms a buffer. Disk caches are better performers because they have more "intelligence" than buffers. You may find that the performance of a disk cache is hampered whether or not you make the cache too large or too small. Test different applications you use and vary the size of the cache to gain from your system the optimum performance.

A disk cache remembers which sections of the disk have been used most frequently. When the cache must be recycled, the better caching programs keep the more frequently used areas and discard those less frequently used. A buffer is recycled depending on how old it is, regardless of how frequently the buffer is used.

In an absolutely random disk access, with program and data files scattered uniformly across the disk, the cache method of recycling the least frequently used area is more efficient than the buffer method of recycling the oldest area. A cache tends to keep in memory the areas of the disk that are most heavily used.

Like the DOS 4 and 5 BUFFERS directive, many disk caches have *look-ahead* capabilities, a technique in which the cache reads more sectors than the program requests.

In many cases, using a disk cache for improved disk activity is preferable to using a RAM disk program like RAMDRIVE.SYS. A RAM disk helps only with files copied to the RAM disk (loading a program with overlays into a RAM disk may be better than using a cache to speed up a slow disk). Although the cache's activity is effortless and transparent, a RAM disk requires separate directives to access the needed files.

A disk cache also is preferable to a RAM disk because you have a greater probability of losing information when files are written to a RAM disk than when files are written to a disk cache. The cache, like a DOS buffer, holds the information for only a few seconds before writing it to the disk. During this brief period, the information is at risk. If, on the other hand, power is lost to the RAM disk, all files on the disk are destroyed. You have to issue commands to copy information from the RAM disk to the safety of a hard disk; unlike the RAM disk, the disk cache automatically copies data from the volatile RAM to the hard disk.

Cache Controllers

Although the speed and performance of the Intel microprocessors have increased, the requirements for the supporting components have increased also. The corresponding cost for these components also has increased, and computer manufacturers consequently have looked at other ways to improve performance without increasing costs. One method used is a cache controller.

A cache controller is not the same as disk caching software. The *cache controller* is an integrated circuit in the computer that improves the access time to RAM. The fastest type of RAM available, called static RAM, is prohibitively expensive for use in large quantities. Dynamic RAM, or *DRAM*, has a lower cost but a slower access time. To keep costs down, hardware manufacturers have compromised by putting a small amount of static RAM and using mostly dynamic RAM in their computers. The cache controller works by automatically caching the information requested from the dynamic RAM in the static RAM. With the same logic used by disk caching software, the next piece of information requested is likely to be stored in the cache.

Your computer may or may not include a cache controller, but you should understand the difference between the terms *cache controller* and *disk cache* because the term *cache* is applied loosely to both types of caches. You can add only a disk cache to a computer; the cache controller is an integral part of the computer's electronics.

Shadow RAM

Another technique for improving memory access time involves tricking DOS. Because the access time for ROM is significantly slower than for RAM, some computers—most frequently, 386-based computers—set aside some RAM for shadowing ROM. This special portion of RAM is called *shadow RAM*. As part of the computer's initialization, usually directly after POST and before DOS is loaded, the contents of ROM are copied into a portion of RAM. The computer remaps the ROM addresses so they point at the shadow RAM rather than ROM, and DOS is tricked into looking at the RAM rather than ROM. This remapping is possible because of the protected mode of the 80386. 80286-based computers that use the Chips and Technology chip set also have shadow RAM capabilities.

As a part of this redirection, the shadow RAM is write-protected because any write commands to that area of memory are blocked. Consequently, shadow RAM looks like ROM to DOS and all applications software, but because it is RAM and not ROM, shadow RAM's access time is comparatively fast.

Like the cache controller, shadow RAM is an integral part of the computer and cannot be added after its purchase. However, if you have the choice of a computer with shadow RAM or without it, the one with shadow RAM probably will perform faster. Some but not all computers with shadow RAM allow you to enable and disable the shadowing with a jumper setting on the system board. Choosing a computer that cannot disable shadow RAM can make the use of a memory manager program more complicated because more than one apparatus is controlling memory.

386 Memory Managers

The additional modes of the 80386 provide PCs with the opportunity to improve the 8088-based PC's standard. The 80386's protected mode is more advanced than that found on the 80286 and is exploited by 386 memory managers without loss of compatibility for DOS and applications software. Although many 386-based computers are supplied with a memory manager, you also can buy memory managers separately from the computer. Products include Qualitas' 386-to-the-MAX, Quarterdeck's QEMM, and COMPAQ's CEMM.

These products are device drivers and serve many purposes in a single product. 386-to-the-MAX, for example, can manage both extended and expanded memory, as well as swap ROM memory with RAM in your computer. A clear understanding of your computer's current features and the enhancements available through memory managers gives you a level of control over your hardware not previously possible. Chapter 11 discusses the use of 386 memory managers.

Keeping Track of Your System

A clear understanding of your computer hardware, the settings, and installed software utilities enables you to get the best performance from DOS and your applications software. The task is not as daunting as it may seem. Because you are familiar with DOS, you have the advantage of knowing how the computer is supposed to perform. Consequently, you can detect when things are not behaving correctly. You are more than likely conscious even of speed changes in the computer.

Taking Small Steps

You should develop a logical approach to improving DOS's performance. Keep one fundamental rule in mind: Change only one item at a time. Don't install a 386 memory manager and a disk cache at the same time, for example. Install one item and make sure that it works and then install the other. When a new setting doesn't work, remove it and check whether adding the new setting really is causing the problem. Checking does not just mean, "Does my computer boot?" Problems do not always appear in expected places.

For example, I experienced problems with a new 386-based computer's second floppy disk drive. When I formatted a floppy disk, DOS reported a 1.2M capacity (which is a 5 1/4-inch floppy disk capacity) when I had requested a 720K format for a low-density 3 1/2-inch floppy disk. After some experimenting, mostly focused on checking disk-drive cables and adapters, I discovered that I could make the symptoms appear and disappear by adding and removing my 386 memory manager. The 386 memory manager was trying to remap my system ROM into RAM after my computer already had remapped it into RAM by shadowing. The solution, because this computer doesn't allow me to disable shadow RAM, was to prevent the 386 memory manager from remapping the system ROM area. I had made the mistake of restoring a backup from another computer onto the new system without checking whether the CONFIG.SYS and AUTOEXEC.BAT settings were appropriate. The symptoms occurred when I used DOS commands, such as FORMAT, that access system ROM.

If you use your computer for one purpose only, you can experiment with settings to get the best performance possible. If you use your computer for a variety of tasks, however, your optimum settings are going to be a compromise. For example, a database program probably makes extensive use of your hard disk for such activities as sorting and indexing your data. This setup benefits from a large disk cache because data is regularly being transferred to and from the disk. Alternatively, a spreadsheet program may benefit more from using the memory as expanded memory. This setup enables you to create larger spreadsheets. In a third scenario, a CAD program, such as AutoCAD, operates much faster if you use a RAM disk to store temporary and overlay files. If you are a typical user with only a couple of megabytes of memory, you have to apportion this memory according to your use of applications software. If you have a great deal of memory, the division is easier to make, but it still has to be done.

Optimizing your computer's performance cannot be done instantly. However, minor improvements can be made easily and quickly. Fine-tuning the components to fit your needs takes time.

Breaking Down the Major Elements

Knowledge of five elements enables you to get the most out of your computer system. You need to know the hardware; the software programs, such as disk caches or memory managers; which version of DOS you have installed and its special features; the device drivers and TSRs you regularly install; and the typical way that you use the computer. As explained previously, each element that makes up the whole computer is tied closely to the other parts. As you change settings in one part, the other parts of the computer are affected.

You quickly can determine the software, the DOS version, the device drivers, and the TSRs by printing your CONFIG.SYS and AUTOEXEC.BAT and by looking at the DOS manual. You should look carefully at these files to find any other files that possibly are being used with specific settings. In your CONFIG.SYS file, for example, a device driver may list a configuration file name that contains the current settings. 386-to-the-MAX, on the other hand, enables you to create a profile file that lists the settings. When you type CONFIG.SYS, you see only the profile file name and not the settings. In this case, you need a printout of the profile file to see the settings. Your AUTOEXEC.BAT may call other batch files that load TSRs that you may not see directly from AUTOEXEC.BAT's listing.

To check your typical usage, the fifth element in getting to know your computer system, you should keep a written log of your daily use. For example, you can keep a diary for a week of the programs you use. Don't try to do this task from memory. If you use more than one applications software, the actual results may surprise you. From memory, for example, you may think you did only word processing on a particular day. However, a log may show 30 minutes of telecommunicating that day to collect and send electronic mail, 30 minutes of using DOS commands to tidy up files on a hard disk, 30 minutes of backing up the hard disk, and an hour of using an accounting program.

In some ways, knowing your hardware, the first element in getting to know your computer system, is the easiest element to understand. However, knowing your hardware also can be the hardest. One of the first things to do is gather all the documentation together and ensure that it is current. For example, you probably have manuals for the computer, video display, and video adapter, as well as for each expansion board in the computer. However, if you have upgraded part of the system, perhaps replacing an EGA with a VGA monitor, you may not have put the VGA manual with the other documentation. When you are altering device drivers, you need to know each device installed and what effect any changes may have.

Using Tools To Assist

Although some documentation may give you the required information, other documentation may not. For example, your video adapter, if it is an EGA or VGA, contains ROM and RAM. The location of this RAM in the 1M address space may affect where you can place expanded memory page frames. If these addresses are not listed in the documentation, you may have to use alternative tools to assist.

Removing the cover from a PC to examine the installed expansion boards can be valuable. You can check any switch or jumper settings and make sure that you have all the documentation for your computer. You can check how many physical hard disks are installed and see whether the system has its full complement of memory. Even if you are not mechanically inclined, removing the cover from a computer is relatively easy. The process involves unplugging the computer, removing a couple of screws, and sliding the cover off. However, if you are not allowed by company policy to take the cover off, perhaps your Information Services Department is responsible for computer maintenance and can supply the information. Alternatively, you can find out most of this information through diagnostic software.

Just as the MEM program supplied with DOS 4 supplies information about DOS locations within the 1M address space, other programs can analyze your hardware. A variety of diagnostic programs exist. Some are tailored to a specific task, such as RAM testers; others are more general in nature and give an overview of your computer. Programs such as Ashton-Tate's Control Room and Dariana Technology Group Inc.'s System Sleuth can prove invaluable in tailoring your system for optimum use. Although many of this book's examples make use of these programs for illustrative purposes, you should be aware of their limitations. Because these software programs are loaded after DOS, they can be fooled. If your VGA is set into EGA mode, for example, these programs may report that you have an EGA and not realize that the display adapter is really a VGA.

System Sleuth and Control Room are examples of utility programs that are best avoided by beginners. Both are easy to use, but they give information relevant only to users who are troubleshooting or analyzing their computers. Samples from each program are given in this chapter to show the concepts introduced in Part I.

Control Room

Although Control Room does not require as much extensive technical knowledge as System Sleuth, Control Room's features provide all the necessary information for many applications. Control Room is installed like most applications software, and when run for the first time, the program surveys the computer in detail. You can have the computer resurveyed by using a command line switch when invoking the program.

The surveyed information includes such details as the microprocessor type and speed, DOS version installed, and hard disk(s) performance. Figure 3.4 shows the summary screen from the survey.

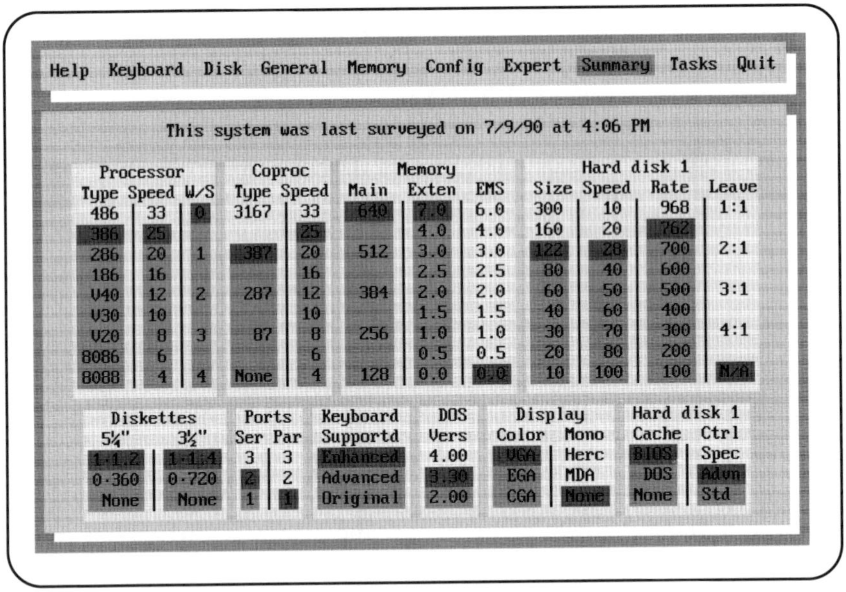

Fig. 3.4. Control Room's summary screen, highlighting the system configuration.

In the example shown in figure 3.4, the surveyed computer shows a 25 MHz 386-based computer with an 80387 math coprocessor, 640K of base memory (called Main Memory in this diagnostic program), and 7M of extended memory. Several other features are listed also, such as the type of floppy disk drives installed and the type of keyboard. The number of serial and parallel ports installed is listed, but detailed information on the installed devices—their addresses and interrupt locations—is not available. System Sleuth can provide this additional information.

Changing the computer's configuration and then resurveying gives different results. For example, installing a 386 memory manager in the computer checked by Control Room in the preceding example gives the survey summary screen shown in figure 3.5.

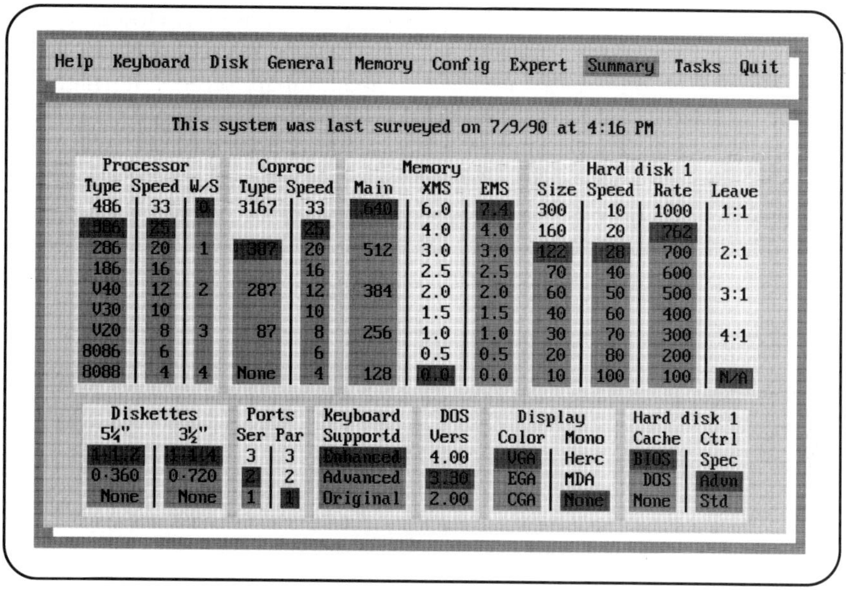

Chapter 3: Extending the Basic Standard

Fig. 3.5. Second sample survey screen.

The memory manager, according to this second sample screen, has created 7.4M of expanded memory instead of leaving the memory as extended memory. The extended memory column labeled Exten in figure 3.4 now is labeled XMS because the memory is capable of doing memory management that conforms with IBM's extended memory specification (XMS). In fact, other changes, such as shadowing video ROM, also have been made, but these changes are not seen by Control Room.

Notice additionally that the values placed in the EMS column are changed to accommodate the full amount of EMS memory. The first screen (see fig. 3.4) shows the EMS column ranging from 0.0 to 6.0; the second screen (see fig. 3.5) shows 0.0 to 7.4 in the EMS column.

The tested computer has 8M of memory installed on an expansion board. The lower 640K of this memory is typical base DOS memory. The remaining 7.384M is configured normally as extended memory. When the memory manager is installed, however, this extended memory configures as expanded memory.

Figure 3.5 shows the performance of hard disk number 1. However, this computer has two more physical hard disks. (Both are an 80M HardCard II from Plus Development Corporation.) The summary screen alternates its display, giving information on hard disk number 1 for a couple of seconds (see fig. 3.5) followed by information on hard disk number 2 for two seconds. Figure 3.6 shows the summary screen with information for hard disk number 2. Control Room doesn't show data on the third hard disk although this diagnostic program does detect its presence. (A computer with three physical hard disks is unusual.)

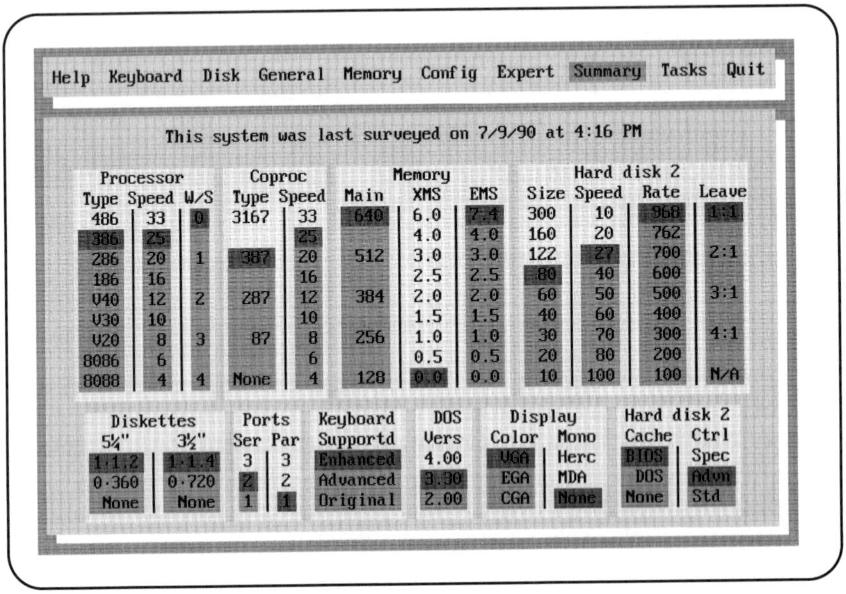

Fig. 3.6. Summary screen for second hard disk.

Besides this summary screen, Control Room provides more information about memory in a memory screen or memory status panel. This type of screen lists such information as the programs currently loaded in memory and the amount of free memory (see fig. 3.7). Again, this screen is general in nature and doesn't, for example, enable you to examine the contents of RAM or the installed device drivers. However, you can see this information by using System Sleuth.

Chapter 3: Extending the Basic Standard

```
Help  Keyboard  Disk  General  Memory  Config  Expert  Summary  Tasks  Quit

                        Memory status panel.

Total main memory:       640 KB    Total EMS memory:         7,504 KB
Programs loaded:                   Programs loaded:
  1 DOS 3.30       39.6               1 (unknown)     576.0
  2 CONFIG.SYS     38.8
  3 COMMAND.COM     3.5             Total in use:               576 KB
  4 INSET.EXE     131.0
                                    Available EMS memory:     6,928 KB
Total in use:            213 KB       (LIM Version 4.0)
                                    · Program name tracking disabled
Available main memory:   427 KB
                                    Total XMS memory:             7 KB
                                    Total in use:                 0 KB
Setup storage:      CMOS memory
                                    Available XMS memory:         7 KB
                                      (XMS Version 2.0)
        ROM BIOS Memory
       Copyrighted 01/15/88 by
```

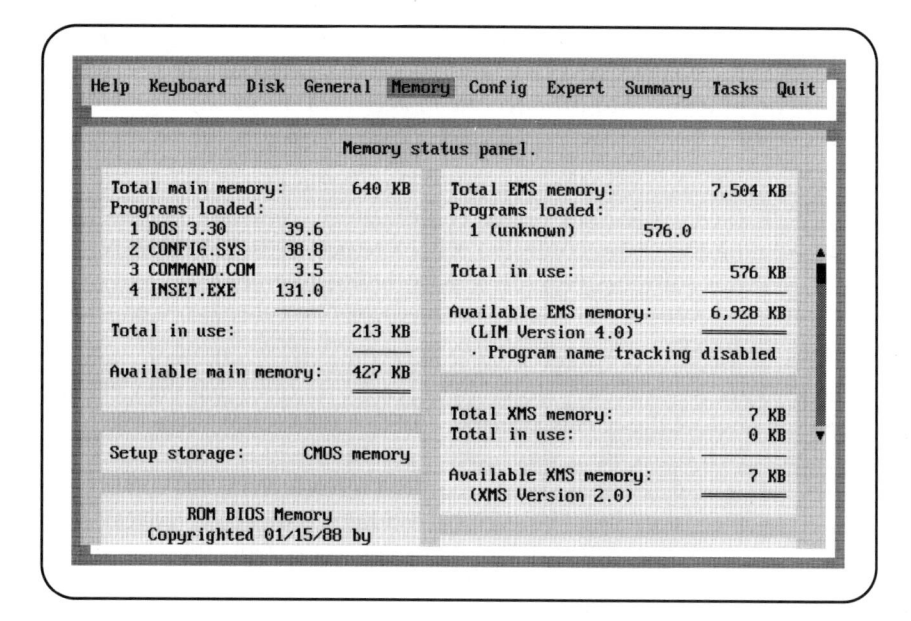

Fig. 3.7. Control Room's memory status panel.

You can display the remaining portion of the memory status panel by using the mouse or arrow keys (see fig. 3.8).

```
Help  Keyboard  Disk  General  Memory  Config  Expert  Summary  Tasks  Quit

                                    · Program name tracking disabled
Available main memory:   427 KB
                                    Total XMS memory:             7 KB
                                    Total in use:                 0 KB

Setup storage:      CMOS memory     Available XMS memory:         7 KB
                                      (XMS Version 2.0)
        ROM BIOS Memory
       Copyrighted 01/15/88 by
      Phoenix Technologies Ltd     Total CPU cache memory:      32 KB


                                    Memory    Wait states w/o cache

                                    Main         3 - Double Word
                                    CPU cache    0 - Double Word
                                    VGA video   30 - Word
```

Fig. 3.8. Control Room's memory status panel, part 2.

These memory screens show four utilities installed in memory: DOS 3.3, CONFIG.SYS, COMMAND.COM, and INSET.EXE. (INSET is the screen capture program used to produce the images for this book.)

The memory information in the lower right corner illustrates the relative access times of memory in the computer. Three areas of memory are shown: main, CPU cache, and VGA video. The diagnostic software is capable of circumventing the cache controller where necessary to get these results. (The diagnostic software does this task by timing memory reads and writes from random locations in memory so the cache controller is not effective.)

The results for this computer show that reading data from main memory when the data is not already stored in the cache requires that the CPU wait for 3 cycles before the data is available and that data is read a double word at a time. (Two bytes are a word, and a double word is 4 bytes. In other words, data is read 32 bits at a time. Chapter 1 introduced bus width.) When the data required is in the CPU cache, no waiting is required and data is read 32 bits at a time. Data written to the video memory in preparation for display on the screen requires the CPU to idle for 30 cycles. The memory on the video board, known as video RAM, is a more sophisticated type of memory than dynamic RAM or static RAM used for normal memory purposes. As a consequence, video RAM has a larger access time than DRAM or SRAM.

Control Room can be used as an educational tool. Instead of just listing the computer's parameters, Control Room provides detailed explanations of the parameters in a report format. You display the report by selecting Expert from the main menu. After the report is displayed, you can print the report to a disk file for future printing by pressing **P**. You can read this report on the screen or print it for further examination. A short extract from a created survey follows:

```
Math coprocessor

This computer has a 387 math chip running at 25 MHz and
is enabled and available at this time.

This math chip is running at the fastest possible speed
for this system because it is running at the same speed
as the main processor. The 387 math chip, more formally
the Intel 80387 Numeric Data Processor, abbreviated
NDP, is a math coprocessor that off-loads the math-
ematical functions from the main CPU and performs them
much faster. Most, but not all, calculation-intensive
programs offer support for the Intel 87-series math
chips, and some support the newer, very fast, Weitek
3167 and 4167 math chips.
```

Support of math chips varies from program to program, so be sure to verify that any calculation-intensive software you plan to purchase takes full advantage of at least one of these chips. Otherwise the math chip will lay idle in the system and never be called upon. Anyway, the 387 chip is the most powerful math chip Intel provides for use in 386 systems.

For ultimate number-crunching performance though, many 386 systems and 486 systems also provide support for the even faster Weitek 3167 and 4167 chips. The 3167 and 4167 chips are the most powerful math coprocessors available today for 386 and 486 systems, respectively. Unlike the other math chips available for personal computers, these chips do not come from Intel but rather from Weitek. Performance gains of 3 to 4 times over those provided by the 80387 chip have been measured! They do not replace the need for a 80387 on a 386 system to provide high speed number-crunching. Instead, the Weitek chips supplement the Intel coprocessor when present.

You may use Control Room to determine your current system configuration. Control Room gives information on the hardware installed in your computer and limited information on the hardware's detailed specifications. You also can read the contents of your CONFIG.SYS and AUTOEXEC.BAT without leaving Control Room.

Control Room provides many additional features for customizing your system. For example, you can adjust the keyboard so that Num Lock, Scroll Lock, and Caps Lock are in a particular state when the computer is booted. Many of these features are examined in later chapters of this book.

System Sleuth

Because System Sleuth not only includes information but also tests parts of the computer, System Sleuth presents information at a more technical level than Control Room. Therefore, you can find all the information you may need for adjusting device drivers or locating free interrupts in your computer, for example. System Sleuth tracks the device driver chain and finds which TSR is causing problems.

When started, System Sleuth presents a screen summarizing your computer's configuration. A system overview screen similar to the one in figure 3.9 is displayed.

Part I: Examining PC and DOS Basics

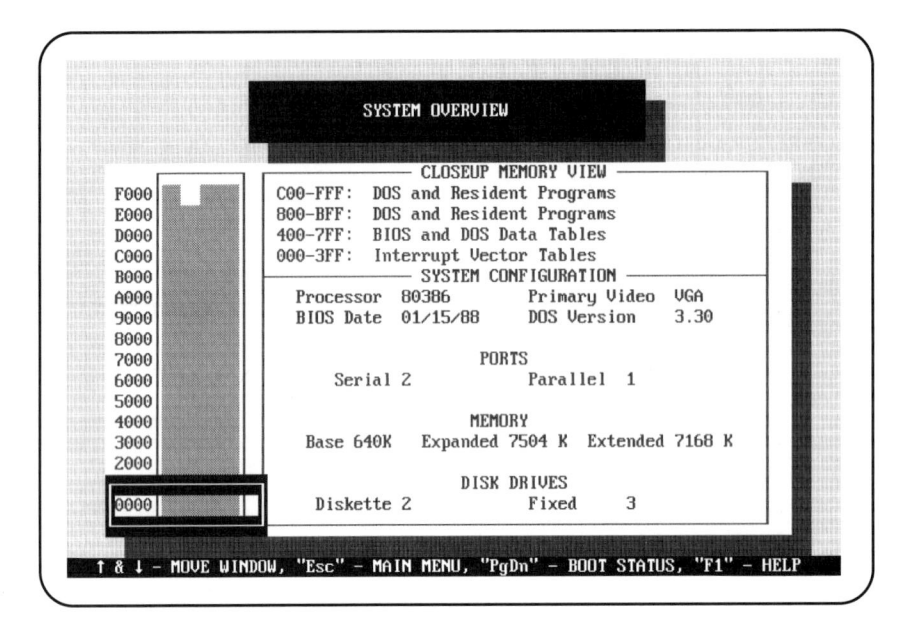

```
                        SYSTEM OVERVIEW
                    ┌─── CLOSEUP MEMORY VIEW ───
         F000       │  C00-FFF:  DOS and Resident Programs
         E000       │  800-BFF:  DOS and Resident Programs
         D000       │  400-7FF:  BIOS and DOS Data Tables
         C000       │  000-3FF:  Interrupt Vector Tables
         B000       ├─── SYSTEM CONFIGURATION ───
         A000       │  Processor  80386        Primary Video  VGA
         9000       │  BIOS Date  01/15/88     DOS Version    3.30
         8000       │
         7000       │                    PORTS
         6000       │       Serial 2           Parallel  1
         5000       │
         4000       │                    MEMORY
         3000       │  Base 640K   Expanded 7504 K   Extended 7168 K
         2000       │
                    │                  DISK DRIVES
         0000       │       Diskette 2           Fixed     3

    ↑ & ↓ - MOVE WINDOW, "Esc" - MAIN MENU, "PgDn" - BOOT STATUS, "F1" - HELP
```

Fig. 3.9. System Sleuth system overview screen.

Like Control Room, System Sleuth describes the computer as an 80386 computer with a VGA monitor, running DOS 3.3, and having one parallel and two serial ports. However, this system overview also contains an address map similar to the address map in figure 2.2, giving the memory layout for DOS's 1M of addressable memory.

Using the arrow keys to move the window up the address map changes the information in the Closeup Memory View window. In many cases, you are referred to another part of the program for more detailed information. Figure 3.9 shows that the first segment of memory contains interrupt vector tables, BIOS and DOS data tables, and DOS and resident programs. Moving to segment A000H, shown in figure 3.10, shows that this area of memory is used by the video adapter.

System Sleuth gives detailed information about each part of memory. First access the main menu by pressing Esc and then choose the Interrupt Table Information option. For example, in figure 3.11, you can examine the interrupt vector table in detail.

Chapter 3: Extending the Basic Standard

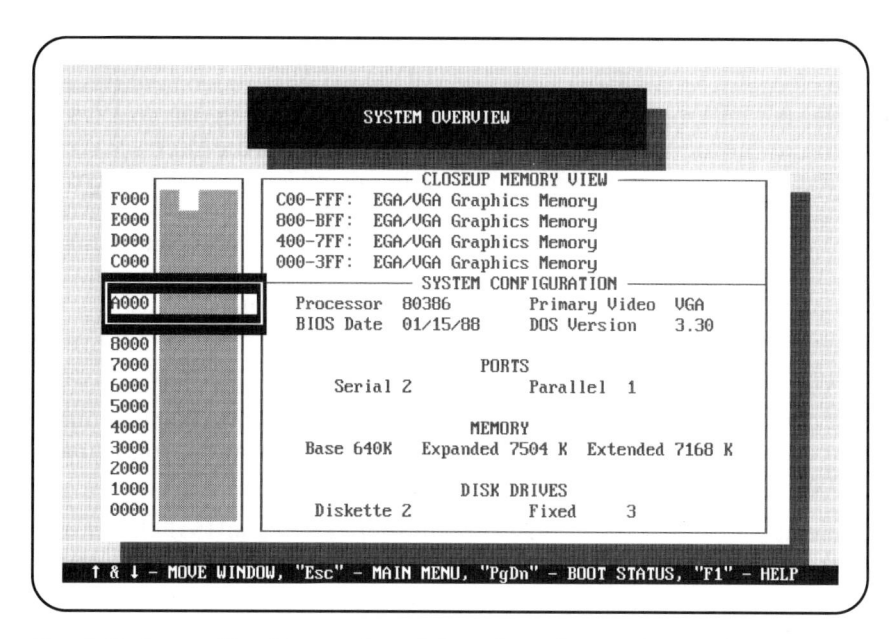

Fig. 3.10. System Sleuth's overview of the video adapter portion of memory.

Fig. 3.11. Interrupt vector table.

Although the table shown in figure 3.11 may appear intimidating, your knowledge of DOS's memory layout will help you to understand this list. When the interrupt controller detects an interrupt, it signals to DOS by giving an interrupt level value (a number). DOS looks in the interrupt vector table at the position indicated by the interrupt level for the interrupt handler at the address listed at this position. This System Sleuth screen lists the interrupt levels in the left column and the addresses in the right column, labeled NORMALIZED. The addresses listed in this column are missing the right-hand zero (for example, 00E5H is really 00E50H) because all the addresses fall on a 16-byte increment known to programmers as a paragraph.

The two central columns express the address listed in the right column as they are normally stored by the computer, a form familiar to programmers and explained in Appendix B.

Remember that BIOS is located in the address range F8000H to FFFFFH. The last three items on this list show that if an interrupt level of 5, 6, or 7 occurs, BIOS contains the interrupt handler. You can use this information to track interrupt handlers. If, for example, you install a TSR and find that interrupt level 5 doesn't point to BIOS anymore, you can examine memory at the address listed to see which device driver is now handling the interrupt.

An understanding of your system's configuration gives you many opportunities for improving productivity and enhancing computer performance. Tools such as Control Room and System Sleuth can be invaluable in the quest for an optimized computer. You don't have to understand all the elements to gain some improvements in your system's performance. Optimization is a gradual evolution.

Chapter Summary

DOS works in conjunction with the hardware to make a complete system. As new versions of DOS are released, more features are added to the core as well as optional features such as device drivers.

The hardware standard also has evolved from the original PC. Computers include not only more powerful microprocessors but also more features such as shadow RAM and cache controllers.

Some enhancements involve both DOS and the hardware. Disk caching software and expanded memory device drivers enable the PC to meet the growing needs of PC users.

Chapter 3: Extending the Basic Standard

Part I introduced the basics of DOS and its interaction with hardware and applications software. The subsequent parts of this book assume this basic knowledge in their explanations. Part II shows how to improve disk performance, and Part III covers managing memory resources.

Part II

Enhancing Disk Performance

Includes

Examining Disk Architecture
Employing Routine Maintenance
Examining Disk Performance
Improving Disk Performance

Examining Disk Architecture

4

Hard and floppy disks have a virtual monopoly on file storage in PCs. Although increasing in popularity, tape and CD ROM (compact disk read-only memory) drives finish a distant second and third. Disk drives offer convenience, reliability, reusability, and rapid access to files. Because disks play the primary role as a file's storage medium, you must know how disks perform their job.

Magnetic media deteriorate with use and abuse. You can wear out floppy disks through continual use and damage a hard disk by jarring your computer. DOS's file system loses efficiency over time. Storing and deleting files eventually fragments files across the disk, forcing DOS to hunt for space to fit files—slowing the system's performance.

This chapter introduces disk architecture, explaining how information is stored on a disk, high- and low-level formatting, and important disk parameters that affect your disk's performance.

Examining the Disk's Magnetic Storage Technique

Disk drives are electromechanical components that record and play back data using the magnetic surfaces of a disk. Normally, the data is in the form of a file. The magnetic medium is an oxide coating on a rotating disk. During the writing of a file, an electronic circuit translates the PC's electrical data into a series of magnetic fields. Because the medium is moving relative to these fields, each part of the disk sees a different magnetic field. Applying a magnetic field to the medium magnetizes the magnetic particles that make up the medium. This process leaves a pattern on the disk that mirrors the applied magnetic fields. In effect, the original data is imprinted magnetically on a disk.

During the reading of data from the disk's surface, an electronic circuit translates the magnetic fields into electrical signals. The disk's original magnetic imprint is not affected by the reading operation. Under normal use, only recording over the old imprint—*overwriting*—changes the imprint. The magnetic imprint resists weakening and lasts for years under perfect conditions. Other magnetic fields, however, such as those produced by motors, magnetic paper clip holders, ringing telephones, and televisions, can weaken the magnetic imprint on a disk, and the disk can become unreadable in a short time.

Magnetic recording of electrical signals is not new technology. Recording computer data on disks is similar to recording music data on cassette tapes, but computers don't tolerate errors as well. If a music cassette suffers a momentary loss of fidelity, the tape player can tolerate the tape's error and continue. If a computer disk suffers a momentary loss of integrity, however, your computer cannot fill in what's missing or wrong. The result is a read error. Read errors can end a work session unpleasantly.

Although designers of cassette tapes can be satisfied with high-fidelity music reproduction, designers of floppy and hard disks must strive for perfect data reproduction. One bad spot on a disk can result in a message such as `General Failure error reading drive A:`.

Understanding Disk Drives

Disk drives are electromechanical computer components. Their mechanical parts and their electrical circuits are complex. Although disk drives are parts of PC systems, the drives are machines in their own right. DOS relies on the driver programs of the BIOS to signal a drive's electronic circuitry to control the actions of the drive's mechanical components.

All disk drives have certain components in common: read/write heads, head positioner mechanisms, and disk-spinning motors. Some disks are removable; some are built into the drive. Both types of disks are spun on a center spindle within the disk drive.

Many systems units contain both fixed and removable disks. DOS includes provisions in its BIOS extensions for both types of drives. Despite their common features, fixed and removable disk drives have some important distinctions. Knowing these distinctions can help you understand each drive type's operation in your system.

Hard Disk Drives

Nonremovable media disk drives have their disks built in. Drives with built-in disks are called *fixed-disk drives*, a term that is often shortened to *fixed disk*. Fixed disks also are called *hard disks* because they are made of a hard, rigid metal. You may hear a long-time user refer to hard disks as Winchester drives, derived from IBM's code name for the sealed disk drive it developed.

Figure 4.1 shows a cutaway view of a typical hard disk. The circular platters in the figure are the drive's magnetic disks. A hard disk drive can contain more than one hard disk or platter. Multiple platters are arranged in a stack, with space between the individual platters. Each surface of the platter is coated with a thin layer of magnetic oxide. A head positioner arm holds the read/write heads above and below the surface of each platter.

Hard disks have the advantages of quick operation, high reliability, and large storage capacities. The disadvantage is that because the hard disk's platters cannot be removed, the data is tied to the drive. Most hard disks are installed with mounting hardware and interconnecting power and data cables. Moving an entire hard disk to another computer just to use the hard disk's data is impractical.

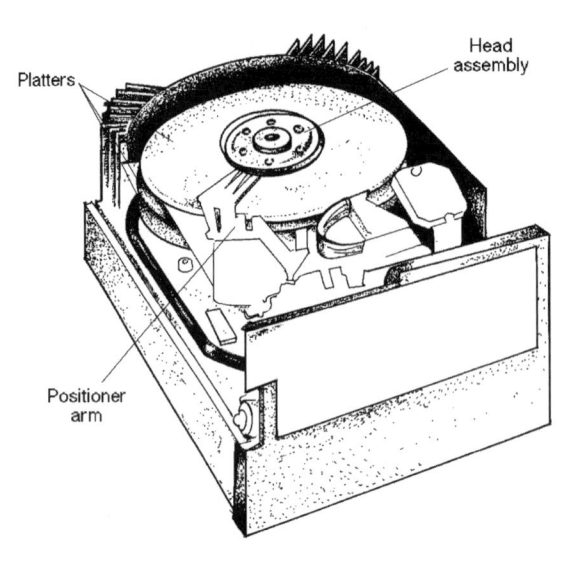

Fig. 4.1. A diagram of a hard disk.

Floppy Disk Drives

In most systems, the disadvantages of tying data to the hard disk are compensated by a floppy disk drive. By far the most common class of removable disk, the floppy disk is a flexible mylar disk that is coated with a film of magnetic oxide and protected by a permanent jacket.

The typical floppy disk drive installed in early PCs supported 5 1/4-inch floppy disks. At that time, the 5 1/4-inch disk was the smallest floppy commonly available. The 3 1/2-inch disk became available later and has surpassed the 5 1/4-inch disk in popularity. Not only is the 3 1/2-inch disk smaller, but it also incorporates a rigid plastic case as a protective cover. The 3 1/2-inch mylar circular medium inside, however, is flexible like the medium in a 5 1/4-inch floppy.

The term *floppy disk* (or just *floppy*) refers to any lower capacity disk enclosed in a jacket and removable from your PC's drive. If identifying the type of floppy is important, many users use the size qualifiers—3 1/2-inch versus 5 1/4-inch—to make a distinction.

Understanding Disk Drive Dynamics

The dynamics of the disk drive are a function of the drive's electronics. The drive contains many components that interact with each other to provide performance. These components are covered in this section.

Disk Drive Heads

Disk drives use one or more *read/write heads*. The heads of a disk drive are analogous to the pickup cartridge of a phonograph, which "picks up" vibrations from the stylus riding in the track and converts the vibrations to electrical energy. Disk heads convert magnetic energy to electrical data. Although several heads can be included in a disk drive, the electronics of the disk drive accept data from one head at a time.

In spite of the similarity between disk heads and phonograph pickup cartridges, note that the data storage method differs. The data in a computer always is stored *digitally*, as bits of data in a series of sections of the disk—magnetized in one direction and then the opposite direction. This pattern translates into 0s and 1s for use within the computer. On a phonograph, the stored information is *analog*; more than two levels of vibrations are stored.

Disk drive heads come in various shapes. Figure 4.2 illustrates two common head configurations. The heads themselves are held in position by flexible metal head-holder assemblies. A set of wires carrying electrical signals connects to the head, passes through the head-holder assembly, and connects at the other end to a flexible ribbon cable. The ribbon cable absorbs wire movements when the head assembly moves. The hard disk head assembly is lower in mass than the floppy disk head assembly to allow for greater start-stop control during high-speed head positioning.

Most floppy disks have data recorded on both sides of the disk. Floppy drives that have a head on each side of the floppy disk are called *double-sided* drives. Hard disk drives can accommodate more than one double-sided platter.

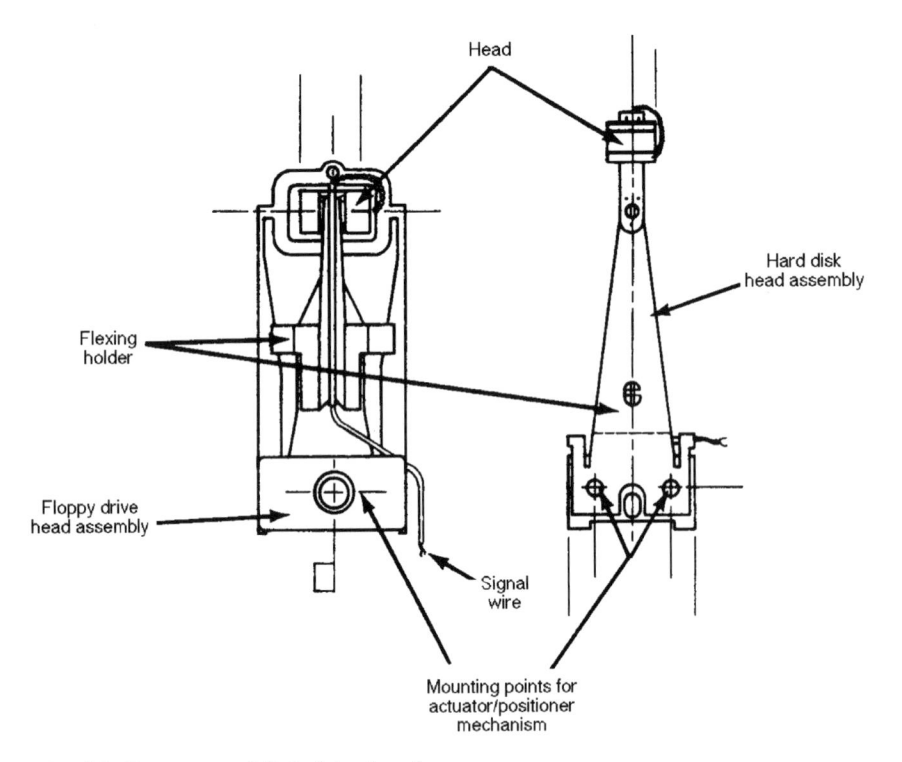

Fig. 4.2. Two types of disk drive heads.

Disk Tracks

Disks spin on a center axis like a record spinning on a phonograph. A floppy disk spins at 360 revolutions per minute (rpm). The rotational speed of a hard disk is 10 times higher (approximately 3,600 rpm). The heads, which are positioned above the spinning surfaces of the disks, are moved by an actuator arm and head positioner. The heads of a floppy disk drive touch the medium's surface; the heads of a hard disk ride above the surface of the medium on a cushion of air. At each step position, the alignment of the hard and the spinning disk produces a circular *track*.

The track is not a physical track like the groove in a record; a track is a ring of magnetically recorded data. Unlike the phonograph, which plays a record's contents by following a single, spiraling track, the disk drive steps from track to track to retrieve the data. Figure 4.3 shows the position of the tracks. Notice that the tracks are not depicted as a spiral; the tracks on a disk's surface are concentric circles. The number of concentric tracks available on a disk's surface is determined by the head positioner's mechanical movements. A small stepping distance creates a tight track pattern and more tracks.

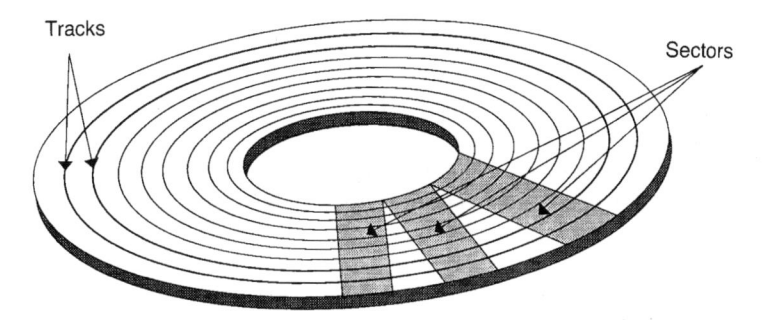

Fig. 4.3. The tracks on a disk surface.

Disk Cylinders

A disk drive's multiple heads are affixed to a single positioner mechanism. Picture a top head riding over track 10 of side 1 of a platter and the bottom head riding under track 10 of side 2. If the disk has more than one platter, the other heads of the disk are positioned on track 10 of the other platters. The alignment of heads on the same track position on different sides and platters of the same disk is called a *cylinder*. The term cylinder is derived from the imaginary shape of the stacked circular tracks at any stopping point of the positioner mechanism (see fig. 4.4).

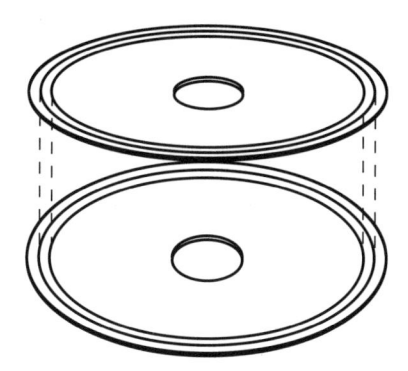

Fig. 4.4. The alignment of tracks into cylinders.

Because only one head can be active at one time, the drive must activate its heads in sequence to write (or read) all tracks at the cylinder position. Head activation starts at the top head. To fill a cylinder, a head drive writes a track with head 1, head 2, head 3, and finally head 4. The head positioner moves one cylinder, and the sequence repeats. Processing all tracks of a cylinder before moving to the next cylinder is efficient, because all heads are already at new track positions.

Seek Time

The time required for a drive to move the heads from one cylinder to another cylinder is called the drive's *seek time*. Hard disk drives can move the heads from one cylinder to another quickly and therefore have low seek times. On the average, a hard disk can seek a cylinder within 65 milliseconds (ms). Some high-performance hard disks can perform the same seek in 10 ms. The seek times of floppy disk drives can be more than 10 times slower than the seek times of a slow hard disk. The specifications quoted by manufacturers for disk performances usually refer to average seek time or track-to-track seek time. *Average seek time* is an average of the time taken to move the heads from one extremity of the disk to the other and the time taken to move the heads from one track to another. The *track-to-track seek time* is the time taken to move the heads a single track. When comparing disks, be sure to compare the same parameters; track-to-track seek time is shorter than average seek time.

The process required to get a track of data involves three steps that can be timed:

1. *Seek time* is the electronic signal to the head-moving mechanism that the head must move to a new location.

2. *Settling time* is a delay. When reaching the new position, the head waits before reading the data, because the head may misinterpret the first few bits of data. This delay guarantees that the data being read isn't distorted by the head's motion.

3. *Latency time* is the rotational latency while the head waits for the beginning of the data to reach the head. Some manufacturers do not include the latency time in their figures.

Although these factors produce different numbers on the manufacturers' specification sheets, in reality small differences in the numbers do not matter. Hard drive speeds range from about 16 ms to 85 ms. One or two milliseconds either way isn't going to affect your productivity. Buying a 20-ms drive rather than an 85-ms drive, however, will affect your productivity positively and your pocketbook negatively.

Seek time is an important measure of disk drive performance. Heads often seek several nonadjacent cylinders to collect the parts of a file. You may have noticed that many applications programs seem sluggish when they use a floppy for file operations, but when using a hard disk, the same programs seem quite speedy. Seek time, rotational speed, and the drive's interfacing electronics affect a drive's relative access time performance.

Although you cannot change any of these parameters after a drive is purchased, you can improve effective seek time by using disk caching software. You also can ensure that DOS is as efficient as possible by defragmenting files. (Chapter 7 covers disk caching, and Chapter 5 covers defragmenting files.)

Wherever possible, use a hard disk rather than a floppy disk because of the faster access time. For example, when copying files from one floppy disk to several others, copy the files into a temporary subdirectory on the hard disk and then copy the file from the hard disk to the other floppies.

Disk Drive Alignment

A floppy disk does not come with its tracks or cylinders identified when it leaves the manufacturer (unless you purchase preformatted disks). Putting the data in tracks is the disk drive's job. Furthermore, the disk drive has no grooves or markings to use as a guide for where a track should be. To ensure the interchangeability of floppies among different drives (of the same type), the drives must be aligned to a standard.

Technicians use alignment disks, which contain carefully positioned tracks, to achieve this standardization. With the alignment disk in the drive, the technician adjusts (mechanically or electrically) the positioning mechanism of the drive until the heads are one to one with the special tracks of the alignment disk. Drives are designed so that once aligned, they resist drifting out of alignment. An out-of-alignment drive often lays down tracks of data on a new disk and reads them back with no error. The alignment problem usually becomes apparent when a different drive attempts to read the disk that came from an improperly aligned drive. Heads do not align to track positions, and read errors may result.

Because disk drives are subject to a variety of environments, a drive's performance may change over time. Large swings in temperature and humidity can cause disk heads to drift. Moving a hard disk to a new position also can make the alignment change. If you move a desktop computer into a vertical position, the effect of gravity may change the alignment of the heads. Utilities such as SpinRite can help ensure that the data is in the correct position (see Chapter 5).

Applying Drive Dynamics to Data Storage

As you have seen, the dynamics of a disk drive are a function of the drive's mechanics. Understanding how DOS uses a disk drive to store data requires you to look deeper into how disks lend themselves to standardized data formats. Since the introduction of the IBM PC, disk drive technology has evolved rapidly. Today, even with the same disk dynamics, higher storage capacities are available from the same size of medium.

DOS sees a disk as a logical device. In DOS, disks of all sizes and capacities are organized with the same file-system approach. In your work with the computer, you see a disk as a file system because DOS connects you or your program to the working computer at a level above the details of disk technology.

Before examining how DOS sees a disk, you need some background on how disks work with data. This section explores disk drives as the primary medium of data storage.

Track Density

Getting more storage capacity from the same disk is desirable. One way to get more capacity from the same disk is to put the tracks closer together on the disk so the same disk contains more tracks or cylinders. With more tracks, the disk can hold more data. If the distance between tracks is halved, for example, you get double the density of the disk because you can fit in twice as many tracks.

Unfortunately, a limit exists on the number of distinct tracks allowed by this capacity-increasing method. The tracks get so close that the disk drive cannot tell where one track ends and the next track begins. On the surface of a disk, the magnetic fields of the tracks interfere with adjacent tracks. The effect is similar to the distortion that results from tuning a radio between two close signals.

To reduce the potential of "blurring," you can make the magnetic head smaller or change the magnetic material composition. Floppy disks basically are the same—a mylar disk coated with magnetic material and covered with a protective jacket—but they vary in quality. The composition of the magnetic material on the mylar disk is tailored for the proposed data density. A 1.2M floppy disk, for example, has a magnetic coating that contains finer particles and has different magnetic properties than a 360K floppy disk, with its relatively coarse magnetic particles. The 360K disk cannot be formatted at 1.2M because the magnetic coating cannot support the required higher bit density. The more refined coatings cost more to manufacture, and so the higher density disks cost more.

Floppy disks are specially designed for the various disk formats. Just as you cannot use a low-density floppy disk with a high-density format, you shouldn't use a high-density disk with a low-density format. The magnetic fields supplied by the disk drive to encode the data onto the disk should vary according to the type of magnetic coating. Using the wrong type of floppy disk can result in the encoding being too faint or insufficiently defined.

Not only does the floppy disk require tailoring to the proposed data density, but the disk drive does as well. The smaller steps taken to put more tracks onto a disk require the magnetic head to be smaller and the head alignment controls to be more accurate.

Data Density

Data is not recorded in tracks as a constant stream of magnetic signals. Instead, data is written as a series of magnetic energy pulses. During data reading, the magnetic fields created by the pulses are deciphered by the drive's electronics and converted back into data.

Consider a compass. The needle is magnetized so that the same end always points to the north pole and the opposite end points to the south pole. The magnetic coating on a disk consists of millions of small needle-shaped particles that can behave like compass needles. The magnetic field is created by the passing of an electric current through the write head. When you apply this magnetic field to the magnetic coating, you cause all the particles in the coating to be magnetized in the same direction. (All the north poles point one way, and all the south poles point the other.) If you reverse the current in the write head, you reverse the direction of the magnetic field and cause the particles to be magnetized in the opposite direction.

The information in a file is encoded as a series of areas magnetized in opposite directions. The drive's electronics read the information stored on the disk by detecting where the magnetization in the particles changes from one direction to the other. This information is translated within the drive circuitry to binary data, which is a series of bits usable by the computer.

In theory, if you increase the number of pulses in a track, you increase the capacity of the disk. You can pack more pulses in a track by reducing the duration of each pulse. If you reduce the space required to hold one bit of information, you can hold more bits of information in any given space.

You are limited, however, to how tightly you can pack magnetic fields in a track before an individual field begins to blur into its neighboring fields. If the magnetic information is too tightly packed, the drive's electronics cannot read it properly. Precision heads and special magnetic disk coatings help increase data density in each track, but even with these precision components, limits to disk technology exist.

Disk Sectors

When a disk is blank, as it is when it comes from the factory, the disk contains no tracks and therefore no information. DOS has to prepare the disk to accept data. You know this preparation as *formatting*. (You can, for a premium, purchase disks that are preformatted.) Formatting, as the name implies, puts a uniform pattern of format information in all tracks while stepping through each cylinder of the disk. This format information within each track enables DOS to slice each track into smaller, more manageable, fixed-size component parts. These component parts are called *sectors*. Figure 4.5 shows the sectors of a floppy disk represented as slices of the disk's surface. The figure shows the boundaries for every other sector. The concentric arcs between the indicated sectors are the disk's tracks. Notice that each track has the same number of sector boundaries (and therefore the same number of sectors).

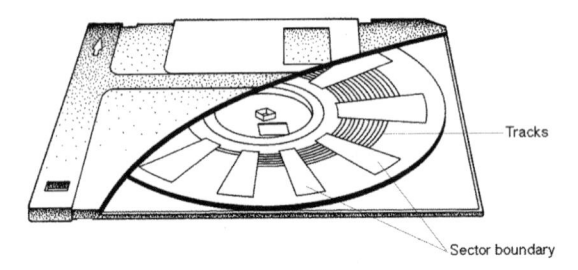

Fig. 4.5. A diagram of a floppy disk's sectors.

DOS prefers to read and write data one sector at a time. Some of the operating system's internal file-system bookkeeping is done by sectors. To DOS, a sector is the disk's most manageable block of data. DOS uses 512-byte sectors with disks but has provisions to use a different sector size. Because the system has been using 512-byte sectors since its beginning, a change in sector size is unlikely (but not impossible) in the future. This fixed number can vary from operating system to operating system or even from disk to disk. During formatting, each cylinder is segmented into 512-byte sectors, starting with the first sector of the first track (the top head) and working to the last sector of the last track (the bottom head). Remember that a drive is more efficient if it completes all track work at each cylinder position before moving the heads, because physically moving the head from track to track takes time.

The number of sectors formatted into each track is tied to the data density that the drive uses when reading or writing data. The more dense the recording in a track, the greater the number of sectors that can be formatted. The more tracks, the greater the number of sectors per disk.

Designers select the number of tracks and the number of sectors per track with reliability in mind. Floppy disk drives are designed with more margin for error than hard disks. You easily can figure out why some margin for error is desirable for a drive that must ensure the mechanical alignment of each disk a user shoves in the door. Floppy disk drives must read disks that may have been stored in a place where the disk's magnetic information has been weakened. Even with the protective jacket, the magnetic-coated surfaces of many floppy disks become contaminated with smoke, dust, or fingerprints. The drive must be capable of tolerating some contamination on a disk and still perform the appropriate functions without numerous errors. Of course, no disk drive can avoid errors if the disks it uses are abused. Drive heads cannot read through liquid spills or ballpoint pen dents.

Hard disk drives have higher capacities than their floppy cousins. The higher capacity is due in large part to the precision of the drive's critical components in conjunction with the special oxides used to coat the platters magnetically. In addition, the working parts of the drive are sealed at the factory in a way that protects the platters, positioners, and heads from particles and contamination. With outside influence over these critical components sealed out, the hard disk drive can offer more tracks and sectors in the same physical space. When you consider that most hard disks have more than one platter, each capable of two-sided operation with more tracks, you can begin to see how hard disks get their large storage capacities.

To find the correct location of the first sector, the disk drive needs some additional help. Remember that a blank disk has no track or sector divisions. To locate sector 1, the drive relies on an index pulse from a sensor in its circuitry. In a 5 1/4-inch floppy, the small hole you sometimes see in the disk surface helps provide this index pulse (see fig. 4.6). As the hole is rotated under a sensor, light passes through the hole to actuate a response in the sensor. The electrical response from the sensor then is relayed to the drive's electronics for use as a start-of-track indicator. With this reliable indicator, the drive can begin to record sector 1's information.

Both 3 1/2-inch and hard disk drives also rely on index pulse indicators; the method of sensing, however, isn't exactly the same. By detecting sector 1 of track 1, the disk drive can extract some specially coded data that helps DOS determine how to manage the disk. The one location on every disk that DOS is guaranteed to find is this first track and sector. It always will be at cylinder 1, head 1, and immediately after the index pulse. After the special data is known, DOS can determine the location of any other sector on the disk.

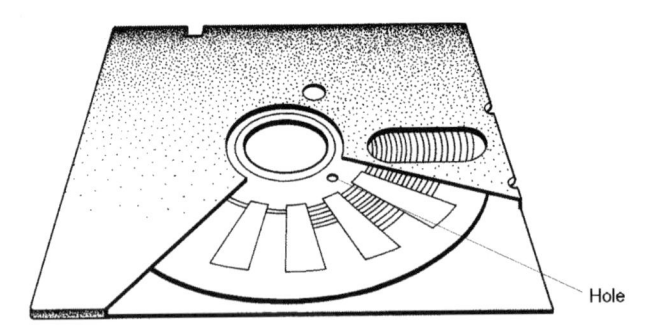

Fig. 4.6. The hole that provides the index pulse for a 5 1/4-inch floppy disk.

Understanding Disk Formats

Disk drives have a universal way to divide logically a disk's available physical space. The number of platters, the number of sides, the number of tracks, the number of bytes per sector, and the number of sectors per track are the specific details that enable this logical division of a disk's physical space. The specification for a disk's use of its physical space is called its *format*. PCs employ a variety of disk drive sizes and formats. PCs equipped with both 5 1/4-inch and 3 1/2-inch floppies are available. Most PC users and software manuals differentiate one format from other formats by using the byte-capacity figure for the desired format. Each new version of DOS has maintained support for disk formats supported by its predecessors. This design ensures that disks made with older drive formats are usable with current versions of DOS.

Floppy Drive Formats

The first DOS-supported disk drives for a 5 1/4-inch floppy disk allowed for double the number of tracks than the standard 5 1/4-inch disk formats of the time. These DOS formats were called *double-density formats*. The original PC disk size and format were 5 1/4-inch, single-sided, with 40 tracks, 8 sectors per track, and 512 bytes per sector. These disks are called *single-sided, double-density disks*, or SSDD. The capacity of this 8-sector single-sided format is 160K.

The early format was extended by the making of the disk format double-sided in DOS 1.1. All floppies are double-sided in the sense that they have two sides. The term double-sided in the formatting sense means that data is recorded onto both sides of the disk. Only drives equipped with a second head can accommodate double-sided recording. By using the other side of the disk, the drive doubles the disk capacity. To differentiate these two-sided disks from disks that used only one side for storage, disk makers called them *double-sided, double-density disks,* or DSDD. With both sides available for storing data, the format capacity was increased to 320K. Today you rarely find a PC with a single-sided disk drive. The majority of 5 1/4-inch floppy drives are equipped with two heads.

As disk drives became more sophisticated in design and magnetic materials made great improvements, the number of sectors per track was increased from 8 to 9 in DOS 2.0 with no reliability problems. Both DSDD and SSDD formats were given the extra sector per track. The extra sector per track enabled this format to store more data than the previous DSDD and SSDD formats had, and the new format quickly became popular with users. To differentiate between the DSDD and SSDD 8-sector formats and these DSDD and SSDD 9-sector formats, you can think of the latter formats as DSDD-9 and SSDD-9. Of course, referring to the DSDD and SSDD 8-sector formats as DSDD-8 and SSDD-8 provides additional clarification. The single-sided, 9-sector version has a capacity of 180K; the double-sided version has a capacity of 360K.

The evolution of DOS to Version 3.0 provided for drives with quadruple the number of tracks of those early standard disks. These new 80-track quad-density formats were applied to 5 1/4-inch drives and also the newer 3 1/2-inch drives. DOS provided one quad-density format of 9 sectors per track, used primarily on 3 1/2-inch drives. This quad-density, 9-sector format is called QD-9, and sometimes just *quad*. The QD-9 disk capacity is 720K. A second quad-density, high-capacity format of 15 sectors per track was incorporated by DOS designers at the same time. This high-capacity format is used primarily on 5 1/4-inch drives. The quad-density, 15-sector format is called HC for high capacity, even though referring to it as QD-15 is just as proper. The QD-15 format, with a capacity of 1.2M, was popularized by the IBM PC/AT.

DOS 3.3 added a high-capacity format for 3 1/2-inch drives that supports the 80-track quad-density but provides 18 sectors per track. The high-capacity format offers 1.44M of storage space on a disk. This QD-18 format is sometimes called 3 1/2-inch HC.

Table 4.1 summarizes the common floppy disk formats. Some versions of DOS enable you to use the FORMAT command to place on a disk a format other than the normal format.

Table 4.1
DOS Floppy Disk Formats

Format	Tracks	Sectors per Track	Total Sectors Usable	Capacity
SSDD	40	8	320	160K
DSDD	40	8	640	320K
SSDD-9	40	9	360	180K
DSDD-9	40	9	720	360K
QD-9	80	9	1,420	720K
QD-15	80	15	2,400	1.2M
QD-18	80	18	2,880	1.44M

Raw Capacity and Usable Capacity

The process of formatting a blank disk places some data on the disk that is not part of the total capacity of the disk. A 1.44M disk, for example, holds more than 1.44M of information. If you buy disks for a 1.44M drive, the disk's identification label may say that the disk has a 2M capacity. Disks for a 720K drive may indicate a 1M capacity. This extra space is not available to you, though. It is the space used by the sector-identification and error-checking information.

You can understand the apparent discrepancy in capacities by looking at the difference between total or raw capacity and formatted or usable capacity. The larger of the two numbers for the same disk is considered the *raw capacity* of the disk. Raw capacity includes the capacity that the formatting information uses at format time. The lesser of the two numbers for the same disk is the *usable capacity* of the disk. This number of bytes is available for storing files after the formatting information has been put on the disk.

Fortunately, most hard disk manufacturers state the capacity of their drives as the formatted capacity. Hard disks also lose some overhead space. If you have any doubt as to the meaning of a hard disk's stated capacity, ask the dealer if the capacity is determined before or after formatting. In this book, disk capacity refers to usable capacity after formatting; overhead information has been applied to the disk.

Hard Drive Formats

Formats for hard disks nearly always employ 17 512-byte sectors per track. You can understand the concept of hard disk capacity by remembering the concept of cylinders. Hard disks, as you recall, have two or more heads. Remember that a cylinder is the alignment of all the heads on the same track on both sides of each platter. If a disk has 306 tracks on one side of one platter, the disk has 306 cylinders. The total number of tracks on the disk is the number of cylinders times the number of heads. The disk's capacity in bytes is the number of tracks times the number of sectors per track times the number of bytes per sector. To obtain the capacity in kilobytes, divide the result by 1,024. To obtain the capacity in megabytes, divide the kilobyte total by 1,024. For approximations of capacity, you can divide by a rounded 1,000.

Table 4.2 shows some typical hard disk formats. An increasing number of hard disk sizes are being used in PCs, and each size or type uses the same basic principle of format.

Table 4.2
Hard Disk Formats

Typical System	Sectors per Track	Heads	Cylinders	Capacity
IBM PC/XT	17	4	306	10M
IBM AT	17	4	615	20M
Late Model IBM AT	17	5	733	30M

The hard disk itself, with its platters that can contain data, does not plug into the PC directly. The hard disk is attached to a hard disk controller, and the hard disk controller is plugged into the PC's expansion bus. Some newer computers incorporate the hard disk controller into the motherboard. The precise method of interfacing between the hard disk and disk controller is independent of the PC and can vary with the manufacturer of the hard disk, disk controller, or both.

For the hard disk to work in the PC, two levels of formatting are required. The first, known as low-level formatting, makes the disk controller work with the hard disk. The second, known as high-level formatting, is the more familiar formatting by the operating system. In the case of DOS, this formatting involves the use of the FORMAT command. Normally, in a discussion of hard disk formatting, the term *format* refers to the high-level format initiated by the DOS FORMAT command. Most users are explicit when referring to low-level formatting.

You may never have to do a low-level format on a hard disk. Disks often are supplied preformatted by the manufacturer or supplier when you buy a hard disk and controller combination. When you buy a computer with a hard disk installed, it usually is configured already for use.

Because the low-level format affects the way the disk controller interfaces with the hard disk, not the way the operating system interfaces with the disk controller, you don't have to understand low-level formatting to use DOS. In fact, you can upgrade to a new version of DOS or to a new operating system such as OS/2 without changing the low-level format. DOS does not provide the low-level format data for a hard disk as it does for a floppy disk, but DOS uses the low-level format information when performing its high-level format. During the formatting of a hard disk by DOS, DOS initializes its bookkeeping tables and then writes "dummy" data into the disk's tracks. DOS keeps the details of the low-level format hidden and out of your way for normal use. The low-level formatting, however, can affect your computer's performance dramatically. The interleave factor used in low-level formatting is discussed in detail in Chapter 5.

When the hard disk is manufactured, the magnetic coating is placed onto the metal platter as a wet, paint-like solution and then dried. The method used to apply the solution varies, but in most cases the solutions are sprayed onto a large piece of metal and then the platters are cut out. The orientation of the magnetic particles, the needle-shaped objects that are magnetized by the head, is random. Only when the hard disk is assembled and paired with a hard disk controller is the situation changed and the particles magnetized in a specific manner. Note that the position of the particles remains random; the *magnetization* of the particles is changed by the hard disk controller. A low-level format lays out where the tracks will lie on the disk and where the sectors will be within the tracks, and numbers the sectors in a track.

You perform a low-level format by running a specialized program. On some disk controllers, the program is stored in ROM on the circuit board itself. Other disk controllers come with a floppy disk containing the program. Performing a low-level format can be thought of as laying down the roads for a new town, marking where the junctions and roads will be. The high-level format, done by the operating system, adds the road signs, in the language applicable for the inhabitants, that enable you to find your way around.

As previously discussed, the hard disk is divided into tracks, with each track divided into sectors. The platter is rotating rapidly (approximately 3,600 rpm) under the head, and data can be read from the disk as the sector goes by. A single track with the typical 17 sectors, each 512 bytes long, contains 8.5K of data. If the sectors were numbered sequentially around the track, the disk controller would have to translate and pass on the data at a rate of 29.8M per second (8.5K times 3,600 rpm). For many disk controllers, particularly the early ones, this speed is too fast. To reduce the required transfer rate, the sectors are not numbered sequentially. Rather than pick up a whole track of data in a single rotation of the disk, the disk controller uses multiple rotations. The number of rotations required is known as the *interleave factor*.

Consider the hard disk platters shown in figure 4.7. On the left, each sector is numbered in sequence, and the disk controller would read each sector in turn. On the right, the disk controller would read every third sector, and a minimum of three revolutions would be required in order to read the full track. The disk's interleave normally is expressed as a number, referring to the number of rotations required to obtain a full track of data, or as a ratio. In this example, the interleave of the disk on the right is 3, or 1 to 3 in ratio form.

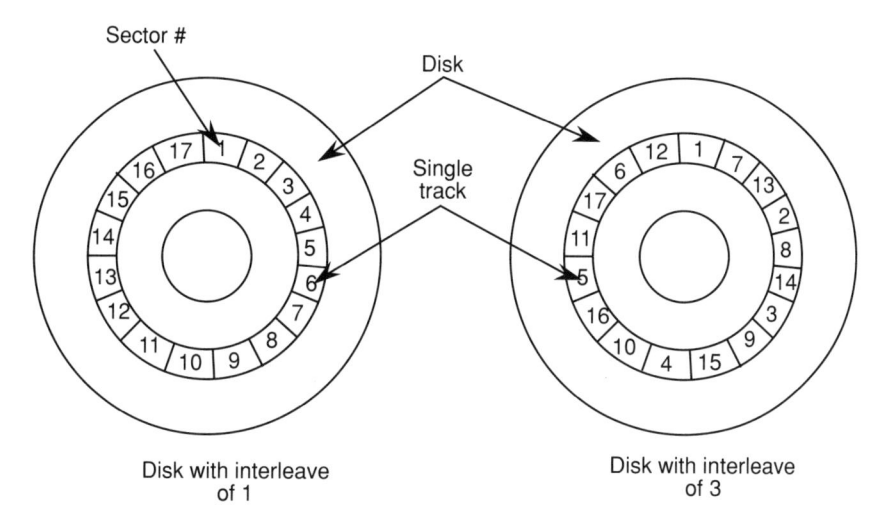

Fig. 4.7. Comparing interleave factors.

At first glance, you may think that the lower the interleave, the faster the data transfer rate. But consider the situation in which the interleave is 1, and the disk controller cannot collect and pass on the data at that transfer rate. The disk controller reads the first sector and processes it; then, when the disk controller looks at the disk again to read the second sector, the second sector already has started to go by the head. The disk controller must wait a full revolution before picking up the second sector. Then the controller just misses the third sector and must wait again. Collecting a track of data would take a full 17 revolutions. If the interleave is set at 2, however, and the disk controller can cope with the data transfer rate, the data can be collected in two revolutions. Now consider the same disk set with an interleave of 3. Instead of being capable of collecting a full track in two revolutions of the disk's platter, the disk controller would require three revolutions. An interleave factor that is too large reduces the data transfer rate of the disk but not as significantly as an interleave that is too low.

You can change your disk's interleave by using the low-level format program. The optimum interleave factor depends not only on the disk controller's capacity to collect the data but also on how fast the PC can accept the supplied data. In an AT-class computer, the typical interleave factor is 3, and in XT-class systems the typical interleave is 5 or 6. Many computer manufacturers set the interleave more conservatively than necessary to ensure that the interleave is not set too low. On 386-based systems, an interleave of 1 is often possible, particularly with new, faster hard disks.

You can use one of several utility programs to check your interleave. Some only assess the disk performance, and you then have to change the interleave and retest the performance. Others evaluate and suggest the correct interleave, or evaluate and change the hard disk to the correct interleave. The most sophisticated can detect the best interleave and change to the optimum without destroying any of the data stored on your disk. Low-level formatting procedures and disk optimizers are covered in detail in Chapter 5.

Understanding Disk Partitions

The growing storage capacity of hard disks offers an opportunity for people to use their PCs as hardware platforms for operating systems other than DOS. Many hard disks today have the storage capacity to support the files of more than one operating system. Without some provision to host more than one operating system on the same hard disk, however, a PC needs a different hard disk for each operating system.

Luckily, such a provision is available. It is the *disk partition table*. IBM introduced the concept of a partitionable disk with PC DOS 2.0. The provision for partitions was introduced to coincide with the introduction of the IBM PC/XT computer. Every version of DOS introduced since Version 2.0 has included provisions for partitions.

The disk partition table is located at the start of a hard disk's sectors, in the track(s) of the disk reserved for operating system tables. There the table is available for any operating system to examine. The disk partition table has entries for logging up to four partitions. Each partition is a number of cylinder and head units of the hard disk. In other words, a partition is a subsection of the disk. Of course, if the disk is given only one partition, the entire disk is devoted to the operating system that controls that partition.

DOS cannot claim to own the partition table as one of its bookkeeping features. The partition table is a hard disk-level bookkeeping provision to which all operating systems have equal access. The partition table indicates which cylinders are controlled by which operating systems. This partition table is added after the low-level format and before the operating system's format.

QNX, a UNIX-like PC operating system, can access the partition table of an IBM PC or compatible's hard disk. When you "mount" the hard disk's QNX partition, QNX accesses the disk partition table and scans the entries to find the first QNX partition. Other PC operating systems access partition table data in a way similar to DOS and QNX. The XENIX operating system also honors the disk partition table's entries.

Two or more tenants who share a warehouse facility may draw a yellow line in an agreed location to divide the warehouse space. On a hard disk, the disk partition table formalizes this type of imaginary line. Figure 4.8 can help you visualize how the physical space of the hard disk can be divided into partitions.

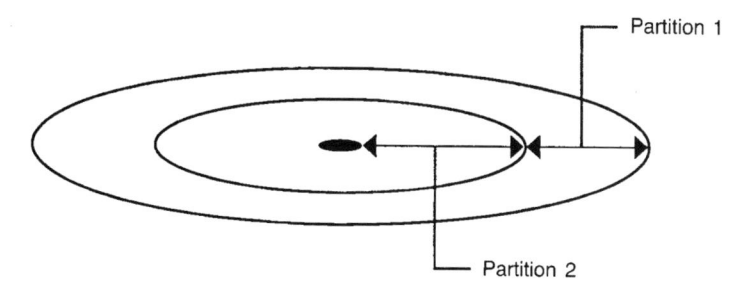

Fig. 4.8. The physical division of a single disk through partitions.

Partition 1 in figure 4.8 is on the outer cylinders of the disk. Partition 2 begins at a cylinder boundary and extends to the centermost cylinder of the disk. Although one disk is present, the two partitions defined in the partition table of the disk act as two disks.

Unlike the warehouse example, only one operating system can be active at a time. The division of the hard disk, however, is still respected by the active operating system. The active operating system confines its file-management activities to its partition. Each operating system has a utility to access and maintain its part of the partition table. DOS uses the FDISK utility to manage its partition definitions. QNX, as well as other operating systems, also names its partition-table maintenance command FDISK. DOS's FDISK is covered in detail in Chapter 5.

When DOS gets its starting and ending cylinders from the partition table, it uses the starting cylinder of the partition as though that cylinder were the first cylinder on a physical disk. The FAT and root directory table, as well as other DOS-reserved information, start in the first cylinder. QNX lays out its partition as though the partition was the entire disk. Internally, QNX uses the first cylinder of its partition as though that cylinder were the first cylinder of the disk. QNX also can read DOS's partition table information and mount the DOS partition to the QNX file system. With a special command, you can convert DOS files to QNX files.

Although you may never use the flexibility that the partition table offers in multiple operating system functioning, the partition table is there on the hard disk if you need it.

A hard disk's flexibility is further enhanced when this same partitioning concept is extended so that DOS can manage more than one partition. Starting with Version 3.3, this extended partition capability was included with DOS. The physical hard disk can include a standard or primary DOS partition as well as an extended DOS partition. The extended DOS partition can be one or more logical drives. The concept of logical drives is illustrated in figure 4.9. Logical drives are not real disk drives; rather, they are defined sections of a real disk drive.

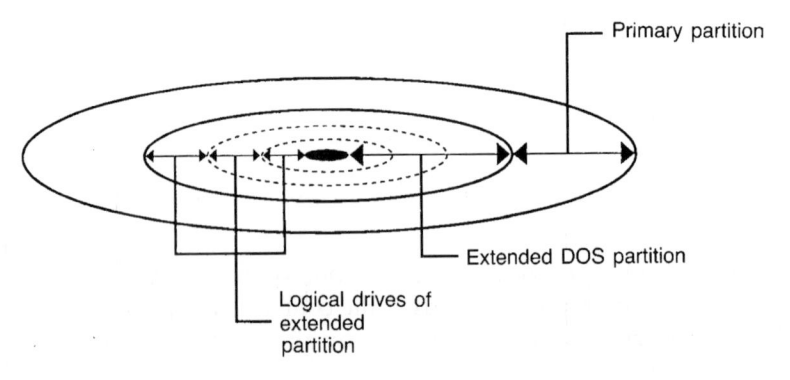

Fig. 4.9. An extended partition with logical drives.

In figure 4.9, the outer cylinders of a hard disk have been allocated to the primary DOS partition. The extended DOS partition begins after the last cylinder of the primary partition. The extended partition extends to the last cylinder of the disk. Notice the two dotted circles further dividing the secondary DOS partition. Each of the dotted circles marks the beginning of a logical drive. In this example, drives C, D, E, and F have been created through the partition table.

The commands that work with disks and files behave in the same way on both logical and physical drives. DOS is the agent that makes the behavior of the logical drive appear the same as it would if the drive were a physical drive. Each logical drive contains its own file system and has its own disk name.

The extended DOS partition is similar to a primary or standard DOS partition. The big difference is that DOS cannot boot from an extended partition. The FDISK partition-maintenance command provided by DOS has no provision to designate the extended partition (or any of its logical drives) as a bootable partition. Other operating system partitions, such as a QNX partition, are not affected by DOS's extended partition.

Only the primary DOS partition can be bootable, but at the command-issuing level of DOS, no practical difference exists between physical and logical drives. Files stored on a logical drive D appear to you as though they were on their own drive, but they are on the same physical hard disk as the files on logical drive E. Each logical disk has no log of what is stored on another disk or logical disk. From DOS's bookkeeping point of view, logical drives are totally separate entities.

After the disk has been low-level formatted and partitioned as necessary, you can install the operating systems. Each operating system can have a different method of using the disk, but all must have some method of indexing where information is kept on the disk and must be capable of recognizing areas that are in use so as not to overwrite data. The next section examines how DOS's filing system makes use of the sectors on disks.

Examining How DOS Manages Disks and Files

You can think of blank disks as empty warehouses in which DOS intends to store files. Floppy disks are relatively small file warehouses; hard disks are large warehouses. If you enter a completely empty warehouse, you see nothing but a shiny floor. No material is stored in the empty warehouse, and the floor space has not yet been organized with aisles, shelves, or storage bins.

This empty space is an example of how DOS sees a blank disk. The disk has no tracks, cylinders, or sectors. After DOS formats the blank disk, the heads, cylinders, and sectors act as aisles, shelves, and bins for data organization and storage. To DOS, receiving a new file is like receiving a shipment of a particular product. The quantity of the file's data bytes is like the shipment's quantity. When DOS stores files, it places the bytes in empty disk "bins" for future retrieval. At the lowest level, DOS uses one sector as one bin. Just as in a warehouse, if the number of bytes of data (quantity of an item) in the file (shipment) is greater than one data sector (storage bin) can hold, another sector (storage bin) is used for additional storage. In fact, some files may require hundreds of sectors as data storage bins.

DOS, however, doesn't use every sector on the disk for storing files. DOS reserves a small part of the disk (normally track 0 sectors) for the operating system's own bookkeeping space. This reserved amount still leaves most of the disk available for data storage. Although the exact makeup and the amount of space reserved on a disk can vary, the difference is never a significant amount. You will see more clearly what DOS does with the reserved area as components of the reserved area of a disk are introduced in this chapter.

Understanding Storage Allocation Logging

To keep track of which sectors it has used, DOS keeps a log of all available sectors. In a warehouse, the warehouse manager may keep in a log book a record of all the warehouse's bin locations. The warehouse manager then can consult the log book when allocating bins to a newly arrived product that needs to be warehoused. DOS uses the log of a disk's sectors to allocate storage space for new file data on the disk. Consulting the log book to determine which bins are available saves the warehouse manager a tedious search for empty bins in the warehouse. Consulting the sector log saves DOS from searching the disk for sectors that are available for allocation.

Figure 4.10 illustrates a simplified allocation log. Because of its role in storage allocation, DOS's sector log is called the *FAT* (file allocation table). Each disk formatted by DOS has at least one FAT stored in the reserved area of the disk. DOS provides for a backup FAT in the reserved area also, but inclusion of the backup is not a fully supported feature of DOS. Many of the utility programs discussed in this book, however, make use of this second copy of the FAT. For example, Norton Utilities sometimes can reconstruct the directory structure on a disk when the first copy of the FAT is damaged but the second copy is intact.

WAREHOUSE BIN	
Allocation Log	
BIN #	USED
1	☑
2	☑
3	☑
4	☑
5	☑
6	☐
7	☐
8	☐
9	☐
10	☐

Fig. 4.10. A simple storage allocation log.

Depending on the disk type, DOS assigns sectors individually; in adjacent pairs or in units of four, eight, or more sectors per unit. The FAT lists the storage locations of the disk in these sector units rather than in individual sectors. Whether a unit contains one sector or more than one sector, each unit is called a *cluster*. DOS always uses adjacent sectors to make a cluster. The number of sectors in a cluster is always an even number because DOS uses cluster sizes based on powers of 2. Table 4.3 lists the common cluster sizes for disks.

Table 4.3
Typical Disk Cluster Sizes

Disk Type	*Capacity*	*Sectors per Cluster*
5 1/4-inch floppy	360K	2
	1.2M	1
3 1/2-inch floppy	720K	2
	1.44M	1
PC/XT hard disk	10M	8
PC AT hard disk	30M	4

The logic of the cluster is simple. If DOS needs to store an additional number of bytes in a file, the last cluster of the file may have space to hold these additional bytes. DOS then does not have to allocate additional storage space every time a user adds to a file. Multiple-sector clusters therefore reduce the number of FAT entries. A disk with 1,000 sectors and 2 sectors per cluster, for example, would need only 500 FAT entries.

On the other hand, a FAT with 1,000 available entries can track 8,000 sectors if each cluster has 8 sectors. Multiple-sector clusters increase the number of total sectors that a given FAT can track. If DOS must allocate space for a 2,048-byte file, DOS needs to make just one FAT entry if the cluster size is 4 sectors (512 x 4 = 2,048). Increased cluster size makes DOS more efficient. If the space given to a FAT remains the same, more disk space can be allocated to data per FAT access when multiple-sector clusters are used.

DOS, however, does not want to group too many sectors into the established cluster. Many clusters of a typical PC operator's disk are partially filled with bytes because of small file sizes, and the unfilled portion is wasted. On a disk using the cluster approach described in the preceding paragraph, for example, DOS minimally allocates 4 times the 512-byte sector size, or 2,048 bytes. Consequently, even a file consisting of 1 byte of data reduces the available disk space by 2,048 bytes. In a warehouse, this system would be as inefficient as storing one screw in each bin. If most of the files stored on the disk are smaller than 512 bytes, one sector per cluster is the most efficient ratio. Because users save larger files frequently or add to many small files such as memos, multiple-sector clusters generally are space-efficient.

DOS uses a coded indicator in the FAT for each cluster allocated. Use of an indicator is similar to how a warehouse manager may place a check mark to indicate "in use" beside a bin number in the log book. With this system, the bin log is clear and simple. DOS marks the clusters in the FAT in a similar fashion, in that DOS can see immediately whether a cluster has been used (or is defective) or whether it is free. During each search of the FAT for available clusters, DOS starts at the first cluster and searches toward the last cluster. The first available cluster in the FAT's list of all the disk's clusters is the next one that DOS marks and uses for storage. This process is DOS's "first found, next used" cluster-search method.

On a newly formatted disk, all clusters (except the first two used by DOS) are available for storing files. As successive clusters are allocated, the disk begins to fill from sector to sector and from cylinder to cylinder uniformly. Cluster entries in the FAT are marked from the start downward uniformly. All files receive as much contiguous cluster space as they need and perhaps a little to spare when the files are smaller than the cluster size.

DOS marks in the FAT—in order from the top of the list and then down—the cluster entries being used. When all new files have been allocated, the FAT has an entry that is the point at which DOS allocated the last file its last cluster. The remaining cluster entries in the FAT are not yet marked as being used. When files are stored in consecutive clusters in this way, they are said to be *contiguous*. Figure 4.11 demonstrates this concept. In the simplified version of the FAT shown in figure 4.11, the first three clusters belong to LETTER.1. Clusters 4 and 5 belong to MEMO.1. Clusters 6 and 7 are allocated to BUDGET.YTD. In this example, clusters 8, 9, and 10 have never been allocated.

CLUSTER	USED	NAME	
1	☑	LETTER.1	
2	☑	LETTER.1	3 clusters to LETTER.1
3	☑	LETTER.1	
4	☑	MEMO.1	2 clusters to MEMO.1
5	☑	MEMO.1	
6	☑	BUDGET.YTD	2 clusters to BUDGET.YTD
7	☑	BUDGET.YTD	
8	☐		
9	☐		Never-used clusters
10	☐		

Fig. 4.11. A simple example of how the FAT keeps track of file storage.

If the next disk activity is the adding of a new file, some of the "never used" clusters are used. This storing of a file's bytes in one contiguous block of clusters isn't always possible, however.

When a file is erased (removed from the disk), the clusters that the file occupied are available for DOS to reuse. To indicate the availability of the freed clusters, DOS "erases the check marks" in the FAT for the removed file's clusters. Figure 4.12 is the conceptual view of this freeing process. The left-side view of the FAT in figure 4.12 shows MEMO.1 being deleted. Clusters 4 and 5 are returned to DOS for later use. Notice in the resulting right view that BUDGET.YTD sits between two blocks of available cluster entries. The freed clusters are higher on the FAT's list than the empty block of clusters farther down the list where files have never been allocated.

	FAT During file deletion			FAT After file deletion		
CLUSTER	USED	NAME	CLUSTER	USED	NAME	
1	☑	LETTER.1	1	☑	LETTER.1	
2	☑	LETTER.1	2	☑	LETTER.1	
3	☑	LETTER.1	3	☑	LETTER.1	
4	☒	~~MEMO.1~~	4	☐		⎫ Next
5	☒	~~MEMO.1~~	5	☐		⎬ available
6	☑	BUDGET.YTD	6	☑	BUDGET.YTD	⎭ cluster
7	☑	BUDGET.YTD	7	☑	BUDGET.YTD	
8	☐		8	☐		
9	☐		9	☐		
10	☐		10	☐		

Fig. 4.12. Understanding how the FAT keeps track of freed clusters.

When a new file (or an addition to an existing file) needs to be stored, DOS scans from the top of the list in the FAT, looking for free clusters. In the example in figure 4.12, DOS first encounters the reusable clusters (clusters 4 and 5) and then allocates them to the new file. If all the freed clusters are used for the new file before it is completely allocated, DOS resumes allocating "never used" clusters farther down the FAT. Figure 4.13 demonstrates this situation. The file NEWFILE.ADD requires that DOS allocate three clusters. Clusters 4 and 5 are the first available clusters; part of NEWFILE.ADD is entered in these clusters. The remaining part of NEWFILE.ADD is recorded in cluster 8, the next available cluster. Now NEWFILE.ADD is fully allocated, but another file sits between the parts of NEWFILE.ADD.

Not only the FAT entries for the new file but also the sectors of the storage area are noncontiguous. The file and its FAT entries exist in chunks, or fragments. By itself, allocating a file in fragments doesn't pose a problem for DOS, but actual file storage isn't always as simple a concept as keeping a group of papers tucked neatly inside a file folder. A highly fragmented file easily can be spread out all over the disk (see fig. 4.14). Fragmented files can be traced by DOS with no problem, provided nothing goes wrong. For the power user, however, nonfragmented disks are preferable. Fragmented files take longer to be retrieved from the disk. Additionally, if you delete a file and then want to undelete it by using a utility program, you may have problems. Fragmented files are less likely to be undeletable because the data is not stored contiguously. Chapter 5 details how to check for fragmented files and how to defragment your disk.

FAT		
CLUSTER	USED	NAME
1 →	☐	LETTER.1
2 →	☐	LETTER.1
3 →	☐	LETTER.1
4 →	☐	NEWFILE.ADD
5 →	☐	NEWFILE.ADD
6 →	☐	BUDGET.YTD
7 →	☐	BUDGET.YTD
8 →	☐	NEWFILE.ADD
9	☐	
10	☐	

Fig. 4.13. How a new file is allocated and becomes fragmented.

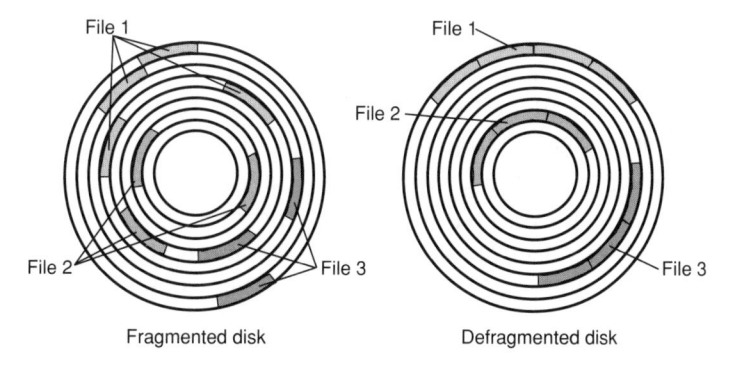

Fig. 4.14. Disk fragmentation.

Understanding Coordinates and Logical Sectors

DOS works with both hard and floppy disk drives to locate a cluster of data by using each disk's FAT with its cluster numbers. Remember that the disk is arranged according to the head/cylinder/track coordinate system built into the formatting directions for the particular disk. A 360K floppy disk has 2 heads, 40 cylinders, and 9 sectors per track. DOS formats other types of disks differently, using other formatting directions. In all cases, any given data can be located at the convergence of the desired head, cylinder, and sector.

Remember, though, that disk drives have varying numbers of heads, cylinders, and sectors per cylinder. How can DOS act as an efficient warehouse manager for stored data when the disks DOS manages are so diverse in their underlying design? DOS doesn't try to track disk data by coordinates. DOS views a disk at a higher level.

The warehouse manager uses a bin log with bin numbers rather than aisle, shelf, and bin coordinates. The warehouse manager uses the numbered bins because all warehouses finally come down to bin space. DOS disks finally come down to clusters. DOS "sees" all disks as a number of clusters made of a number of sectors. To DOS, the disk is an addressable group of logical sectors. As long as DOS knows the ordering method of the sectors and clusters, DOS doesn't need to log storage information in terms of cylinders and heads.

Cylinders and heads are disk-drive specific; sector numbers are general. A DOS-formatted disk may be a removable 160K floppy or an 80M hard disk. Both disks, however, have a first sector and a last sector. By numbering the sectors from 1 and counting the sectors cylinder by cylinder and from head to head within cylinders, DOS can use the same basic space-allocation strategy without regard to the disk's physical attributes.

The low-level driver routines are programmed to deal with disk specifics. DOS relies on the low-level routines in the BIOS layer to interface directly with the disk drive's electronics. DOS merely communicates file needs to the driver. At the point where DOS and the driver communicate, cluster numbers are translated to disk coordinates of cylinder, head, and sector and passed on by the driver to the disk drive. Because each driver routine is familiar with the disk type that it supports, DOS doesn't need to know the disk's hardware details. The lower level service provided by the go-between driver enables DOS to view the disk more generically. The lower level service keeps DOS from being bogged down with details such as starting the drive's motor, activating a particular head, or determining when the correct sector is passing under the activated head. DOS doesn't have to memorize every disk type and predict future disk types just to make a simple disk access. The same basic numbered-cluster allocation system works for DOS whether the disk is small or large.

You can use in a PC, however, only hard disks that are supported by the BIOS. The BIOS contains a list of drive types, which includes a drive's number of cylinders, heads, and sectors per track. Many new larger capacity disks are not fully supported by the BIOS. DOS versions prior to 5.0 cannot support the full capacity of drives with more than 1,024 cylinders. These drives are made to work by the drive controller lying to DOS about the number of cylinders, heads, and sectors.

Consider a Microscience 120M hard disk being used with an Adaptec disk controller. The hard disk has 1,314 cylinders, 7 heads, and 17 512-byte sectors per track. If DOS is told these drive parameters, it formats the first 1,024 cylinders and ignores the remaining ones. The Adaptec, however, can do what is known as *sector translation*. DOS is made to believe that the drive has 146 cylinders, 7 heads, and 63 sectors per track. The disk drive and controller are installed as a Type 1, according to the computer's setup routine. The disk controller assumes the responsibility of translating all DOS's requests into a form usable by the hard disk.

The other method of installing disks that normally would not be formattable by DOS, due to the large number of cylinders, is to use a disk manager program that usually is supplied with the hard disk and controller. This program provides a device driver that is installed through CONFIG.SYS. The device driver makes the disk look compatible to DOS and does the translation necessary to enable the disk controller and hard disk to perform correctly.

Knowing What DOS Stores— The Directory

So far, this discussion of DOS's storage management has focused on allocating storage space from a record kept in a file allocation table. The discussion hasn't covered one important consideration: How does DOS find what it has stored? Although the use of a FAT indicates that *something* is being stored in the appointed clusters, the FAT has no record of *what* is being stored. On the surface, DOS shows you a file as a named collection of data. DOS doesn't record the file's name within the file's disk storage area, so the name must be stored somewhere else. DOS needs some convenient means to tie a file name to where it can be found quickly on the disk. Most disk operating systems incorporate some sort of catalog or directory that indicates what is being stored as well as storage locations. Every disk formatted by DOS thus has a *directory*.

The directory is stored in a portion of the disk's reserved space in the sectors in the first track. Each file stored in the directory is listed once by name. The DOS file directory lists other information about each file, including the total number of bytes of storage space occupied by the file, and some status information, such as the time and date of creation or last modification of the file.

Table 4.4 summarizes some important inclusions in DOS directories. This directory information is handy, but the directory seems to have no way to indicate which of the disk's clusters holds a file. DOS, however, provides an even better method. The FAT and a directory are linked so that they can work together to locate named files.

**Table 4.4
The Main Features of DOS Directories**

File Type	What Is Stored	Example
File name	Eight-character file prefix	THANKYOU
File-name extension	Three-character file suffix	THANKYOU.OLD
Time	Time of creation or last modification	10:22
Date	Date of creation or last modification	11-19-90
Starting cluster	The number of the first cluster allocated to this file by DOS in the FAT	576
File attributes	Special status information about this file, used by DOS	Read-only/ hidden archive/ system

You probably recall that the FAT contains a list of cluster numbers, one for each cluster on the disk. In a simplistic view of a FAT, you may picture that a box appears beside each cluster number (see fig. 4.10). If the cluster is in use, the box is check-marked; if the cluster is available, the box is empty (not check-marked). DOS can allocate clusters with this FAT because DOS can determine easily the first free cluster by looking for an unmarked box. Now, if you replace the box with an entry blank beside the cluster, DOS can enter a variety of information in the blank. If the cluster can be allocated, for example, DOS can enter a binary value that it interprets as meaning "free." The meaning signified by "free" is the same as the meaning signified by the absence of a check mark in a box in figure 4.10.

Figure 4.15 shows the visualization of the improved FAT with its entry blank as a link status. Each cluster in the FAT has an entry for a link status. When a cluster logs part of a file, the link status shows the cluster number of the next cluster that is allocated to the file. Clusters that are available because they are no longer part of a linked list of clusters (in this case, clusters 4 and 5) are "free" clusters. You can presume that clusters 4 and 5 once were allocated to a file that has since been erased. Clusters that have never been part of a linked list are also "free." In figure 4.15, clusters 9 and 10 (and those that would follow in the complete FAT) have never been allocated. DOS is responsible for marking a usable FAT entry as being "free."

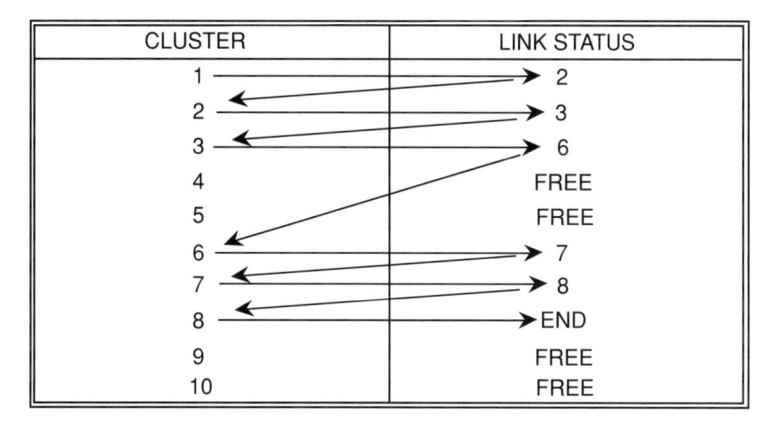

CLUSTER	LINK STATUS
1	2
2	3
3	6
4	FREE
5	FREE
6	7
7	8
8	END
9	FREE
10	FREE

Fig. 4.15. An improved version of the FAT showing the link status of each cluster.

DOS has two ways of using the entry in the FAT to indicate that the cluster is part of a file. The first way is by placing in a FAT entry the linking number to the next cluster used for the file. The other way is to put in the file's last cluster entry a value that indicates the "end." Not only do the linking number and the "end" entries indicate that the clusters are unavailable for allocation, but also these entries form a traceable chain for each file allocated.

In practice, DOS allocates a cluster to a file and then determines whether the entire file will fit into the cluster. If the entire file will not fit, DOS stores as much as it can in the cluster. DOS then finds and allocates another cluster. When the next cluster is found, DOS puts the number of the second cluster back in the entry blank of the previous cluster. DOS has chained the two clusters together by using the entry in the first to point to the location of the second. If the remaining bytes of the file do not fit in the second cluster, DOS again stores what it can and finds another cluster. DOS repeats this partial-store-and-allocate process until the entire file is allocated to clusters. Each cluster except the last has the number of the next cluster as its entry. Because the last cluster is the end of the file's chained allocations, the last cluster has a value of "end" in its entry.

The example in figure 4.15 shows the linkage of clusters 1 through 3 and 6 through 8 for a file allocated by DOS. You can assume that clusters 4 and 5 were allocated to some other file when the rest of the clusters were allocated. Even with the fragmentation of the file between two blocks of clusters, the entry in cluster 3 that points to cluster 6 as the next cluster leaves DOS a trail.

Using this "point to the next cluster" method, the contents of the blank for any cluster number in the FAT is either "free," "end," or the number of the cluster to examine to find additional bytes of the file. Utilizing this chain, DOS can start at the first cluster number entry in the FAT for a file and quickly trace that file's other clusters through the chain to the end cluster. DOS then knows where all the bytes of the file are stored. This use of the FAT is a sort of scavenger hunt, with each clue giving the exact location of the next clue. DOS needs to know only where the first entry for a file is located in the FAT, and DOS then can access the entire file. DOS therefore needs a link between the FAT's "where" values and the directory's file names.

Remember that the directory entry for each file contains the starting cluster number for the file. DOS makes these entries when files are allocated. Figure 4.16 shows the same FAT as the previous example but also shows the directory's link to the FAT through the directory's starting cluster number for the file.

DOS DIRECTORY		DOS FAT	
NAME	FIRST CLUSTER	CLUSTER	LINK STATUS
BUDGET.YTD	1	1	2
		2	3
		3	6
		4	FREE
		5	FREE
		6	7
		7	8
		8	END
		9	FREE
		10	FREE

Fig. 4.16. The linking of DOS's file directory to the FAT.

DOS enters the directory information for BUDGET.YTD and then allocates to the file the first available cluster listed in the FAT. DOS puts that first cluster number in the directory for future access. DOS allocates the rest of the space for the file and chains the allocated clusters together in the FAT. DOS's method for file allocation and access is the same for all files.

With this system, DOS allocates free space quickly and finds all the bytes of a file—regardless of where the file is stored—by using the FAT. The file name, file status, and pointer to the first entry in the FAT for each file are available in the directory.

Now apply this FAT-plus-directory system to DOS file management. Every disk formatted by DOS has some space reserved in the first track of the disk to serve as a directory table. DOS also uses some of this space to create a FAT that matches the number of clusters on the disk. Each file stored on a disk is entered in the directory table by DOS. When a new file is added to the disk, DOS consults the FAT to find the first cluster that can store the file and puts the first cluster number in a field in the directory entry for that file.

As clusters are allocated to store the file, the current cluster number is entered into the preceding cluster's pointer entry. If the file has been stored completely on the disk, the final cluster entry for that file in the FAT is marked with a value DOS takes as "end."

When DOS gets a request for a file (such as from a COPY command), DOS looks for the file's name in the directory. When it finds the name, DOS uses the first cluster entry to access directly that cluster's entry in the FAT. DOS calls for low-level service from the BIOS routines to read the cluster's data at the cylinder, head, and sector coordinate that the disk understands. If the cluster entry in the FAT points to another cluster, DOS consults that other cluster's entry in the FAT and repeats the read steps. DOS continues to move to each cluster in the chain until the last cluster's data is retrieved. If the file is fragmented (in noncontiguous sectors), the disk drive has to work a little harder, but DOS has no problem following the file's cluster chain. The directory and the FAT work together to make DOS more efficient.

The directory is good for storing file names and associated status information. If the disk capacity is small, the number of entries in the directory will be small because the directory's "living quarters" in the reserved area of the disk is limited. The dedicated reserved space for the directory accommodates all the limited number of entries; searching the entries for a file name is therefore reasonably fast. If the disk capacity is huge, however, the number of files the disk can accommodate is proportionally large. The space reserved by DOS for the directory on a large-capacity disk may become filled before the disk becomes filled.

DOS designers faced this limited directory problem in DOS 1.0 when hard disks began to catch on with users. The DOS designers facing the larger disks solved the directory limitation problem. But, before you see how they solved the problem, you should see how they could have handled it and why some solutions were not implemented.

One solution would have been to enlarge the reserved space for the directory. This approach would have allowed more directory entries, but establishing how much directory space is enough is an arbitrary judgment call. If DOS designers provided for 5,000 files to be stored in the directory, those users who needed 10,000 files would be disappointed. If the designers provided for 10,000 entries in the directory, those users who needed only 1,000 entries would be sacrificing usable disk space to hold a directory that couldn't be fully utilized.

Unless some cap were established on the number of entries, the directory could take the lion's share of the disk. Besides, because DOS makes directory entries on a first-come, first-served basis, file names are not in any particularly useful order in the directory. To find a file, DOS has to search from the start of the directory until finding the correct name. This long search would be cumbersome with a filled, over-sized disk directory.

In addition, you wouldn't have a way to instruct DOS to divide files into categories. For example, you may want to group files by their purpose, by what programs normally use them, by what special functions they support, or in other categories. Searching a category is much faster and to the point than searching every entry in a large directory.

Considering the disadvantages of simply expanding the directory size to accommodate more files on a hard disk, DOS designers had to answer one question: How can you use the same basic directory system and gain the benefits of categories of your choosing without having a confusing, slow-to-use directory that may fill with file entries long before the disk filled with files? The DOS designers answered this question in Version 2.0 by introducing hierarchical directories.

Understanding the Root Directory and its Subdirectories

An earlier mainframe operating system, UNIX, solved the directory problem by enabling users to create their own subdirectories as expansions of the main directory. Borrowing this UNIX-like directory system, DOS incorporated subdirectories into its file system.

To maintain the functionality of a directory-based system, DOS designers designed one master directory with a predetermined number of entries to keep the reserved space small. The designers first established a cap on the number of entries in this master directory to fix its size. The cap number was proportional to the capacity of the disk with which the designers were dealing. Floppies had fewer file entries in the master directory (less bytes) than hard disks had.

The master directory was not intended to list the names of every file on the disk (unless the disk was a floppy used to store a few files). The master directory, as the root of the system, was called the *root directory*. Many of the disk's files could be entered into subcategory expansion directories or *subdirectories*. Ideally, the subdirectory system would not limit the number of files it could manage. Like a single directory system, the subdirectory system was efficient and easy to use. This subdirectory system had the root directory as its only required directory and optional subdirectories subordinate to the root.

In the root directory or in a subdirectory, DOS still can enter the name and the first cluster number of a file's FAT entry. The DOS subdirectory is a special file that DOS uses the same way it uses the root directory. On the surface, you cannot tell that the root directory is a reserved section of the disk and that the subdirectory is a special file. DOS manages the root directory and subdirectory difference internally and provides uniformity on the surface. For this reason, DOS users commonly call subdirectories "directories." Unless the context of the term dictates otherwise, subdirectories can be called directories.

DOS can implement an entire system of subdirectories and still retain the general advantages of a single directory. From a space-economy point of view, a subdirectory system overcomes many of the drawbacks of a single directory system, such as an excessively large number of dedicated file entries. Of course, DOS has to provide a few commands for managing the subdirectory system. Commands to create, remove, and change the current directory are examples.

On a freshly formatted disk, you have access to the disk's only directory, the root directory. With the MKDIR (Make Directory) command, you can create a subdirectory called LETTERS. You can use the name LETTERS as the subdirectory name to categorize the letter files that you plan to keep in this new subdirectory. To focus DOS's attention on the LETTERS subdirectory as though it were the only directory on the disk, you can use the CHDIR (Change Directory) command to change the current directory to LETTERS. If you later want to remove the LETTERS subdirectory because you no longer need it, you can use the RMDIR (Remove Directory) command to do so. DOS's subdirectories, as well as the commands that support them, are a great advance over the single fixed directories of Version 1.0.

Examining Subdirectories as Files

DOS can utilize subdirectories while maintaining a fixed-size reserve area on a disk because DOS is in charge of files. DOS makes a subdirectory out of a file. A subdirectory can be considered DOS's personal file.

A subdirectory is not placed in the reserved area with the root directory. Instead, a subdirectory is located in the main storage area of the disk just like other files are. Unlike the master directory, which is fixed in size, a subdirectory can grow as more file's entries are added to it. All subdirectories have names similar to files; to DOS, a subdirectory's name is a modified file name. Because only one root directory exists, and its space is reserved, the root directory has no recorded name and is known always as the root. Naming subdirectories gives you the ability to categorize the contents of a subdirectory by the meaning of its name. But DOS attaches no special meaning to your choice of a subdirectory's name. Internally, DOS can search for a subdirectory name in a manner similar to the way it searches for a file name.

Looking at DOS's File System from the Ground Up

As you can see, the DOS file system and its related mechanics aren't as simple as they appear on the surface. At the DOS command prompt, you issue a command and rightfully don't expect to be responsible for the success or failure of the command's execution. Command execution is the responsibility of DOS. Needless to say, DOS cannot be held accountable for failed commands that are poorly formed or inaccessible. But a big difference exists between your learning to issue commands correctly and your learning to control hardware at the binary level.

Through the hardware, the driver software, and DOS's own internal organization, the complexities of the file system remain in the capable hands of DOS. When you have some insight into what DOS is up to behind the scenes, however, you stand a better chance of mastering those aspects of DOS for which you are responsible. Figure 4.17 puts in perspective the role of DOS in disk-based activity. The figure shows a series of transformations or refinements of organization that become the structure for your disk and file work.

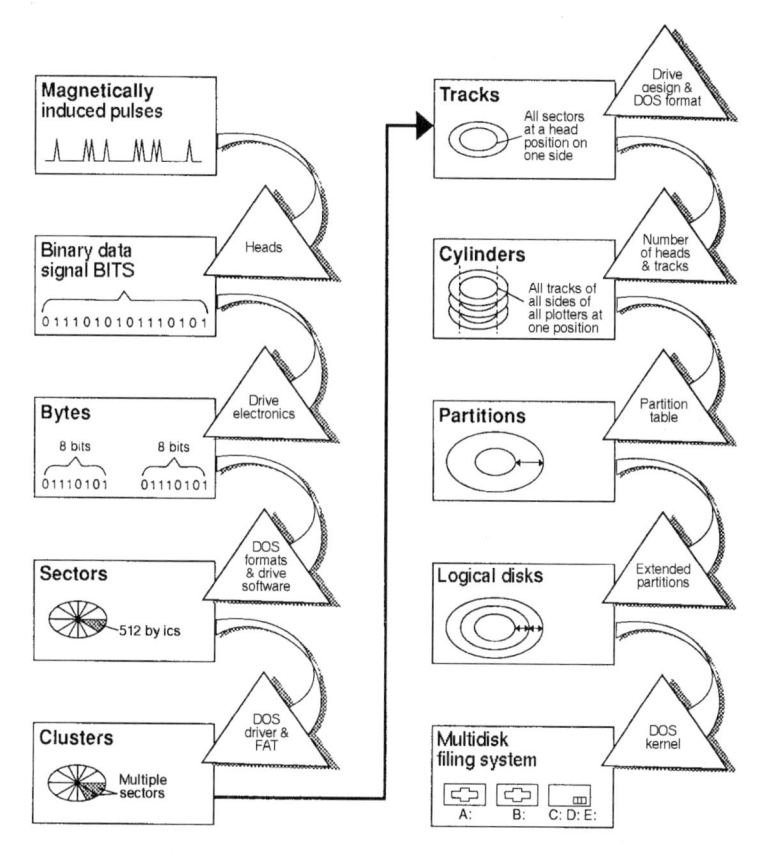

Fig. 4.17. The underlying organization of the DOS file system.

Figure 4.17 shows boxes containing levels of data organization. Connecting the boxes is a series of arrows. Each arrow head references the method used to transform the level of data organization from the preceding box to the next box. Follow the transformation of magnetic pulses and fields through to the multidisk file system that DOS offers.

From magnetic pulses, the drive head extracts the electrical signals that the drive electronics can transform into electrical binary data. The drive electronics, in cooperation with the disk-driver program, package these binary signals into bytes and deliver them to the PC's memory in 512-byte sectors. DOS's format-defined clusters keep the bookkeeping of the sectors efficient. The sectors give rise to tracks; tracks give rise to cylinders.

DOS keeps a logical map of this disk real estate in the FAT and matches file names to file locations on the disk through the directory. DOS knows a disk's organization immediately after reading the disk's boot record. DOS transparently treats one hard disk as many disks when DOS finds the disk's division into partitions in the partition table. DOS uses names for both physical and logical drives so that you can manipulate a multidisk filing system by using hierarchical directories.

When you consider that DOS manages this range of details from magnetic pulses to multidisk filing systems, you may have trouble believing that DOS has its "disk act together" in the moment it takes the drive light to glow.

Chapter Summary

This chapter introduced the fundamentals of magnetic disk storage on PCs. A magnetic head is positioned over a rotating disk. Data is written onto the disk by the creation of a magnetic field in the head. The drive read electronics detect the positions on the disk where the magnetic recording changes from one orientation to another and translate this information into bits of data for use in the PC.

The low-level formatting of hard disks lays out the positions for the tracks and sectors. The interleave for a hard disk is established during a low-level format. Having an incorrect interleave dramatically affects the performance of a hard disk.

DOS's FDISK program defines partitions for the disk. You can divide a partition further into logical drives if you prefer. DOS's FORMAT command adds the directory and FAT information on a hard disk.

On a floppy disk, DOS's FORMAT command is equivalent to both the low-level format and the high-level format. Because of the low access time and slow rotation speed of a floppy disk, you should use a hard disk to store and retrieve data whenever possible. A floppy disk, however, is a convenient backup data storage medium.

Through the directory and the FAT, DOS's filing system keeps track of where data is placed on the disk. The starting cluster number for a file is stored in the FAT. Each subsequent cluster containing parts of the file is chained together. DOS reads the first cluster and then is referred to the next cluster in the chain. When fragmentation occurs, with files not being stored in contiguous sectors, DOS's storage becomes inefficient because DOS has to search more of the disk to find data.

Employing Routine Maintenance   5

Although magnetic media is generally reliable and convenient to use, it benefits from routine maintenance. This chapter covers the wide variety of things you can do to ensure that the magnetic media, whether hard disks or floppy disks, are working to their full potential.

DOS supplies tools, such as CHKDSK, that can help at a basic level, and these tools are introduced first. Computers, particularly if they are relatively new, may come with diagnostic software that can assess their performance. Both commercial and public domain software can improve the testing and evaluation process. This chapter illustrates some of the evaluation procedures available. The low-level formatting process is explained, and examples of how you can test the hard disk's interleave are given.

Examining Fragmentation of Files

Even though you may have tested the computer and hard disk extensively when you first obtained it, its performance may have degraded with time. This loss of efficiency may not be due to the deterioration of computer parts but instead to normal computer use. This seemingly illogical situation is not an indication that you need to buy new equipment. You need only perform routine maintenance.

As you use the computer, you probably add new files and delete unwanted ones regularly. Because of DOS's filing methods, which place new files in the first available cluster on the disk, you can end up with parts of files scattered all over the disk. When you retrieve one of these scattered files from the disk, DOS can fetch it successfully, but the disk head has to move to several different areas of the disk and retrieval is slow.

If a disk contains *fragmented files*, you may notice degraded speed and increased noise. Remember that the hard disk is rotating at about 3,600 rpm and can pick up a full track of data in a few revolutions. With an interleave of 3, for example, one track is read from the disk in 0.8 milliseconds (ms). A typical hard disk has an average seek time of 28 ms. For every different track that data is read from, at least an additional 28 ms is taken. Although you will not notice one 28 ms period, not much fragmenting of files is needed to add seconds to either the retrieval or save time for files. As a beginner, you don't notice these couple of seconds, but as you become a more advanced user, you grow conscious of every second.

Remember that DOS doesn't move data already on the disk; DOS assigns new clusters when data is added. This new cluster may not be contiguous with the preceding cluster. Unless special steps to assemble files are taken, data is saved to the disk as fragmented files.

Removing fragmentation from the disk also improves a utility program's chances of recovering an erased file. When a file is deleted, its name is marked in the directory as being deleted, and the clusters it occupied are marked as being available. An *undelete utility* program, such as Norton's UnErase, is capable of looking at the deleted directory entry and finding the first cluster number. If the file is not fragmented and you haven't written something into the clusters that were used by the file, you can get the whole file back. A fragmented file is harder to reconstruct because it is scattered over the disk, which makes the chain in the FAT harder to follow.

One of the side effects of fragmented files is that the disk's head thrashes around as it retrieves data. This thrashing around not only adds to the wear and tear of the disk but also is noisy. *Defragmenting* a hard disk so that all parts of a file are written to contiguous sectors can lessen significantly the noise made and the amount of time wasted by the computer.

Lost clusters can add indirectly to the fragmentation on the disk. If you turn off the computer without exiting applications programs properly or reboot the computer in the middle of a program, you can produce lost clusters on the disk. The most common occurrence of lost clusters is when you reboot the computer after it apparently has hung in a program. Just before rebooting, DOS and the applications program were handling several different files on the disk. Rebooting doesn't give DOS a chance to note where every cluster in use is located and to name all the files correctly in the directory and FAT. As a consequence, the chain of sectors that make up some of the files is broken. You have certain clusters on the disk marked as in use, but DOS doesn't know to which file they belong.

You may not be aware of these lost clusters. These clusters are marked as in use, so DOS does not reassign them. However, the clusters are not used by anything because they don't belong to a particular file. When DOS tries to find room on the disk, DOS ignores these clusters and may fragment a file to fit it around a lost cluster.

Lost clusters can be a significant problem. I tested some computer-aided design (CAD) software that would not work properly with my VGA, and I had to keep rebooting the system. Within three reboots, I ran out of disk space. A single reboot left 9M of lost clusters on my disk. After three times, 27M of my hard disk was marked as in use but wasn't assigned to any file DOS understood. Although this is an extreme case, lost clusters can take up a great deal of disk space—particularly if you are installing and testing new software and have to reboot at unusual times.

Analyzing a Disk with CHKDSK

The first step in removing lost clusters and defragmenting the disks is knowing you have a problem. DOS's CHKDSK command can supply this information easily and quickly. A good policy is to run CHKDSK regularly on the computer. I, for example, check my disks immediately before doing my weekly backup. Because the FAT and the hierarchical directory system work together to manage file allocation, identification, and status, a problem in either the FAT or one of the directories is always a serious problem.

The external command CHKDSK analyzes the FAT, the directories, and, if you want, the fragmentation status of a disk's files. Optionally, CHKDSK repairs problems in the FAT due to lost clusters and writes the contents of the lost clusters to files. CHKDSK also provides an option to display all of a disk's files and their paths. On completion, CHKDSK displays a screen report of its findings. Chapter 4 discusses both the structure of DOS's FAT and directories.

Understanding the Operation of CHKDSK

CHKDSK checks the FAT for the following problems:

- Unlinked cluster chains (lost clusters)
- Multiple linked clusters (cross-linked files)
- Invalid next cluster-in-chain values (invalid cluster numbers)
- Defective sectors where the FAT is stored

CHKDSK checks the directory system for the following problems:

- Invalid cluster numbers (out of range)
- Invalid file attributes in entries (attribute values DOS does not recognize)
- Damage to subdirectory entries (CHKDSK cannot process them)
- Damage to a directory's integrity (its files cannot be accessed)

CHKDSK then produces a screen report that summarizes disk and system RAM usage. A typical CHKDSK report for a normal hard disk follows:

```
Volume HARD DISK D created 12-26-1990 5:05p
Volume Serial Number is 2E79-18CA

21344256 bytes total disk space
    2048 bytes in 2 hidden files
   40960 bytes in 20 directories
 8058880 bytes in 300 user files
13242368 bytes available on disk
```

```
   2048 bytes in each allocation unit
  10422 total allocation units on disk
   6466 available allocation units on disk
 655360 total bytes memory
 133760 bytes free
```

Note that you should issue the CHKDSK command without the /F (fix) switch the first time you use this command. CHKDSK can make a "dry run" of its checking routines. CHKDSK with no /F prompts you if it finds a problem as though you used the /F switch. Take advantage of CHKDSK's "dry run" capacity to review reported problems. After you assess the findings of CHKDSK and take remedial actions (such as those that follow), you can issue CHKDSK with the /F switch so that the command can fix the problems found.

The directory entry contains the starting cluster number for a file. CHKDSK can take this number and look in the correct position in the FAT to find the next cluster assigned to the file. By following the chain of clusters until the end-of-file indicator is found, CHKDSK checks the file's allocation integrity (see Chapter 4).

CHKDSK processes each directory starting at the root and following each subdirectory. The indicated cluster chain is checked using the directory entry's FAT pointer. The size of the file in bytes also is compared with the size of the FAT's allocation in clusters.

CHKDSK expects to find enough chained clusters in the FAT to accommodate the file but not more than necessary. If CHKDSK finds too many clusters, it issues the following message:

```
Allocation error,
size adjusted
```

The file is truncated (excess clusters deallocated) if the /F switch is in effect. You should copy the reported file to another disk before running CHKDSK with the /F switch in case the number of bytes indicated in the directory entry for the reported file is incorrect. If the directory entry has an errant (too low) number of bytes indicated, CHKDSK effectively "chops off" some of the file. With a copy of the file on another disk, you can recover the data in the unlikely event that the directory entry was wrong.

CHKDSK makes sure that each of the FAT's clusters is allocated only once. In rare circumstances such as power problems or hardware failures, DOS may give two different files the same cluster. By checking each cluster chain for cross-linked files, CHKDSK can report "mixed up" files. Each time you see the message *filename* `is cross-linked on cluster` *X,* copy the file reported in *filename* to another disk. CHKDSK normally reports another file with the same message. Copy the second file to another disk also. The contents of the two files probably are mixed up, but you have a better chance of recovering the files if you save them to another disk before CHKDSK "fixes" the problem.

Unfortunately, if CHKDSK encounters a file allocation chain that loops back to itself, CHKDSK runs in a circle reporting errors. If the /F switch is active, the root directory becomes swamped with CHKDSK-produced recovery files. In all likelihood, the action that terminates CHKDSK when it is chasing a circular allocation chain is the filling of all root directory entries. Pressing Ctrl-C stops the process. If you detect that a circular reference episode is taking place, don't reissue the CHKDSK command with the /F switch. Try erasing the file and restoring it from the backup.

Finding Lost Clusters with CHKDSK

CHKDSK expects that every cluster in the FAT is available for allocation, part of a legitimate directory-based cluster chain, or a marked bad cluster. If CHKDSK encounters any clusters or cluster chains not pointed to by a directory entry, CHKDSK issues the following message:

```
X lost clusters in Y chains
```

CHKDSK then prompts you as follows:

```
Convert lost chains to files (Y/N)
```

If the /F switch is active, CHKDSK turns each cluster chain into a file in the root directory. Each created file is named FILE*nnnn*.CHK, with *nnnn* representing a number that is increased for each file created by the CHKDSK command's current execution.

You can use the DOS TYPE command to examine the contents of a text file, and you may be able to put the text back into its original file using a word processor. If the file is a binary (program or data) file, the TYPE command will not do you any good. If the problem is due to a program file, you may need to use COMP or FC (File Compare) to compare the disk's binary files with their counterparts from the backup disks.

A lost cluster report does not indicate that the clusters are bad and that the disk has physically lost any sectors. Lost clusters only indicate that DOS made a bookkeeping error in the FAT that makes a cluster or some clusters appear to be lost to DOS. The clusters aren't tied to a directory entry, but the clusters are marked as being in use. The lost cluster problem is most likely to occur when you are running disk-intensive programs such as dBASE IV or WordPerfect. These programs are not to be blamed for lost clusters, but the programs increase DOS's exposure to bookkeeping errors. Programs that use disk files to swap sections of a program or data too large for memory may ask DOS to read and write work files hundreds of times during a single computing session. Power "glitches" or interruptions, heated hardware components, and electrical interference can turn a cluster chain number into a different number at the critical moment that DOS is writing the number into the FAT. Still, when you consider the millions of bytes that DOS is responsible for in a typical PC, DOS's reliability record is superb. CHKDSK recovers most clusters that DOS bookkeeping errors lose.

Most lost clusters are, however, user-induced. Not properly exiting a program such as WordPerfect, for example, can create lost clusters. Suppose that while working with WordPerfect you use the DOS Shell command and get a DOS prompt. Instead of returning to WordPerfect and exiting to the proper DOS prompt, you assume that you have exited already and turn off the system. When you are in an applications program and use the DOS prompt from within the program, the program puts many of its parts into temporary storage on the disk. These temporary copies of parts of files can be lost when you turn off the computer while within the program. WordPerfect takes the precaution of changing the DOS prompt to say `Enter 'EXIT' to return to WordPerfect`, but other applications programs, such as Lotus 1-2-3, do not, and you can be confused. If in doubt, try typing **EXIT**. If the command prompt returns without anything happening, you aren't in an applications program and you can turn off the computer safely.

When you issue the CHKDSK command, DOS reports whether lost clusters are found and prompts to check whether you want to convert the lost clusters to files. If you used the /F switch and press N at this prompt, DOS marks the lost clusters as free and available and doesn't give you the chance to check the clusters' contents. Although you usually cannot salvage the contents of these lost clusters, a wise precaution is to convert them to files and check them anyway. If you find that you are getting lost clusters regularly, you may be able to decipher enough data to identify the applications program generating the lost clusters. You may see the word AutoCAD in most of the recovered files, leading you to assume that you—or someone else using the computer—is not exiting AutoCAD completely before turning off the computer.

Using CHKDSK To Find Fragmented Files

DOS provides a way for you to find fragmented files on a disk: CHKDSK. Using CHKDSK is not very efficient because you have to run it for each subdirectory. Because CHKDSK is supplied with DOS, however, it is an economical approach. You can use third-party programs that do the same thing but more efficiently. Two of these programs are discussed later in this chapter.

Type **CHKDSK *.*** at the DOS prompt to check each file in the current directory. When checking a directory with contiguous files, you may see a message similar to the following:

```
Volume HARD DISK D created 12-26-1990 5:05p
Volume Serial Number is 2E79-18CA

 21344256 bytes total disk space
     2048 bytes in 2 hidden files
    40960 bytes in 20 directories
  8062976 bytes in 300 user files
 13238272 bytes available on disk

     2048 bytes in each allocation unit
    10422 total allocation units on disk
     6464 available allocation units on disk

   655360 total bytes memory
   569760 bytes free

All specified file(s) are contiguous
```

If *noncontiguous* or fragmented files are found, however, the message may resemble the following screen:

```
Volume HARD DISK D created 12-26-1990 5:05p
Volume Serial Number is 2E79-18CA

 21344256 bytes total disk space
     2048 bytes in 2 hidden files
    40960 bytes in 20 directories
  8062976 bytes in 300 user files
 13238272 bytes available on disk

     2048 bytes in each allocation unit
    10422 total allocation units on disk
     6464 available allocation units on disk

   655360 total bytes memory
   569760 bytes free
```

```
D:\QUE\DOSBOOK\CHAP3.TOC Contains 2 non-contiguous blocks
D:\QUE\DOSBOOK\CHAP1.WP  Contains 2 non-contiguous blocks
D:\QUE\DOSBOOK\CHAP4.WP  Contains 2 non-contiguous blocks
D:\QUE\DOSBOOK\CHAP3.WP  Contains 2 non-contiguous blocks
D:\QUE\DOSBOOK\CHAP5.WP  Contains 3 non-contiguous blocks
```

CHKDSK looks up the starting cluster number from the file in the directory and follows the chain through the FAT. Any file that doesn't occupy sequential clusters is listed as being noncontiguous. CHKDSK counts the number of separate parts into which the file is split. This example shows that the noncontiguous files are split into two or three sections. On a badly fragmented disk, however, you get many times this number of blocks and get seriously degraded performance while using these files.

Although DOS can report noncontiguous files, it doesn't have a command to put files back together. You can remove fragmentation manually. If fragmented files are on a floppy disk, you can use the COPY or XCOPY command to move them onto a freshly formatted disk. Because either command copies each file in turn to the first available sectors on the new disk, each file is stored contiguously.

Do not use DISKCOPY for defragmenting because DISKCOPY replicates the first floppy disk, sector by sector, onto the second disk. Consequently, DISKCOPY duplicates the noncontiguous blocks on the second disk just as they appear on the first disk.

If fragmented files are on a hard disk, the principle is the same, but recopying is more involved because of the large amount of data normally on a hard disk. First, back up all hard disk files, using either DOS BACKUP or another backup program. Next, reformat the hard disk, using DOS FORMAT, and restore the files from the backup. As with the floppy disk example, when you restore files to the hard disk, each file is restored whole. Because DOS isn't hunting all over the disk for space to fit the file, each file is placed contiguously on the disk.

You can use several third-party products to defragment files without having to reformat the hard disk. Products such as Central Point Software's PC Tools Deluxe or Peter Norton Computing's Norton Utilities include a defragmenting utility program.

Although data fragmentation on floppy disks is just as likely as on a hard disk, using disk utility programs to fix the problem usually is not worth the effort. Simply format a new floppy disk and copy the files from the fragmented disk to the freshly formatted disk. This procedure not only makes an unfragmented disk but also ensures that the floppy disk is formatted at the current head alignment.

I have a couple of floppy disks that I use for transferring files between the computers in my office. These disks quickly fill with files. I normally delete some of the old files and add new ones. After a couple of months of adding and deleting, the files become fragmented. At that point, I simply reformat the disks and start all over. When the disks show signs of wear, I throw them out.

Using Third-Party Software To Defragment

Products such as Central Point Software's PC Tools Deluxe or Peter Norton Computing's Norton Utilities include utilities that remove file fragmentation from disks. As this book demonstrates, using one of the commonly used utility programs solves most of the DOS configuration problems efficiently and inexpensively.

Most of these products are not just disk optimizers but are a collection of utility programs. PC Tools, for example, includes a file manager, backup programs, and restore programs, as well as a variety of disk utilities that can unerase files, improve the disk's performance, and keep information that helps to recover data from a crashed disk.

PC Tools' Compress Program

One feature of PC Tools' Compress program enables you to defragment disk files. Additionally, you can rearrange the files and directories and remove the data stored in unused clusters.

You may choose to rearrange a disk's files so that all executable files are together and the directories are all in alphabetical order. The appropriate choice from among the various options varies with the application. If you put all executable files first, followed by data files, for example, you reduce the likelihood of getting fragmented files. Because you normally change data files frequently, these are the files most likely to become fragmented. By placing these files later in the disk, you do not end up with fragmented executable files. Sorting directories into alphabetical order makes them easier to use.

You can run Compress directly from the DOS command prompt by using optional switches. However, because you will use Compress occasionally rather than daily, the menu-driven method of accessing Compress usually is easier.

Chapter 5: Employing Routine Maintenance

You start the program by typing **COMPRESS** at the DOS prompt. A screen showing a map of one of the logical drives appears (see fig. 5.1).

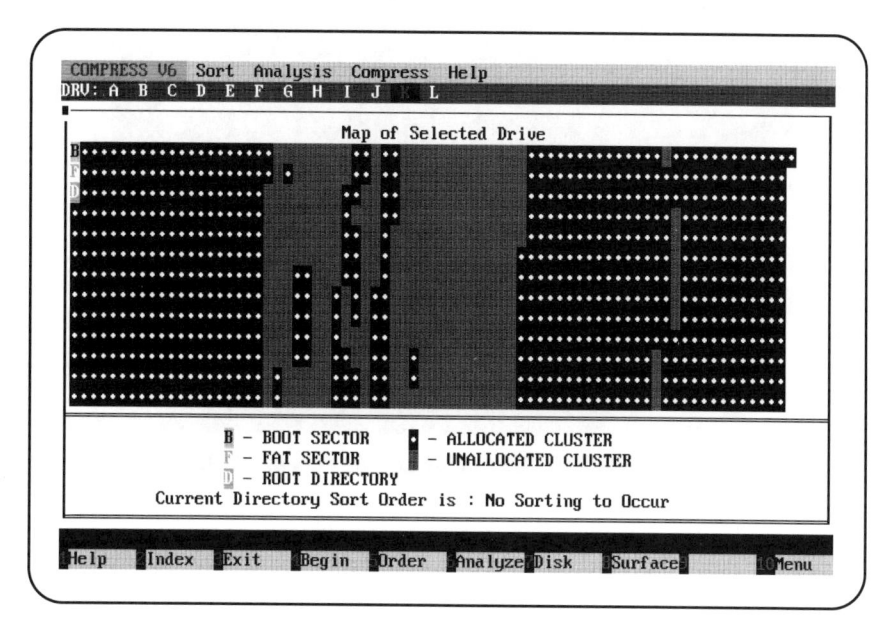

Fig. 5.1. A map showing a logical drive.

The top line is a menu bar, and the line below the menu bar lists all the drives available on the system. In this example, drives A through L are available. The central portion of the screen is a map of the hard disk—in this example, drive K. Each character on the map area of the screen represents several clusters on the hard disk. The number of clusters represented by a single character on this map depends on the size of the hard disk being analyzed.

The map in this example shows that the hard disk has a large number of files at the start, a few scattered in the middle, and a large number of files at the end. You can make assumptions about the history of this disk's use. After it was formatted, files were added to the disk until it became full. A group of files that had been located near the middle of the disk then was deleted, leaving a large gap. Using Compress on this disk removes the gap in the middle and puts the files in sequential clusters starting at the beginning of the disk.

Although this screen shows the data scattered over the hard disk, this screen doesn't specify the degree of fragmentation. Pressing F7 reveals a screen that is PC Tools' equivalent of DOS's CHKDSK (see fig. 5.2).

Part II: Enhancing Disk Performance

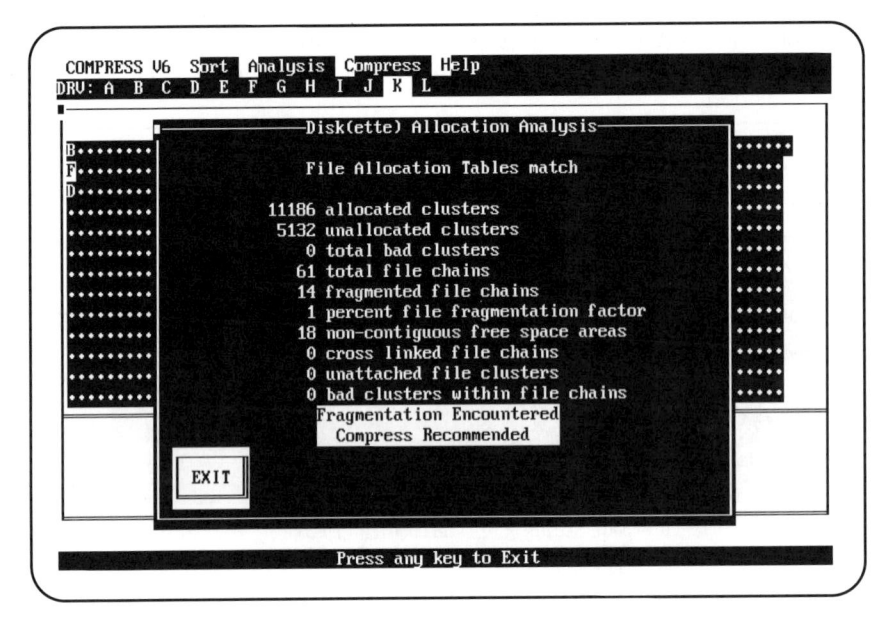

```
COMPRESS V6  Sort  Analysis  Compress  Help
DRV: A  B  C  D  E  F  G  H  I  J  K  L
```

```
                  Disk(ette) Allocation Analysis
                       File Allocation Tables match

                   11186 allocated clusters
                    5132 unallocated clusters
                       0 total bad clusters
                      61 total file chains
                      14 fragmented file chains
                       1 percent file fragmentation factor
                      18 non-contiguous free space areas
                       0 cross linked file chains
                       0 unattached file clusters
                       0 bad clusters within file chains
                  Fragmentation Encountered
                     Compress Recommended

                  EXIT

                     Press any key to Exit
```

Fig. 5.2. The Disk(ette) Allocation Analysis screen.

The first three items list the number of used, free, and bad clusters, respectively. You can see that 5,132 unallocated clusters—or roughly 1/3 of this disk's clusters—are available for use. This number corresponds with the map, which shows about 1/3 of its characters as unused clusters.

Compress reports a total of 61 file chains with 14 of them fragmented. The number of file chains, including subdirectories and user files, is found by PC Tools when it looks through the directory area. Remember that a subdirectory is only a special type of file and has a cluster, or more, assigned to it. The top-level subdirectory name is stored in the system directory area, and the contents of the subdirectory are listed in the cluster pointed to by the directory entry.

If you used DOS's CHKDSK on this disk, you would see one additional subdirectory listed that doesn't appear as a file chain. This subdirectory is the volume name for the disk. Because it is only a name and doesn't need to point to another area of the disk, PC Tools doesn't list this type of subdirectory as a file chain.

Compress reports that 1 percent of the data stored on this disk is fragmented. This percentage may not sound like much, but this fragmentation includes 14 of the 61 file chains. The program recommends running the Compress utility to remove the fragmentation and to place the data on the disk more efficiently.

You can choose one of two ways to organize the data. You can organize files in the same order that they are stored on the disk (which clusters contain which files), or you can organize files in the same order that they appear in the directory listing.

Compress's Standard option places all subdirectories at the disk's start followed by files in any order. When using this strategy, Compress selects the order and operates fastest. Other options are available, however, that may be more suitable in certain situations.

The COM & EXE First option, which puts executable files at the start of the disk, followed by data files, should be used on hard disks containing programs that don't change often. All the program files are at the front of the disk. Because these files don't change often, you are adding and deleting files only toward the end of the disk. When you run Compress again, it is fast because it deals with fragmentation and unused space only at the end of the disk.

Two other options arrange files following the directory structure on the hard disk. One option places all subdirectories at the disk's start and then places the files in the order they are listed in the directory. The other option places each subdirectory, with its associated files, in order on the disk.

For certain directory structures, placing the subdirectories at the start and then the files in subdirectory order is the most efficient. Consider a disk sorted by the COM & EXE First option. The hard disk head reads the program from the beginning of the disk and then has to move a long way to reach the data. With the files placed on the disk in directory order rather than executable-files-first order, however, the data and program files are close and the disk operates efficiently.

Most well-organized hard disks don't have the data files in the same directory as the program files, so the option of placing the subdirectories at the start and then files in subdirectory order may not prove more efficient for the way you use DOS. The second option—grouping all the data into subdirectory order—is best for situations where whole subdirectories are added and deleted at a time.

I partition my hard disk so that one logical drive contains the programs I normally use, programs such as DOS, WordPerfect, and 1-2-3. The next logical drive contains my data files, such as memos, articles, and spreadsheets. This system of relegating data files to a particular drive greatly simplifies my backup procedures. I have to back up the program drive only occasionally, such as when I upgraded from WordPerfect 5.0 to 5.1. Because the data drive has constantly changing contents, the data drive is backed up weekly—if not daily. I use the Compress executable-files-first ordering option for the program drive and the subdirectory-with-files option for the data drive. Each of my computers has a similar arrangement of files on the first two logical drives, which greatly increases my efficiency when I swap computers. Regularly used items are always in the same place on each computer.

PC Tools can rearrange files in a directory with its PC Shell disk-management program. However, you have to arrange each directory in turn. If you select file sorting options before compressing the disk, Compress sorts the directories while it rearranges the disk. Sorting options include sorting by DOS's date and time stamp, file name, extension name, and size. You can choose ascending or descending for each of these options, or you can choose no ordering of files.

Pressing F4 starts the compression process. Depending on the options chosen, size of disk, and current organization of files, the process may take a few minutes. If a disk has a great deal of fragmentation, after you run Compress you will notice improved performance of applications programs.

After Compress is finished, the hard disk map illustrated in figure 5.1 is altered to the map shown in figure 5.3. The free space is at the end rather than the middle of the disk, and the disk analysis shows no fragmentation of file chains.

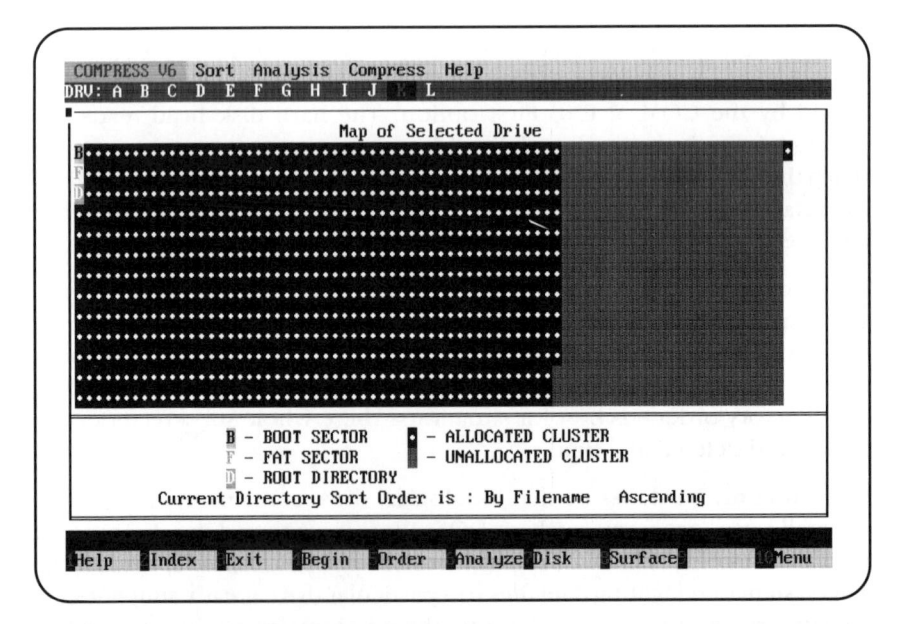

Fig. 5.3. The hard disk map after compression.

Compress performs a more extensive analysis than just defragmenting files. Compress, like CHKDSK, finds cross-linked files and lost clusters, but unlike CHKDSK, Compress also checks for media errors such as defective or worn out areas of the disk. DOS eventually finds these clusters and gives a data error when reading the cluster. However, you can use Compress to check before data loss becomes a problem. Compress tests each cluster in turn. If a cluster is bad, Compress marks it as bad in the FAT and, if the cluster was in use by a file, moves the data in the bad cluster to another cluster. The moved data may not be correct because the media defect may have caused some of the data to be missing or wrong, but moving the data may enable you to recover some of the information stored in the cluster.

Compress is only one of many programs supplied with PC Tools that can improve the computer's performance. Some of these programs, such as PC Shell, can increase productivity through their file management tools. Others, such as DISKFIX, can help recover corrupted files.

Norton's Speed Disk Program

PC Tools is not the only utility program available for defragmenting files. Norton Utilities' Speed Disk is similar to Compress. Other utility program collections have similar utilities, or you can buy products that specialize in defragmenting files.

Type **SD** alone or with command switches at the command prompt to start Speed Disk. You then are prompted for a drive name, and Speed Disk fetches the relevant information from the disk. Figure 5.4 shows a representative map of a hard disk.

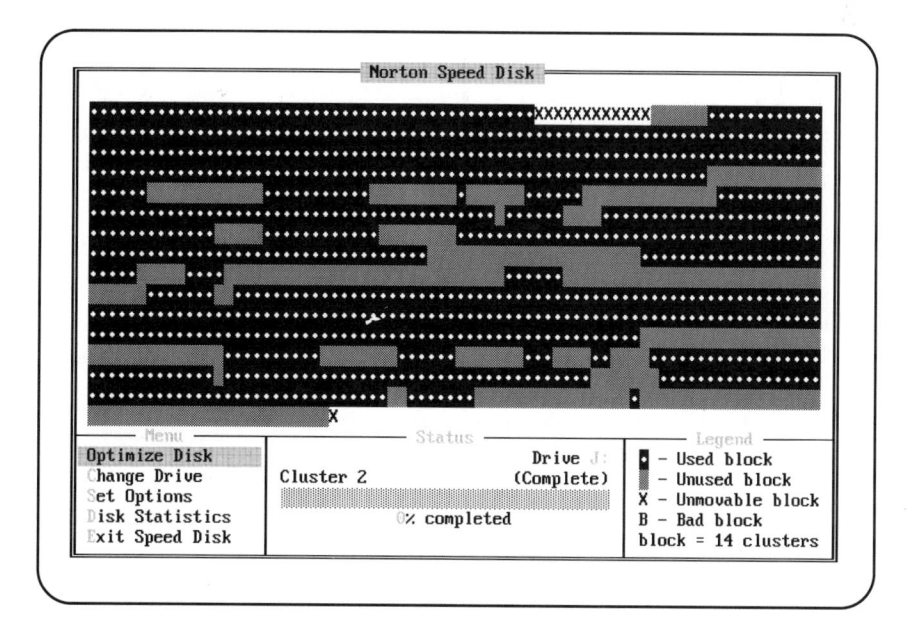

Fig. 5.4. Speed Disk showing a hard disk map.

Part II: Enhancing Disk Performance

Instead of using a column arrangement as Compress does, Speed Disk lists clusters horizontally, starting its rows near the top of the screen. The information available is similar to that of a Compress screen. The whole disk is shown on a single screen, and as an improvement over Compress, the number of clusters represented in a single block is listed in the lower right corner.

This map shows some free but scattered space on this disk. Choosing the Disk Statistics option from the menu shows that 4 percent of the data on the disk is in fragmented files. The number of files, directories, and free disk space also is shown.

Speed Disk's options, like those of PC Tools, fall into either one of two general ordering strategies. Speed Disk enables you to reposition disk files or to arrange directories.

If you want to reposition files, Speed Disk offers the following options: remove fragmentation, move free space to the end of the disk, move files and directories, or use all three options at once.

You rearrange directories by using a screen similar to that found in figure 5.5. The current tree listing is shown, and you add, delete, or move directories to fit your needs. When you run Speed Disk, the current option settings are used for optimization.

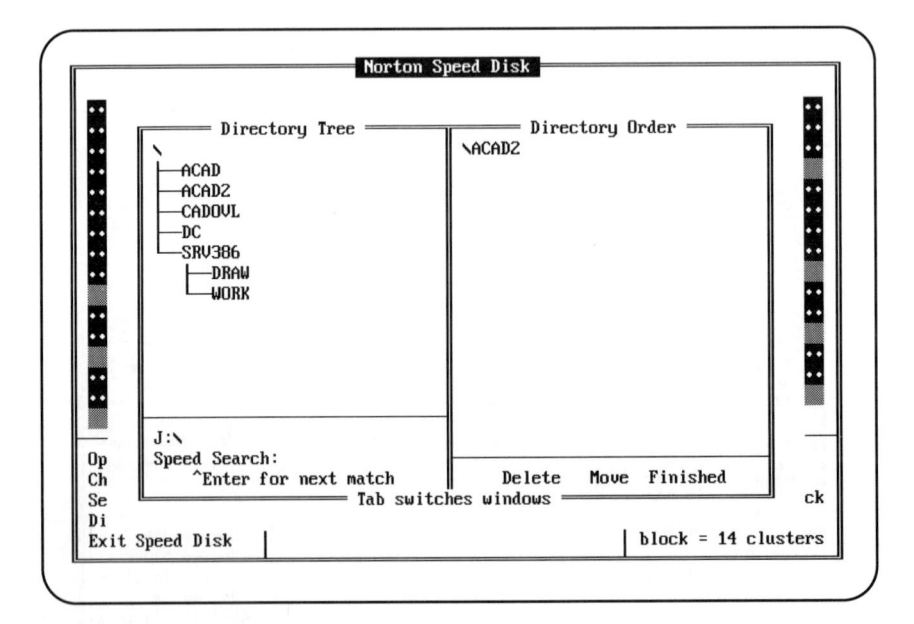

Fig. 5.5. Speed Disk showing a directory tree.

Speed Disk, Compress, and other third-party disk-optimization products can improve a disk's performance quickly and easily. Choosing a utility program is a matter of finding the one you like best for the programs you run. I happen to like Compress better than Speed Disk for my applications, but I prefer some of the other Norton Utilities over their PC Tools counterparts. No matter which product you choose, make a policy of checking each disk for fragmentation, lost clusters, and cross-linked files as part of a backup routine to keep the computer disk working at its peak performance.

Choosing Benchmarks

The quotation "There are three kinds of lies: lies, damned lies, and statistics" can be applied to computer benchmarks. You can produce a benchmark that makes anything appear to perform well. Nevertheless, with some careful thought, benchmarks can be useful.

Consider the physical specifications of Plus Development Corporation's Hardcard II. It has a quoted average seek time of 25 ms and an effective access time of 19 ms. Because of its disk controller's caching circuitry, Hardcard II improves the physical hard disk performance. If you run a benchmark program that tests the seek time of the disk, you probably get results around 25 ms. If you retrieve a file from the disk, however, you may realize an access time of 19 ms. The reason for this discrepancy is that the benchmark that measures the seek time of the disk is not measuring a "real world" value. However, the real world varies with each individual.

Benchmarks should not be ignored, but they should be used for comparative purposes and not taken too literally. When testing a variety of hard disks on different computers, use the same benchmark on each computer and, at the same time, run the same version of DOS and similar software configurations. Comparing one disk with its disk cache turned on to another disk with its disk cache disabled doesn't give valid data. Comparing the same disk with its cache turned on and then off, however, should give more useful information.

Many public domain testing programs give you a feel for a computer's performance. Many utility programs also include a performance program. For years manufacturers would quote Norton's SI (System Index) in their advertising. However, as microprocessors improve and manufacturers discover ways to make the System Index look high, the SI benchmark is becoming less significant. The Landmark CPU test, often run on computers at exhibitions, serves only two purposes: You see that the computer can run the Landmark test, and you get a number only used as a comparison with other Landmark test results.

Benchmarks are like IQ tests. IQ tests test one's ability to take IQ tests. As a general indication of intelligence, however, IQ tests are only one part of a measure of intelligence. When used in isolation, neither benchmarks nor IQ tests have much practical use.

The best approach to evaluating a computer involves a mixture of benchmarks and specifications. For example, you may have some public domain testing programs, your own benchmark tests, and sales brochures from a variety of manufacturers. By testing and comparing several different systems, or a single system with different configurations, you can determine how well your computer performs. You then can use these results as a basis for checking the computer's performance over time—detecting, for example, how much fragmentation of files is affecting the system's performance.

Benchmarks can take any form but should reflect the type of work done with the computer. If, for example, you use AutoCAD most of the time and occasionally use a word processor, create a test that involves zooming out and in, to test the display's speed. Create a different test that loads and saves a drawing, to test the hard disk's capability. Although other benchmarks may test the word processor and confirm the AutoCAD results on other computers, you will have more confidence in the computer that runs your customized AutoCAD benchmark the best.

Your benchmarks should test not only applications programs you use but also the specific application features of that program most commonly used. If you always use 1-2-3, don't invent a benchmark that sorts database records in dBASE. If you never use 1-2-3's graphing features, don't build a benchmark to test 1-2-3's graphing performance. If you often use 1-2-3 with complex trigonometric functions in formulas, invent a benchmark that recalculates trigonometric values.

My set of benchmarks encompasses database, spreadsheet, word processing, and graphics applications. Whenever I change my computer's configuration, such as adding a cache or new DOS version, I rerun and time the benchmarks to evaluate performance. The database benchmark, which exercises the hard disk, sorts a database containing about 200 records. If I used my database more extensively, I would increase the test's complexity and add more database tests. However, I generally use a database only as an electronic Rolodex and only display an address. Because word processing is an important part of my work, I have several benchmarks that require a word processor. These tests include retrieving and saving files; sorting, merging, and moving around documents; and a global search and replace exercise.

Although your benchmarks probably include some tests that exercise many parts of the computer, create some that test specific parts of the computer, such as the hard disk, the display, or the math coprocessor. Benchmarks that use applications programs or DOS do not analyze the hardware literally. Your benchmarks written using WordPerfect, for example, tell you the time taken to load a certain size file into WordPerfect. Rarely can you create a benchmark that tests only one item of a computer system. However, you can pick disk-intensive activities, such as database sorting or math-intensive calculations.

Armed with a customized set of benchmarks, you can improve the computer's performance. Each time you change a feature, you see the results. If a configuration change only makes a benchmark number look better but doesn't improve a computer's performance, the change is not worth doing. In an extreme example, adding a hard disk to a computer is going to improve the file access time only if you store files on it. The floppy disk drive continues to be a slow device and is unaffected by the hard disk's installation.

You don't have to run every benchmark for every configuration change. Pick benchmarks that test particular parts of the computer that interest you. To test the hard disk, for example, pick benchmarks that include saving and retrieving files from within an application, sorting database records in a database or word processor, or copying files in DOS. You quickly see how much a specific change, such as altering a disk cache size, affects the computer. After choosing an optimum value for the change, you can see how it affects the system's overall performance by running more general benchmarks.

Assessing Hard Disk Performance

You can use benchmarks that test the hard disk to check the hard disk's interleave setting. Alternatively, public domain programs, such as SpinTest, measure the interleave and tell you whether it is optimum.

Chapter 4 discusses in detail the effect of changing the interleave. If the interleave is set too high, the disk spins at least one extra time before a full track of data transfers. If the interleave is set too low, the disk spins one extra time for each sector that transfers. By measuring the time to save and retrieve files at different interleave settings, you can determine the optimum interleave for the hard disk.

The other methods of improving performance, such as disk caching software discussed in Chapter 7, are easier to alter and can affect the disk's performance dramatically. However, you need to ensure that the interleave is set to the maximum before optimizing any of the other disk enhancers. You see different optimum settings for disk enhancers for different interleave factors. If you cannot reformat the disk, perhaps because of company policy, you still can optimize disk performance using other disk enhancers, but you have to assume that the interleave is correct or at least that it is as optimum as it's going to get.

Changing a Hard Disk's Interleave

Changing a hard disk's interleave is done through the low-level formatting program. Chapter 4 explains that low-level formats define the positions of tracks and sectors. Low-level formatting marries the hard disk to the disk controller. The DOS FORMAT command creates the interface between DOS and the hard disk subsystem. The operating system can store files on the hard disk because of DOS's FORMAT, created when the directory and FAT is established. The low-level format doesn't determine a sector's contents, just its position.

> *Warning*: Because low-level formatting removes all data on the disk, back up all data onto floppy disks or tape before using a low-level formatter. Restore the data after the formatting, partitioning, and DOS formatting is complete.

Although it's relatively easy to do, low-level formatting takes a long time. You easily can spend a couple of hours carrying out all the steps. However, after the hard disk's interleave is set correctly, you need to change it only when you buy a new disk or disk controller or when you install the disk in a different computer. While testing for the best interleave factor, only restore essential files—DOS and a couple of disk-intensive benchmark programs—to the hard disk between settings.

The low-level formatter is supplied with the hard disk controller, not with DOS. You use the same formatter regardless of the operating system you use. The formatter comes either stored in the ROM on the disk controller card or as a software program on a floppy disk. Products such as Speedstor or Disk Manager, which often are bundled with hard disks, include low-level formatters.

The operation of the formatter varies depending on the hard disk and disk controller. However, the user interface is similar for almost all formatters; you need to supply the same information, although possibly in a different order, to format the hard disk. Examples of a ROM-based formatter and a floppy disk-based formatter are discussed later in this chapter.

To prepare a new, unformatted hard disk, perform the following steps:

1. Run the computer's SETUP program to specify the type of hard disk. (This step doesn't apply to XTs.)

2. Run the low-level formatter.

3. Run FDISK to partition the disk.

4. Run DOS's FORMAT to format the disk. (Don't forget the /S if you want the disk to be bootable.)

5. Add program and data files to the disk.

Keeping this sequence in mind helps when you're checking the interleave factor. Because you go through the process several times, losing your place or getting confused is easy. Having this checklist assists you through the formatting procedure.

For new disks, prepare the disk for data using the preceding sequence and following any manufacturer's instructions. Make a note of the interleave factor used as listed in the instructions. You supply this number to the formatter.

If you have an IBM PC AT and are setting up a new disk, you must run the SETUP program before low-level formatting. The information about SETUP is located in the installation and setup manual. In the setup procedure, you are asked for the disk drive type. Currently, all IBM 20M disk drives are type 2, and all IBM 30M disk drives are type 20. If you are unsure of your disk drive type, remove the cover of the AT and read the large number on the front of the disk drive. You cannot always find a number on the front of the disk drive. You may have to call the manufacturer to get the number.

If you have an IBM PS/2 Micro Channel computer (Model 50, 50Z, 60, 70, or 80) and are setting up a new disk, you should boot the system from the Reference disk. Follow the instructions, and the system automatically configures itself for the hard disk and adapter cards you have installed.

The only files you need to transfer (see step 5) onto the hard disk each time you change the interleave are those you need for running the benchmarks. These files typically include all the DOS files, a couple of applications programs, and the sample data files. When you have chosen an interleave, copy all the files and programs to the disk for normal use.

I have a complete backup with all the contents of my disk and a partial backup with the files I need to evaluate the disk's performance. If you don't do this partial backup set, you either waste time restoring far more data than you need or you have to select the data for restoring on a file-by-file basis. Be sure to include in the partial backup any necessary CONFIG.SYS statements. For example, your hard disk may need a device driver to run. You also need a copy of FORMAT.COM and FDISK.COM on a separate system floppy disk for use in steps 3 and 4.

For all disks, whether new or not, next you should run the benchmarks and record the results. Create a table similar to the one shown in figure 5.6. If you know the current interleave factor, you can fill in two columns before you begin testing. Or you can complete the initial interleave. Although you need to check only one partition (logical drive) on each physical hard disk, be sure to use the same size partition for each interleave factor tested. While testing, turn off any disk caches or other software features that enhance disk performance. Making sure that you are changing only one variable at a time is easier if you reduce the number of possibilities to a minimum of variables.

	Initial Interleave	1:1	1:2	1:3	1:4	1:5
Benchmark #1						
Benchmark #2						
Benchmark #3						
Benchmark #4						

Fig. 5.6. A sample table for recording benchmark results.

In most cases, you will not need to rerun SETUP when you change the interleave factor. However, you must know the physical characteristics of the hard disk because the formatter prompts you for the number of heads and cylinders. You also are prompted to enter any bad sectors on the disk.

The manufacturer lists the bad sectors on the disk and provides a label listing the number of heads and cylinders. These bad sectors are found by the manufacturer during testing. If your disk doesn't have a label attached, listing the number of cylinders and heads, you may find that the documentation cites these specifications. If you are unable to find the drive specifications, call the manufacturer for this information before running the formatter.

My MicroScience disk, for example, has two labels. One lists the model number and the number of cylinders, heads, and sectors. The other, which is like a calculator printout, lists the defective sectors. My Seagate disk, however, has only a model number on it. The Seagate documentation, which comes with the hard disk and controller, includes a table listing the specifications for the various model numbers.

Hard disks usually have defects. Although you can pay a premium for defect-free disks, the defects amount to a small proportion of the total disk space. Manufacturers consider a disk with less than 1 percent of defects acceptable. However, the defect count is typically nearer to 0.1 percent.

The manufacturer can list bad sectors because the manufacturer formats disks as part of the testing process. As mentioned earlier, however, you do need to perform a low-level format before you use a hard disk because the disk controller you attach may not be the same type as the manufacturer used.

Entering the defective-sector information into the formatter from the defect list is optional because the formatter looks for defects itself. Data you store on a disk is precious, however; if the manufacturer found a fault, chances are it's real and you should avoid putting data in that sector. The best time to mark off defective areas of the disk is during the initialization process. Don't take chances putting valuable data in questionable sectors and discovering that you cannot retrieve the information when DOS gives you error messages.

After you know the current performance of the disk, the physical characteristics of the disk, and any supplied defects, you are ready to change the interleave.

Because formatters do not work in exactly the same way, follow the instructions supplied with your low-level formatter to format the hard disk. The discussion of a typical low-level formatter in the next section gives only a general idea of what a formatter does.

Low-Level Formatting with a ROM-Based Formatter

The ROM-based low-level formatter is run through DOS's DEBUG program. You don't have to be an expert with DEBUG to run it. Remember, though, that because you are going to format the hard disk, you cannot use the copy of DOS on this hard disk.

Create a system floppy disk using FORMAT with the /S option and copy the debug program (DEBUG.COM) from the DOS directory to this disk. DEBUG is supplied on DOS's Supplemental disk, so you may not have copied it onto the hard disk.

Next, check to see whether you can boot the computer from this disk. After you do a low-level format on the hard disk, you cannot boot from the disk until you have both partitioned and formatted it for DOS. Make sure that you also have copies of a restore program for restoring the backup disks (or tapes) of the hard disk. If you use DOS's backup and restore program, for example, you need to copy RESTORE.COM to a floppy disk. The backed-up version of RESTORE.COM is unusable until it is restored because BACKUP doesn't store the files on backup disks in the same format as ordinary files are stored on disks. You also want copies of FORMAT.COM and FDISK.COM on a disk for use in the reformatting process.

For an example, suppose that I boot my computer from the DOS floppy disk and type **DEBUG** at the DOS prompt. I see the following:

```
A>debug
-
```

The hyphen is DEBUG's command prompt. I next enter the command that starts the formatter program. Remember that the formatter is located in the ROM on the disk controller board. The PC address space (see Chapter 1) and hard disk ROM is located starting at segment address C800H. The absolute address where the program that can low-level format varies slightly with the disk controller. In this example, using an Adaptec controller (Model # ACB-237XC), the absolute address is offset 5 bytes into the segment. I issue the debug "go" command that sets the address of the instruction counter to a new address and consequently starts the formatter. I type **G=C800:5** and press Enter at the DEBUG command prompt, and the following information appears:

```
Adaptec Disk Preparation Program Version 3.0
Copyright (C) Adaptec Inc. 1987, 1988. All rights
reserved.

Choose:    1 - to primary-format drive 1
           2 - to primary-format drive 2
           3 - for the special options menu
           q - to quit this program

Enter your selection:
```

The first option formats the first physical hard disk attached to the controller, and the second option formats the second hard disk. You see both options whether one or two hard disks are attached to the controller. The third option is used after the low-level formatting is complete.

I press 1 to format the first disk. The following information appears:

```
Drive 1 has 1313 cylinders, 7 heads, 26 sectors
Are the above correct (y/n) ? [y]
```

The label on the MicroScience disk attached to the controller has the same values for the cylinders, heads, and sectors per track as shown, so I press Enter to accept the values. If these values were wrong, I could change them by pressing N, pressing Enter, and typing the new values at the prompt. The saved defect list is displayed next:

```
Saved defect list (cyl/physical sct):
Surface 0:
    1278/1
Surface 1:
    1256/17
Surface 2:
Surface 3:
Surface 4:
    258/20  257/20
Surface 5:
    1169/1  65/9  64/9  63/9  62/9  61/9  2/25
Surface 6:

Do you want to ERASE the saved defect list (y/n) ? [n]
```

This list contains all the sectors that were marked bad the last time I formatted the disk. The defects for each surface are listed in turn beginning with surface 0 and ending with surface 6. For example, surface 1 has a defect on cylinder 1256, sector 17. I decide to keep this list because it includes the defects on my disk label and ones that were found during the last low-level format, so I press Enter. The following information appears:

```
Please specify format of additional defects:

    1 - No additional defect
    2 - Cyl/Head/RLL byte offset
    3 - Head/Cyl/RLL byte offset
    4 - Cyl/Head/Logical Sector

Enter your selection: [1]
```

I can add any defects listed on the disk label or depend on the formatter to find any additional defects. Because all the defects I know of are listed, I press Enter to accept the default of no additional defects. The defect list is redisplayed as follows:

```
Total defect list (cyl/physical sct):
Surface 0:
    1278/1
Surface 1:
    1256/17
Surface 2:
Surface 3:
```

```
Surface 4:
    258/20 257/20
Surface 5:
    1169/1 65/9 64/9 63/9 62/9 61/9 2/25
Surface 6:
Interleave (1 to 12): [1]
```

Because I didn't add any defects, this list is the same as the first. Any added defects would be listed at this time. Next, as you can see, I choose the interleave factor, selecting any value from 1 to 12.

The current interleave factor normally is displayed by the formatter at this prompt. A good approach for checking the best interleave is to try lowering it by one factor on each pass of the benchmark until the performance results get slower. At this point, raise the factor by one. A typical XT, for example, is set by the manufacturer with an interleave of 5. You test it with an interleave of 4, then 3, and then 2. The performance should degrade at an interleave of either 2 or 3. After you discover the point when slowing down occurs, raise the interleave factor until the higher factor begins slowing down the performance again. Suppose that a benchmark takes 40 seconds to run with an interleave of 5. The benchmark may take 35 seconds with an interleave of 4, 30 seconds with an interleave of 3, and 100 seconds with an interleave of 2. You set the interleave to 3 for optimum performance.

Because my computer is a 25 MHz 386 and this disk drive and controller are specified to work together with an interleave of 1, I know the interleave factor I want. In many cases, however, you don't know that this interleave factor is optimum. If it's currently set at 1, you may want to change the interleave factor to 2, check whether the performance degrades, and then lower it back to 1. If the performance improves when you set the factor to 2, then you know that 2 is a better interleave factor than 1 for the disk. With the interleave factor set at 1, the disk spins more often than necessary.

I select an interleave value of 1 for this disk and press Enter. The following prompt appears:

```
Allow a spare sector for defects (y/n): [n]
```

The spare sector option is a feature of this particular disk subsystem. Instead of formatting the disk to its maximum capacity of 120M, you can allocate one sector per track as a spare sector. This extra sector is set aside so that if a defect is encountered during use, the spare sector is swapped with the defective one, and the disk capacity remains constant. Because I want the full capacity of the drive and am not overly concerned about losing a sector, I press N and the following prompt appears:

Chapter 5: Employing Routine Maintenance 163

```
Ready to primary-format the drive. All data in it will
be lost !!!
Continue (y/n) ? [y]
```

This message signifies the point of no return. Accepting this prompt starts the formatting process. As shown in the following listing, the first cylinder formatted is the highest number (1313), and each head in cylinder 1313 is formatted in turn before the heads are moved to the next cylinder:

```
Formatting and Verifying Drive ...
Head 0 Cyl 1313
```

After each cylinder has been formatted (a process that took about an hour on my computer), the main menu reappears with the following message:

```
Format Complete! Now Select "Q" to quit, and go to your
Operating System Installation (e.g. DOS FDISK and
FORMAT).
```

To make full use of this disk with the version of DOS I am installing, I have to use the Special Options menu. Because DOS can accommodate only drives with fewer than 1,024 cylinders, I have to set up my hard disk controller to lie to DOS about the number of cylinders it contains. I can create this setup by using the Special Options menu, which I reach by pressing 3 at the main menu. The following menu appears:

```
Special Options Menu:

Choose:  1 - to enable 17-sector translation
         2 - to enable 63-sector translation
         3 - to disable translations
         4 - to generate Adaptec auto-configuration
             device driver
             q - to return to main menu

Enter your selection:
```

To accommodate operating systems that require 17 sectors per track, the Adaptec controller appears to the operating system as if it has 17 sectors rather than the actual 26 (using option 1). For DOS, which accepts a different number of sectors but is limited in the number of cylinders it can handle, the 63-sector translation of option 2 is necessary. This translation makes the disk look to DOS as if it has 63 sectors on a track. This disk has 1,313 cylinders, 7 heads, and 26 sectors per track, for a total of 238,966 sectors on the disk (1,313 x 7 x 26). When you select 63-sector translation, DOS is told by the controller that 63 sectors per track, 236 cylinders, and 16 heads are available. Although this procedure wastes a few sectors, it enables DOS to use the disk.

The other options disable translations and create a device driver. I select option 2 and see the following screen:

```
DOS has a limit of 1024 cylinders per drive. This
option will allow use of drives with more than 1024
cylinders up to 528M capacity. The drive parameters are
translated to a 63-sector equivalent. Run your Operat-
ing System Installation after using this option. Any
previous partitions on the drive will be erased.

Translate drive 1 or 2 ?:
```

I select drive 1 for the first hard disk in my system and get the following message:

```
Drive 1 is currently in standard (no translation) mode.
Enable 63-sector translation on drive 1 ? (y/n)
```

After I press Y, the Special Options menu reappears with the message `The drive is now in 63-sector translation mode.`

I press Q twice to return to the main menu and exit the program. The drive is now low-level formatted with a new interleave and is ready for partitioning with FDISK and formatting with DOS, the operating system.

Low-Level Formatting with Disk Manager

Not all hard disk controllers include low-level formatters in ROM. Instead, these other controllers are supplied with floppy disks containing low-level formatters. These disks often include additional programs that replace FDISK to partition and format hard disks. Storage Dimensions' SpeedStor and Ontrack Computer Systems Inc.'s Disk Manager are two examples of additional programs sometimes provided with controllers. Many of these programs are customized for and bundled with a particular hard disk. They also can be bought separately for use with other disks.

My 80M Seagate drive was supplied with a Western Digital hard disk controller that did not contain ROM and a customized version of Disk Manager for low-level formatting and partitioning. Disk Manager can be run in either automatic or manual mode. Manual mode provides more flexibility in configuration, but automatic mode is appropriate for most situations.

Chapter 5: Employing Routine Maintenance

The following paragraphs depict the use of this type of low-level formatter. Because the program doesn't have to fit into a small area of ROM, the program has a better user interface and is easier to use. However, a disadvantage is that the program is not permanently attached to the hard disk and controller. You are likely to lose the program because you normally don't use it often.

You can start Disk Manager with a variety of options. To check the appropriate interleave value, add a single switch to the command line. This extra switch enables you to select the interleave. Thus, when you start Disk Manager by typing **DM /I**, you see a screen similar to the one shown in figure 5.7.

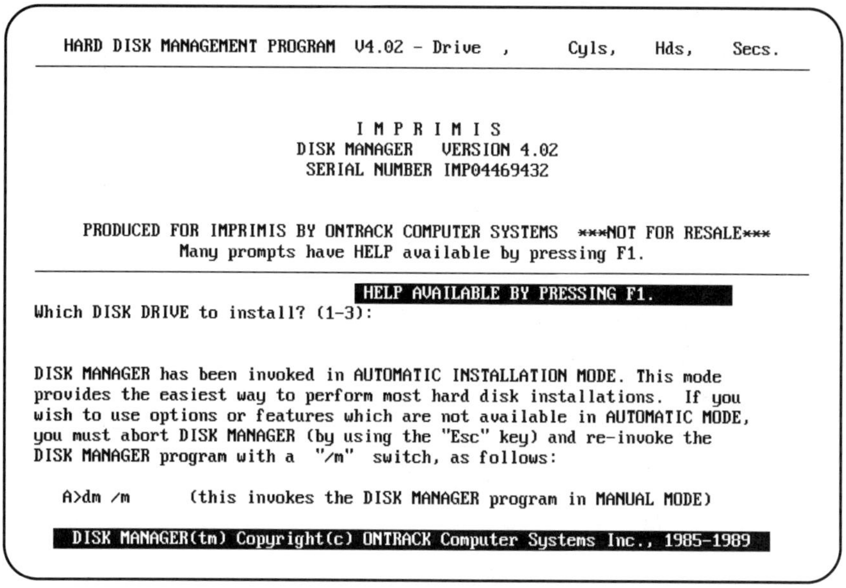

```
HARD DISK MANAGEMENT PROGRAM  V4.02 - Drive  ,    Cyls,    Hds,    Secs.


                              I M P R I M I S
                        DISK MANAGER    VERSION 4.02
                        SERIAL NUMBER IMP04469432

        PRODUCED FOR IMPRIMIS BY ONTRACK COMPUTER SYSTEMS  ***NOT FOR RESALE***
                  Many prompts have HELP available by pressing F1.
                                      HELP AVAILABLE BY PRESSING F1.
Which DISK DRIVE to install? (1-3):


DISK MANAGER has been invoked in AUTOMATIC INSTALLATION MODE. This mode
provides the easiest way to perform most hard disk installations.  If you
wish to use options or features which are not available in AUTOMATIC MODE,
you must abort DISK MANAGER (by using the "Esc" key) and re-invoke the
DISK MANAGER program with a   "/m"  switch, as follows:

   A>dm /m       (this invokes the DISK MANAGER program in MANUAL MODE)

      DISK MANAGER(tm) Copyright(c) ONTRACK Computer Systems Inc., 1985-1989
```

Fig. 5.7. The Disk Manager invoked in automatic installation mode.

You first select the disk drive you want to install. In my case, I press 1 for the first hard disk in the system. The screen shown in figure 5.8 appears.

Part II: Enhancing Disk Performance

```
┌──────────────────────────────────────────────────────────────────────┐
│  HARD DISK MANAGEMENT PROGRAM  V4.02 - Drive  ,    Cyls,  Hds,  Secs.│
│                                                                      │
│                           I M P R I M I S                            │
│                      DISK MANAGER   VERSION 4.02                     │
│                      SERIAL NUMBER IMP04469432                       │
│                                                                      │
│       PRODUCED FOR IMPRIMIS BY ONTRACK COMPUTER SYSTEMS ***NOT FOR RESALE***│
│                Many prompts have HELP available by pressing F1.      │
│──────────────────────────────────────────────────────────────────────│
│ Please SPECIFY DRIVE 1:                                              │
│ USE ↑↓←→ keys to select a MODEL.         **** PGUP/PGDN FOR MORE MODELS ****│
│ ENTER when ready, or ESC for a STANDARD drive.                       │
│ DRIVE PARAMETERS:     697 CYLINDERS    5 HEADS    17 SECS    30 MB   │
│   ┌────────────────────────────────────────────────────────────────┐ │
│   │ 9415-536     9415-538     94155-48    94155-56    94155-57    │ │
│   │ 94155-67     94155-77     94155-85    94155-85P   94155-86    │ │
│   │ 94155-96     94155-96P    94155-120   94155-120P  94155-135   │ │
│   │ 94155-135P   94156-48     94156-67    94156-86    94166-101   │ │
│   │ 94166-141    94166-182    94186-383   94186-383H  94186-442   │ │
│   │ 94196-766    94204-65     94204-71    94205-51    94205-77    │ │
│   │ 94216-106    94244-383    94246-383   94354-90    94354-126   │ │
│   └────────────────────────────────────────────────────────────────┘ │
└──────────────────────────────────────────────────────────────────────┘
```

Fig. 5.8. Selecting the disk drive for installation.

The five columns of numbers refer to the various Seagate drives distributed with Disk Manager. You can highlight the drive you want and press Enter, or press Esc to select a standard drive. The screen shown in figure 5.9 appears next.

```
┌──────────────────────────────────────────────────────────────────────┐
│  HARD DISK MANAGEMENT PROGRAM  V4.02 - Drive 1,  236 Cyls, 16 Hds, 63 Secs.│
│                                                                      │
│  Cyl--Hd  Cyl--Hd  Cyl--Hd  Cyl--Hd  Cyl--Hd  Cyl--Hd  Cyl--Hd  Cyl--Hd│
│                                                                      │
│                                                                      │
│                                                                      │
│                                                                      │
│                    ──────── CURRENT DEFECT LIST ────────             │
│                        HELP AVAILABLE BY PRESSING F1.                │
│  Do you wish to INITIALIZE this drive? (y/n):                        │
│                                                                      │
│                                                                      │
│                                                                      │
│                  Press Esc key to ABORT DISK INSTALLATION            │
└──────────────────────────────────────────────────────────────────────┘
```

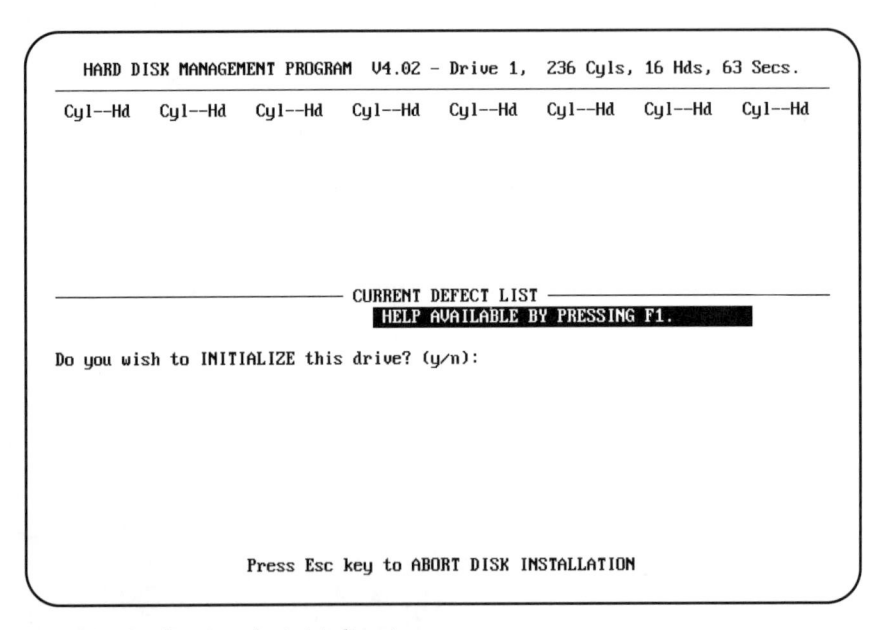

Fig. 5.9. Confirming the initialization.

Chapter 5: Employing Routine Maintenance

The top half of the screen lists the current defect list for the drive. In this case, no defects are listed yet. By confirming that you want to initialize this drive, you see the screen shown in figure 5.10.

```
 HARD DISK MANAGEMENT PROGRAM  V4.02 - Drive 1,  236 Cyls, 16 Hds, 63 Secs.
  Cyl--Hd    Cyl--Hd    Cyl--Hd    Cyl--Hd    Cyl--Hd    Cyl--Hd    Cyl--Hd




                         ─── CURRENT DEFECT LIST ───
                           HELP AVAILABLE BY PRESSING F1.
 Do you wish to enter the bad-track map for this drive? (y/n):




                    Press Esc key to ABORT DISK INSTALLATION
```

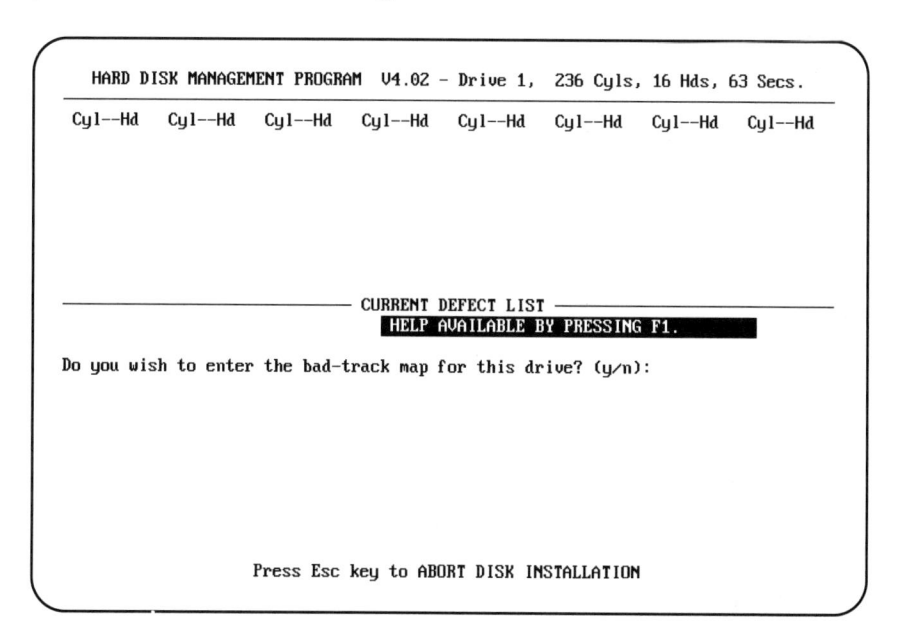

Fig. 5.10. Entering the bad track map.

Pressing Y in response to the question `Do you wish to enter the bad-track map for this drive` enables you to add the known defects, as listed on the hard disk label, to the table. The Defect List Management menu assists with the process (see fig. 5.11).

Press A to add known defects to the list. The formatter prompts you for the cylinder number (see fig. 5.12) and then the head number (see fig. 5.13).

Part II: Enhancing Disk Performance

```
┌─────────────────────────────────────────────────────────────────────┐
│   HARD DISK MANAGEMENT PROGRAM  V4.02 - Drive 1,  236 Cyls, 16 Hds, 63 Secs. │
│                                                                     │
│  Cyl--Hd   Cyl--Hd   Cyl--Hd   Cyl--Hd   Cyl--Hd   Cyl--Hd   Cyl--Hd   Cyl--Hd │
│                                                                     │
│                                                                     │
│                                                                     │
│                                                                     │
│                          ─── CURRENT DEFECT LIST ───                │
│  DEFECT LIST MANAGEMENT MENU:    HELP AVAILABLE BY PRESSING F1.     │
│  (G)et, (W)rite the defect-map FILE                                 │
│  (C)lear, (A)dd to, (D)elete from, (L)ist the defect-list           │
│  (R)eturn to initialization menu                                    │
│  Select an option (R):                                              │
│                                                                     │
│                                                                     │
│                                                                     │
│                                                                     │
│                 Press Esc key to ABORT DISK INSTALLATION            │
└─────────────────────────────────────────────────────────────────────┘
```

Fig. 5.11. Adding the known defects to the list.

```
┌─────────────────────────────────────────────────────────────────────┐
│   HARD DISK MANAGEMENT PROGRAM  V4.02 - Drive 1,  236 Cyls, 16 Hds, 63 Secs. │
│                                                                     │
│  Cyl--Hd   Cyl--Hd   Cyl--Hd   Cyl--Hd   Cyl--Hd   Cyl--Hd   Cyl--Hd   Cyl--Hd │
│                                                                     │
│                                                                     │
│                                                                     │
│                          ─── CURRENT DEFECT LIST ───                │
│  DEFECT LIST MANAGEMENT MENU:    HELP AVAILABLE BY PRESSING F1.     │
│  (G)et, (W)rite the defect-map FILE                                 │
│  (C)lear, (A)dd to, (D)elete from, (L)ist the defect-list           │
│  (R)eturn to initialization menu                                    │
│  Select an option (R): a                                            │
│                                                                     │
│  *** Strike "ESC" to ABORT ***                                      │
│  Enter Cylinder Number (   0):                                      │
│                                                                     │
│                                                                     │
└─────────────────────────────────────────────────────────────────────┘
```

Fig. 5.12. Entering the cylinder number.

```
       HARD DISK MANAGEMENT PROGRAM  V4.02 - Drive 1,  236 Cyls, 16 Hds, 63 Secs.
    Cyl--Hd    Cyl--Hd    Cyl--Hd    Cyl--Hd    Cyl--Hd    Cyl--Hd    Cyl--Hd    Cyl--Hd




                              ─── CURRENT DEFECT LIST ───
    DEFECT LIST MANAGEMENT MENU:    HELP AVAILABLE BY PRESSING F1.
    (G)et, (W)rite the defect-map FILE
    (C)lear, (A)dd to, (D)elete from, (L)ist the defect-list
    (R)eturn to initialization menu
    Select an option (R): a

    *** Strike "ESC" to ABORT ***
    Enter Cylinder Number (   0): 65
    Enter Head Number (  0):
```

Fig. 5.13. Entering the head number.

The defect number is added to the list (see fig. 5.14), and you are prompted for further defects until you press Esc.

```
       HARD DISK MANAGEMENT PROGRAM  V4.02 - Drive 1,  236 Cyls, 16 Hds, 63 Secs.
    Cyl--Hd    Cyl--Hd    Cyl--Hd    Cyl--Hd    Cyl--Hd    Cyl--Hd    Cyl--Hd    Cyl--Hd
    65- 5



                              ─── CURRENT DEFECT LIST ───
    DEFECT LIST MANAGEMENT MENU:    HELP AVAILABLE BY PRESSING F1.
    (G)et, (W)rite the defect-map FILE
    (C)lear, (A)dd to, (D)elete from, (L)ist the defect-list
    (R)eturn to initialization menu
    Select an option (R): a

    *** Strike "ESC" to ABORT ***
    Enter Cylinder Number (  66):


    Cylinder   65, Head  5 added to the Defect-List.
```

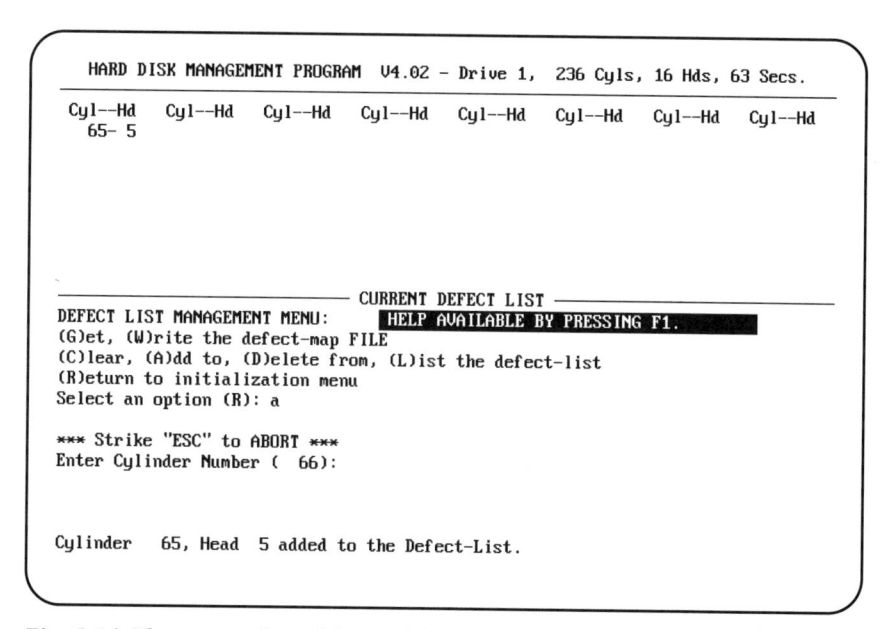

Fig. 5.14. The prompt for additional defects.

Other options from this menu enable you to clear the whole defect list, delete individual defects from the list, get a previously stored defect list, or save the defect list to a file. Continue to modify the list until all defects listed on the hard disk's label are added. You then can save the defect list and return to the initialization menu.

In automatic mode, you are prompted next for information about partitioning the disk. Partitioning is done after the low-level format and before putting DOS on the disk. This partitioning step was not included in the preceding low-level formatter example.

The partitioning menu is shown in figure 5.15. Three typical arrangements are listed as the first three options. A fourth option enables you to specify a different division.

```
HARD DISK MANAGEMENT PROGRAM  V4.02 - Drive 1,   236 Cyls, 16 Hds, 63 Secs.

Installing drive 1.

The formatted capacity will be 121.8 Megabytes.

It has  236 Cylinders,  16 Heads, and 63 Sectors per track.



                                HELP AVAILABLE BY PRESSING F1.
Select one of the following options:

Option A-- 1 partition  with   1.5 Megabytes, and
           1 partition  with 120.2 Megabytes
Option B-- 3 partitions with  33.5 Megabytes each, and
           1 partition  with  21.1 Megabytes
Option C-- 4 partitions with  30.4 Megabytes each
Option D-- CUSTOMIZED PARTITIONS other than option A thru C above.

    Select an option:

              Press Esc key to ABORT DISK INSTALLATION
```

Fig. 5.15. The partitioning menu.

After you supply the partitioning information, you see one more screen (see fig. 5.16) before the low-level format begins.

Just in case you missed the point, Disk Manager warns that a low-level format is destructive to any data previously stored on the disk. After you accept the selected options, the low-level format and partitioning occurs automatically. Because you selected the /I switch when you invoked the program, you are prompted for an interleave factor, as shown in figure 5.17. Disk Manager automatically responds to most questions without prompting you for an answer. However, Disk Manager pauses at the interleave factor setting and then continues without further input from you.

```
┌─────────────────────────────────────────────────────────────────┐
│    HARD DISK MANAGEMENT PROGRAM   V4.02 - Drive 1,  236 Cyls, 16 Hds, 63 Secs. │
│                                                                 │
│  Installing drive 1.                                            │
│                                                                 │
│  The formatted capacity will be 121.8 Megabytes.                │
│                                                                 │
│  It has  236 Cylinders, 16 Heads, and 63 Sectors per track.     │
│                                                                 │
│  The drive will be partitioned into  3 partitions with  33.5 Megabytes each, and │
│            1 partition  with   21.1 Megabytes.                  │
│  ─────────────────────────────────────                          │
│                                                                 │
│                                                                 │
│  This is your LAST CHANCE TO ABORT the installation.            │
│                                                                 │
│  ****** ALL EXISTING DATA, IF ANY, ON DRIVE 1 WILL BE DESTROYED ****** │
│                                                                 │
│  Do you wish to proceed with the installation as described above? (y/n): │
│                                                                 │
│                                                                 │
│                                                                 │
│              Press Esc key to ABORT DISK INSTALLATION           │
│                                                                 │
└─────────────────────────────────────────────────────────────────┘
```

Fig. 5.16. The final warning before the low-level format begins.

```
┌─────────────────────────────────────────────────────────────────┐
│    HARD DISK MANAGEMENT PROGRAM   V4.02 - Drive 1,  236 Cyls, 16 Hds, 63 Secs. │
│  Cyl--Hd    Cyl--Hd    Cyl--Hd    Cyl--Hd    Cyl--Hd    Cyl--Hd    Cyl--Hd    Cyl--Hd │
│   65- 5                                                         │
│                                                                 │
│                                                                 │
│                                                                 │
│                                                                 │
│                        ─── CURRENT DEFECT LIST ───              │
│  INITIALIZATION MENU:        HELP AVAILABLE BY PRESSING F1.     │
│  (I)nitialize or (V)erify surface                               │
│  (D)efect-list management, (R)eturn to main menu                │
│  Select an option (R): INITIALIZE                               │
│  Is the above DEFECT-LIST accurate for this disk? (y/n): YES    │
│  Do a (T)rack, (P)artition, entire (D)isk,  (R)eturn to initialization menu │
│  Select an option (R): DISK                                     │
│  Enter Interleave Value ( 3):                                   │
│                                                                 │
│                                                                 │
└─────────────────────────────────────────────────────────────────┘
```

Fig. 5.17. Entering the interleave factor.

After you choose the interleave value, low-level formatting begins, followed by disk partitioning. Disk partitioning saves using FDISK. The whole process can take some time because low-level formatting requires several seconds per cylinder.

When the low-level formatting is completed, use DOS's FORMAT program on each partition to add the operating system to the boot disk and to prepare the partitions for accepting data.

If, however, you have used the ROM-based low-level formatter or a floppy-disk-based low-level formatter that doesn't partition the disk, you need to complete the next section, which describes how to use FDISK. Because the FDISK program is supplied as a standard part of DOS, you can follow its steps more exactly than the steps for low-level formatters whose operations vary with different hard disk controllers and hard disks.

Partitioning the Hard Disk

The next step after low-level formatting the disk is to add the partition information. You use the FDISK.COM program supplied with DOS. *Partitioning* (see Chapter 4) is a method of dividing up the disk into logical drives. When you format each partition (logical drive), the operating system knows where the beginning and end of each drive occurs.

FDISK differs for DOS 3 and DOS 4, and this chapter addresses each version of FDISK in a separate section. FDISK for DOS 5 is similar to DOS 4.

Using FDISK with DOS 3.2 and Earlier Versions

FDISK works a little differently with DOS 3.2 and earlier versions than it does with DOS 3.3. The differences are noted as they occur in the following instructions.

The computer's hard disk can be used by more than one disk operating system. To accommodate people who use more than one operating system, DOS's FDISK program divides the hard disk into partitions. Each partition can be used with a different operating system.

Most people use only DOS. The instructions given in this first section are for setting up the hard disk for a single DOS partition:

1. Boot the computer from the DOS system floppy disk.

2. If you are not using a Personal Computer AT, type the correct date and press Enter. If you are using an AT, check the date. If the date is incorrect, enter the correct date and then press Enter. Remember that the date was incorrect.

3. If you are not using an AT, enter the correct time. Because DOS uses a universal, 24-hour clock, add 12 to afternoon and evening hours. If you are using an AT, check the time. If the time is incorrect, enter the correct time and press Enter. If the time is off by more than a minute or two, remember this fact.

   The date and time settings are worth checking for accuracy because the disk is time- and date-stamped during the formatting process. This process enables you to see when you last formatted the hard disk for reference purposes.

   Now you should see the DOS prompt.

4. Type **FDISK** and press Enter. The screen should look something like the following:

   ```
   IBM Personal Computer
   Fixed Disk Setup Program Version 3.20
   (C) Copyright IBM Corp. 1983, 1985

   FDISK Options

   Current Fixed Disk Drive: 1

   Choose one of the following:

       1. Create DOS Partition
       2. Change Active Partition
       3. Delete DOS Partition
       4. Display Partition Data
       5. Select Next Fixed Disk Drive

   Enter choice: [1]
   ```

5. Choose option 1 by pressing Enter. If you have DOS 3.2 or an earlier version, the screen should look something like the following:

   ```
   Create DOS Partition

   Current Fixed Disk Drive: 1
   Do you wish to use the entire fixed
   disk for DOS (Y/N) ............? [Y]
   ```

6. Press Enter to inform FDISK that DOS should use the entire hard disk. The hard disk light should come on briefly, and the following message should appear:

   ```
   System will now restart
   Insert DOS disk in drive A:
   Press any key when ready...
   ```

7. Press any key. Because the DOS disk is already in drive A, DOS restarts. Answer the date and time questions again (steps 2 and 3) and then proceed to the next section on formatting the hard disk.

Using FDISK with DOS 3.3 and 4

1. After you boot DOS, load the disk with FDISK in drive A.

   For DOS 3.3, this disk is the Operating disk; for DOS 4, this disk is the Install disk. At the A> prompt, type **FDISK**.

   You see a screen like this one:

   ```
   IBM DOS Version 4.00
   Fixed Disk Setup Program
   (C) Copyright IBM Corp. 1983, 1988

   FDISK Options

   Current fixed disk drive: 1

   Choose one of the following:

       1. Create DOS Partition or Logical DOS Drive
       2. Set active partition
       3. Delete DOS Partition or Logical DOS Drive
       4. Display partition information
       5. Change current fixed disk drive

   Enter choice: [ ]

   Press Esc to exit FDISK
   ```

   For DOS 3.3, option 1 of this display is `Create DOS Partition`, option 3 is `Delete DOS Partition`, and option 2 is `Change Active Partition`. DOS 3.3 enables you to have more than one bootable partition, so you can use FDISK to change the active (bootable) partition from one to another. DOS 4 enables you to activate only the primary DOS partition.

   With either version of DOS, option 5 is displayed only if the system has more than one hard disk.

2. Choose option 1.

   A menu appears, which looks like this one:

   ```
   Create DOS Partition or Logical DOS Drive
   Current fixed disk drive: 1
   ```

```
1. Create Primary DOS Partition
2. Create Extended DOS Partition
3. Create Logical DOS Drive(s) in the Extended DOS Partition
Enter choice: [ ]
```

The DOS 3.3 screen produces a slightly different heading, but the menu choices are the same. The primary DOS partition is the bootable partition (with DOS 4 and 5) and cannot be divided into more than one logical drive. If you want to have more than one logical drive, you must divide the disk into both primary and extended DOS partitions. Menu option 3 enables you to create those logical drives.

DOS 4 and 5 also enable you to create a primary DOS partition larger than 32 megabytes. The extended DOS partition can be larger than 32M, and the logical drives there *also* may be larger than 32M. Note, however, that you cannot create a partition of exactly 32M; if you choose 32, FDISK substitutes 31.

3. Choose option 1 to create the primary DOS partition. The following screen appears:

```
Create Primary DOS Partition

Current fixed disk drive: 1

Do you wish to use the maximum available size for a Primary DOS
Partition and make the partition active (Y/N).....? [Y]

Press Esc to return to FDISK options.
```

4. Decide how much of the hard disk you want to allocate to the primary partition.

   If you want to use the entire hard disk for a single partition, even if you are using DOS 4 or 5 and the partition is more than 32 megabytes, press Y. If you press N, DOS reports on available space and asks you to enter the amount to be set aside for this partition. If you're using DOS 3.3, enter the number of megabytes to be allocated. If you're using DOS 4 or 5, enter either the number of megabytes or the percentage. For example, you can type either **22** or **50%** to allocate half of a 44M disk as the primary partition. After selecting the amount of space to allocate, press Enter. You automatically return to the main menu.

5. Choose option 2 from the main menu to make the primary partition active so that you can use it to boot the computer.

If you want to create additional DOS partitions, because you have another physical hard disk or have not set aside the entire disk as the primary partition, follow the next steps. Otherwise, press the Esc key to exit FDISK. The next section, "Using FORMAT To Prepare the Hard Disk," explains how to format hard disks.

If room is available for additional partitions on the disk, FDISK automatically takes you to the next menu, which looks like this one:

```
Create Extended DOS Partition

Current fixed disk drive: 1

Partition Status Type     Size in Mbytes   % of Disk Used
C:1        A     PRI DOS  22               50%

Total disk space is 22 Mbytes (1 Mbyte = 1048576 bytes)
Maximum space available for partition is 22 Mbytes (50%)

Enter partition size in Mbytes or percent of disk space (%)
to create an Extended DOS Partition..........[22]

Press Esc to return to FDISK options.
```

`C:1` in the first column indicates the drive letter and the number assigned to the DOS partition. The `A` indicates that the partition is active; `PRI DOS` shows that it is the primary DOS partition. The `Size` and `%` columns show the amount of space already in use for the primary partition and the presence of any other DOS partitions.

DOS 5 has an additional column labeled `System`. This column lists the size of the file allocation table used for the partition. Large partitions need a larger file allocation table to assign data to all the available clusters. DOS 5 supports disk partitions up to 2 gigabytes (GB).

6. Enter the amount of space to be allocated to the next partition.

    Just as when creating a primary partition, you may enter the size of the extended partition(s) in megabytes or (if using DOS 4) in percentages.

7. Now create logical disk drives in the partition if you want separate drives.

    Each time you create an extended partition, FDISK shows you the following screen:

```
Create Logical DOS Drive(s) in the Extended DOS Partition
No logical drives defined
Total Extended DOS Partition size is 22 Mbytes
(1 MByte = 104857 bytes)
Maximum space available for logical drive is 22 Mbytes (50%)
Enter logical drive size in Mbytes or percent of disk space
(%)...[ ]
Press Esc to return to FDISK options.
```

Although the DOS 3.3 screen does not show the size of a megabyte or the percentage of the disk used, the concept is the same. Enter the space in megabytes rather than percentages if you have DOS 3.3.

8. Repeat steps 5 through 7 to create additional partitions.

After you have created all the partitions and logical drives you want, press Esc to return to the FDISK menu and exit to DOS.

Using FORMAT To Prepare the Hard Disk

The FORMAT command performs several functions. It lays out individual sections of the disk for DOS to store programs and data. FORMAT creates housekeeping areas so that DOS can keep track of the programs and files. FORMAT also places key parts of DOS on the hard disk. To use FORMAT, do the following steps:

1. With the DOS start-up disk in the floppy disk drive and the door closed, start the FORMAT program by typing the following:

   FORMAT C:/S/V

   Next press Enter. The floppy disk drive red light goes on for a few seconds, and you see this message:

   ```
   WARNING, ALL DATA ON NON-REMOVABLE DISK
   DRIVE C: WILL BE LOST! Proceed with Format (Y/N)?
   ```

2. Because you do want to format the hard disk, press Y and then press Enter. The following message appears:

```
Formatting...
```

The hard disk's red light stays on for two to four minutes, depending on the type of hard disk you have.

After FORMAT completes its first stage, the message `Format complete` appears. Within a few seconds, FORMAT provides the message `System transferred`, which informs you that DOS has been placed on the hard disk. Next the following message appears:

```
Volume label (11 characters, ENTER for none)?
```

3. Type a volume name that contains up to 11 characters.

   This name appears whenever you display a list of files on the hard disk and at several other times also. After you type a name, press Enter.

4. Test the setup of the computer.

   Open the floppy disk drive door and press Ctrl-Alt-Del (hold down the first two keys with your left hand while pressing the Del key with your right). This sequence restarts DOS from the hard disk.

   The floppy disk drive light comes on, followed by the hard disk drive light. The computer beeps and then attempts to load DOS from the floppy disk drive. Several seconds later, the computer tries to load DOS from the hard disk. Within 20 seconds, DOS prompts you for the date.

   Answer the date and time messages if they appear, as you did in steps 1 and 2 in the first section. You now successfully have prepared the hard disk to start DOS.

In a normal situation, when you are about to transfer all files to the disk and continue using the computer, you format each logical drive. However, you need to format only one logical drive for testing purposes because each drive's performance is affected similarly by the interleave. After you choose and set the interleave, you need to format the logical drives in order to store files on them.

Now the disk is low-level formatted with a known interleave and is ready for data. Restore the partial backup set that includes DOS and the files needed to run the benchmarks. Run the benchmarks and time the results. Enter the results into the table and see how changing the interleave has affected the disk's performance.

You have to repeat the low-level formatting, partitioning, and formatting for each interleave setting you try. Although this task may seem like a large time investment, you can have significant performance degradation from using the wrong interleave factor.

Using SpinRite

Fortunately, an alternative to this laborious process is available. SpinRite II from Gibson Research Corporation can check the hard disk, change it to the optimum interleave, and correct myriad problems you may encounter eventually with the hard disk. All these procedures can be done without data loss. This utility program is not suitable for new computer users, but most intermediate users—particularly those who understand the principles of interleave, low-level formatting, and bad sectors—can benefit from SpinRite.

Although it is a fine program, SpinRite does not work on all disks, and on some disk types SpinRite cannot change the interleave. The program can perform routine maintenance on most hard disks and has an excellent reputation for reliability. If SpinRite cannot handle a particular type of hard disk, SpinRite does not work at all and gives an error message explaining that the drive type is not supported, or—in the case of disk drives that have interleaves the program cannot alter—SpinRite gives messages explaining how many of its features you can use.

Choosing the Best Interleave

SpinRite can determine the hard disk's optimum interleave more quickly than you can by using DOS and benchmarks. SpinRite also performs routine maintenance, data integrity checking, and recovery of defective data.

Even though SpinRite performs its checking without damaging data, you should have a complete backup of the disk before you run the program. If, for example, you have a power surge at a critical moment during the process, you may lose data and need that backup. You also need to ensure that no memory-resident programs are running on the computer during the process. You also should run DOS's CHKDSK on each drive to remove lost clusters before using SpinRite.

Temporarily remove the CONFIG.SYS and AUTOEXEC.BAT files from the root directory or create a system floppy disk from which to boot. Look in CONFIG.SYS for any disk device drivers. In order to use SpinRite, you need to create a temporary CONFIG.SYS containing any applicable hard disk device drivers. Other programs, such as memory managers, disk caches, and TSR utilities, are not needed and must be removed for safety.

Remember that SpinRite performs tasks at a low level on the computer. If, for example, you have a disk cache active, SpinRite may succeed in moving the data around, but the cache, as a consequence of SpinRite's activities, may become confused and write data in the wrong place.

Because SpinRite is used only periodically, it isn't a utility that always should be on the hard disk. I keep on hand a DOS System disk containing SpinRite, and when I do want to use it, I run SpinRite from the floppy disk drive.

After you boot the computer, you run SpinRite by typing **SPINRITE** at the DOS prompt. After the introductory screens appear, you see a display similar to that shown in figure 5.18.

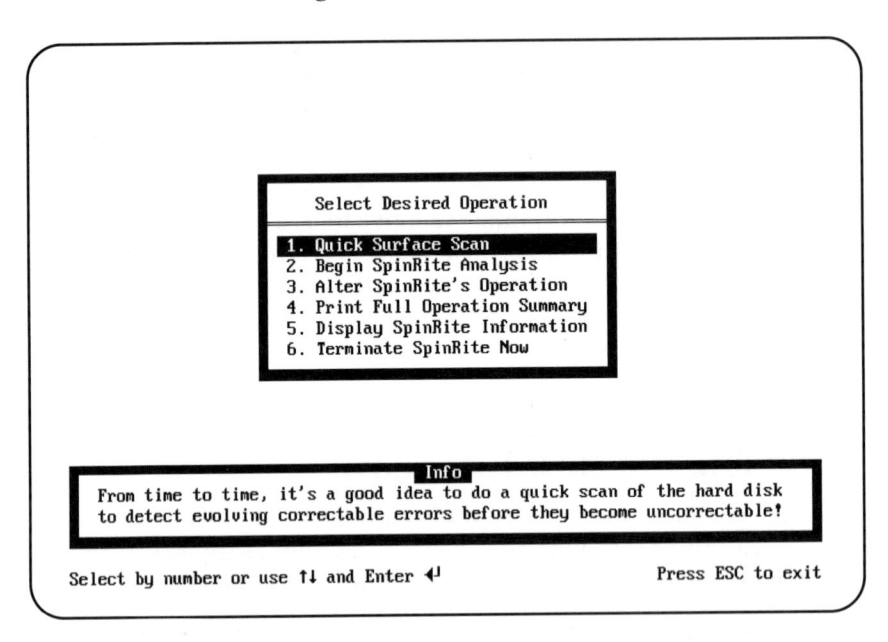

```
          Select Desired Operation
       1. Quick Surface Scan
       2. Begin SpinRite Analysis
       3. Alter SpinRite's Operation
       4. Print Full Operation Summary
       5. Display SpinRite Information
       6. Terminate SpinRite Now


                        Info
   From time to time, it's a good idea to do a quick scan of the hard disk
   to detect evolving correctable errors before they become uncorrectable!

Select by number or use ↑↓ and Enter ↵          Press ESC to exit
```

Fig. 5.18. *The first menu of SpinRite.*

If you haven't used SpinRite before on the disk, which will be the case if you're checking for the optimum interleave factor, do a complete analysis of the hard disk. Press 2 (or use the arrow keys to highlight option 2 and press Enter) to begin the analysis. A screen similar to the one shown in figure 5.19 appears.

On the computer I tested, two hard disks were installed. One (44M) was partitioned into two logical drives, and the other (20M) was a single partition. Obviously, a differently configured computer will produce a different list of available partitions.

Choose one of the drives from the list of the hard disk partitions by pressing a letter (or using the arrow keys to highlight the drive and then pressing Enter). In this case, choose drive E. The screen shown in figure 5.20 appears.

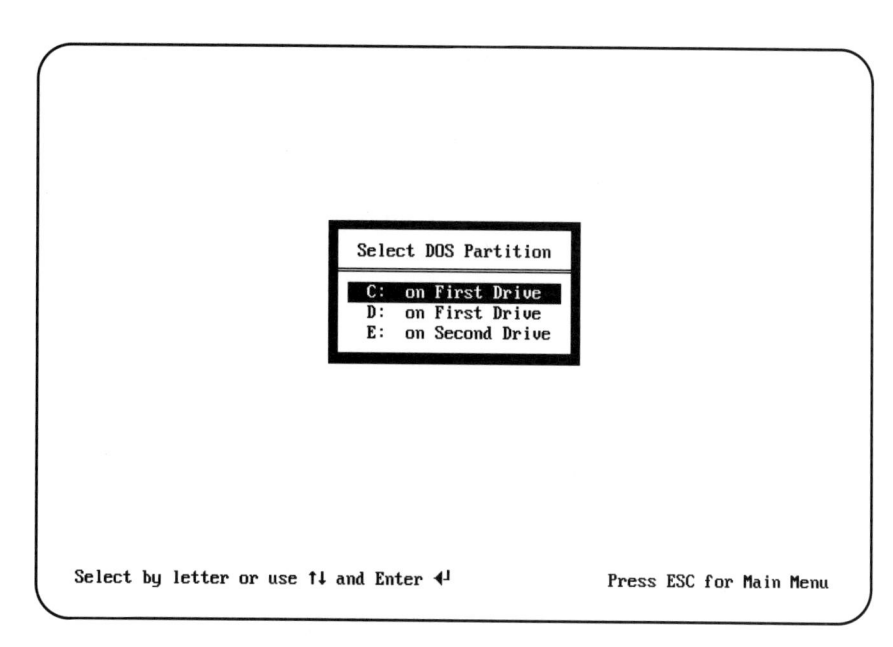

```
                    ┌──────────────────────────┐
                    │   Select DOS Partition   │
                    ├──────────────────────────┤
                    │  C:  on First Drive      │
                    │  D:  on First Drive      │
                    │  E:  on Second Drive     │
                    └──────────────────────────┘

Select by letter or use ↑↓ and Enter ↵          Press ESC for Main Menu
```

Fig. 5.19. *Selecting the DOS partition.*

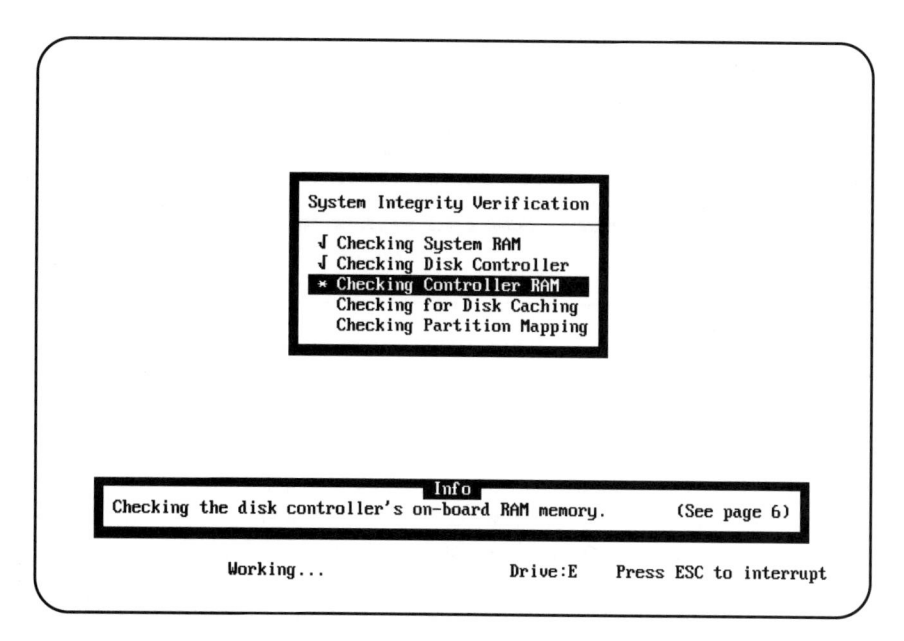

```
              ┌──────────────────────────────────┐
              │   System Integrity Verification  │
              ├──────────────────────────────────┤
              │  √ Checking System RAM           │
              │  √ Checking Disk Controller      │
              │  * Checking Controller RAM       │
              │    Checking for Disk Caching     │
              │    Checking Partition Mapping    │
              └──────────────────────────────────┘

        ┌─────────────────── Info ────────────────────────┐
        │ Checking the disk controller's on-board RAM     │
        │ memory.                          (See page 6)   │
        └─────────────────────────────────────────────────┘
              Working...          Drive:E   Press ESC to interrupt
```

Fig. 5.20. *SpinRite checking the system's integrity.*

Part II: Enhancing Disk Performance

SpinRite checks the system first. As shown in the list, the program checks the system RAM, disk controller, and RAM on the disk controller; ensures that no disk caches are active; and checks for unusual partition mapping that its further tests may not understand. If SpinRite doesn't support your particular disk, an error message appears explaining the reason. Your disk controller, for example, may have a cache that SpinRite cannot deal with. In this case, you need to disable the cache permanently (usually by moving a jumper on the disk controller) or not run SpinRite.

After SpinRite determines that it can analyze the hard disk, the Performance Evaluation screen is displayed (see fig. 5.21).

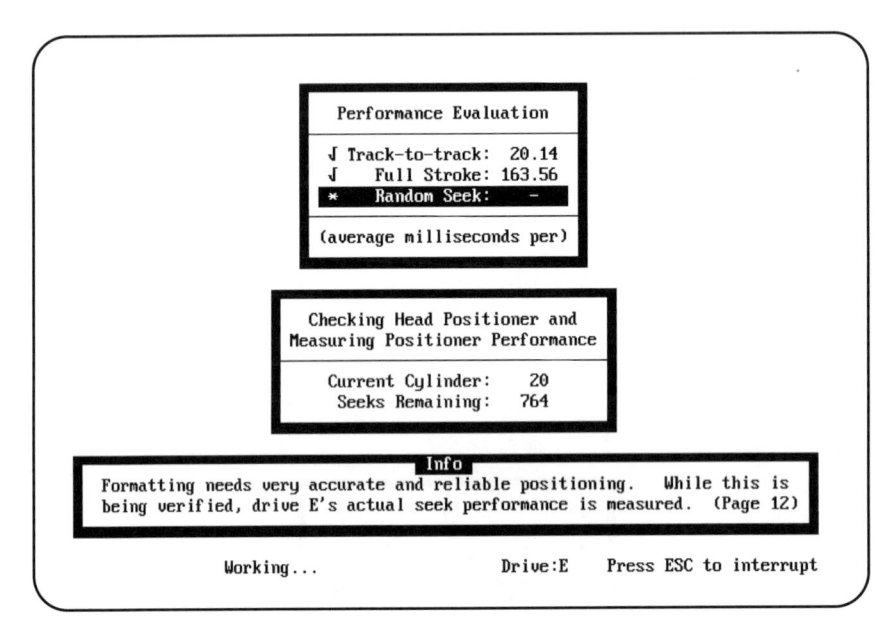

```
            Performance Evaluation
         √ Track-to-track:  20.14
         √    Full Stroke: 163.56
         *    Random Seek:    -

         (average milliseconds per)


         Checking Head Positioner and
         Measuring Positioner Performance

           Current Cylinder:   20
           Seeks Remaining:   764

                      Info
   Formatting needs very accurate and reliable positioning.  While this is
   being verified, drive E's actual seek performance is measured.  (Page 12)


         Working...           Drive:E    Press ESC to interrupt
```

Fig. 5.21. The Performance Evaluation screen.

SpinRite uses three tests to analyze the disk's speed. A track-to-track test measures the time taken to move the head from one track to an adjacent track. Results are averaged over several track-to-track movements. In my case, the track-to-track time averaged 20.14 ms. A second test records the time needed to move from the first track to the last track (163.56 ms in the example). Next a random seek test times the head movements between tracks. In order to achieve an accurate result, the program performs several hundred seeks. Figure 5.21 shows the screen in the middle of the random seek test.

After these timing tests are complete, SpinRite displays the screen shown in figure 5.22. In this example, the head positioning is found to be satisfactory.

Chapter 5: Employing Routine Maintenance 183

```
              Performance Evaluation
          √ Track-to-track:   20.14
          √     Full Stroke: 163.57
          √    Random Seek:  74.50

          (average milliseconds per)


      Press ANY KEY to analyze sector transfer timing.

                          Info
      *** Drive E's head positioning sub-system is operating perfectly. ***
      The average seek overhead for this system, which was subtracted from
      each of these measurements, is:   0.73 milliseconds.  (See page 12)


  Press ANY KEY to proceed...           Drive:E   Press ESC for Main Menu
```

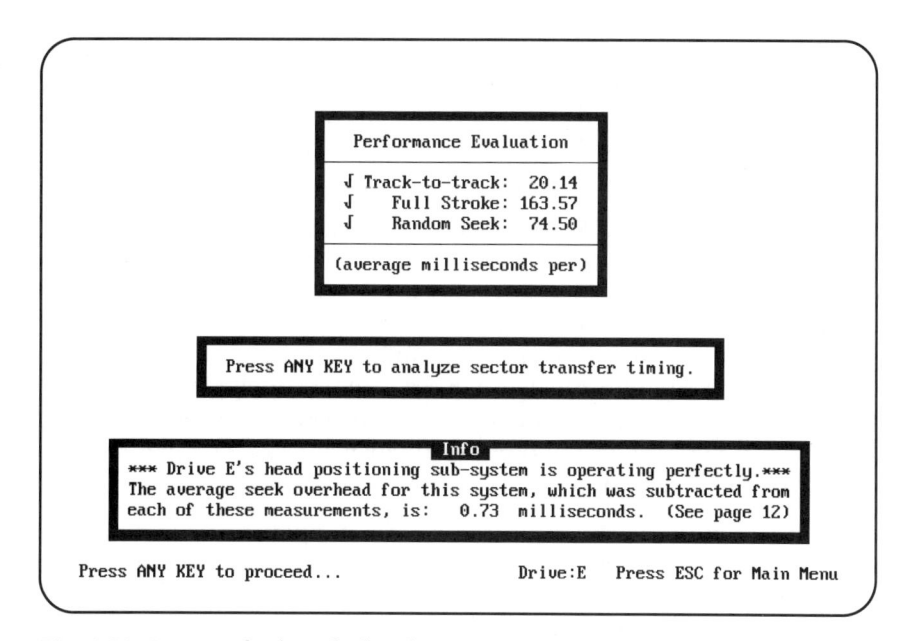

Fig. 5.22. SpinRite finding the head positioning satisfactory.

SpinRite next analyzes the sector transfer timing. The screen that appears is shown in figure 5.23.

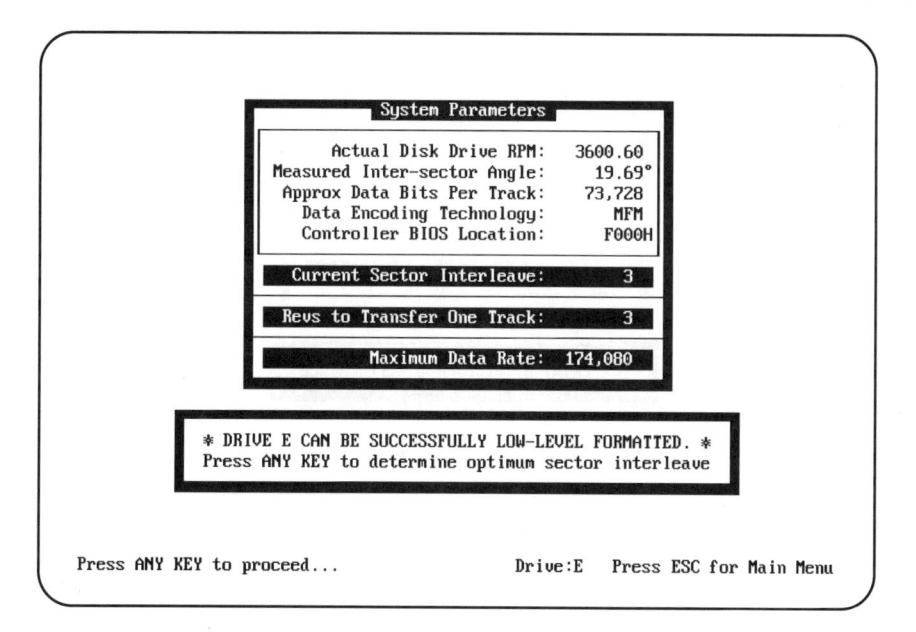

```
                      System Parameters
              Actual Disk Drive RPM:    3600.60
          Measured Inter-sector Angle:    19.69°
           Approx Data Bits Per Track:   73,728
              Data Encoding Technology:     MFM
              Controller BIOS Location:    F000H

           Current Sector Interleave:        3

           Revs to Transfer One Track:       3

                   Maximum Data Rate:  174,080


       * DRIVE E CAN BE SUCCESSFULLY LOW-LEVEL FORMATTED. *
       Press ANY KEY to determine optimum sector interleave


  Press ANY KEY to proceed...           Drive:E   Press ESC for Main Menu
```

Fig. 5.23. A listing of the system parameters.

Part II: Enhancing Disk Performance

SpinRite calculates the values displayed in the top box of this screen and uses them when measuring the interleave, number of rotations required to transfer a track of data, and maximum data rate. Although only of academic interest, the typical disk drive rotation rate and hard disk BIOS location (discussed previously) are listed.

The message in figure 5.23 states that this disk can be low-level formatted. SpinRite cannot do a low-level format (and therefore change the interleave) of all disks. For example, SpinRite cannot low-level format my MicroScience and Adaptec disk drive. The reason is that the Adaptec controller has sector translation activated to enable use of the full disk capacity (with more than 1,024 cylinders). SpinRite can detect that the values supplied to DOS for the number of cylinders, sectors, and heads are not actually correct. However, SpinRite can perform all the other maintenance tasks. Pressing any key moves you to the next step.

As displayed in the next screen (see fig. 5.24), SpinRite determines the present interleave setting in a couple of minutes, a job that takes hours using the procedures shown earlier in this chapter. If you use SpinRite to check a 16 MHz 386 computer, the process takes about a minute. On a PC/XT, SpinRite takes about five minutes.

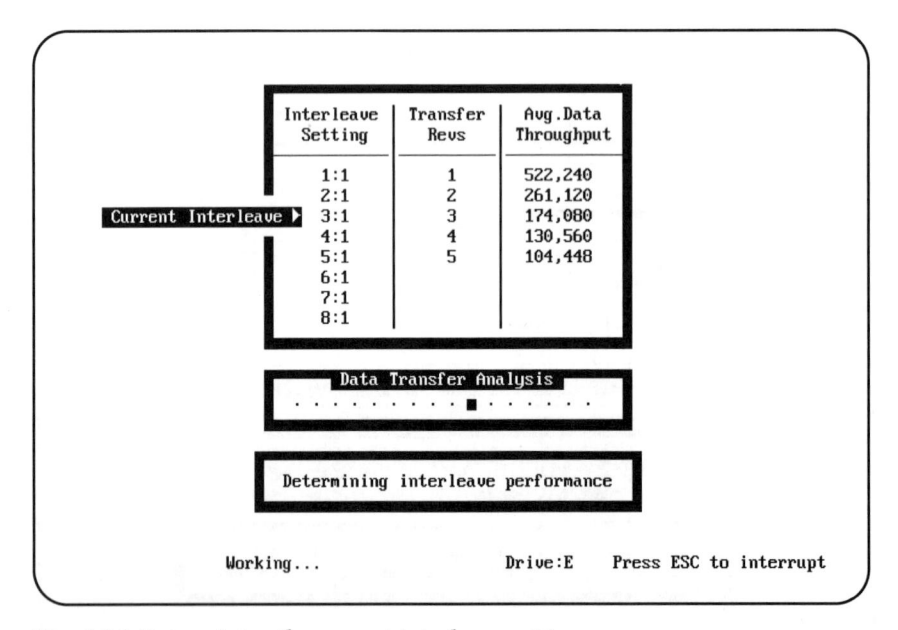

```
                  Interleave  | Transfer | Avg.Data
                  Setting     | Revs     | Throughput

                     1:1      |   1      |  522,240
                     2:1      |   2      |  261,120
 Current Interleave ▶ 3:1     |   3      |  174,080
                     4:1      |   4      |  130,560
                     5:1      |   5      |  104,448
                     6:1      |          |
                     7:1      |          |
                     8:1      |          |

                    ┌─ Data Transfer Analysis ─┐
                    │ . . . . . . . . ■ . . . .│
                    └──────────────────────────┘

                  ┌──────────────────────────────┐
                  │ Determining interleave performance │
                  └──────────────────────────────┘

       Working...               Drive:E    Press ESC to interrupt
```

Fig. 5.24. Determining the current interleave setting.

SpinRite has worked out, in the preceding step, the current drive's interleave setting. Using this information as a base and requesting data from the disk bypassing the usual BIOS routines, SpinRite gathers data from the disk as if it has a different interleave. By requesting data from adjacent sectors on the disk, SpinRite determines the transfer rate for the disk as if it has a 1 to 1 interleave. The calculations are repeated, but this time the data is taken from every other physical sector. The results are for an interleave factor of 2.

This table is equivalent to the table shown in figure 5.6. The faster the times you obtain for the benchmarks, the faster the data is being transferred from the disk.

Compare this screen with the results given on my PC's hard disk, shown in figure 5.25. In the PC's case, the optimum interleave is 5, which is the current setting. If the interleave is set to 4, the performance degrades by 81 percent. Increasing the interleave to 6 drops the performance by 20 percent from the optimum.

Interleave Setting	Transfer Revs	Avg. Data Throughput
1:1	26	30,706
2:1	27	29,562
3:1	28	28,522
4:1	26	30,706
5:1	5	159,744
6:1	6	133,120
7:1	7	114,088
8:1	8	99,840

Current Interleave ▶ 5:1 — Optimum Interleave

Press ANY KEY to select a new interleave.

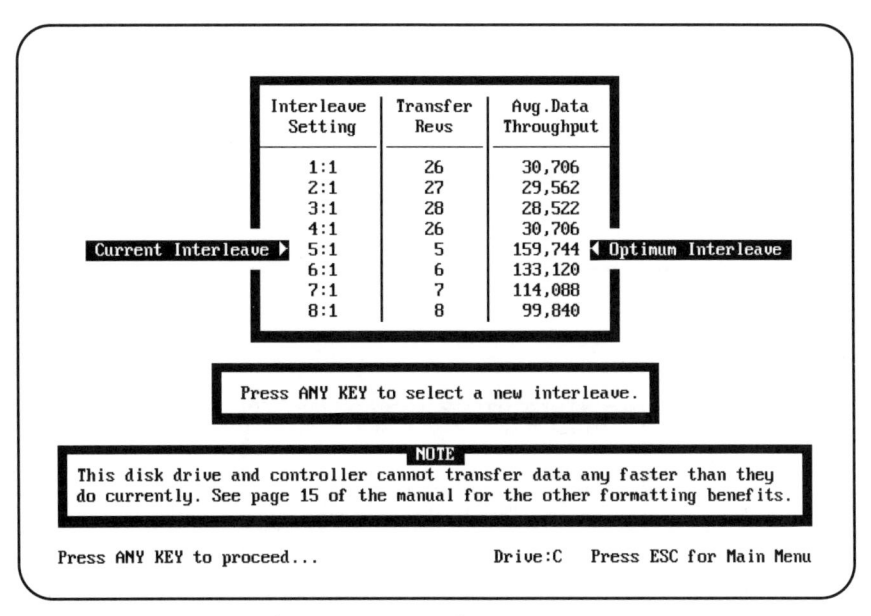

NOTE
This disk drive and controller cannot transfer data any faster than they do currently. See page 15 of the manual for the other formatting benefits.

Press ANY KEY to proceed...   Drive:C   Press ESC for Main Menu

***Fig. 5.25.** Determining the optimum interleave.*

The completed table for drive E is shown in figure 5.26. The disk's optimum interleave is different from the current interleave. SpinRite reports that you can improve performance 300 percent by changing the interleave setting.

Part II: Enhancing Disk Performance

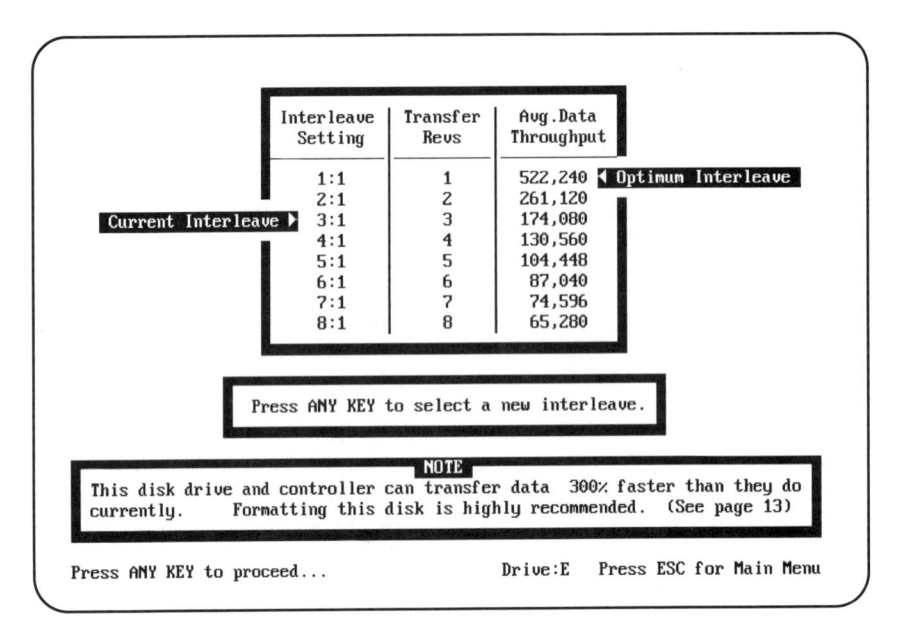

```
            Interleave   Transfer   Avg.Data
             Setting       Revs    Throughput

              1:1           1       522,240  ◄ Optimum Interleave
              2:1           2       261,120
Current Interleave ▶ 3:1    3       174,080
              4:1           4       130,560
              5:1           5       104,448
              6:1           6        87,040
              7:1           7        74,596
              8:1           8        65,280

            Press ANY KEY to select a new interleave.

                              NOTE
        This disk drive and controller can transfer data 300% faster than they do
        currently.   Formatting this disk is highly recommended.  (See page 13)

        Press ANY KEY to proceed...         Drive:E   Press ESC for Main Menu
```

Fig. 5.26. A current interleave setting that should be changed.

Using the arrow keys, if necessary, select the optimum interleave value and press any key. SpinRite now prepares to start its surface testing, as shown in figure 5.27.

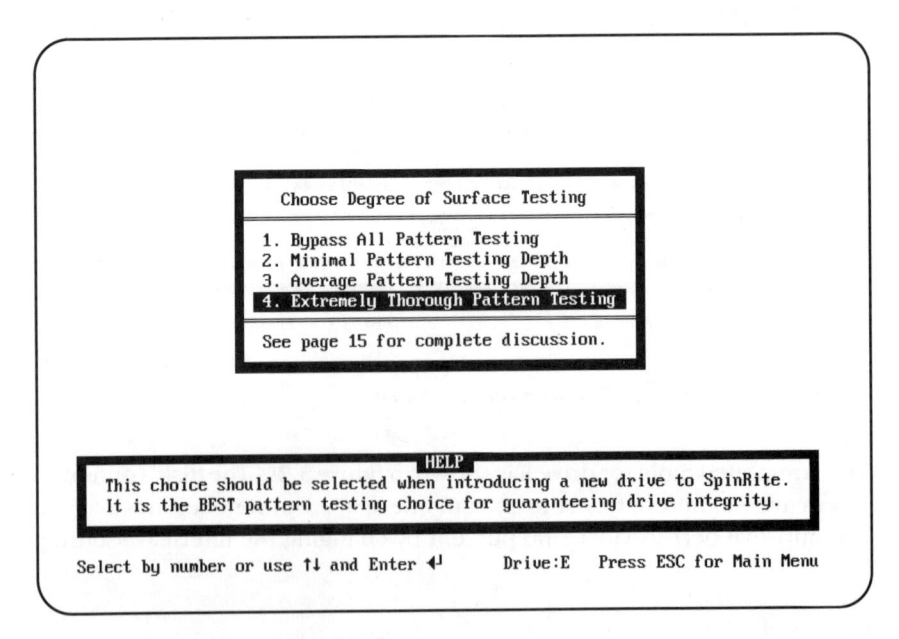

```
              Choose Degree of Surface Testing

             1. Bypass All Pattern Testing
             2. Minimal Pattern Testing Depth
             3. Average Pattern Testing Depth
             4. Extremely Thorough Pattern Testing

             See page 15 for complete discussion.

                              HELP
        This choice should be selected when introducing a new drive to SpinRite.
        It is the BEST pattern testing choice for guaranteeing drive integrity.

        Select by number or use ↑↓ and Enter ↵    Drive:E   Press ESC for Main Menu
```

Fig. 5.27. Selecting a testing level.

Chapter 5: Employing Routine Maintenance 187

SpinRite offers four levels of testing. One extreme, option 1, just checks the data on the disk; the other extreme, option 4, checks the data in a sector, places it in memory, writes a variety of testing patterns onto the sector, verifies that they can be read, and then replaces the data. The thorough testing procedure (option 4) takes several hours for a 32M partition; the quick scan (option 1) takes only an hour or so for the same size partition. The advantage of the tests are discussed in the next section, "Performing Routine Maintenance."

Although you can select an option that does less testing, and consequently finishes testing faster, you should choose the thorough test the first time you run the program. If SpinRite cannot change the interleave, the surface testing still can be done but the sector numbering cannot be changed.

Selecting any testing option from this menu starts the disk media analysis. A screen similar to the one shown in figure 5.28 is displayed.

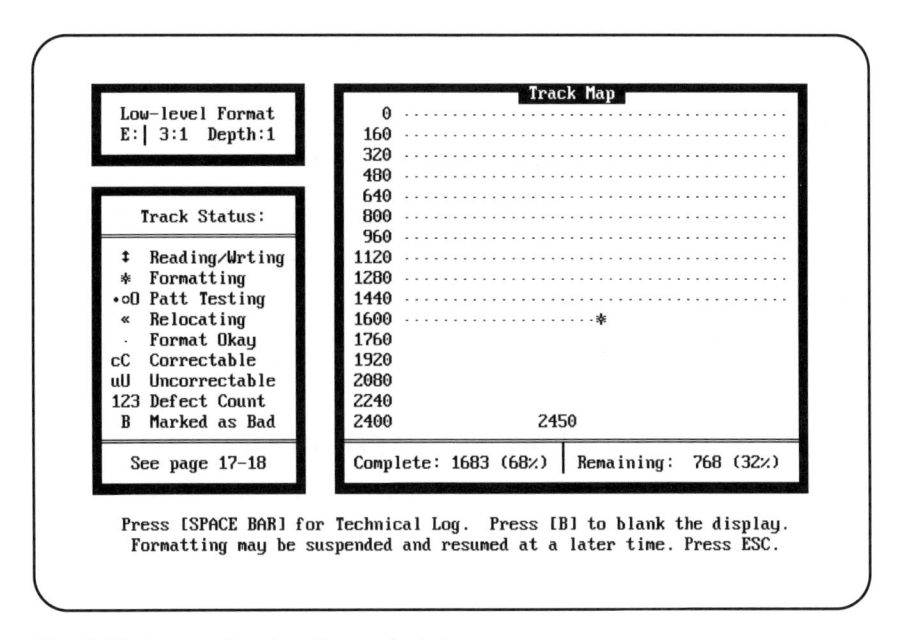

```
┌─────────────────────────────────────────────────────────────────┐
│                                    Track Map                    │
│  Low-level Format        0   ..................................│
│  E:| 3:1  Depth:1      160   ..................................│
│                        320   ..................................│
│                        480   ..................................│
│                        640   ..................................│
│    Track Status:       800   ..................................│
│                        960   ..................................│
│    ‡  Reading/Wrting  1120   ..................................│
│    *  Formatting      1280   ..................................│
│   •oO Patt Testing    1440   ..................................│
│    «  Relocating      1600   ....................*             │
│    .  Format Okay     1760                                     │
│   cC  Correctable     1920                                     │
│   uU  Uncorrectable   2080                                     │
│   123 Defect Count    2240                                     │
│    B  Marked as Bad   2400                2450                 │
│                                                                 │
│    See page 17-18     Complete: 1683 (68%) | Remaining: 768 (32%)│
│                                                                 │
│   Press [SPACE BAR] for Technical Log.  Press [B] to blank the display.│
│   Formatting may be suspended and resumed at a later time. Press ESC.  │
└─────────────────────────────────────────────────────────────────┘
```

Fig. 5.28. *A map showing the analysis in progress.*

Similar to the Norton Utilities Speed Disk program's map, SpinRite represents the disk area as a series of characters. The disk represented in figure 5.28 has 2,450 such divisions because 2,450 sectors are on the disk.

SpinRite starts at the first sector and takes each sector in turn. Different symbols are used for showing how the testing is proceeding. Figure 5.28 shows the 1,684th sector being formatted at the new interleave. SpinRite has not yet discovered any bad sectors on this disk. If any problems are discovered, the period is replaced by a number or marked as bad. The legend on the left side of the screen shows the symbols used.

SpinRite gives an estimated time for completion, information about the current status of the test, and information relating to any data problems found and corrected. The summary information shown in figure 5.29 gives the results from drive E. In this case, no data errors are found.

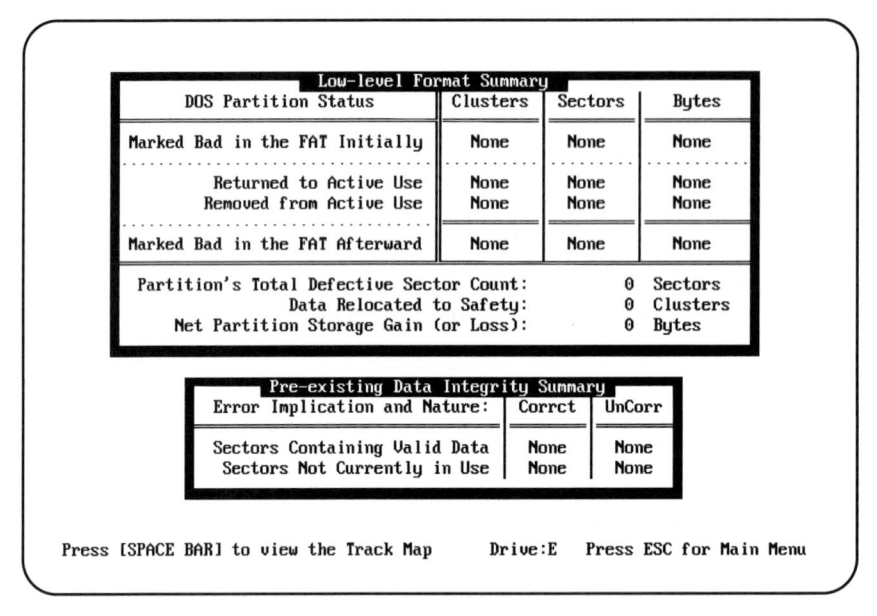

```
                  Low-level Format Summary
       DOS Partition Status    | Clusters | Sectors | Bytes
  Marked Bad in the FAT Initially | None   | None    | None
       Returned to Active Use  |  None    |  None   |  None
       Removed from Active Use |  None    |  None   |  None
  Marked Bad in the FAT Afterward |  None  |  None   |  None
       Partition's Total Defective Sector Count:  0  Sectors
                   Data Relocated to Safety:      0  Clusters
          Net Partition Storage Gain (or Loss):   0  Bytes

              Pre-existing Data Integrity Summary
       Error Implication and Nature:   | Corrct | UnCorr
       Sectors Containing Valid Data   |  None  |  None
       Sectors Not Currently in Use    |  None  |  None

  Press [SPACE BAR] to view the Track Map    Drive:E  Press ESC for Main Menu
```

Fig. 5.29. The low-level format summary.

Performing Routine Maintenance

You should use SpinRite on any newly purchased disk and also use SpinRite for routine hard disk maintenance. The maintenance procedure is identical to the preceding section, but you do not change the interleave. Routine maintenance of hard disks corrects data errors before you're aware of their presence, ensures the validity of the data, and removes bad sectors from use while returning incorrectly marked bad sectors to use.

What, you may ask, can go wrong with a hard disk over time? To understand the usefulness of regular hard disk maintenance, you should be aware of several things that can go wrong.

When you first turn on the computer, the hard disk is cool. With time, however, the disk's temperature rises substantially. This rise in temperature causes the platters to expand, and, consequently, track positions may move with time.

For example, Hardcard II has special circuitry that makes adjustments for temperature expansion of its magnetic material every 10 minutes of operation. Plus Development Corporation has found that maintaining data integrity on a densely packed, small disk requires special considerations.

Normal hard disks are larger, have more platters, and are less densely packed with data. However, expansion and contraction because of temperature changes still occur.

This constant shifting of the hardware because of expansion and contraction can change the alignment of the heads with the tracks. When SpinRite checks each sector, the program rewrites the data onto the disk. Tracks not completely under the head when read are realigned. As you write files to the disk, you actually are performing a similar process but in a localized way, because you are not writing to every sector of the disk. For example, you write word processor program files to the disk only when you upgrade to a new version. SpinRite's refreshing of the track data ensures that infrequently used files remain aligned with the head.

Another effect of head alignment changes resulting from temperature and time has to do with bad sectors. Flaws on a disk are typically small. Remember that the head is floating a few microinches above the surface of the disk. Any big bumps would have wreaked havoc long before the disk left the manufacturer. As the head alignment changes, the head may move off some flaws and move onto others. SpinRite's checking includes the sectors marked as bad, and in some cases, the previously flawed sectors are returned to use when no flaws are found due to the new position. Additionally, the new head alignment may place a flaw in an area of the disk marked as usable. SpinRite removes any data in this sector to a safe area of the disk and removes any bad data areas from the disk.

Just as the change in head alignment can move a flaw under the head, causing a sector to go bad, the head alignment can move a flaw off the head to make the sector clean.

Another potential problem that SpinRite can address is corrupted data. All data is encoded in sectors as a series of bytes. The disk controller adds extra information to each sector to help check the validity of the data stored there. When the data found doesn't match the expected value, DOS error messages such as `Data error reading drive C Abort, Retry, Ignore, Fail` occur. By the time DOS detects this type of error, your data is corrupted.

The disk controller corrects some errors it finds. DOS ignores this type of error because it can get the correct data, even if corrected by the disk controller en route. SpinRite finds these errors and, by redoing the low-level format, removes them. If the data is so corrupted that the controller cannot fix the problem, SpinRite retrieves the data (DOS gives you the data error message and refuses to read it) and moves the data to another area of the disk. You then can examine the data and reclaim the parts not corrupted.

SpinRite is an invaluable tool for the PC. Running SpinRite every three months not only refreshes and renews the data of the hard disk but also extends the life of the hard disk by correcting minor errors before they become serious. The program takes time to run but is well worth the investment. SpinRite is best for people who understand the implications of its use, however. If SpinRite adds bad sectors every time you run it, for example, you should understand that the hard disk's life is limited. You should replace the hard disk soon.

Chapter Summary

This chapter covered optimizing the hard disk at the hardware level.

You should defragment files by using DOS or a disk optimizer to improve the disk's file retrieval performance.

Your disk's interleave factor changes the computer's performance significantly. Either check and choose the optimum interleave manually through low-level formatters or use a product, such as SpinRite, to do this task for you.

Routine hard disk maintenance can be done by specialized programs such as SpinRite. The time invested in running SpinRite can extend the hard disk's life and improve the data's integrity.

Examining Disk Performance

6

Chapter 5 discussed techniques that alter disk performance at a fundamental level. Using the best interleave factor enables the hard disk to operate as fast as possible. Removing fragmentation and sorting files on the disk are the most efficient methods of storing files. Consequently, DOS and your applications programs retrieve files in the most efficient manner.

After establishing the best interleave, you don't need to consider interleave again until you change hardware. Check the file arrangement, however, on a regular basis. Consider using a disk optimizer immediately after routine disk backups to ensure that optimizing is done regularly.

Other methods of enhancing the disk drive depend on how you use the computer. Chapter 3 explains how the fastest system does not use disks but relies on RAM for optimum performance. The access time for RAM is many times faster than a disk. Data stored in RAM is volatile, however, and disappears when the computer is rebooted or turned off. Consequently, although computers using only RAM as memory would be best in terms of speed, magnetic media, such as hard disks and floppy disks, are a necessary "safety net."

This chapter shows how use of the DOS environment can affect computer performance. The use of RAM disks and other types of disks, such as high-density floppy disks, disks on a card, and removable hard disk cartridges, also are discussed.

Understanding the DOS Environment

The environment is an area of RAM set aside by DOS to hold strings that can be examined and used by either DOS commands or user programs. Strings typically are names of directories or frequently used switches for programs, although any information can be used. DOS makes information placed in the environment available to programs.

Information is placed in the environment by programs like DOS or by you, the user. DOS places information in the environment through the PATH, APPEND, or PROMPT command. Executable files, including batch files, also may put information in the environment. To place your own information in the environment, use the SET command.

The following line, for example, sets or shows the environment variable EXAMPLE:

SET EXAMPLE=C:\WORDS\EXAMPLE

When programs find and examine EXAMPLE, they find the string C:\WORDS\EXAMPLE. The environment provides a noninteractive method to give programs information. Later, programs can locate the variable and use the string associated with the variable.

SET also displays the current environment variables. If you type **SET** with no arguments, DOS displays a list of the current settings.

For optimizing DOS's use of the disk, the most important environment setting is PATH. For DOS 3.3 and later versions of DOS, the APPEND setting also is important. The PATH setting has a list of directories. After you type a command at the DOS prompt, DOS searches each directory listed in the PATH to find an executable file matching the typed command name.

The APPEND setting also has a list of directories that can be used to search for nonexecutable files (usually data files). Typically, applications programs use this list. A database program can use the APPEND setting, for example, to find a database file not located in the current directory. Depending on the parameters you use with APPEND, the list of directories is stored in the environment or main memory. Use APPEND judiciously to increase the computer's performance. Don't use the approach of putting every subdirectory into the APPEND setting so that every data file is found regardless of its position. The discussion that follows about the PATH statement applies equally to the APPEND statement.

Most computers list directories in the PATH at random. When you install a new program that adds its directory to the PATH, the installation program inserts the relevant information to either the beginning or end of the existing PATH. In time, you also may add a couple of your own directories to the PATH. The net result is a long, disorganized PATH statement.

Note that PATH settings cannot exceed 127 characters, with each path name no longer than 63 characters. If you use many levels of subdirectories, especially if you utilize extension names, you rapidly can use up this 63-character limit. DOS truncates paths exceeding this length, thereby "demolishing" the disk if you aren't careful. You have to reformat the disk to recover. The moral is "Keep your path names as short as possible."

After you type a command at the DOS prompt, DOS searches for an executable file with the typed root name in a specific order. First, the current directory is searched for a file with the typed root name and a COM, EXE, or BAT extension. Next, DOS looks at the PATH and searches the first directory listed for the file. Each directory in the PATH is searched in the order listed for the executable file.

Note that in a directory having files with the same name but different extensions, the order of search precedence is COM, EXE, and BAT. DOS finds the file named COM and executes it instead of finding the batch file with the same root name.

This search process of a PATH with many files and directories can take several seconds each time the search is performed on a hard disk. You dramatically improve file retrieval time by choosing an appropriate order for the directories listed in PATH. This careful arrangement of directories gives the appearance of improving the speed of the hard disk.

Suppose that you regularly use a word processor whose subdirectory is the 15th directory in the PATH listing. Each time you start the word processor, 14 other directories are searched before the executable file is found. Additionally, when you're in the program, the possibility exists (depending on how the program is written) that the program uses the PATH setting regularly to find files in the word processor's directory. Again, 14 other directories are searched before the appropriate file is found.

The ideal solution is to place every subdirectory first in PATH's list. Obviously, this approach is impossible. However, two ways are available to reduce search time. You can optimize the sequence of directories in the PATH, and you can use different PATH settings for different applications.

Placing all files in one directory instead of using many directories would not speed up the process because DOS would have to search through many directory entries looking for the appropriate file. This approach would take longer for many files. To optimize this situation, you would want to place every file as the first file listed in the directory. This arrangement is even more unlikely than placing every subdirectory first in the PATH statement.

Optimizing the PATH Sequence

To optimize the PATH sequence, first print a copy of your current PATH setting. You can use the SET command to display the setting or copy the AUTOEXEC.BAT file to a printer.

Next, using the log that shows your typical computer use (see Chapter 3), you can analyze the directory sequence. Place the directories accessed by your most frequently used applications at the front of the list. Remove any subdirectories listed in PATH that are associated with programs you no longer use.

For example, I had a PATH setting (before sorting) similar to the following example:

```
PATH=C:\;C:\DOS;C:\UTIL;C:\BATCH;C:\UTIL\ARC;C:\UTIL\PCTOOLS;
    C:\WP51;C:\FONTSPAC;D:\HL;
```

Most parts of this PATH show a familiar directory structure, as described in the following list:

C:\ and C:\DOS	Contains the DOS files
C:\UTIL	Contains small utility programs such as Norton Utilities' File Find program
C:\BATCH	Contains all the batch files I use to start my applications programs
C:\UTIL\ARC	Contains the file compressor and uncompressor—PKZIP and PKUNZIP from PKWARE Inc.
C:\UTIL\PCTOOLS	Contains the file for PC Tools Deluxe, including my backup and restore programs

C:\WP51	Contains WordPerfect
C:\FONTSPAC	Contains Isogon's FontSpace utility, which automatically compresses and uncompresses LaserJet font files
D:\HL	Contains the files for Hotline, General Information Inc.'s electronic Rolodex program

I use drive C to store all program files so that I don't have to back up this drive continually. The Hotline electronic Rolodex, however, is on drive D (my data disk) because I keep notes about phone calls and frequently add names and numbers. Consequently, Hotline is backed up with the other data files every week.

When I look at a week of log entries, I discover that I use WordPerfect most extensively, then PC Tools, Hotline, and utility programs in C:\UTIL. I use PKZIP and print to the LaserJet with files compressed by FontSpace only once or twice a week. I use the files in C:\BATCH every time I start an applications program and use DOS and the root directory about as frequently.

From this information, I rank the directories and change my PATH to the following:

```
PATH=C:\WP51;C:\;C:\DOS;C:\BATCH;C:\UTIL\PCTOOLS;D:\HL;
    C:\UTIL;C:\UTIL\ARC;C:\FONTSPAC;
```

This rearrangement, for example, means that the time taken to load PKZIP has increased but makes my Rolodex, which I use many times a day, load more rapidly.

Note that DOS doesn't check the PATH settings for validity. If you misspell a directory name or include a directory that doesn't exist, DOS will not know. When searching, DOS takes each directory in turn and searches for the file. When a directory doesn't exist, DOS attempts to find the directory and goes onto the next directory in the list without comment. DOS is capable of detecting an invalid drive listed in PATH, however, and gives the following error message:

```
Invalid drive in search path.
```

A side effect of checking the PATH setting and prioritizing the contents enables you to remove unused paths because you don't use the program or you no longer need a path setting for that program. Although I use 1-2-3 regularly, for example, I don't have my 1-2-3 subdirectory on the PATH because I don't need it. When I run the program, I use a batch file (stored in my batch file subdirectory, which is on the PATH) and run 1-2-3 from within the 1-2-3 subdirectory.

Changing the Environment Size

Each character that is part of an environment variable takes up space in the DOS area reserved for the environment. The environment space is not available memory for you to use for a program. You may have a line in your CONFIG.SYS that increases the environment size, reducing the remaining memory that you can use for running applications programs. You should make sure that the environment size is not set larger than necessary.

Chapter 2 shows the memory map of how DOS loads itself into memory. Increasing the size of the environment causes each item loaded into memory after the environment to be at a higher address. The net result is that the top of DOS is at a higher memory location, leaving less base memory free.

The environment size is established at DOS's default size or by the setting in the CONFIG.SYS file. You may be advised to increase the size of your environment to overcome the `Out of environment space` error message. Whereas increasing the environment size is necessary for some applications, most notably sophisticated CAD programs, the error message may be due to bad management of the computer's environment space.

If you run programs, such as DESQview or Windows, that enable you to load multiple programs into memory, your environment size is that much more important. Even if you use the DOS Shell command only from within such applications programs as 1-2-3 and WordPerfect, you reduce available memory by having an unnecessarily large environment.

Each program you start (and the DOS Shell command in an applications program is a second program) has its own copy of the environment. If you have four programs loaded into DESQview, for example, four copies of the environment are in use. Having multiple copies of the environment is a necessary part of running multiple programs because you must ensure that each program continues to work even after you change the environment associated with one of those programs.

On more powerful computers that run a variety of programs, users more commonly increase the environment size by means of CONFIG.SYS. You can use the SHELL directive to change the command processor's settings. You can increase the environment size from 160 bytes (128 bytes in DOS 3.1) to a larger value.

The syntax for the SHELL directive for DOS 3.1 through 5.0 is as follows:

   SHELL = *d:path***COMMAND**.*COM d:path* /P /E:*size*

If you want to use a different command processor than COMMAND.COM, replace the file name COMMAND.COM in this SHELL directive with the new command processor's name.

d:path is the full path name to COMMAND.COM. If omitted, DOS looks for the command processor in the root directory of the boot drive.

COMMAND, with its optional extension *COM*, is the name of the command processor COMMAND.COM.

d:path also is the full path name to COMMAND.COM. This parameter is passed to COMMAND.COM when the SHELL directive starts COMMAND.COM. COMMAND.COM uses this parameter to set a value for the environment variable COMSPEC. Although *d:path* is optional in both cases, you probably want to include it.

The */P* switch instructs DOS to load and keep resident a copy of the command processor. Without the */P* switch, DOS loads COMMAND.COM, executes the AUTOEXEC.BAT file, and immediately exits. You therefore must reboot the system using a different disk if you omit the */P* switch. This switch is optional, but in almost all cases, you want to include */P*.

The */E:size* switch is the optional switch that sets the amount of RAM used for the environment. If you see the `Out of environment space` message, use the SHELL directive with the */E* switch to specify a larger space for environment variables.

If you use */E*, the size of DOS increases automatically by the amount of space specified as the normal starting value for the environment. The SHELL directive does not use any additional memory except when the directive increases the size of the environment.

DOS 3.2, 3.3, 4.0, and 5.0 start with an environment size of 160 bytes. You can specify a size from 160 to 32,767. If you give a size number larger than 32,767, DOS uses 32,767. If you give a number smaller than 160 or give a nonsense size (such as a letter), DOS uses a default size of 160 bytes for the environment.

If the size you specify is not evenly divisible by 16, DOS adjusts the environment to the next higher multiple of 16. If you specify 322, for example, DOS automatically adjusts the size to 336.

DOS 3.1 uses a different system for size: the number of 16-byte paragraphs for the environment. DOS 3.1 starts with an environment size of 128 bytes. You can change the size with the SHELL directive from 11 (11 x 16, or 176 bytes) to 62 (62 x 16, or 992 bytes). If you use a number less than 11 or greater than 62, DOS 3.1 displays an error message and ignores the */E* switch.

DOS 4 enables an additional switch for COMMAND.COM, /MSG, which tells DOS to load DOS messages into RAM when it loads COMMAND.COM. This enhancement speeds up operation somewhat and increases the amount of memory DOS uses by only about 1K.

Using Multiple PATH Settings

Although certain programs require a larger environment than DOS's default, many environment expansions are due to a computer having a long PATH and the SHELL directive being added arbitrarily.

If your path is long because of using a variety of programs rather than a particular program, consider using multiple, shorter PATH settings. This technique eliminates the need to extend the environment and saves RAM. Also, the response time is faster because DOS doesn't need to search through as many subdirectories to find (or not find) a file.

Batch files commonly are used for starting applications programs. For example, you may start WordPerfect with a batch file named WORDP.BAT containing the following lines:

```
C:
CD \WP51
WP /R /NC
CD \
```

This file can be used from any subdirectory on any disk, provided that the subdirectory containing the batch file is listed in PATH. The current drive and path is changed to C:\WP51, and WordPerfect is started using the parameter that uses expanded memory and the parameter that disables the Cursor Speed feature. When you exit WordPerfect, the current path is changed to the root directory.

Using a series of similar batch files to start applications programs can streamline your computer use. You don't need to remember your preferred start-up options for programs, and when you leave a program, you are always in the root directory of the drive.

You can extend this concept further by including PATH statements in your batch files. Establish a PATH for a particular program, and the next applications program—when run—has its own PATH setting. Each PATH setting can be shorter than one setting that serves all purposes. DOS completes its searches faster, and the hard disk appears to work faster.

You can change the batch file for WordPerfect to the following:

```
C:
CD \WP51
PATH=C:\WP51;C:\;C:\DOS;
WP /R /NC
CD \
```

If you use this approach, remember that the PATH setting remains the same until it is altered. If your AUTOEXEC.BAT file includes the directory C:\123 in its path setting and you run this batch file, C:\123 is no longer on the path.

Depending on your use of the computer, this technique may be a useful approach. If you swap between applications programs every few minutes, for example, this probably is not a good approach. However, if you use a word processor in the morning, delete some files and perform other disk maintenance, and then use a spreadsheet all afternoon, using multiple PATH settings can improve response time.

If you use only three different programs in a day, you need three batch files—one batch file for each program. The disk maintenance, even if you only use DOS commands, may need a different PATH setting from that set in the applications programs' batch files.

Beware of using the %PATH% parameter (available in DOS 3.3 and later versions) in batch files. This parameter permits you to add to the existing PATH setting. You can end up with huge PATH settings that include multiple mentions of the same directory. DOS follows your instructions, and if you tell DOS to look in a particular directory four times, DOS blindly obeys.

The way to use %PATH% is as follows:

PATH=%PATH%new directories

Note that this line uses the replaceable parameters feature of batch files and must be in a batch file to work. Typing this line at the command prompt causes the string %PATH% rather than the value for PATH to be placed in the environment.

Suppose that your PATH is set to C:\;C:\DOS; and you include the following in a batch file:

PATH=%PATH%C:\;C:\DOS;

Your new PATH setting is C:\;C:\DOS;C:\;C:\DOS;. DOS searches four directories before reporting that an executable file isn't found with the message Bad command or file name.

Saving the existing PATH setting, using a new setting, and then returning to the first setting when finished would be nice. With DOS, the closest you can come to this technique is to use the COMMAND command and start a second command processor with new environment settings. This method causes a whole new command processor and its supporting memory areas to be loaded, however, significantly reducing the amount of free base memory.

The method involves issuing a COMMAND command, using the new command processor to change the environment settings, and running a program. When you finish with the program and return to the DOS prompt for the second command processor, you use EXIT to leave the second command processor. The second command processor is dumped from memory, and you are returned to the first command processor, which has an intact environment.

Another way to save your old PATH setting is to use an environment variable to save the PATH temporarily, use a new setting, and then restore the old setting. Because one of the objectives of shortening the PATH in the first place is to reduce the space used by the environment, however, you should use the following with discretion.

You save the old PATH setting, use a new PATH, and restore the old setting by using the following steps:

1. Create an environment variable (called OLDPATH in this example) that is set to the current PATH by issuing the following SET directive from within a batch file:

    SET OLDPATH=%PATH%

2. Change the PATH setting as needed.

3. Restore the old PATH setting by including the following in a batch file:

    PATH=%OLDPATH%

4. Remove the environment variable OLDPATH to preserve environment space by issuing the following directive:

    SET OLDPATH=

Using PATH can make using a hard disk that much easier. Judicious use is required, however, to ensure that you don't pay a speed penalty or lose RAM space unnecessarily.

Comparing Disk Drive Types

All disk drives are devices in the PC. The data on the disk is transferred from the disk to the CPU through the expansion bus. The speed at which data is transferred is limited by the speed of the bus.

On PCs running at 4.77 MHz, particularly XTs or their equivalents, the transfer rate possible by the bus is slower than the hard disk can deliver. The

8-bit expansion bus and slower microprocessor speed are the limiting factors. Regardless of how fast a hard disk operates, the bus cannot transfer data any faster. With a few exceptions, hard disks for PCs are capable of transferring data as fast as the bus can demand.

On ATs and 386- and 486-based computers, the expansion bus is at least 16 bits wide. Additionally, the microprocessor is operating at faster frequencies ranging from, for example, 8 MHz to 33 MHz. For compatibility reasons, however, the expansion bus on these systems usually is only 8 or 10 MHz. Some newer systems have a special hard disk drive connector, which is different from the typical expansion bus connector. The principle is the same, however: The disk is a device in the PC that transfers data between the magnetic media and the CPU as requested.

In some of these faster systems, data can be transferred from the disk to the CPU as fast as the disk can supply the data. On the faster versions of these systems, you may be able to wring more performance out of the computer by buying a faster disk than the currently installed device.

Two trade-offs exist. First, you don't want a disk so fast that the bus becomes the limiting factor. Second, you reach a point of diminishing returns in which the cost of buying a new disk outweighs the performance advantage gained.

The next section discusses the various types of hard disks available. If you are purchasing a new hard disk, you can choose from the various technologies that work best for your system. You may find, however, that using RAM disks and disk caches improve your existing hard disk performance more than adding a new hard disk would.

To get better performance, consider equipping the computer with more RAM and using this memory as a disk substitute before purchasing a hard disk. If you need a new disk for additional capacity or for replacing a defective device, however, the new hard disk is not an option but a necessity.

Typical Hard Disks

The most common hard disks are devices that fit into a computer's drive bay. The hard disks have either 3 1/2-inch or 5 1/4-inch platters and are supplied with mounting rails that enable you to slide them into the drive bay and screw them into place. Connectors on the rear of the drive link the drive to the power supply and the disk drive controller. The most common disk drive controller occupies a single slot in the expansion bus and may be an 8-bit or 16-bit device. Some computers have their hard disk controllers built into the system board itself.

A wide variety of disks can be used in a PC. Disk technology is one PC feature that has improved substantially in the last few years. User demand for both higher capacity and faster disk drives has helped bring about this evolution.

Disk types differ as to the way data is encoded on the disk drive and as to the way the disk controller interfaces with the expansion bus.

As Chapter 4 explains, the head encodes data onto the disk as a series of "pulses." These pulses magnetize magnetic particles on the disk in one direction or the opposite direction. The head reads data from the disk by detecting the transitions between particles oriented in one and then the opposite direction.

Lengths of the various bits and encoding methods used to represent bytes of data are determined by the disk controller and hard disk combination. Two main encoding techniques used are *MFM* (modified frequency modulation) and *RLL* (run-length limited). Although the details of these techniques are academic, the important thing to remember is that you need to buy a disk controller and hard disk that use the same encoding technique.

The RLL encoding system packs a great deal more data than the MFM technique into the same space. To store its data satisfactorily, however, RLL-certified disks use a finer quality and more expensive magnetic surface. RLL disks have a faster access time than MFM disks because the head doesn't need to move as far to reach the data.

Using the correct disk with the correct disk controller is similar to matching the right floppy disk with the right disk drive. Although formatting a low-density floppy disk with a high-density setting is possible, the floppy disk is not reliable. Similarly, you can format a high-density floppy disk with a low-density setting, but the disk does not store data reliably. The effect on hard disks is compounded. Because hard disks contain many times the amount of data that a floppy disk holds, you chance losing many times the amount of data if you try to economize by using an incompatible disk and controller.

The method of interfacing between the disk controller and expansion bus varies with the hard disk but conforms with one of several standards. All PC hard disks originally used the ST-506 standard, but as hard disks became more important in PCs, additional standards were adopted. Some of these standards were invented for other types of computers and adapted to PCs.

The next section discusses the current major standards and their advantages and disadvantages.

ST-506

The ST-506 is the original standard and the most common interface for PC hard disks. This type of disk is slow but also is the least expensive. Since the

ST-506 was established, a new standard has evolved—ST-412—which is a superset of ST-506. Most ST-506 drives currently available include the additional features found in the ST-412 standard.

The ST-506 drive, with its separate hard disk and controller, typically is depicted in articles about hard disks. The controller board fits into an expansion slot in the computer, and the hard disk drive, which contains a minimal amount of electronic circuitry, is placed in a drive bay. The hard disk is linked to the disk controller by cables, and the disk controller is linked to the computer by being plugged into the expansion slot.

IDE

Many newer computers have both disk drive and controller in a single package. This type of disk is commonly called *IDE* (intelligent drive electronics). Advances in hard disk technology are making the magnetic part of the hard disk smaller, leaving room for the controller electronics to be an integral part of the hard disk. You now can buy an IDE hard disk similar in size to the ST-506 standard drive but which incorporates the disk controller.

IDE drives plug into a specialized connector on the system board. Four main standards exist: one for the XT, one for the AT, and two for the PS/2. The XT and AT standards use a similar 40-pin connector but with different pin assignments. You need to check that the drive is suitable for installation in an XT or AT computer. Although the magnetic material used on the disk drive's platters is probably similar, the electrical signals are connected differently. IBM has its own proprietary standard for its PS/2 computers that have IDE drives. One PS/2 standard uses a 44-pin connector; the other standard uses a 72-pin connector.

IDE disks perform better than ST-506 drives but can be used only in computers with the correct type of connector.

ESDI

ESDI (Enhanced Standard Device Interface) drives have "intelligent drive electronics" but don't conform to the same standards as IDE drives. ESDI drives perform better than ST-506 drives, transferring data at 10 megabits per second, which is twice as fast as the ST-506. The storage capacities of ESDI drives usually are significantly higher than ST-506 drives, frequently with more than 100M. Not surprisingly, ESDI drives cost more. Like the ST-506 drives, the hard disk and controller card are separate. But like the IDE drives, the ESDI drives incorporate some electronics on the hard disk itself. Because several variations of the ESDI exist, be certain to buy a matched hard disk and controller card that conform to the same standard.

SCSI

SCSI drives (pronounced *scuzzy*) have been used in computers for a long time. These Small Computer System Interface drives are found in many workstations. They are high-performance drives with sophisticated drive controllers. You can install several SCSI devices in the same system, and they don't all have to be disk drives. Most I/O devices, such as printers and tape units (conforming to the SCSI standard), can be attached.

Several SCSI standards are available: SCSI, SCSI-2, and an anticipated SCSI-3. Additional sophisticated controller electronics relieve the CPU of some of its burden and result in better performance. These drives tend to be the most expensive. They likely are to be the most commonly used in the future, however, because users demand higher capacities and higher performances.

Table 6.1 shows the comparative performance of these different drive types. Note that the values given are an average of several manufacturers' models, and a particular model may have different specifications.

Table 6.1
Relative Disk Performances by Type

Type	Transfer Rate (megabytes/sec)	Average Seek Time (milliseconds)	Wattage (watts)
ST-506/ST-412 (MFM)	5	18-40	8-29
ST-506/ST-412 (RLL)	7.5	18-70	8-28
IDE (XT)	5.5-10	29-50	3-7
IDE (AT)	7.5-15	15-70	5.5-20
ESDI	10-15	14-28	9-32
SCSI	8-22	14-70	3.8-35

Other Large Capacity Disk Types

In addition to the typical hard disk, other disk types that store large amounts of data are available. These disks fall into three main categories: disks on a card, removable media disks, and extremely high-density floppy disks.

Each of these disk types has advantages and disadvantages. The next few sections cover specific examples of each disk type.

Hardcard

Plus Development's series of Hardcards is an excellent alternative to conventional hard disks. Instead of using a separate disk controller and hard disk, the Hardcard's single expansion board has the hard disk mounted on one end and the controller at the other end, as shown in figure 6.1.

Fig. 6.1. Plus Development's Hardcard II 80.

Other manufacturers make equivalent products. Plus Development was the first, however, and has taken the technology further than other manufacturers. The Hardcard occupies only a single expansion slot, thereby cramming more into a small space but still working well. Some other manufacturers' disks on a card, however, plug into a single expansion slot connector but take up several (typically two or three) slots' worth of space.

Hardcards can be used in most computers, and they are the only alternative in certain configurations. The Hardcard is useful particularly in PCs that don't have drive bays that can take hard disks. The large, early "portable" PCs are a typical candidate.

Hardcards also can be used as substitute hard disks when no additional drive bays are available. On some computers, particularly those with a small *footprint* (the space on a desk top occupied by the computer case), only three half-height drive bays are available. If you have two floppy disk drives and a tape backup unit, you will not have room for a conventional hard disk.

Finally, Hardcards can be used in computers that have two hard disks attached to an ST-506 controller. Only one ST-506 controller can be in a single system, and you cannot use an ESDI or SCSI drive in the same PC that has an ST-506. The Hardcard, on the other hand, can coexist with another disk controller in the same computer and can provide additional storage space in a computer that normally would not be capable of accepting another hard disk. The ESDI and SCSI standards accept more than one disk controller at a time.

Part I of this book explains that each device in the computer is an asynchronous device, and when the device requires attention, it signals to the CPU by setting an interrupt. The interrupt controller determines the interrupt level and signals to the CPU that an interrupt number X requires servicing. The interrupt number indicates a position in the interrupt vector table. The CPU looks for the address stored in the relevant position in the interrupt vector table and jumps to the indicated service routine. Because each device operates differently, a different service routine is required for each device. Computers with many devices, such as LAN boards, scanner boards, and a mouse, may be short of free interrupts. One method that helps to compensate for this shortage is to install two Hardcards in a computer and set them to share an interrupt. The apparent disadvantage of each Hardcard having a different disk controller, and therefore being a different device and requiring a separate interrupt, is overcome by this sharing of interrupts.

A Hardcard's power requirements are less than that of a conventional disk. In portable computers, therefore, which are not designed to use devices with high power needs, the Hardcard doesn't put undue stress on the system. Some clone computers, however, may not be capable of handling several conventional hard disks because their power supply is underrated. This discovery of an inadequate power supply also can occur when you upgrade a PC to an AT by replacing the motherboard in the old PC case.

Lower power requirements and smaller size also put less long-term stress on the computer. A computer equipped with a Hardcard rather than a conventional hard disk generates less heat, and the Hardcard's smaller size permits air flow from the cooling fan to move around components more easily.

The Hardcard's performance and storage capacity are comparable to that of a conventional hard disk. A 40M or 80M configuration is available with the Hardcard II. If you need hundreds of megabytes of storage space, a conventional hard disk is more suitable.

Historically, Hardcards have been expensive. Now, however, they are priced comparably to conventional hard disks having similar disk performance.

Hardcards have two disadvantages. First, they are not compatible with all computers. The level of compatibility varies, and some clone computers are not supported at all. In some cases, the restriction is physical: The Hardcard's large expansion board does not fit in a slot in which system board components stick up substantially from the system board. In other cases, particularly in old PCs, the BIOS doesn't support the Hardcard's device driver, and you may not be able to boot the computer. So that the Hardcard can coexist with other devices, its configuration is more specialized than, say, a scanner board. Consequently, you may not be able to use Hardcards in certain computers. I have experienced problems with the original Hardcard not working in one of two nearly identical computers.

The second disadvantage of Hardcards is that you cannot perform a low-level or physical format on them. When the Hardcard crashes, as all hard disks do in time, you must return it to the manufacturer for repair. Some conventional hard disks allow a low-level format that removes damaged areas by marking them as bad in the drive table and that enables continued hard disk use without sending it away for repair. You can run a high-level format on a Hardcard using the DOS FORMAT command, but a high-level format does not test as exhaustively as a low-level format. To offset the disadvantages of not being able to run a low-level format on its Hardcard, Plus offers a two-year warranty rather than the typical hard disk one-year warranty.

You cannot do a low-level format on a Hardcard because it is not laid out like a typical hard disk. The Hardcard is formatted unconventionally so that large amounts of data can be squeezed onto a physically small disk. Formatting is proprietary and includes such techniques as placing more sectors on the outer tracks than on the inner tracks.

Hardcard II includes a new feature, an error-correcting technique that reduces the likelihood of complete hard disk failure. Hardcard II has spare sectors that are utilized when the controller detects an error on the disk. The offending sector is mapped out of use, and the data is moved to a spare sector. DOS is unaware of the transfer and continues to function normally.

Because you cannot alter Hardcard's low-level format, exercise great care when running a low-level format on a conventional hard disk installed in the same system as a Hardcard. You also should exercise caution when using utility programs, such as SpinRite, that can do low-level formats. SpinRite can identify Hardcards in a given system and either disable its own low-level formatter or refuse to operate. Competing products, however, may not be as sophisticated.

Although the procedure is not recommended by Plus Development, some people use Hardcards as removable hard disks. They place a Hardcard in a computer, for example, use it, and then take the Hardcard out and place it in another computer. This procedure, in a kludgey way, enables you to share one hard disk between two computers. Another way to use Hardcards as removable hard disks is to use Hardcard's mirroring program to make a copy of the hard disk. After it is copied, the Hardcard is removed and stored as a backup in case the other hard disk fails.

Removable Media Disks

An alternative to typical hard disk technology is to use high-density removable media disks. These hybrid disks are a cross between floppy disks and hard disks. They access data faster than floppy disks and store about as much data as smaller hard disks. You can insert and remove media disks as conveniently as floppy disks. With only a single disk drive, you can use multiple disk cartridges to get the job done.

Removable media drives normally fit into a typical floppy disk drive bay and have plug-in disks. Some disks are in a typical 3 1/2-inch jacket, but other jackets are slightly larger. You use removable media disks in the same way as floppy disks. You install the drive as a device driver in CONFIG.SYS, insert a removable media disk into the drive for use, and use it as a normal disk drive. DOS assigns the drive a logical drive name and treats the drive in the same way as other disk drives. Each removable media disk can contain as much data as a low-capacity hard disk (typical sizes range from 10 to 80M). Currently, these secondary storage devices are expensive.

Trade-offs are involved when you use these devices. In general the higher the capacity, the lower the access time. Iomega's Bernoulli box, for example, has a storage capacity of 44M and access time of 22 ms, whereas Brier Technology's Flextra drive has a formatted capacity of 21M and an average access time of 35 ms. Brier Technology's product is shown in figure 6.2.

Fig. 6.2. Brier Technology's Flextra drive.

Although these drives are an excellent solution for certain situations, use them with care if you want optimum performance from the computer. Whenever possible, use the fastest storage medium for general use and slower devices as backups.

If you have a removable drive and a conventional hard disk, for example, use the hard disk in preference to the slower device. You can buy a mirroring program, which replicates the contents of one disk onto another. These mirroring programs are roughly equivalent to DOS's DISKCOPY command but allow the transfer of data between dissimilar drive types. The best plan may be to use the hard disk during the day and copy the changed files onto the removable disk when you change projects or as part of a backup procedure at the end of each day.

Speed degradation as a result of using a removable hard disk is not as pronounced as the degradation from using a floppy disk as primary storage, but the effect is the same. Each time you access the slower disk, the computer is operating at less than its optimum performance. As the next chapter demonstrates, you may be accessing a disk thousands of times a minute. Even if the hard disk is only 1 ms faster than the removable medium, you save a second each minute. These saved seconds mount up and are a plus when you make the best use of your computer to gain optimal performance.

RAM Disks

Despite advances in technology, hard disks are relatively slow devices. RAM is much faster by several orders of magnitude. You can use one of the device drivers supplied with DOS to set up a RAM disk, which operates many times faster than the fastest hard disk.

However, don't forget RAM's volatility. If you reboot the computer or if a power outage occurs, the RAM disk's contents are lost. Transfer changed files to a disk, therefore, if you want to keep the contents after the computer's power is turned off.

RAM disks are given a drive allocation such as D or E. You can use RAM disks just like ordinary drives, but you lose the contents when you turn off the computer.

You can use the DOS-supplied device driver called RAMDRIVE.SYS (also called VDISK.SYS in some implementations of DOS). This program installs an imaginary or virtual disk in memory. *Virtual disk* is another name for RAM disk. Like buffers and disk caches, RAM disks are much faster than ordinary disk drives. You also can purchase third-party RAM disk programs that may provide more functionality. You can install and remove some of these third-party RAM disks without rebooting the computer. DOS's RAMDRIVE.SYS offering is placed in CONFIG.SYS and is removed only by rebooting.

To install RAMDRIVE and create a virtual disk, just insert a line in CONFIG.SYS. The syntax to invoke RAMDRIVE from CONFIG.SYS is as follows:

DEVICE = *d:path***RAMDRIVE.SYS** *bbbb sss ddd /E:max or /A*

In this syntax, *d:path* is the drive and directory path for RAMDRIVE.SYS. The options for RAMDRIVE are listed in table 6.2 and described in the following section.

Table 6.2
Parameters for Using RAMDRIVE.SYS

Option	Description
bbbb	The size in K of the RAM disk
sss	The size in bytes of the RAM-disk sectors
ddd	The number of directory entries for the RAM disk
/E:max	The switch for extended memory use (DOS 5.0 just includes a /E switch with no maximum value)
/A	The DOS 4 switch for expanded memory use (some versions of DOS use /X rather than /A)

Understanding the RAMDRIVE Options

The RAMDRIVE *bbbb* option can range from 1K to the maximum amount of memory available minus the 64K DOS requires for other programs. For most PCs and compatibles, the maximum amount of memory is 640K. ATs and compatibles can have up to 16M of RAM, so you can set up more than one RAMDRIVE. For example, you conceivably can set up one 3M and three 4M virtual disks.

The default value of *bbbb* is 64K. When you're using DOS 3.2 and later versions of DOS, RAMDRIVE automatically reduces the RAM disk's size if you forget to leave 64K of memory free for your programs. With DOS 3.0 and 3.1, if you specify a value for *bbbb* larger than the amount of the computer's RAM, RAMDRIVE uses the default of 64K. If you have less than 64K of memory available, RAMDRIVE displays an error message and is not installed.

The *sss* option is the size of the sectors for RAMDRIVE. You can specify one of three sector sizes: 128, 256, or 512 bytes. The default value in DOS versions before 5.0 is 128 bytes. DOS 5.0 uses the default value of 512 bytes, and this sector size works well unless you are using a very small RAM disk. (You are allowed to specify the sector size for a RAM disk; DOS disks usually use a sector size of 512 bytes.)

In Chapter 4, you learned that files are allocated disk space a cluster at a time. On a RAM disk, as on all disks, the cluster size depends on the disk size, sector size, and number of directory entries. If you create a file only 1 byte in length, the whole cluster is set aside for that small file.

If a value for *sss* is given, you also must include a value for *bbbb*.

The *ddd* option is the number of directory entries or files for the RAM disk. Each file stored on the RAM disk uses one directory entry. Because the volume label RAMDRIVE creates takes one of the directory entries, *ddd* actually specifies the number of files, minus one, that the RAM disk can hold. You can specify a value for *ddd* from 2 to 512 files; the default is 64. Set the number of directories based on the size of the RAM disk and the size of the files you are storing.

/E is the switch RAMDRIVE uses to access extended memory. If you use the /E switch, RAMDRIVE uses 768 bytes of base memory but places the RAM disk itself in extended memory, with a maximum size of 4M for the RAM disk. You can use multiple RAM disks, limited only by the amount of available extended memory and DOS's regular memory. Because each RAMDRIVE uses 768 bytes of regular memory, specifying many RAM disks may reduce regular memory below 64K. If the amount of memory drops below 64K, the last RAM disk you try to install is not installed.

DOS 3.0 and 5.0 use the /E switch alone; other versions add the *max* parameter to the switch; *max* is the maximum number of sectors that can be transferred at one time from the RAM disk. Certain programs, primarily communications programs, may lose characters if the CPU's attention is directed to the RAM disk for too long. If you have such a problem, set *max* to 7 or less. Otherwise, omit the parameter or specify /E:8.

DOS 5.0 requires that an extended memory manager, such as HIMEM.SYS, be installed before you activate the RAM disk in CONFIG.SYS when using the /E switch and making use of extended memory.

If you have enough extended memory, you can set up several RAM disks. Just specify additional DEVICE=RAMDRIVE statements in CONFIG.SYS. Each statement invokes a fresh copy of RAMDRIVE and installs additional RAM disks.

To use a RAM disk that has the features of a 360K, double-sided floppy disk, for example, use the following command line:

DEVICE = RAMDRIVE.SYS 360 512 112

If you want a RAM disk that uses all the extended memory on a computer with 1M of RAM, use this command line:

DEVICE = RAMDRIVE.SYS 384 512 112 /E:8

This statement creates a RAM disk of 384K (384K is the difference between 1M of RAM and 640K of conventional memory), with 512-byte sectors and 112 directory entries. The /E:8 switch tells DOS to install the RAM disk in extended memory and transfer 8 sectors to and from the RAM disk at a time. If the /E switch is omitted, DOS installs the RAM disk in the 640K of DOS memory.

If you use DOS 4 or 5.0, you can use the /A parameter, which enables you to use expanded memory (rather than extended memory) for the RAM disk. To use this switch, you must load the expanded-memory driver (such as XMA2EMS.SYS) before loading RAMDRIVE.SYS. You cannot use both the /A and /E switches for the same RAM disk. You may create different RAM disks, however—some using extended memory and others using expanded memory—if you have enough memory available. Simply insert multiple DEVICE statements in CONFIG.SYS.

Learning More about RAM Disks

The amount of a computer's RAM, the programs you use, and the convenience of a RAM disk determine the size of the RAM disk you use—or whether you should use a RAM disk at all. This section helps establish whether you should use a RAM disk, and if so, what size is probably best.

A RAM Disk in 640K of Memory

Although all computers can accommodate a RAM disk, the computer may not be capable of accommodating a RAM disk while using other programs. When DOS 4.01 is loaded on a computer with 640K of memory, for example, 581K is left for programs to use. DOS 4.01, using the CONFIG.SYS FILES and BUFFERS directives and the ANSI.SYS device driver, uses about 59K of RAM.

If you use 1-2-3 Release 2.2 with this computer, you must have 223K of RAM for 1-2-3, plus enough memory left over for worksheets. Loading 1-2-3 leaves 358K for worksheet creation. If you create a RAM disk in the remaining 358K of conventional memory, you decrease the amount of memory available for a worksheet.

As another example, dBASE IV uses 412K of RAM, leaving 169K of memory. Although dBASE IV does not use RAM for workspace in the same way that 1-2-3 does, you may limit some features of dBASE IV, such as running DOS commands from dBASE, if you create a RAM disk.

The bottom line is this: If you have only conventional memory, you may find that a RAM disk does not optimize your use of memory. Exceptions exist, of course. If the program you use does not take up a great deal of memory, you may be able to use a RAM disk. You may want to limit the size of the RAM disk to no more than 100K, however.

If you set up a 100K RAM disk, you cannot store a large quantity of information on the RAM disk. You probably would use the RAM disk only for temporary storage of rather small files. You may want to use the following directive in your CONFIG.SYS file:

DEVICE = C:\RAMDRIVE.SYS 100 128 64

This statement creates a 100K RAM disk, with 128-byte sectors and 64 directory entries. Because the RAM disk uses some of the allocated space for the directory and FAT, only 98.9K actually is usable.

The small sector size of 128 bytes is assigned in this example to maximize the performance of the RAM disk. If you set up the disk with 128-byte sectors, and the disk contains 10 files of 600 bytes each, 92.5K is available for further storage. If you set up the RAM disk with 512-byte sectors and have the same files, only 89K is available.

Because one file does not share a sector with another file, a single 600-byte file requires five 128-byte sectors, wasting 40 bytes. This same 600-byte file, on the other hand, needs only two 512-byte sectors; however, 497 bytes are wasted. From this example, you can see that using a small sector size has advantages.

If you plan to store only one or two large files on a 100K RAM disk, you may be better off setting a large sector size. You realize a time savings when a few large sectors rather than several small sectors are read from or written to the RAM disk.

The size of the directory also influences the usable size of the RAM disk: The larger the directory, the more room is needed to track files. A 100K RAM disk set up to store 64 files has 98.9K available for storage. The same 100K RAM disk with a 192-file directory has only 94.9K for storage. You get a 4 percent larger disk by using the smaller directory size. Practically speaking, you rarely store more than 64 files on a 100K RAM disk, anyway.

A RAM Disk in Expanded or Extended Memory

If the computer has either extended or expanded memory, you may find that a RAM disk is worthwhile. The actual memory used by the RAM disk in systems with expanded or extended memory is located outside the conventional memory used by programs. You can create a RAM disk without giving up program memory. If you decide to use a RAM disk on a computer with expanded or extended memory, the issue is how large the RAM disk should be and what settings to use.

If you have expanded memory and use a program like 1-2-3 Release 2.01 or 2.2, you have more of a decision of how much expanded memory to dedicate to a RAM disk because 1-2-3 can store data in expanded memory. Creating a RAM disk in expanded memory decreases the amount of expanded memory that 1-2-3 can use. If you have 2M of expanded memory, for example, you may find that you can set aside as much as 512K for a RAM disk without affecting programs that use expanded memory.

If the computer has extended memory, you must decide how much extended memory to use as a RAM disk, if any. Programs such as 1-2-3 Release 3 use a DOS extender to make extended memory available to the program for data storage. Creating a RAM disk in extended memory, therefore, decreases the amount of memory available to programs that use DOS extenders.

Regardless of whether you have extended or expanded memory, you also must decide what you can use that memory for in addition to programs. You may want to use some of that memory for SMARTDRV.SYS or IBMCACHE.SYS, for example. (Chapter 7 discusses the use of disk caches supplied with DOS.) If the programs you use are disk oriented rather than RAM oriented (dBASE is disk oriented; 1-2-3 is RAM oriented), you can use expanded or extended memory for a large disk cache. The use of a large disk cache may make a RAM disk obsolete because the disk cache may enable you to access your files just as fast as when using a RAM disk. Furthermore, the disk cache has other advantages. You don't have to copy files from the disk to the RAM disk, and all changes to files are written to the disk without the need for you to copy the changed files from the RAM disk back to the hard disk. The disk cache also works automatically.

If you create a RAM disk in expanded or extended memory, you probably create a disk larger than one created in conventional memory. When you create a larger RAM disk, you can vary the settings for sector size and directory size. The values given for these settings, however, still depend on the quantity and size of the files to be stored on the RAM disk.

If you create a 512K RAM disk, for example, you may find that a sector size of 512 bytes is adequate, even if you store small files on the RAM disk. You also may find that a directory size of 64 is adequate because you seldom store more than 64 files on a RAM disk. If you plan to use the RAM disk to help you copy files from one floppy disk to another, however, change the directory value to 112, which is the total number of files that can be stored on a 360K floppy disk.

If you have only one floppy disk drive of a particular type, you can use a RAM disk for replicating disks. You can do this technique with batch files by copying the current CONFIG.SYS and AUTOEXEC.BAT to a backup, creating a new CONFIG.SYS with the RAM disk specification, and rebooting the computer. You create a RAM disk that is the same size as the floppy disk to be copied and use the copy command to copy from the floppy disk into the RAM disk. Next, you copy from the RAM disk onto the new floppy disks without having to swap disks as frequently. When you finish copying to the floppy disks, you restore your normal CONFIG.SYS and AUTOEXEC.BAT and reboot again.

To create a 512K RAM disk with 512-byte sectors and 112 directory entries in expanded memory, include the following directive in CONFIG.SYS:

DEVICE = C:\RAMDRIVE.SYS 512 512 112 /A

To create the same RAM disk in extended memory, include this directive:

DEVICE = C:\RAMDRIVE.SYS 512 512 112 /E

These directives create a RAM disk adequate for temporary storage. Remember the word *temporary*; when the power goes out, you lose what is on the RAM disk. Back up important files on the RAM disk to the hard disk or floppy disks.

Many applications programs use temporary files to hold information briefly. A word processor may store the current settings, for example, when you invoke a spell checker. When you finish checking the spelling, the program retrieves the information from the temporary file. Temporary file creation and use varies with each program.

You may be able to improve the response time of your programs if you use a RAM disk to store these temporary files. Some applications programs store the temporary files in the location specified in an environment variable. If you create an environment variable that indicates that the temporary file should be placed on the RAM disk, the files are placed on the RAM disk rather than the hard disk, and you see a speed improvement. The SET command, which is placed in AUTOEXEC.BAT, has a form similar to the following:

    SET TEMP=E:\

In this command, E: represents the RAM disk. Different programs use different spellings of the variable TEMP, however. dBASE IV uses DBTEMP for its variable name, for example, but TEMP and TMP are used frequently by other programs.

If you are using WordPerfect 5.1, you can direct your overflow files to the RAM drive by using the /D start-up option. You can start WordPerfect by using the following form:

    WP /D-E:\

This command indicates that the RAM disk drive has the logical letter E. Substitute a different letter if the RAM disk is not drive E. An alternative to typing this start-up each time is to create an environment variable named WP. You can use the following command, for example:

    SET WP=/D-E:\

Alternatively, you can place your WordPerfect options into a batch file as discussed earlier. WordPerfect starts faster if you use the SET command rather than a batch file, but you use additional precious environment space. Allocation of your resources depends on your particular use of the computer. If you use only WordPerfect, your PATH setting is small, and you can spare the environment space. If you use a wide variety of programs, however, environment space may be scarce.

Chapter Summary

This chapter provided several tools for improving the apparent performance of your hard disk.

You can rearrange the directory list in your PATH environment variable so that the most frequently used subdirectories appear first. This way, DOS does not search needlessly through infrequently used subdirectories before loading your program.

Similarly, you can optimize the contents of your APPEND variable. Or you can—using batch files for convenience—use several different PATH variable values, depending on the APPEND program you are running.

You may improve the performance of your hard disk by replacing the disk. Technological advances have created a wide array of high-capacity disks that can fit most needs of most users. In general, the faster the disk or the higher the capacity, the more expensive. Some alternatives, such as Plus

Development's Hardcard, can increase the total number of hard disks in a system. Others, such as Iomega's Bernoulli box, give you the advantage of having a removable magnetic media.

Although a RAM disk always is faster than a hard disk, you may prefer a hard disk with a cache. This chapter explained when using a RAM disk is best, such as when a drive is used for storage of a program's temporary files.

Improving Disk Performance

7

Chapter 5 covered how to ensure that the disk is working at its best performance, and Chapter 6 introduced alternative disk types. This chapter covers how the use of memory can improve your disk drive's performance.

DOS provides several tools that change how DOS uses some of the memory in your computer; these tools include RAMDRIVE, BUFFERS, FASTOPEN, and caching programs. Refer to Chapter 6 for information on RAMDRIVE. This chapter covers BUFFERS, FASTOPEN, and caching programs.

These tools can improve the computer's performance. You shouldn't just assume, however, that more of each thing is a good choice. This chapter covers each of the available tools so that you have an understanding of how each tool works. Using this knowledge, you can decide how much of each feature you want to use. This selection requires being familiar with the typical tasks you do on your computer and is best done through the suite of benchmarks you developed in Chapter 5.

Using BUFFERS

The BUFFERS directive tells DOS how many disk buffers to use. Before the introduction of disk-caching programs (which also keep disk information in memory), BUFFERS had potential for great impact on disk performance. This command was changed significantly for DOS 4 and again for DOS 5. The older version of BUFFERS is discussed first, followed by a discussion of DOS 4 enhancements and DOS 5 changes.

As this book emphasizes, RAM is much faster than disk memory. Whenever possible, use RAM in preference to disks. RAM access speed is rated in nanoseconds (billionths of a second) in contrast to hard disk access speed, which is rated in milliseconds (thousandths of a second).

Clearly, when you can fetch data from RAM rather than from disk, you can improve your performance. You see how this concept is taken to its near-ultimate in the discussion of SMARTDRV.SYS and IBMCACHE.SYS later in this chapter. For now, consider the improvements that can be made with the BUFFERS directive.

A *buffer* is a reserved area of RAM set up by DOS to store information read from disk. If you configure your system with enough buffers, DOS frequently finds the information it needs in buffered memory. Instead of idling for a few hundred million cycles during a disk access, the microprocessor goes back to work in as little as a thousand cycles if the information is in a buffer.

A single buffer is about 512 bytes long (plus 16 to 20 bytes for overhead). The BUFFERS directive controls how many disk buffers your computer uses. The syntax for this directive is as follows:

BUFFERS = nn

In this syntax, **nn** is the number of disk buffers you want. With versions of DOS except DOS 4, you can have any number of buffers from 1 to 99. If you do not give the BUFFERS directive, DOS uses a default value of 2 to 15. The default number of buffers depends on the type of disk you have, the amount of memory in your computer, and the version of DOS you use. Table 7.1 lists the different default buffer configurations.

**Table 7.1
Default Number of Disk Buffers**

DOS Version	Buffers	Hardware
DOS pre-3.3	2	Floppy disk drive
	3	Hard disk
DOS 3.3 or later	2	360K floppy disk drive
	3	Any other hard or floppy disk drive
	5	More than 128K of RAM
	10	More than 256K of RAM
	15	More than 512K of RAM

You can use fewer BUFFERS than the default numbers shown in table 7.1. Unless you use a disk-caching program, however, you may want more rather than fewer buffers.

Understanding How DOS Uses Disk Buffers

When DOS is asked to get information from a disk, DOS reads information in increments of whole sectors (512 bytes). You can transfer data on and off the disk more efficiently in sectors than in small increments. Most programs usually don't consider this fact when asking for data, however, but ask for specific information, regardless of the information's size. DOS tries to be more efficient and takes data in sectors and passes on only information requested specifically. Excess data not required from a sector is left in the buffer. If this unused data is needed later, DOS doesn't have to do another disk access to retrieve the data.

Similarly, DOS tries to reduce disk activity when writing information to the disk. If less than a full sector is to be written to the disk, DOS accumulates the information in a disk buffer. After the buffer is full, DOS writes the information to disk. This action is called *flushing the buffer*. To make sure that all pertinent information is placed into a file, DOS also flushes the buffers when a program "closes" a disk file. If you turn off the computer without exiting an applications program, you lose any information stored in the buffers and not yet written to the disk.

When a disk buffer becomes full or empty, DOS marks the buffer to indicate that the buffer has been used recently. When DOS needs to reuse the buffers for new information, DOS takes the buffer that hasn't been used for the longest period of time. This marking takes place in the bytes (16 or 20 depending on the DOS version) used as overhead. The net effect of DOS's use of buffers is a reduction in the number of disk accesses DOS performs because DOS retains information likely to be needed next. Your programs and DOS, therefore, run faster.

If your program does much *random* disk work (reading and writing information in different parts of a file), you may want to specify a higher number of buffers. The more buffers you have, the better the chance that the information DOS wants is already in the disk buffer holding area of memory.

Some programs do not benefit much from using disk buffers. If your program mainly does *sequential* reads and writes (reading or writing information from the start of the file straight through to the end), using disk buffers doesn't help you much.

Fine-Tuning with BUFFERS

The number of disk buffers you should have depends on the programs you use and how much memory your computer has. If your day-to-day use of the computer does not involve accounting or database work (both of which use files with small groups of data), the right number of buffers is from 10 to 20. If you do accounting or database work, you should have between 20 and 40 buffers (more, if you use expanded memory with DOS 4). If you use many subdirectories, using more disk buffers optimizes your computer's performance. Many applications programs check your CONFIG.SYS when you install them and recommend a minimum value.

Because each disk buffer takes approximately 530 bytes, every two disk buffers you use cost just over 1K of RAM. If you use many memory-hungry programs and *TSR utilities*—terminate-and-stay-resident programs designed to stay in RAM and to be activated with a keystroke—you may need to use a minimal number of buffers to preserve precious RAM. If you are using disk-caching programs, however, you may have different reasons (discussed later in this chapter) for keeping the number of buffers low.

Even if memory is no problem, DOS has a "magic" range for disk buffers. DOS Versions 3 and 4 slow down if you specify between 40 and 60 disk buffers. DOS 5 slows down with more than 50 disk buffers. This slowing effect happens because DOS spends more time searching the buffers for information than reading or writing to disk. Depending on the programs you run, specifying more than 30 buffers may saturate memory and cause the system to become sluggish.

If you use a floppy disk system, start with 10 disk buffers; start with 20 buffers for hard disk systems. Fine-tune the number by increasing or decreasing the number 1 to 5 buffers every few hours or once a day. Reboot DOS and examine its performance. Keep doing this procedure until you think you have the best performance. You can use your benchmark programs (see Chapter 5) for this purpose. You don't need to be exact but just get the general "feel" of the computer's performance with different numbers of buffers.

These rules of thumb are not valid if you use sophisticated programs with memory management routines of their own. If you have a disk cache, for example, most of the work done by buffers is handled automatically and more intelligently. (Disk-caching programs are covered later in this chapter.) Memory managers for 386 computers, such as Quarterdeck's QEMM-386, set up their own disk buffers. (Memory managers are covered in Chapter 11.) If you fall into either one of these categories, set the CONFIG.SYS BUFFERS directive to a relatively low number, such as 2. This action enables DOS to read a whole sector or two into memory but doesn't waste memory on buffers that really aren't needed.

If you use a large number of buffers as well as a disk cache, you are not making the most efficient use of memory. Instead, you essentially are double-caching. Data first is taken into the buffer memory (assuming that you set BUFFERS prior to loading the cache) and then is passed to the cache program before being passed onto the requesting program. Setting a low number for BUFFERS restricts the buffer memory to handle only requests for small amounts of data and enables the caching program to handle the majority of data requests.

Using BUFFERS in preference to a disk cache, such as Microsoft's SMARTDRV.SYS, is particularly inadvisable when using programs with advanced memory management capabilities. Microsoft Windows, for example, makes special use of SmartDrive's disk cache memory. Windows enables you to run several applications programs at once. Windows achieves this memory feat by keeping control of memory in your computer and sharing memory between applications as much as possible. Windows can share the same memory assigned to the disk cache with other applications requiring memory. If you use a large buffers setting rather than SmartDrive, the memory used by BUFFERS cannot be shared with other applications. This inefficient use of memory reduces the computer's flexibility.

Understanding DOS 4 BUFFERS Options

DOS 4 added important options to the BUFFERS directive. The number of buffers you can set with DOS 4 was increased to 10,000—if you have expanded memory. In addition, you now can use "look ahead" buffers to increase disk efficiency.

DOS 4 introduced support for expanded memory, and BUFFERS is one of the features that can use it. If you add the /X switch to the BUFFERS directive in your CONFIG.SYS file, DOS uses expanded memory to store buffered information. Calculate the number of buffers you can fit in the memory you have (each buffer is just over 512 bytes).

If you don't have expanded memory, 99 is the maximum number of buffers that can be specified. You cannot use the /X switch without expanded memory, but you can use the look-ahead buffer feature.

Look-ahead buffers (also called *secondary caches*) are special buffers that DOS uses to store sectors ahead of the sector requested by a DOS read operation. A look-ahead buffer requires exactly 512 bytes of memory. You can specify from 0 to 8 look-ahead buffers. If you specify 5 look-ahead buffers, for example, every time DOS reads a sector from your disk, DOS also reads the next 5 sectors. Reading the additional sectors is simple (and rapid) for DOS because the read/write head already is positioned and operating to read the first sector.

If your application or DOS needs one of the sectors already read, DOS finds the sectors in the look-ahead buffer and does not have to make another disk access. Look-ahead buffers improve the computer's performance because the buffers are fetching information from RAM rather than from disk. RAM access time is more than ten thousand times faster than disk access time.

The following syntax is used for the expanded-memory and look-ahead buffer features:

BUFFERS = buffers,*look-ahead_buffers* /X

For example, the command **BUFFERS = 1000,8 /X** tells DOS to set aside 1,000 buffers and 8 look-ahead buffers, using expanded memory. If enough expanded memory is not available, the directive is ignored and DOS reverts to the default buffer value. To be sure that you have sufficient memory for the buffers you want to specify, use the DOS 4 MEM command. The default is 1 look-ahead buffer; if you want to use look-ahead buffers, a good value to start with is 8.

Understanding DOS 5 BUFFERS Options

DOS 5 also enables you to specify look-ahead buffers as part of the BUFFERS directive. The expanded memory switch is not available, however, and the maximum number of buffers allowed is 99. If you don't have extended or expanded memory, the function is unchanged from DOS 4.

If you have expanded memory, however, you may think that DOS 5 is a step backward by not continuing to support expanded memory. If you look at DOS as a whole, you can use expanded memory in better ways than by assigning a large number of buffers. A disk cache, such as SmartDrive, is a more sophisticated alternative that significantly improves your computer's performance and makes better use of your resources.

The syntax for DOS 5's BUFFERS directive with its look-ahead buffer feature is as follows:

BUFFERS = buffers, *look-ahead_buffers*

For example, the command **BUFFERS = 40,8** tells DOS to set aside 40 buffers and 8 look-ahead buffers. The default is 1 look-ahead buffer; if you want to use look-ahead buffers, a good value to start with is 8. You should not specify any look-ahead buffers if you are using a disk cache.

If you are using an 80286, 80386, or 80486 microprocessor, DOS 5 can load part of itself into high memory instead of taking up as much low DOS memory as previous versions. This feature requires the use of HIMEM.SYS in your CONFIG.SYS file. HIMEM.SYS and other memory managers are discussed in Chapter 10.

If you load part of DOS into high memory, your buffers also are located in high memory. At the same time, DOS sets aside 512 bytes of low DOS memory for its use in association with the buffers.

The discussion of BUFFERS settings for early versions of DOS applies equally to DOS 5 BUFFERS. Whenever possible, use a disk cache in preference to a large buffer setting. If you're using a disk cache, set a BUFFERS value of 2. If you're not, perhaps because of memory constraints or compatibility problems between the disk cache and your applications programs, you should use a value between 20 and 50.

The best solution for choosing an appropriate BUFFERS setting is to alter the value until you are comfortable with the performance. Start your testing by altering the setting in large increments and then fine-tune your chosen setting by altering it one buffer at a time. Run your benchmarks (see Chapter 5) and see which setting gives you the best value.

Use this value for a while in normal use and then try altering the setting one buffer higher or lower to see whether you notice an improvement. If during normal use you do notice an improvement that you did not detect through the benchmarks, you may want to add to your set another benchmark that makes use of this faster feature. Perhaps the spell checker in your word processor is faster, for example, and you weren't using the spell checker as a benchmark test. Adding a benchmark test that spell-checks a standard document is a valuable addition because, in this example, it detects the difference between two close buffer settings. A spell-checking benchmark also may prove to be valuable in optimizing your disk cache.

Gaining Speed with FASTOPEN

If you use many of the same files during the day—particularly small files that DOS can read or write in one cluster—BUFFERS is not a major benefit. The time DOS spends traversing the subdirectory system and opening the files may be greater than the time spent actually reading or writing the files.

FASTOPEN, introduced with DOS 3.3, is only for hard disks. Whereas buffers store information moved from disk to user memory, FASTOPEN allocates memory to store directory information. FASTOPEN partially solves a performance problem not resolved by the CONFIG.SYS BUFFERS directive. BUFFERS helps when your computer reads or writes information to several files and helps most when disk activity is isolated to a file's few key portions.

FASTOPEN caches directory information, holding in memory the locations of frequently used files and directories. As Chapter 4 explains, directories are a type of file that DOS reads and writes in a manner similar to that of other files. A part of the directory entry for a file or subdirectory holds the starting point for the file in the FAT. Because DOS typically holds the FAT in the disk buffers, FASTOPEN was developed to hold directory entries in memory.

You must exercise a little care to use FASTOPEN effectively. FASTOPEN's syntax for use at the command prompt with a single drive is as follows (substitute your drive letter for **d**):

*d:path***FASTOPEN**.*EXE* **d:**=*nnn*

You can add this command to your CONFIG.SYS by using the DOS 4 or 5 INSTALL directive as follows:

INSTALL = *d:path***FASTOPEN.EXE d:**=*nnn*

Note that you must use the full file name in CONFIG.SYS.

The *d:path* parameter is the disk drive and path to the FASTOPEN.EXE file. The **d:** following the file name is the name of the hard drive you want FASTOPEN to act on and is a mandatory part of the command. The *nnn* parameter is the number of directory entries that FASTOPEN should cache. Each file or subdirectory requires one directory entry, and you can enter a value from 10 to 999. If you do not specify a value for *nnn*, most DOS versions default to 10. DOS 5 defaults to 48.

You can use FASTOPEN on several disks at once. However, you can issue the command only once. To change the settings, you must reboot the computer. You can use different settings for each drive by using the following syntax:

*d:path***FASTOPEN**.*EXE* **d1:**=*xxx* **d2:**=*yyy*

You specify each disk drive and the number of directory entries to be held in memory for that drive. Just leave a space between the information for each drive. For example, to install FASTOPEN (located in drive C's DOS directory) onto drive C so that 30 directories are kept in memory and also onto drive D so that 50 directories are kept in memory, type the following:

C:\DOS\FASTOPEN.EXE C:=**30 D:**=**50**

DOS 3.3 enables you to specify up to four logical drives at a time. Later versions, discussed next, allow different numbers of logical drives.

If you use DOS 4, you can use two additional parameters with this command, as shown in the following syntax line:

*d:path***FASTOPEN**.*EXE* **d:**=(*nnn,mmm*) /X

The *mmm* parameter refers to the number of fragmented entries for the drive. Using this parameter improves performance when files on your hard disk become fragmented. The values you can use for *mmm* range from 1 to 999. If no value for *mmm* is given, the feature is not active. Because your disk performance deteriorates with fragmented files, you should keep your files unfragmented by using a disk optimizer (see Chapter 5). The /X switch enables FASTOPEN information to be kept in expanded memory.

If you don't have a disk optimizer, however, you may want to use this parameter. The value you specify for *mmm* depends on how fragmented your files are. Use the CHKDSK *.* command in subdirectories where you store data files to get a report of fragmentation. The more fragmentation, the larger the value you should assign to *mmm*. A general rule is to use a value for *mmm* twice the number of *nnn*.

If you omit *nnn*, FASTOPEN uses 10. If you want to specify a value for *mmm* but not *nnn*, you should include the equal sign, parentheses, and comma.

As with DOS 3.3, you can specify more than one logical drive on a single command line. The syntax is as follows:

d:path**FASTOPEN**.*EXE* **d1**:=*(xxx,aaa)* **d2**:=*(yyy,bbb)* /X

For example, to use FASTOPEN (located in the DOS directory on drive C) to keep 100 directory entries and 200 fragmented entries for drive C as well as 50 directory entries and 100 fragmented entries for drive D, all in expanded memory, type the following:

C:\DOS\FASTOPEN.EXE C:=(100,200) D:=(50,100) /X

The /X switch enables FASTOPEN information to reside in expanded memory. You can choose to omit the *xxx* and *yyy* parameters. If you want to specify a value for *aaa* but not *xxx* or for *bbb* but not *yyy*, for example, you should include the equal sign, parentheses, and comma.

DOS 5 does not include the *mmm* parameter but does include the /X feature. The syntax therefore is the same as for DOS 3.3 but with an optional /X switch, as shown in the following example:

d:path**FASTOPEN**.*EXE* **d:**=*nnn* /X

DOS 4 enables you to use FASTOPEN on up to four hard disks and to store up to 999 directories on each hard disk. DOS 5 has increased this capability, enabling you to use FASTOPEN on up to 24 hard disks at a time and to store up to 999 directories on each disk.

The practical limit of *nnn* is between 100 and 200 directories per disk. If you specify a value much higher, DOS wades through the internal directory entries slower than it reads information from the disk. Additionally, each directory entry stored in memory takes approximately 40 bytes in DOS 3.3 and 48 bytes in DOS 5. In DOS 4, FASTOPEN takes 48 bytes for each file name (*nnn*) and 16 bytes for each fragmented entry (*mmm*). Considering the trade-off between the speed improvements possible with FASTOPEN and the amount of memory FASTOPEN needs to give you that speed improvement, the 100-to-200 limit yields adequate performance.

Using too small a number for *nnn* can be a disadvantage as well. When directory entries are recycled, the least recently used entry is discarded if a new entry is needed. If the *nnn* value is too small, DOS discards entries it may still need. The object is to have enough entries in memory so that FASTOPEN operates efficiently but not so many that FASTOPEN wastes time looking through many directory entries.

At the very least, *nnn* must exceed the number of subdirectories through which you travel to get to the "deepest" subdirectory. The minimum value for *nnn* is 10; this value often exceeds the number of levels in your directory organization. Suppose that you have a directory structure like \DOS\BASIC\TEST. The deepest level is three down from the root, much less the default of 10. A reasonable starting value for *nnn* is a number equal to the number of megabytes of the hard disk. For example, you should try *nnn* equal to 80 for an 80M hard disk.

FASTOPEN stores files and directories for files that you or your applications program open. If you are using only one file, for example, FASTOPEN isn't going to improve the computer's performance. Programs that open and close a great deal of files (such as databases) show the most improvement in performance with a FASTOPEN setting. When you are determining this value, run your benchmarks that test this feature first. For example, a benchmark testing the sorting of a database probably shows different performances with different FASTOPEN settings. If none of your benchmarks shows a change, you don't use programs that use a large number of files, and you may decide that the memory you are giving up to the FASTOPEN setting should be used for another purpose.

You should observe two restrictions when using FASTOPEN. First, the disk drive you name cannot be one on which you use JOIN, SUBST, or ASSIGN, because these commands do not create "real" drives. Second, if you load a disk-drive device driver through AUTOEXEC.BAT rather than through CONFIG.SYS (some manufacturers provide a driver that must be started from a batch file or from the DOS prompt rather than from CONFIG.SYS), you must use FASTOPEN *after* you define all disk drives. FASTOPEN can become confused if you add additional disk drives after you have invoked FASTOPEN.

The choices involved when using a cache with BUFFERS are different from those involved when using a cache with FASTOPEN. Because data retrieved from the disk is placed into BUFFERS in a similar way as into a cache, BUFFERS and caches appear to do the same thing. A good caching program, however, is more flexible and has more intelligence than the BUFFERS command. A disk cache offers many advantages over the BUFFERS directive, and you should choose a good disk cache in preference to using the BUFFERS directive.

On the other hand, using FASTOPEN is sensible even if you are using a disk-caching program (unless the disk-caching program has an equivalent function). Whereas FASTOPEN caches the directory information, a disk cache may or may not store this information depending on the particular product. If the disk-caching program has an equivalent FASTOPEN function, you shouldn't use FASTOPEN and the disk cache because they duplicate each other, performing a double cache.

Understanding Disk Caches

Strictly speaking, the IBMCACHE.SYS device-driver file is not part of DOS. (IBMCACHE.SYS comes on the Reference floppy disk for IBM PS/2 Models 50, 60, and 80.) Some versions of DOS come with the SMARTDRV.SYS file; other versions of DOS don't. If your version of DOS doesn't come with the file, you have to purchase Windows to get SMARTDRV.SYS. An understanding of disk-cache systems aids you in getting the best performance out of your computer. The concepts discussed in this section apply to both programs as well as other caching programs.

This section discusses disk-caching programs, which are not the same as hardware-caching controllers. The cache controller, particularly popular on 386-based computers with speeds of more than 16 MHz, increases the CPU's interaction with memory. A disk-caching program, on the other hand, quickens the computer's interaction with the hard disk. A hardware cache controller is an integral part of the computer, whereas a disk cache can be installed and removed from a computer at will. Chapter 3 discusses this difference in detail.

You can think of IBMCACHE.SYS and SMARTDRV.SYS as large, smart buffers. Like a buffer, a disk cache operates from a section of RAM you request from DOS. A disk cache and a disk buffer accumulate information going to or coming from the disk. When information is read from the disk, the information is placed in a buffer or cache; only the specific information requested by the program is sent on to the program. Like a buffer, a disk cache can read more information than was requested by the program. When information is written to the disk, the information may be stored in the buffer or cache until it is full and then written to the disk. (Most caches have a "write through" feature: The cache frequently writes information to disk to avoid data loss if the system is turned off or loses power. Smart caches eliminate redundant writes by putting information on a disk only when the data is different from what is on the disk already.) If you use a cache or buffers, your program performance improves because slow disk accesses are replaced by higher speed, memory-to-memory transfers.

Although a DOS disk buffer is a type of disk cache, a good caching program outperforms a buffer. Disk caches are better performers because they have more "intelligence" than buffers. You may find that the performance of a disk cache is hampered if you make the cache too large or too small. Test different applications you use and vary the size of the cache to find its optimum performance.

A disk cache remembers which disk sections have been used most frequently. When the cache must be recycled, the program keeps the more frequently used areas and discards those less frequently used. Buffers, as you recall, are recycled based on how old the buffer is, regardless of how frequently the buffer is used. Because a cache tends to keep in memory the most heavily used areas of the disk, the cache method of recycling the least frequently used area is more efficient than the buffer method of recycling the oldest area.

Like the DOS 4 BUFFERS directive, many disk caches have look-ahead capabilities, a technique that has the cache read more sectors than the program requests.

In many cases, using a disk cache to help with disk activity is preferable to using a RAM disk program like RAMDRIVE.SYS (see Chapter 6). A RAM disk helps only with files copied to the RAM disk (loading a program with overlays into a RAM disk may be better than using a cache to speed up a slow disk). Whereas the cache's activity is effortless and transparent to the user, a RAM disk requires separate directives to access the needed files.

A disk cache also is preferable to a RAM disk because the danger of losing information with a cache can be less. You have a greater probability of losing information when files are written to a RAM disk than when files are written to the cache. The cache, like a DOS buffer, holds the information for only a few seconds before writing it to disk. During this brief period, the information in the cache is at risk. If power is lost to the RAM disk, however, all files on the disk are destroyed. You have to issue commands to copy information to the safety of a hard disk because the RAM disk does not copy to the disk automatically.

In two situations, however, a RAM disk is preferred to a disk cache. When you need to copy files between floppy disks on a computer with a single floppy disk drive, copying to and from the RAM disk is convenient. You first copy the files to the RAM disk, change floppy disks, and then copy the files from the RAM disk to the second floppy disk. A disk cache cannot help you copy files between floppy disks.

You also may prefer to use a RAM disk if you frequently use resource files with contents that do not change and can be placed completely on the RAM disk. A good example is Turbo Lightning, whose dictionary and thesaurus files can be placed on a RAM disk. Because you access these files frequently—but rarely the same spots in the file—having the files on a RAM disk provides better performance than having the files in a disk cache.

Many disk-caching programs are available, each with different performance features. For the same reasons that you shouldn't use a large BUFFERS setting and a disk-caching program together, you shouldn't use two disk-caching programs together. In fact, the situation may be worse than just losing performance. The two disk caches may not interact with each other correctly and may not write data to disk because one program thinks that the other has done it, or your program may be given out-of-date information because the disk cache supplying the information doesn't know that the information in memory isn't current.

Installing IBMCACHE.SYS

IBMCACHE.SYS is a file that accompanies any IBM PS/2 that uses extended memory (which excludes Models 25 and 30). IBMCACHE is a disk-caching program made specifically for PS/2 computers. IBMCACHE.SYS is found on the Reference disk that comes with the computer.

To install IBMCACHE.SYS the first time, you must run the program IBMCACHE from the Reference disk. Because the IBMCACHE.COM program and the IBMCACHE.SYS disk cache itself are hidden files on the floppy disk, you cannot copy the files to your computer using the DOS COPY command. Norton Utilities and PC Tools Deluxe include programs that enable you to copy hidden files, if you prefer.

A detailed installation procedure is listed next. Even if you are experienced with typical installation programs, you may want to read this section because it examines the terms used for describing caching program settings.

First, start up DOS on your PS/2 system. After DOS is running, insert the Reference disk into drive A and type the following:

A:IBMCACHE

Your screen should look similar to figure 7.1. The highlighted bar should be on the first option, Install Disk Cache Onto Drive C. When you press Enter to select the option, a window pops up, giving the information shown in figure 7.2. Press Y to install the cache. The pop-up window goes away, the floppy disk and hard disk lights go on, and a message stating that the cache is installed appears in another window (see fig. 7.3). Press Enter to continue.

Chapter 7: Improving Disk Performance

```
┌─────────────────────────────────────────┐
│ Disk Cache Main Menu                    │
├─────────────────────────────────────────┤
│ 1. Install disk cache onto drive C:     │
│ 2. View disk cache settings             │
│ 3. Change disk cache settings           │
│ 4. Remove disk cache from drive C:      │
│                                         │
│                                         │
│ Use ↑ or ↓ to select. Then press Enter. │
│ Esc=Quit    F1=Help                     │
└─────────────────────────────────────────┘
```

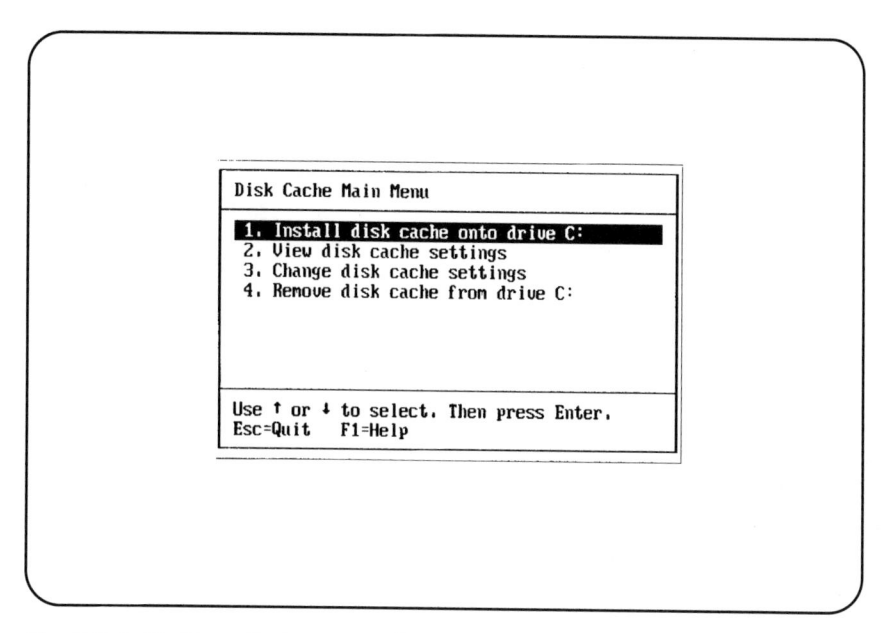

Fig. 7.1. Initial installation screen for IBMCACHE.

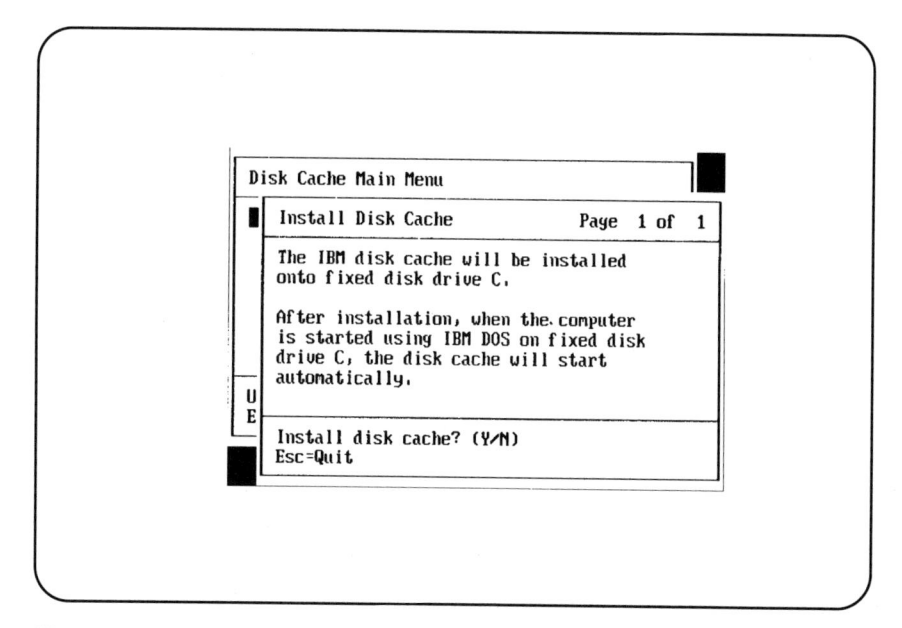

```
┌─────────────────────────────────────────┐
│ Disk Cache Main Menu                    │
├─────────────────────────────────────────┤
│ Install Disk Cache      Page 1 of 1     │
├─────────────────────────────────────────┤
│ The IBM disk cache will be installed    │
│ onto fixed disk drive C.                │
│                                         │
│ After installation, when the computer   │
│ is started using IBM DOS on fixed disk  │
│ drive C, the disk cache will start      │
│ automatically.                          │
├─────────────────────────────────────────┤
│ Install disk cache? (Y/N)               │
│ Esc=Quit                                │
└─────────────────────────────────────────┘
```

Fig. 7.2. IBMCACHE installation information.

Part II: Enhancing Disk Performance

```
Disk Cache Main Menu

1. Install disk cache onto drive C:
2. View disk cache settings
3. Change disk cache settings
4. Remove disk cache from drive C:


Use ↑ or ↓ to select. Then p┌─ Information ──────────────┐
Esc=Quit   F1=Help           │                            │
                             │ The IBM disk cache has been installed
                             │ onto fixed disk drive C.   │
                             │                            │
                             │ Press Enter to continue.   │
                             └────────────────────────────┘
```

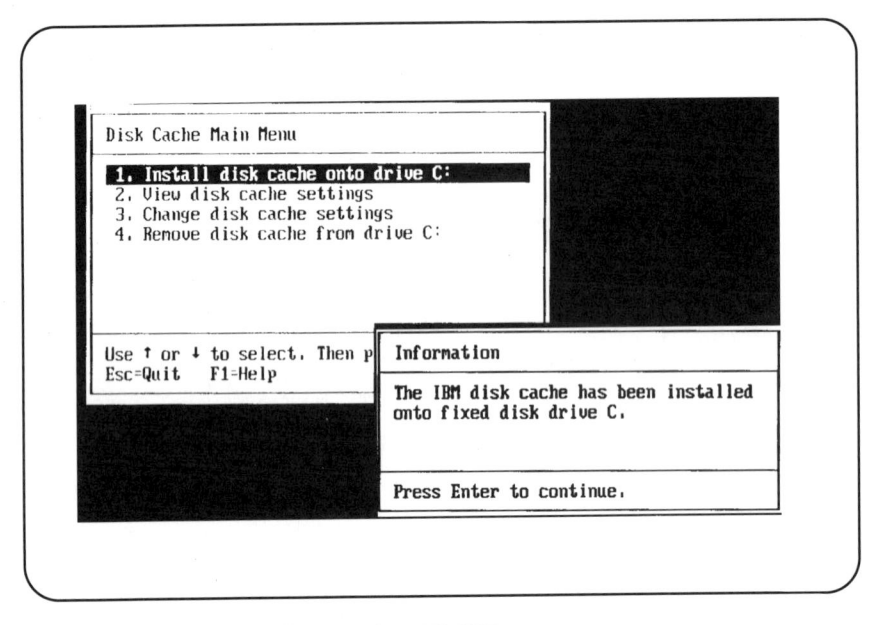

Fig. 7.3. Successful installation of IBMCACHE.

If you have extended memory, move the highlighted bar on the Disk Cache Main Menu screen to option 3, Change Disk Cache Settings, by pressing the down-arrow key twice. Press Enter. The Change Disk Cache Settings screen appears (see fig. 7.4). The following sections explain how to use this screen.

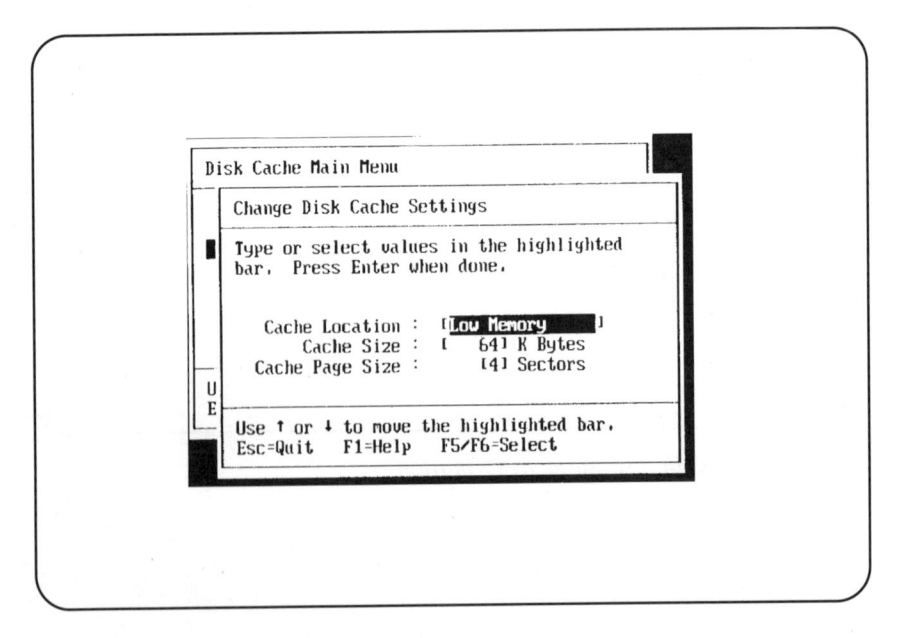

```
Disk Cache Main Menu
┌─ Change Disk Cache Settings ─────────────┐
│                                          │
│ Type or select values in the highlighted │
│ bar. Press Enter when done.              │
│                                          │
│      Cache Location : [Low Memory    ]   │
│          Cache Size : [    64] K Bytes   │
│     Cache Page Size :     [4] Sectors    │
│                                          │
│ Use ↑ or ↓ to move the highlighted bar.  │
│ Esc=Quit   F1=Help    F5/F6=Select       │
└──────────────────────────────────────────┘
```

Fig. 7.4. The Change Disk Cache Settings screen.

Changing Cache Location

Change the first option, Cache Location, from Low Memory to Extended Memory by pressing either the F5 or F6 key. *Low memory* is the area of memory normally set aside for your applications programs and data (the lowest 640K of memory in your computer). *Extended memory* is the memory in your computer above the 1M address space. The area between 640K and 1M is reserved for devices such as the video board, BIOS, and hard disk.

Changing Cache Size

The initial size of the cache is 64K. A computer with 1M of memory has 384K of extended memory. You may want to expand the size of the cache to incorporate all the extended memory, or you may want to save some of the memory for a RAM disk. (The latest computer systems, particularly 386-based systems, may use some extended memory to "shadow" ROM code in faster RAM. If you have a VGA board or other peripherals, some ROM may be mapped into extended memory, which decreases the amount of extended memory that can be used as a cache.)

If you want to change the size of the cache, press the down-arrow key on the Change Disk Cache Settings screen to move to the Cache Size option. Press F5 to reduce the cache size; press F6 to increase the size. Try pressing the F5 and F6 keys to see some of the possible sizes for the cache. Alternatively, you can type the desired cache size.

If you don't use a RAM disk in extended memory, use all the extended memory for the cache by specifying a cache size of 384K. If you use a RAM disk in extended memory, use the leftover memory for the cache: Subtract the size, in kilobytes, of the RAM disk from 384K and use the resulting figure as the size of the cache.

You may notice that the size choices offered when you press F5 or F6 do not match your calculations. If you do not see a number that matches your calculations, simply type the number you want.

Changing Cache Page Size

The final option on the Change Disk Cache Settings screen is Cache Page Size. This option specifies the number of sectors to be read whenever DOS reads any information from disk. Regardless of how many sectors a program requests that DOS read, DOS always reads the number of sectors you specify here (in this respect, the page size is similar to a look-ahead buffer). DOS always reads the minimum amount of sectors required; if you specify a page size larger than what is required, more sectors are read. This strategy is excellent for programs that start at the beginning of a file and read to the end but may not be good for programs that read files randomly.

The starting value for Cache Page Size is 4 sectors. The values 2, 4, and 8 are valid for this option. Do not change this value initially. No single optimum value can be given for the option; you and your programs must determine the best value. If you find the performance of some of your programs declining slightly with the addition of IBMCACHE.SYS, rerun IBMCACHE and change the cache page size to 2. You reduce the number of sectors to be read because your programs are reading files randomly rather than sequentially; DOS is wasting time reading sectors not used by the program.

After you finish changing disk-cache options, press Enter. You see a message stating that the changes you made have been saved (see fig. 7.5). Press Enter again to return to the DOS prompt.

```
Disk Cache Main Menu

 1. Install disk cache onto drive C:
 2. View disk cache settings
 3. Change disk cache settings
 4. Remove disk cache from drive C:



Use ↑ or ↓ to select. Then p┌ Information ─────────────────────┐
Esc=Quit   F1=Help            │                                  │
                              │ The IBM disk cache on fixed disk │
                              │ drive C has been updated with    │
                              │ your changes.                    │
                              ├──────────────────────────────────┤
                              │ Press Enter to continue.         │
                              └──────────────────────────────────┘
```

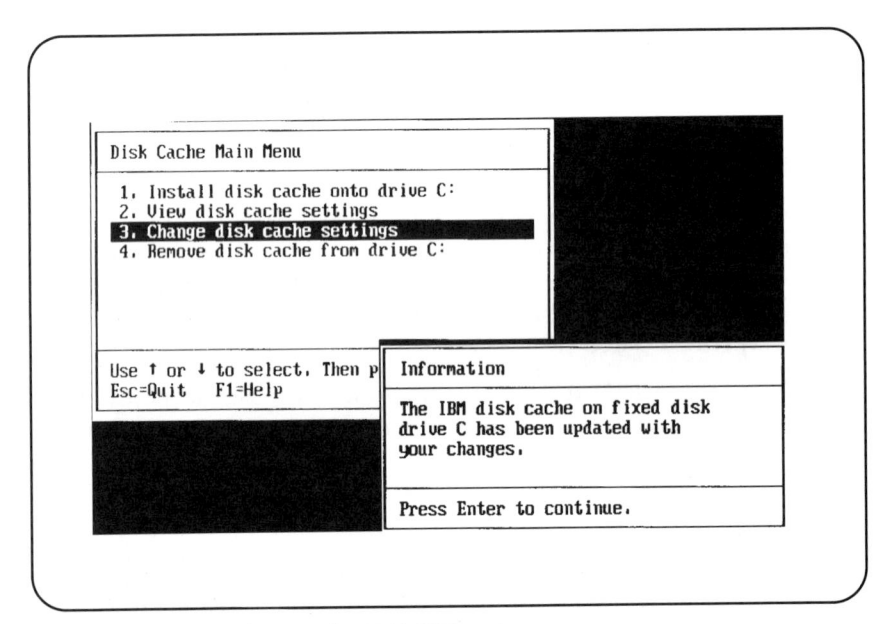

Fig. 7.5. Successful change of IBMCACHE options.

The cache program is activated when you reboot the computer, and the following message is displayed:

```
Disk Cache Version 1.0

Copyright 1987 by IBM Corp.
Allocating Cache Buffers
Cache Initialization Complete
```

As with each of the settings discussed, such as BUFFERS and FASTOPEN, you need to approach selecting a value systematically. Run your benchmarks, change one setting only, and rerun the benchmarks. If performance improvement or degradation occurs, adjust the value again and rerun the benchmarks. Keep changing the value until you get the best performance. Remember, however, to change only one thing at a time.

If you don't see a performance change, either you are not affecting performance or your benchmarks don't test the appropriate feature. Try out your new value for a couple of hours or days. If you see a performance change that was not detected by the benchmarks, create a new benchmark to add to your collection. Using this new benchmark, go back and alter the setting until an optimum value is found.

Note that you see a substantial change in performance by selecting the correct interleave for a hard disk or by defragmenting your files and ordering files regularly. The optimum values for these settings do not change as you alter other DOS settings or add a disk cache. Settings that optimize your use of memory, however, such as BUFFERS and a caching program, depend on each other. The optimum setting for BUFFERS when you're using only BUFFERS is different from the optimum setting for BUFFERS when you're using a disk cache. Learn how each of these settings uses memory and make your choice of values for each, considering their interaction with each other.

Changing IBMCACHE Settings in CONFIG.SYS

If you want to change options after the cache has been installed, you can rerun IBMCACHE or edit the IBMCACHE line in your CONFIG.SYS file (when you installed the cache, the CONFIG.SYS file was altered to include this line). The syntax for the IBMCACHE.SYS program is as follows:

DEVICE = *d:path***IBMCACHE.SYS** *cachesize* /E or /NE /P*sectors*

In this syntax, *d:path*\ is the optional disk drive and path name for the IBMCACHE.SYS program, and *cachesize* is the size of the cache in kilobytes.

The /E and /NE switches designate where the cache is to be placed. /E indicates extended memory, and /NE indicates the 640K of low memory. You can use either switch but not both.

/*Psectors* designates the number of disk sectors that DOS should read at once; *sectors* can be set to 2, 4, or 8. Notice that, unlike many DOS switches, /*Psectors* requires no colon to separate the P from the number of sectors.

Using SMARTDRV.SYS

Microsoft Windows and MS-DOS provide a disk-cache program called SmartDrive. You can use SMARTDRV.SYS rather than IBMCACHE.SYS. No installation program is necessary for SmartDrive. To install this program, you add a directive in CONFIG.SYS. The syntax for installing SMARTDRV.SYS is as follows:

DEVICE = *d:path***SMARTDRV.SYS** *size* */A*

In this syntax, *d:path* is the optional disk drive and path name for SmartDrive, and *size* is an optional parameter that specifies how much memory you want SmartDrive to use. The default size is 256K. If your system doesn't have expanded or extended memory, you may want to specify a smaller size than 256K because not limiting the size of the cache may not leave enough memory for running large programs.

The /A parameter tells SmartDrive to use expanded memory, if available, or to use extended memory as expanded memory. If this switch is not used, SmartDrive uses extended memory.

In general, give a disk-caching program as much memory as possible. Do not, however, make the disk cache so large that it prevents your applications programs from running. A system with only conventional memory has little or no memory to spare for a disk cache, but a system with expanded or extended memory can accommodate a large disk cache. Sizes up to about 2M improve your computer's performance.

A disk cache's performance is optimum when your disk is optimized. Using the correct interleave and keeping files unfragmented help the disk cache work to its full potential. Although you improve performance with a disk cache, you improve performance even more if you provide the disk cache the best performing disk possible.

After you insert SMARTDRV.SYS in CONFIG.SYS and reboot, the cache is activated with a message similar to the following:

```
Microsoft SMARTDrive RAM Cache version x.xx
Cache Size: xxxk in 80286 Extended Memory
```

The version number and cache size vary depending on how SmartDrive was set up.

In all versions of DOS, you must have expanded memory to make use of expanded memory. Expanded memory requires a device driver in your CONFIG.SYS. To use SmartDrive in expanded memory, therefore, you need to install the expanded memory device driver before SMARTDRV.SYS.

For SMARTDRV.SYS to use extended memory in DOS 5, you need to install the extended memory manager HIMEM.SYS. As with the installation of the expanded memory driver, you need to install the memory device driver before the disk cache.

SmartDrive works only on hard disks. Some third-party programs cache floppy disks. You should use this feature with care, however. You typically use a floppy disk only for transferring files because the access time for a floppy disk is many times slower than that of a hard disk.

For example, you may keep all your data files on floppy disks. This system enables you to keep files for particular projects separate, a technique similar to using subdirectories. A small hard disk may not have room for your projects to be stored permanently on its surface. One solution is to keep just applications programs on the hard disk and use floppy disks for storing your data. If you create a subdirectory on your hard disk, copy the files from the floppy disk onto the hard disk at the beginning of the day, use the files all day, and copy the files back onto the floppy at the end of the day, you save a substantial amount of time. This improvement in performance is even better if you are using a disk-caching program.

Because you are using the floppy disk drive only for transferring files, you are not continually taking the same information from the floppy disk, and the disk cache does not have the required information in memory. You frequently change floppy disks in the floppy disk drive and can end up confusing a disk cache because the cache thinks it has the information from a floppy but actually you are requesting information from the next floppy disk.

Disk caches that cache floppy disks are useful, however, on floppy systems with no hard disk. Floppy disk drives in these computers can run applications programs. The disk cache can cache information you need because you are doing more than just transferring files. A disk cache for a floppy-only system may be more economical for improving the floppy-only system than purchasing a new hard disk. Except in extremely unusual situations, however, you do not see the same performance from a floppy disk-caching system as you do from a hard disk.

Applying Your Knowledge

You can improve your hard disk's performance significantly by using some of the features supplied with DOS. Suitable settings for these features vary with the specific computer configuration and the particular mix of applications programs being used. Because computers are used in slightly different ways, some features often are not installed automatically as a part of DOS. Even when a feature is installed automatically, the feature may not be set with an optimum value. Perhaps you have acquired the computer from someone else and, because it works without any problems, have not changed its settings. You may be able to wring some more performance from the system by experimenting with some of the DOS features.

Optimizing your computer's performance is not an instantaneous event. You can set some basic parameters, such as disk interleave, and never touch them again. Some settings depend on other settings, however; if you change one setting, another setting is not at its optimum value. Additionally, your use of the computer may change with time, and you may find that the new program mix you are using requires different system settings.

Most computers don't have sufficient memory. You have to make compromises as to how RAM is used. This division of memory is personal and usually requires different settings for different purposes.

For example, I have three sets of CONFIG.SYS and AUTOEXEC.BAT files on one computer. For me to have this setup, the files cannot all be named CONFIG.SYS and AUTOEXEC.BAT. I use this computer mostly for evaluating software. One set of files is for normal office use and contains things like an electronic Rolodex, a great deal of expanded memory, and a disk cache. Another set enables the computer to use extended memory with a RAM drive, and the third set includes an expanded memory driver.

I use the second two sets of files to evaluate software programs. They don't include any TSRs or extra statements that make my computer work faster. I use these scaled-down sets because the first thing I'm asked when I call technical support for a new program is to remove all TSRs and try again. I have three similar batch files, which copy the configuration files to CONFIG.SYS and AUTOEXEC.BAT. I then reboot to use the new settings. The only set optimized for the computer is the configuration files I use for normal office use. My computer functions normally but not optimally.

A typical situation that benefits from two optimum settings is when you have two distinct modes of operation. Suppose that on Fridays you use 1-2-3 to do your accounts, but the rest of the week you use your computer for CAD. During your testing, you determine that the CAD program works best if you set up a RAM disk to store its overlay files. 1-2-3, however, makes use of expanded memory. You may create two sets of CONFIG.SYS and AUTOEXEC.BAT. Name one set something like CONFIG.CAD and AUTOEXEC.CAD and the other set CONFIG.123 and AUTOEXEC.123. The CAD configuration files should contain a RAMDRIVE device driver, and the 1-2-3-specific configuration sets up expanded memory for 1-2-3's use. Using a batch file, copy CONFIG.CAD and AUTOEXEC.CAD to CONFIG.SYS and AUTOEXEC.BAT, respectively, when you want to run the CAD program. Remember to reboot your computer for the new configuration to be activated.

Even if you think you need only one set of configuration files, because you always do similar tasks on your computer, making copies of your CONFIG.SYS and AUTOEXEC.BAT files before you start making changes is worthwhile. When you see a performance improvement with a new setting, copy this newer configuration file to the backup configuration. With all the testing and timing, you easily can forget what the last setting was that you tried, and mistyping in these files can cause your computer not to run until you correct the error.

You can optimize your computer armed with the knowledge that BUFFERS and disk-caching programs cache data from the disk into memory, FASTOPEN caches directory and file-name information into memory, and a RAM disk is a virtual disk that operates faster than a hard disk.

You should set BUFFERS to 2 if you're using a disk cache. (No setting for BUFFERS results in DOS setting BUFFERS to 10 for most DOS versions.) If you're not using a disk cache, pick a BUFFERS setting appropriate for your hard disk size. Whenever possible, use a disk cache in preference to BUFFERS because the disk cache is more intelligent than BUFFERS and gives you better performance.

Consider your typical use of the computer and whether the program mix involves extensive use of the hard disk, expanded memory, or many files. Compromise between the various settings to suit your program mix. This compromise probably takes both immediate experimentation with your suite of benchmarks as well as longer term evaluation with the settings in normal use.

You can change your CONFIG.SYS or AUTOEXEC.BAT in a few minutes, so don't be afraid to continue refining your settings over a period of time. If you always have a backup copy of CONFIG.SYS and AUTOEXEC.BAT and a system floppy disk, you are able to recover from any incorrect settings you make in tailoring your computer. Ideally, you should keep a current copy of CONFIG.SYS and AUTOEXEC.BAT on the spare system floppy disk. You then can boot from this floppy disk and copy the backup configuration files to the erroneous CONFIG.SYS and AUTOEXEC.BAT.

"Caching In" with Control Room

Many sophisticated, third-party caching programs are available. Multisoft's Super PC-Kwik is a dedicated caching program, for example, whereas PC Tools Deluxe includes PC-Cache as one of its utilities.

Part II: Enhancing Disk Performance

This section briefly covers Control Room's disk-caching program. Control Room includes a report of the time you have saved by using its cache. This program sizes your cache to an optimal value for your program mix. Other caching programs may or may not give you more performance.

You install Control Room's disk cache through the Disk menu, shown in figure 7.6.

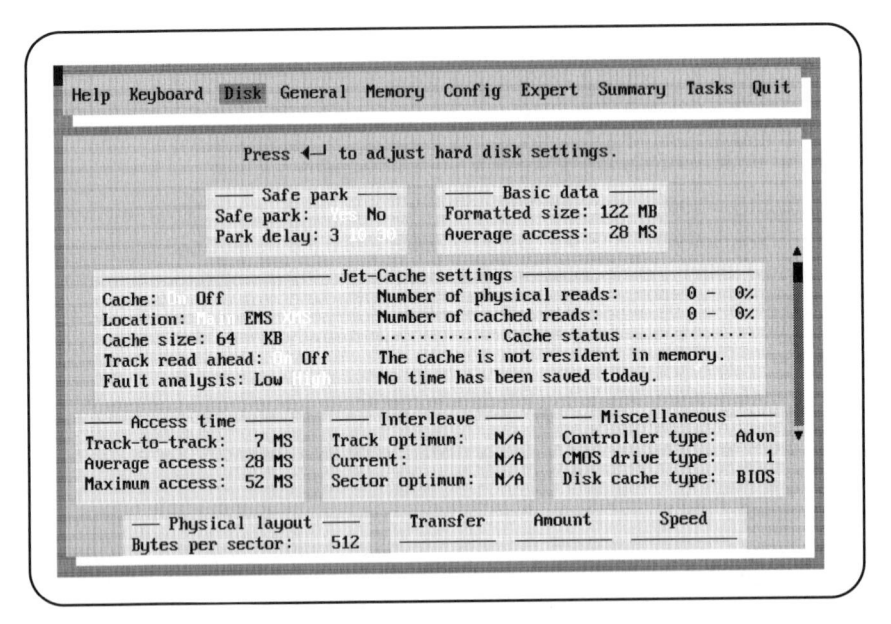

```
Help  Keyboard  Disk  General  Memory  Config  Expert  Summary  Tasks  Quit

              Press ← to adjust hard disk settings.

        ── Safe park ──           ── Basic data ──
        Safe park:    No          Formatted size: 122 MB
        Park delay: 3             Average access: 28 MS

                    ── Jet-Cache settings ──
     Cache:    Off              Number of physical reads:   0 -  0%
     Location:     EMS          Number of cached reads:     0 -  0%
     Cache size: 64   KB        ············ Cache status ············
     Track read ahead:    Off   The cache is not resident in memory.
     Fault analysis: Low        No time has been saved today.

      ── Access time ──       ── Interleave ──      ── Miscellaneous ──
     Track-to-track:  7 MS    Track optimum:  N/A   Controller type:  Advn
     Average access: 28 MS    Current:        N/A   CMOS drive type:     1
     Maximum access: 52 MS    Sector optimum: N/A   Disk cache type:  BIOS

        ── Physical layout ──     Transfer      Amount      Speed
        Bytes per sector:    512
```

Fig. 7.6. Installing the disk cache with the Disk menu.

Point to the Cache option when it's set to On and press the mouse button to select the cache. Next, choose the individual settings, such as the type of memory to be used, size, and read-ahead cache. When you exit Control Room, the appropriate setting in your AUTOEXEC.BAT is made. Rebooting the computer activates the cache.

You can appreciate the effect of four different settings by running benchmark tests. Each setting is chosen, the computer rebooted, and one of my word processing benchmarks run. Although only a few seconds are saved during the time taken to run one benchmark, saving a couple of seconds every minute adds up during the course of a day.

The first test setting is shown in figure 7.7. The 64K cache is located in expanded memory. No other settings are chosen. Only 3 percent of the word processor's read requests are taken from the cache rather than from the disk itself. A total of 1 second is saved. As you can see, programs read from the disk a large number of times. In only a minute, more than 5,000 read requests are made to DOS.

Chapter 7: Improving Disk Performance

Fig. 7.7. The first test setting.

Next, the size of the cache is increased to 1M. Again, no other changes are made to the settings. The computer is rebooted, and the benchmark is rerun. In this case, 42 percent of the disk reads are read from the cache instead of from the disk itself (see fig. 7.8). This increase of cache to 1M saves a substantial 20 seconds.

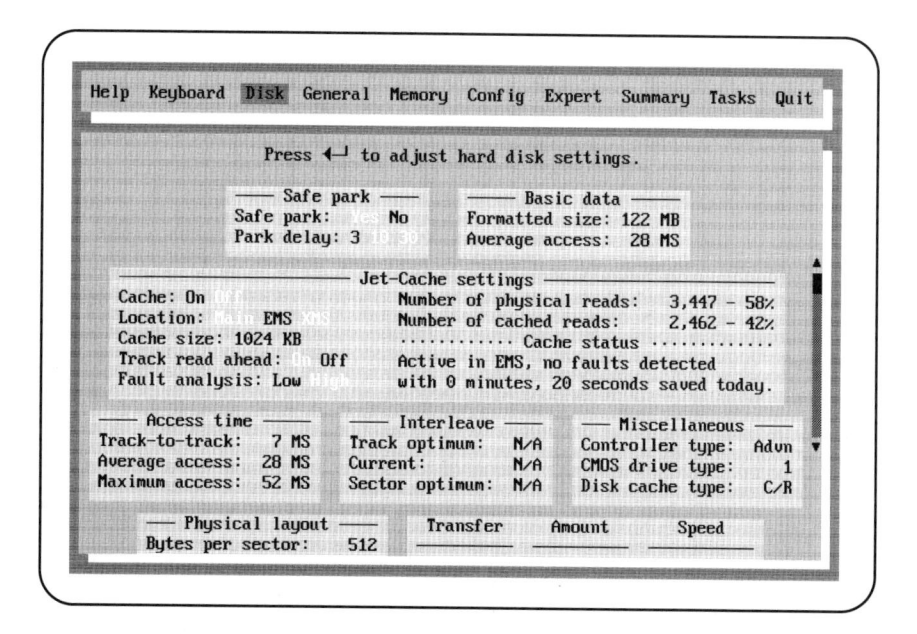

Fig. 7.8. Disk reading from cache 42 percent of the time.

Part II: Enhancing Disk Performance

The settings are changed again to include the Track Read Ahead setting, which is the same as a look-ahead buffer. After the computer is rebooted, the benchmarks are run again. As figure 7.9 shows, 25 seconds are saved with 53 percent of the read requests being satisfied with the cache contents. The settings are changed once again to increase the fault detection process. As shown in figure 7.10, this new setting does not degrade the performance.

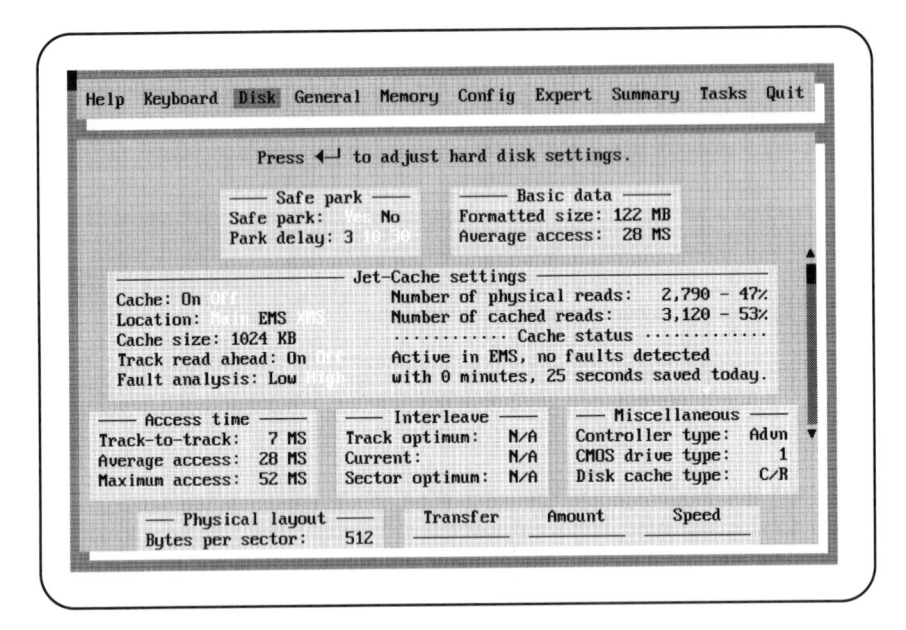

Fig. 7.9. Including the Track Read Ahead setting.

The results of Control Room clearly show the speed improvement gained from a disk cache. Using Control Room's advanced look-ahead feature further improves the disk cache. You should note, however, that the benchmark most used in this example reads files sequentially. This type of benchmark favors caches because the next piece of data requested is available in the cache. If you use a benchmark that accesses the disk randomly, you do not see such dramatic improvements. Your particular program mix may include using a higher proportion of random reading than my benchmark shows. During the course of a typical computing session, however, you are unlikely to use more random than sequential reads. Consequently, the improvement in performance because of a disk cache's sequential read requests probably more than compensates for any degradation as a result of any random reading requests.

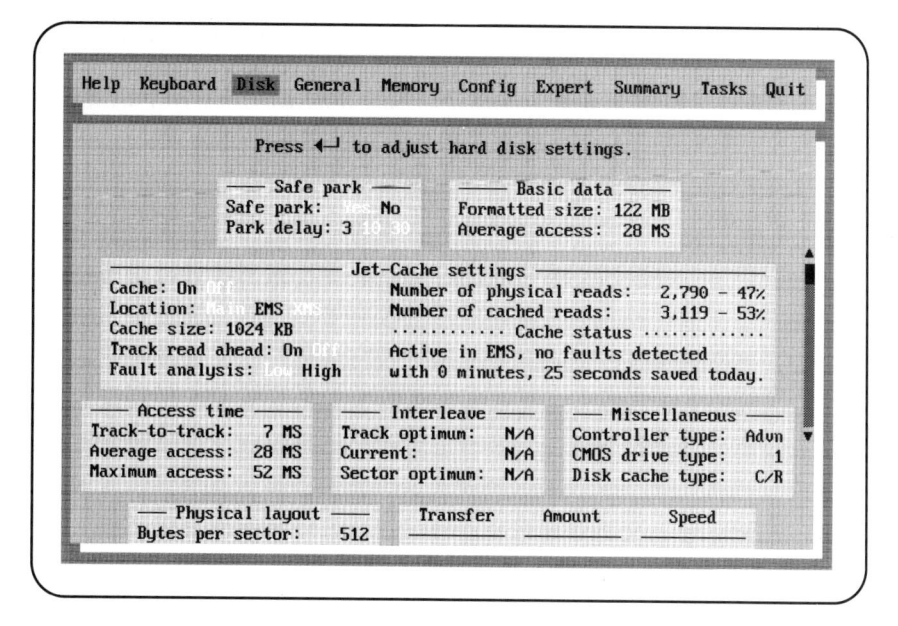

Fig. 7.10. Increasing the fault detection process.

Chapter Summary

DOS includes settings that improve the computer's performance by altering the way DOS collects data from the disk. BUFFERS collects data a whole sector at once, regardless of the size requested by the program. FASTOPEN stores the names of recently used files and directories, speeding DOS's search for a requested file.

Disk-caching programs, such as SmartDrive and IBMCACHE, act like sophisticated buffers. They recycle their reserved area of memory by discarding the least *frequently used* rather than the oldest or least *recently accessed* portion of memory. Look-ahead features (found in most disk caches and the DOS 4 and 5 BUFFERS directive) read even more information from the disk than requested, thereby increasing the chance that the next piece of requested information is already in memory.

You need to analyze your specific use of the computer to determine optimum settings for BUFFERS, FASTOPEN, and a disk cache. If you are using a disk cache, your BUFFERS setting should be low because it competes with a disk cache. Make the disk cache as large as possible (up to about 2M).

If you are using expanded memory with your particular program mix, however, you may want to assign more memory to expanded memory rather than to a disk cache. You need to run your benchmarks to determine the best arrangement of the various settings that use the same memory.

For very specific purposes, a RAM disk may be preferable to a disk cache. For most situations, however, the safety of a disk cache is preferable to a RAM disk. A disk cache automatically writes changed data to the hard disk, whereas files must be copied explicitly from the volatile RAM disk to the hard disk.

Part III

Managing Memory Resources

Includes

**Using Device Drivers
Stretching Your Resources
Regaining Base Memory
Using the Processor's Power
Improving the Operating System**

Using Device Drivers

8

Most advanced users make use of device drivers to enhance their computers. Device drivers expand DOS's functionality by permitting the addition of extra hardware devices, such as external disk drives, software performance enhancers, such as disk caches, and user interface enhancers, such as ANSI.SYS.

This chapter covers some of the most commonly used device drivers and how best to use them in conjunction with each other. Some of these device drivers are supplied as part of DOS; many are supplied with the hardware or as third-party products. Although they all work in isolation (assuming that they're from a reputable manufacturer), problems tend to occur when device drivers from different sources are used.

DEVICE Directives in CONFIG.SYS

The *device driver* is the low-level software responsible for communicating commands and user data from DOS to the device and for relaying device information and user data from the device to DOS. To use a device driver, you must enter a configuration command that identifies the file containing the driver. This command is placed in the CONFIG.SYS file.

You easily can make changes in CONFIG.SYS by using a text editor. Doing so, however, is potentially dangerous. Remember that when you boot the computer, DOS looks for the CONFIG.SYS file right away. If a mistake exists in CONFIG.SYS, perhaps because of a typing error or conflicting device drivers, the computer does not boot. Before adding or changing the CONFIG.SYS, make sure that you have a spare floppy disk with a working CONFIG.SYS. This backup copy doesn't have to include a complete configuration file with all its extra system optimizing tricks. The disk needs just the basic CONFIG.SYS and AUTOEXEC.BAT directives that enable you to access the text editor to change the offending CONFIG.SYS on your normal boot disk.

As explained in Chapter 2, the IO.SYS file of DOS provides device drivers for normal, built-in computer devices. One of DOS's strengths, however, is its capacity to use a wide variety of devices, many of which did not exist when the IBM PC was introduced. DOS can use these different devices by installing device drivers into the system RAM at boot time. The CONFIG.SYS file contains DEVICE directives that load the driver into memory and modify the interrupt vector table as necessary. The CPU then can communicate with the device as if the device was always a standard part of the PC. Occasionally, device drivers are installed externally to the CONFIG.SYS file, but this situation is unusual.

DOS does not place many restrictions on the CONFIG.SYS file. It is a text file that contains a series of commands related to the system's configuration. DOS doesn't care what order the information is in. For example, you can load a couple of device drivers, set FILES, load another device driver, and then set BUFFERS. DOS takes each line in CONFIG.SYS in turn and executes the instructions on that line. You don't have to group the lines together according to type. You don't have to put all the device drivers next to each other, for example. You should pay special attention to their order, however, so the computer behaves in a predictable manner. The individual devices and some of the DOS commands in CONFIG.SYS are affected by their loading sequence as they appear in CONFIG.SYS. In some cases, DOS and your software are not affected by the order; in other cases, however, the order can affect how you use the computer. In certain cases, the device driver or system simply does not work if the directives are out of order.

DOS executes each line of the CONFIG.SYS in order. DOS loads and installs the device driver listed first in CONFIG.SYS, then loads and installs the second device driver, and so on, until all lines in CONFIG.SYS are executed. If a specific device driver needs to be loaded before another, the affected DEVICE directives are order-sensitive.

While adding or changing CONFIG.SYS, be alert. You can identify the latest change that causes the computer to lock up—probably due to a conflict with another DEVICE directive. Whenever possible, run only one device driver at a time and then check whether it works with other device drivers.

When modifying CONFIG.SYS, you don't have to delete the DEVICE directives you don't want to install at that time. Temporarily remove them from CONFIG.SYS by placing a REM (*remark*) statement at the front of the line. DOS 3.3 and later versions ignore any line that begins with REM. Depending on the DOS version, you may see the error message `Unrecognized command in CONFIG.SYS`. This message does not cause problems; you can ignore it. Thus, you don't have to retype long directives and hope that you have remembered how the line should be written.

To save memory, for example, I remark out my scanner device driver except when I actually am going to use the scanner. I don't have to drag out the scanner's manual when I want to reinstall the scanner; I just remove the REM, and all the appropriate switches are still there. I reboot the computer, activate my scanner, and then add the REM back into the CONFIG.SYS after I finish using the scanner.

As Chapter 2 explains, devices are either character or block devices. *Character devices*, devices that transfer data between the device and the CPU one character at a time, include the system console (CON), serial ports (AUX or COM*x*), clock (CLK), and printer (PRN or LPT*x*). *Block devices*, devices that exchange data with the CPU in larger chunks than one character at a time, include floppy disks, hard disks, and tape drives.

Ordering of Character Device Drivers

Most character-oriented device drivers do not depend on a certain order. A device driver that controls a printer, the communications port, or a mouse (bus, serial, or mouse port) usually is independent of other device drivers. If a single device driver supplements or replaces a character device, the order of the device drivers generally does not matter.

On the other hand, these device drivers are order-sensitive when the same device is involved in more than one device driver directive. For example, any console driver that utilizes ANSI.SYS usually is order-dependent, and you need to list the DEVICE directives in CONFIG.SYS in the appropriate order. The EGA.SYS driver provided with Microsoft Windows 2.x, for example, must be loaded after ANSI.SYS. If you reverse the order, you lose the features of EGA.SYS. The DEVICE directive for ANSI.SYS must appear before EGA.SYS's DEVICE directive.

Another example of order sensitivity is when you install an external drive in an IBM XT or AT. You incorporate this hardware configuration into the PC by using an expansion board driven by two device drivers installed in CONFIG.SYS. The first device driver, which IBM calls EXDSKBIO.DRV, enables the computer to recognize the hardware adapter. The second device driver, DRIVER.SYS, tells DOS how to set up the disk drive. EXDSKBIO.DRV must be loaded before DRIVER.SYS; otherwise, the drive is unusable. Other external disk drive manufacturers may use different names for their device drivers.

Character device drivers that use extended memory (regardless of their purpose) can be order-dependent. Several extended memory standards exist. IBM's VDISK, for example, allocates extended memory from the lowest available memory location to the highest. Microsoft's RAM disk and disk cache programs (RAMDRIVE and SMARTDRV, respectively), however, allocate extended memory from the highest available memory location to the lowest. Because of these varying standards, you can get unpredictable results when device drivers clash. Each device driver probably works fine in isolation, but when used in combination, two device drivers can cause the computer to lock up because DOS cannot understand the conflicting device drivers.

Another example of order-dependency occurs when you're using the extended memory manager HIMEM.SYS in association with VDISK.SYS. HIMEM.SYS requires the first 64K of extended memory. You can use HIMEM.SYS with VDISK.SYS by loading HIMEM.SYS before VDISK.SYS. HIMEM.SYS hides the first 64K of extended memory from VDISK.SYS. When VDISK.SYS loads, it places itself in the memory location above HIMEM.SYS, and the two coexist.

Some disk caches make prolific use of extended memory. Not all disk caches conform to the same standard, however. Consequently, you may need one particular order in CONFIG.SYS to use a disk cache in association with other devices that use extended memory. In some cases, a disk cache must be loaded before the RAM disk software; otherwise, the cache does not recognize "footprints" of VDISK or RAMDRIVE and inadvertently destroys the RAM disk's data. In other cases, a disk cache must be loaded after VDISK or RAMDRIVE; otherwise, the RAM disk destroys the cache instead.

Each device driver should supply clear information about the areas of memory it's using currently as well as information about which memory locations are available. In many cases, however, each device driver uses its own rules and doesn't adhere to any standard. IBM has an extended memory specification (XMS), which in theory helps programs coexist in the same computer; in many cases, though, the programs do not coexist unless you give the correct program precedence in CONFIG.SYS. (Expanded memory standards are well established, and most programs conform to a known standard.)

However, you do get memory conflicts when using expanded memory managers. Expanded memory is an extension of the PC standard. Additional memory is mapped into the microprocessor's 1M of addressable memory one page at a time. This memory mapping requires a device driver, typically called an *expanded memory manager*. Because expanded memory doesn't actually exist until the memory manager directs the mapping, the memory manager must be loaded before other device drivers can use expanded memory. If you want to use an expanded memory RAM disk or disk cache, for example, the DEVICE directive for the expanded memory board must appear before the directive that loads the RAM disk or disk cache.

On 386-based computers, the situation can be even more complex. These systems may use a 386 memory manager, which makes use of the advanced 386 microprocessor features in its device driver for managing memory. Chapters 11 and 12 discuss in detail memory managers for the 80286 and 80386.

The following sections provide an example of the potential complexity encountered when you're using a more sophisticated computer. If you are using PC DOS 4 and a 386 computer, the IBM 386 extended-memory control program, XMAEM.SYS, must be loaded before the expanded memory manager, XMA2EMS.SYS, is loaded. Otherwise, XMA2EMS does not recognize that the 386 can use extended memory as expanded memory.

Ordering of Block Device Drivers

Block device drivers can be installed in any order; however, you may not get the desired results from a random order. Block devices are assigned a logical drive letter by DOS when they are installed. When DOS installs a device, the device is assigned the next available drive letter. DOS assigns the names A and B to floppy disk drives. The first hard disk (or disk partition) is designated drive C, the second is designated drive D, and so on.

The drivers for these devices are built into DOS and do not need CONFIG.SYS DEVICE directives. Devices having DOS internal device drivers are constant. You are unlikely to change the drives, and consequently the drive letters assigned remain the same even if you change CONFIG.SYS.

You may have other drives (block devices) installed, however, that require a device driver directive. These drives are affected by the directive's order in CONFIG.SYS because they are assigned a different drive letter depending on that sequence. If you change the sequence of block device driver directives in your CONFIG.SYS, DOS assigns devices different drive letters.

Typical examples of this more transient type of block device include RAM disks, logically remapped drives, tape drives, and CD-ROM drives.

Suppose that you use VDISK.SYS and DRIVER.SYS and that your system has two hard disk partitions, making the current in-use drive names A through D. If VDISK comes first in the CONFIG.SYS file, VDISK gets the next available drive letter, E. The logical drive indicated by DRIVER.SYS receives F. Reverse the order of the directives in CONFIG.SYS and reboot. The logical drive is assigned E and the RAM disk drive F. With this last arrangement, if your batch file or programs expect the RAM disk to be drive E, problems arise.

Ordering Approaches in General

When you add a DEVICE directive to CONFIG.SYS, examine the product's documentation. Your system can contain some unrelated peripheral or software that does not work with the new device driver. Look in the documentation for references to both order dependencies and conflicts. Also, for any product you consider buying, ask the manufacturer whether any known conflicts exist with your existing device drivers.

A product's documentation usually states any known dependencies—whether another driver must appear before or after this driver—or conflicts—whether you shouldn't use this driver with some other driver. An installation program or batch file, when either is provided, also can give clues. Additionally, check the READ.ME file on the installation floppy disk for further device-specific information. Often, this important ordering information is in this file or buried in the manual's appendixes.

In most cases, when the documentation states that its device driver must be first or last, its DEVICE line must appear before all other DEVICE directives (first) or after all other DEVICE directives (last). You usually can place all non-DEVICE directives before or after the DEVICE directives and can intersperse the other directives between the DEVICE statements.

Be organized to minimize unexplainable conflicts between devices. First, arrange your CONFIG.SYS. Group DRIVE directives by device type. Put all console-related DEVICE statements together; put disk-drive-related directives together; and put memory-related device drivers together. This procedure helps locate any conflicts when you later add a new device.

Extend this organization by using remarks in CONFIG.SYS. If you discover that loading device A before device B prevents a conflict, write a REM statement that reminds you of this fact:

REM Device A must be loaded before device B.

DOS ignores this REM statement, but you see it when you edit CONFIG.SYS's contents at a later date. Add remarks to identify devices that have strange names or to comment on a device's drive letter assignment. When optimizing the computer, you easily can remember why you are changing something and what effect the change produces. Three months later, however, installing a new disk-cache program is easier when you're guided by helpful remarks.

When you add a new DEVICE directive, the surrounding group provides a reminder to question any dependencies or conflicts. Also, by keeping interdependent device drivers together, you are less likely to forget the dependency and inadvertently reverse the DEVICE lines when you edit your CONFIG.SYS.

In addition, by keeping block device drivers together and adding a new device driver to the end of the group, you preserve the operating order of disk drive letter assignments and reduce program and batch file maintenance. Because the new block device gets a new letter not used by another drive, you needn't worry about changing program or batch files that use a specific disk drive name.

If your batch files and programs depend on drive E to be the RAM disk, for example, add the DEVICE line for a new block device after the RAM disk directive. The RAM disk remains as drive E, and you do not need to edit the batch file or reinstall programs.

Note that when you add a new block device, be aware of any SUBST commands used at the command prompt or in batch files. The substitution of a drive letter for a subdirectory name occurs after DOS has loaded all CONFIG.SYS devices. When you add an additional device, the next available drive letter for use by the SUBST command has changed.

I keep the files for each of my projects in a separate subdirectory on my hard disk, for example. These subdirectories frequently have long path names. I use the SUBST command to assign them a drive letter so I don't have to type the long path name. When I finish a project, I change the SUBST command to the next project's subdirectory. After adding a second hard disk to my computer, I had to change the SUBST drive letter because the new hard disk was assigned a drive letter by DOS during the boot process before my SUBST could take effect.

Consider two exceptions to these organizational guidelines. First, if two device drivers are order-dependent but are of different types, group them together instead of separating them strictly by type. Second, if you want a new device to take the logical drive letter assigned to another device, change the order of the device driver directives rather than add the new driver to the end of the list.

Place your device drivers in subdirectories instead of placing them all in the root directory. Removing as many files as possible from the root directory is good practice. Remember to put the full drive and path name to the device drivers in the relevant CONFIG.SYS line. The only files that should be in the root directory are those used before DOS has the path established, such as CONFIG.SYS and AUTOEXEC.BAT. DOS can find the device drivers by using the full path name listed in the device driver directive.

Put the device drivers supplied by DOS into the DOS subdirectory and put all other device drivers in another subdirectory. This practice keeps all DOS files together but doesn't mix other files not supplied by DOS in the same directory. DOS-supplied device drivers include ANSI.SYS, DRIVER.SYS, and RAMDRIVE.SYS.

Keep all other device drivers, however, in a separate subdirectory. A good, meaningful name for this subdirectory may be DRIVERS. The easiest location for this subdirectory is either \DRIVERS, which is a subdirectory of the root, or a subdirectory of your main utility directory, such as \UTIL\DRIVERS.

The reason for this placement is threefold. First, maintenance is easier using this scheme. You quickly can replace all old DOS device drivers with new DOS device drivers when you upgrade DOS.

Second, you know exactly where to copy or move the device driver (into \DRIVERS or \UTIL\DRIVERS) when installing a program. Keeping the device drivers in a separate directory also reminds you that all device drivers provided by a program may not be needed. When you install a program, you often copy the entire contents of the installation floppy disk to a subdirectory. When copying or moving the device driver files, you are reminded to copy or move only useful files and delete ones not applicable to your setup. For example, many programs supply a large number of display device drivers—one to drive a CGA, another to drive an EGA, and a third to drive a high-resolution Targa board, for example. If you have a CGA only, why keep the other device drivers on the hard disk? If, at another time, you upgrade the monitor, you can copy the required device driver from the original program floppy disks.

Third, editing the DEVICE directives is easier. You have only two path locations to specify: \DOS and \DRIVERS (or the appropriate names for your subdirectory setup). DOS-provided drivers reside in \DOS; all others reside in \DRIVERS. This scheme is easy to use and remember.

Use a full file name in the DEVICE directive. Don't load ANSI.SYS through the directive \DOS\ANSI.SYS, for example. Instead, use C:\DOS\ANSI.SYS for a hard disk or A:\ANSI.SYS for a floppy disk.

Because the files are not in the root directory, you must give the path name so that DOS can find the files. The reason to give a drive name is less obvious. By using drive and path names, you can copy the hard disk's CONFIG.SYS file to a bootable floppy disk and use that floppy disk without changes, which helps when you are trying to optimize the computer by means of a variety of settings. An emergency floppy disk that contains the same file as the one on your hard disk is a good "insurance policy" when you unwittingly create a CONFIG.SYS that hangs up the computer.

Interaction between CONFIG.SYS Directives

The CONFIG.SYS file is used for all features that need to alter the function of IO.SYS during boot time. Although a major use of CONFIG.SYS is to install extra devices, the file can be used for other modifications to the default DOS function.

The FILES directive, for example, alters the number of files that DOS and, consequently, applications programs can have open (in use) at once. In order to function, many programs require that several files be open at the same time. A word processor, for example, must have at least two files open: the program file and the current document file. In fact, programs often are segmented and have several parts in use at one time. When you install applications programs, they often require a CONFIG.SYS with a FILES directive that allows at least a specific number of files open. This number is often in the 20 to 30 range. You can increase this number to 99. However, doing so causes DOS to use more memory to maintain the status of all those files, and DOS's performance goes down.

Therefore, do not use a higher number for the files' setting than is necessary. Check the programs' manuals for the optimum and minimum settings. Programs do not run properly if you set the value too low. Although some people check this value when they start, not all do, and you can get stuck in the middle of a program without a way to save data if this value is below the minimum. A word processor, for example, may need only 10 files until the spell checker is activated; then the word processor needs 15 files. If you set FILES equal to 10, the program may run fine until you access the spell checker. At this point, the computer locks up because the word processor cannot continue to function without additional files open, and you lose the document.

Some programs set the value high for their own purposes only. Some backup programs, for example, particularly those that back up to floppy disks rather than to tape, set the FILES value at 99 during installation. Although maintaining a large number of open files gives a backup program optimum performance and reduces backup time, this same high value degrades performance for everyday computer use. Accepting a slower performance from your backup program by setting a lower value for FILES keeps normal performance at an optimum.

An alternative to mainstreaming a backup program directive in the primary CONFIG.SYS file is to create a secondary CONFIG.SYS file that has the settings for the backup program. This procedure may be necessary anyway if you run a disk optimizer after the backup program. Disk optimizers must only be run without terminate-and-stay-resident (TSR) programs present. As Chapter 5 discusses, disk optimizers rewrite the FAT and directory structure by reading and writing to the FAT and to the directory at once and circumventing DOS. A TSR can disrupt this process, either by giving bad information or by changing information while it's written to the disk. Instead of running the risk of your disk being corrupted, reboot the computer with a CONFIG.SYS and AUTOEXEC.BAT that uses only the bare minimum features when you are going to back up and optimize.

Understanding DRIVPARM and DRIVER.SYS

Although most CONFIG.SYS directives are independent of devices, DRIVPARM is not. DRIVPARM alters the drive parameters for an installed device. The device driver DRIVER.SYS installs a device using certain parameters. DRIVPARM, on the other hand, alters a device's parameters, regardless of whether the device was installed automatically by DOS or through a device driver in CONFIG.SYS. Understanding the difference between these two configuration options enables you to change your computer's configuration to be compatible with another computer.

The CONFIG.SYS directive DRIVPARM and the DOS-provided device driver DRIVER.SYS have many similarities. Both are activated through CONFIG.SYS, and both enhance primarily floppy disk drives. The switches and default values for both, shown in table 8.1, are identical. However, as the next section explains, the assigned drive numbers differ.

Table 8.1
DRIVPARM and DRIVER.SYS
Syntax and Switches

Syntax

DRIVPARM = **/D:ddd** */T:ttt /S:ss /H:hh /F:f /C*

DEVICE = *d:path\\DRIVER.SYS /D:ddd /T:ttt /S:ss /H:hh /F:f /C /N*

Switches

Switch	Description
/D:ddd	For DRIVPARM: Physical drive number from 0-255; mandatory switch; no default value
	For DRIVER.SYS: Physical drive number; 0-127 for floppy disk drives, 128-255 for hard disk drives; 0-based for floppy disks, 128-based for hard disks; mandatory switch; no default value
/T:ttt	Tracks per side; 1-999 (default of 80 tracks)
/S:ss	Number of sectors per track; 1-99 (default of 9 sectors)
/H:hh	Number of heads per disk; 1-99 (default of 2 sides)
/F:f	Device type or form factor (default of 2); the values for the form factor include

Value	Type
0	160-360K floppy disk drive
1	1.2M floppy disk drive
2	720K floppy disk drive
3	8-inch single-density disk drive
4	8-inch double-density disk drive
5	Hard drive
6	Tape drive
7	1.44M floppy and all other disk drives

Switch	Description
/C	Disk changeline hardware supported (no changeline support if switch is omitted)
/N	Used when a disk drive is nonremovable; should not be used with floppy disk drives or external hard disks

Although both DRIVPARM and DRIVER.SYS establish the physical characteristics for the disk drive, only DRIVER.SYS establishes logical characteristics. When you use DRIVER.SYS, DOS assigns the device a new logical drive letter. When you use DRIVPARM, DOS alters the parameters for the specified device and does not add a new drive letter.

DRIVPARM and DRIVER.SYS work intimately with hardware. Although they are useful commands, be careful when using them. Just as you know to exercise caution when using the FORMAT command, you should consider the implications of using DRIVPARM or DRIVER.SYS before rebooting the computer to activate any settings.

If you use incorrect settings, the drive acts erratically or does not format the disks properly. Using the wrong drive number parameter (/D:ddd) or omitting this parameter can cause problems because you are applying new parameters to a different device from the desired one. This error can destroy the FAT or root directory on the incorrectly specified drive. In particular, this destruction occurs when you indicate that the drive has changeline support when the BIOS or drive does not.

Using DRIVPARM with Floppy Disk Drives

Use the DRIVPARM directive to establish the physical formatting characteristics of any floppy disk drive. You primarily use DRIVPARM with drives not originally supported by the PC. For example, 3 1/2-inch disk drives were not supported at first by most IBM PCs and many IBM Personal Computer ATs. DRIVPARM enables you to use a 3 1/2-inch disk drive plugged into the normal floppy disk controller. Without the DRIVPARM setting, DOS and your BIOS think the drive is a 5 1/4-inch drive because that's all they know about.

The entire IBM Personal Computer family was designed to use 5 1/4-inch disk drives. The system ROM BIOS contains the number of heads, tracks, sectors, motor start time, and other information for the supplied floppy disk drive. Many IBM-compatible manufacturers followed IBM's lead in embedding this information in ROM.

Since the advent of the PS/2 systems and laptop computers, more computers need 3 1/2-inch disk drives. However, the ROM BIOS of earlier computers does not accommodate this smaller disk drive size. Newly designed computers supply the 3 1/2-inch drive information in ROM, and the IO.SYS of newer DOS versions (DOS 3.2 and later versions) looks for this information.

Earlier systems, however, need a method of allowing these new drives to work—hence DRIVPARM. Incidentally, the IO.SYS file for each version of PC DOS except Version 3.1 supports a new or changed floppy drive type.

In the last few years, 3 1/2-inch drives have gained in popularity. Equipped with rigid plastic cases and a sliding door that protects the access hole, the smaller floppy disks are less susceptible to damage than the flimsy 5 1/4-inch floppy disks. In many cases, owners have replaced a 360K or 1.2M 5 1/4-inch floppy disk drive with a 720K or 1.44M 3 1/2-inch floppy disk drive. The new drive works properly when reading or writing floppy disks because DOS, starting with Version 3.2, reads the disk parameter block from the floppy disk and knows the proper characteristics (heads, tracks, and sectors) for the drive.

The problem occurs when you're formatting a floppy disk in the previously unsupported disk drive. In most cases, DOS—on reading the ROM BIOS—assumes that the original disk drive type is installed. Although you can install the disk drive type (also called a *form factor*) in the CMOS memory of many AT-compatible systems, many versions of DOS do not use this information. Therefore, you can use the drive for all operations except formatting new floppy disks.

To solve this problem, Microsoft added the DRIVPARM directive. DRIVPARM modifies the drive parameter block. Because the FORMAT command uses the drive parameter block to determine how to format the drive, any DRIVPARM settings are detected and used during the format process.

Use DRIVPARM on replacement or add-on disk drives that connect to the original floppy disk adapter but are not identical to the replaced disk drive. Usually, the disk drives added that require DRIVPARM are 720K or 1.44M 3 1/2-inch drives. After setting the parameter, you can use the disk drive for formatting floppy disks.

Suppose, for example, that you replace the second disk drive on an AT-compatible system with a 720K disk drive. Use the following full syntax for the directive in CONFIG.SYS:

DRIVPARM = /D:1 /F:2 /T:80 /S:9 /H:2 /C

From left to right, the switches tell DOS that the affected drive is the second physical floppy disk unit; has a 720K form factor, 80 tracks, 9 sectors per track, and 2 recording heads; and supports the drive changeline.

Note that the computer's drives are numbered rather than lettered. DOS's drive letter designation refers to a logical drive, not a physical drive. The reason is that you can have multiple partitions on a single hard disk. Each partition is assigned a different drive letter, but each physical disk has only a single number.

DRIVPARM specifies the disk number in a different way from DRIVER.SYS. Arguably, DRIVPARM's numbering scheme is easier. Each disk is numbered in turn; the two floppy disk drives are numbered 0 and 1, respectively. The first hard disk is drive 2, and subsequent block devices are numbered 3 through 255 in sequence. DRIVER.SYS, which this chapter examines later, uses a different numbering scheme with hard disk numbers starting at 128.

The *changeline* support is the floppy disk drive's "door opened" signal. The disk drive can detect when you open the disk drive door or press the ejector button for the floppy disk drive. When DOS (or any disk-caching software) notices the signal, the software presumes that you have changed the floppy disk and either invalidates all buffered information for the drive or demands that the floppy disk be returned to the drive in order to complete writing information. DOS cannot detect whether you actually have changed the floppy disk in the drive. DOS can detect only that the drive door is open (or that the eject button has been pressed). If you close the drive door on the same floppy disk, DOS assumes that the disk has been changed. Also, note that floppy disk drives for the original IBM PC, IBM Personal Computer XT, and compatibles do not have this support.

Specifying each parameter ensures that you are choosing appropriate parameters for the device. Nevertheless, because DRIVPARM and DRIVER.SYS use certain default values, you instead can use the following shorter directive:

DRIVPARM = /D:1 /C

Or you can use the following brief syntax to add a 1.44M disk drive for drive B:

DRIVPARM = /D:1 /F:7 /S:18 /C

Remember that you need only to use the DRIVPARM directive if the computer doesn't already support the installed drive type with the desired parameters.

Keep in mind the different, although closely related, purposes of DRIVPARM and DRIVER.SYS. DRIVPARM is used for defining or altering the parameters of an existing block device. DRIVER.SYS is used for installing and setting the parameters of an additional device. Also, some implementations of MS-DOS do not respect DRIVPARM because of a conflict with the ROM BIOS and DOS's IO.SYS device drivers.

Unfortunately, DRIVPARM does not control your ability to "autoshift" while formatting. To format a 360K floppy disk in a 1.2M drive or a 720K floppy disk in a 1.44M drive, DOS must use a different disk parameter block of the reduced number of both tracks and sectors for 360K floppy disks or of the reduced number of sectors for 720K floppy disks. Setting DRIVPARM does not control this routine. The DOS FORMAT program uses internal system functions to tell the IO.SYS to make this change. To complete the change, the IO.SYS ultimately calls the routines in the ROM BIOS. The DRIVPARM setting is not consulted during this process.

Because of differences in ROM BIOS and DOS implementations made by computer manufacturers, all but a few older versions of DOS implementations can format a 360K floppy disk in a 1.2M disk drive. Not all versions of DOS can format a 720K floppy disk in a 1.44M disk drive. Some implementations of DOS also do not recognize DRIVPARM. FORMAT either aborts or produces 1.2M on the 1.44M drive.

You may wonder why a floppy disk drive that reads and writes files onto floppy disks with differing capacities, such as a 360K floppy disk in a 1.2M disk drive, cannot always format the floppy disk. However, programs that format floppy disks are not the same programs that read from or write to the disk. The problem, when it occurs, usually is related to the actual implementation of DOS you are using. If the DOS supplier hasn't customized the FORMAT command to work with the relevant device using the correct parameters, you cannot format the lower capacity floppy disk. Note that PC DOS is not one of the implementations that has this problem.

If you have this problem, all is not lost. You can use one of four workarounds. The first workaround is to use a different formatting program. Several programs in users'-group libraries and on bulletin boards or time-sharing services (such as CompuServe Information Service and The Source) set the drive parameters and format the floppy disk correctly. Exact file names vary, but FMT720 and FMT144 are popular. Because the parameter setup is important only when you're formatting a floppy disk, this solution is both practical and efficient. If DOS does not recognize DRIVPARM (as in DOS 4) or mishandles DRIVPARM, this remedy is the only solution.

The second workaround is a program that sets the drive parameter block correctly and responds to unrecognized or mishandled DRIVPARMs. One such program, called DRVPARM, is available through some users'-group libraries and on time-sharing services. The switches for DRVPARM are the same as those for DRIVPARM and DRIVER.SYS. A disadvantage with this program is that a floppy disk with the correct parameters must be in the disk drive when DRVPARM runs. In other words, you place a previously formatted floppy disk into the relevant disk drive, and DRVPARM takes some information from the floppy disk for use during the boot process. Consequently, DRVPARM cannot work if you don't have at least one floppy disk formatted to the correct capacity to begin the process. DRVPARM also is not a solution if you are trying to alter the parameters for drive A on a hard disk-based system. You cannot boot from the hard disk because you need to have a floppy disk in drive A for DRVPARM to run. Remember that DOS boots from drive A in preference to the hard disk if you have a floppy disk in drive A at boot time.

The third solution is to have two CONFIG.SYS files—one for the 1.44M setup and one for the 720K setup. Start DOS using the appropriate CONFIG.SYS file.

The fourth workaround is to use DRIVER.SYS to establish the correct parameters with a new logical disk drive. The single physical disk then is addressed as two different logical drive letters. When you want one capacity, you use the first drive letter; when you want the other capacity, you use the second drive letter.

Before you install a 1.44M disk drive, note that all 1.44M disk drives are not alike. If you look at a 1.44M 3 1/2-inch floppy disk (hold the floppy disk face up with the shutter toward you), notice two holes in the floppy disk—one in each of the upper corners. The right hole is the write-protect hole; the left hole is the high-capacity indicator. Many 1.44M disk drives use this latter hole to sense whether a 720K or 1.44M floppy disk is in the drive. IBM does not use the capacity sensor in disk drives; therefore, IBM disk drives and PC DOS ignore the hole.

Some third-party disk drives, however, do use the sensor, but generic MS-DOS does not. Because of these "smart" drives' capacity to determine whether a high-density disk is in place, these drives do not format a 1.44M floppy disk at 720K, and they do not format a 720K floppy disk at the 1.44M capacity. The stumbling block is the disk drive, not DOS. Usually, changing a jumper on the interface board within the floppy disk drive disables the sensor; however, some drives do not offer this option.

Using DRIVER.SYS with Floppy Disk Drives

DRIVER.SYS is an alternative to DRVPARM, but differences between the two CONFIG.SYS directives exist. As covered in the preceding section, DRVPARM alters the parameters of an existing drive, whereas DRIVER.SYS is a device driver that adds an additional logical drive to the computer.

You can use DRIVER.SYS to copy files between similar-sized floppy disks when you have two physically dissimilar disk drives. You can use DRIVER.SYS in place of DRVPARM when DRVPARM does not work, when FORMAT does not work, or when external floppy disk drives are used on some systems.

The syntax for the DRIVER.SYS device driver is shown in table 8.1; the switches are identical to those for DRIVPARM. DRIVER.SYS performs the same functions as DRIVPARM but with one important addition. Each copy of DRIVER.SYS produces a new logical disk drive from the same physical disk drive. The number assigned to physical drives differs between DRIVPARM and DRIVER.SYS.

DRIVER.SYS has an unusual numbering scheme for disk drives. The first floppy disk drive is number 0, and the second floppy disk drive is number 1. The first hard disk drive is number 128, and the second hard disk drive is number 129. Any additional hard disk drives are numbered in order from 130 upward.

DOS always has two logical floppy disk drives, even if only one physical drive is installed. When one drive is installed, the name drive A or B references the same disk drive. Therefore, you can copy files between floppy disks by using a command such as **COPY A:MYFILE B:**. DOS knows the same physical disk drive is in use and prompts you during the copying process to place the proper floppy disks in the drive.

If you have two dissimilar physical floppy disk drives (such as a 1.2M and a 1.44M disk drive), copying files directly between two 1.2M (or 360K) 5 1/4-inch floppy disks or between two 1.44M (or 720K) 3 1/2-inch floppy disks is impossible. Because two drives physically are present, A and B reference two different drives. The same command (**COPY A:MYFILE B:**) copies files between a 1.2M floppy disk and a 1.44M floppy disk.

You can use DRIVER.SYS to establish additional logical floppy disk drives from each physical disk drive. You can, therefore, copy files between the media that fit each disk drive. To use the new drive letters, you must change only the COPY command. If you make a new drive letter (E, for example) with DRIVER.SYS and the same parameters as drive A, you copy files between A and E (the same physical disk drive) by using commands of the form **COPY A:MYFILE E:**.

External floppy disk drives on some systems may need DRIVER.SYS. When the drive is connected by an additional expansion board or when two internal floppy disk drives are already in use, DRIVER.SYS usually is required. For example, using an external disk drive on an AT-compatible system requires an additional adapter and an additional device driver to DRIVER.SYS. (IBM calls this driver EXDSKBIO.DRV.) The device driver (EXDSKBIO.DRV or its equivalent) enables the computer to use the disk drive but doesn't inform DOS of the specific parameters for the drive. In this case, you must use DRIVER.SYS to inform DOS, so you should load DRIVER.SYS before EXDSKBIO.DRV.

> *Note:* Not all computers that use external disk drives require DRIVER.SYS. You don't need DRIVER.SYS, for example, when you add an external disk drive to a PS/2 that has a single internal drive. The PS/2's ROM BIOS and PC DOS's BIOS recognize the different drive types and can handle a single external drive added to a single floppy system. This type of external disk drive is addressed as drive B because it takes the drive B position in the computer even though the portion of the disk drive that actually holds the floppy disk is separate from the system unit.

To establish another logical disk drive from the same physical disk drive, use DEVICE = DRIVER.SYS once for each additional logical drive. To establish another logical drive for a 1.44M disk drive B, for example, use the following command (assuming that DRIVER.SYS is located in C:\DOS):

DEVICE = C:\DOS\DRIVER.SYS = /D:1 /F:7 /S:18 /C

DOS assigns the next available disk drive letter to the logical device. On a two-hard-disk partition system, this line assigns the name E to the drive. Therefore, to copy MYFILE between 1.44M (or 720K) floppy disks, you use the command **COPY B:MYFILE E:**.

Unlike other device drivers, DRIVER.SYS can be loaded any number of times. You can create as many new logical disk drives as you want. Be sure, however, that the correct physical drive number is specified in each invocation of DRIVER.SYS. The physical drive number has no relationship to the logical drive letter DOS assigns. The difference between physical and logical drives is this: A *physical drive* is a single unit you can hold onto. A *logical drive*, on the other hand, can be a single drive, a partition on a hard disk, or a subdirectory made into a drive using SUBST. Physical drives are given numbers; logical drives are assigned drive letters.

If your version of DOS does not allow formatting at a lower capacity when formatting with DRIVER.SYS (for example, formatting a 720K floppy disk in a 1.44M disk drive), you may be able to use additional copies of DRIVER.SYS and some tricks to solve the problem. One solution is to use the following lines:

DEVICE = C:\DOS\DRIVER.SYS = /D:1 /F:7 /S:18 /C
DEVICE = C:\DOS\DRIVER.SYS = /D:1 /F:7 /S:9 /C

The first line establishes the first additional logical disk drive with the correct parameters for a 1.44M disk drive. The second line establishes an additional logical drive to format a 720K disk drive. These command lines take advantage of DOS's defaults for some parameters and consequently are short. This technique works with some computer and DOS combinations.

Notice that the form factor for both invocations is 7. With most versions of DOS, the form factor must be correct in order for the drive to format with the required recording head write current. If the 7 doesn't work, you may experiment with a form factor of 2 in the second line.

You can use DRIVER.SYS when DRIVPARM doesn't work (because of a faulty DOS-ROM BIOS combination or an incompatible brand of external disk drive) and when you need to copy between like-sized floppy disks (3 1/2-inch or 5 1/4-inch) when the system has dissimilar drives.

The major difference between DRIVPARM and DRIVER.SYS is that DRIVPARM changes the drive in place (the DOS drive name stays the same), and DRIVER.SYS creates a new logical disk drive. DRIVER.SYS displays the letter assigned to the logical disk drive while it loads. You need to remember these drive letter assignments to use them, however.

Because of the way DOS assigns logical drive letters, the new logical drive letter can be several letters later than the original drive letter. DOS assigns new logical drive letters after the last hard disk partition is established. Remember that DOS loads the internal devices before using CONFIG.SYS to add to the configuration. The order assignment happens in the following manner: skip A and B (regardless of the number of physical floppy disk drives), assign each hard disk partition the next drive letter, and then assign others (block device drivers loaded with the DEVICE directive) on a first-come first-assigned basis. The regular name for the floppy disk drive is two to four letters different from its new logical drive name.

Copying files between the physical drive and a new logical drive is an uncommon operation. Although you easily can recall a floppy disk drive with the name A or B, you may not remember a disk drive with the name E, F, or G. To avoid giving the wrong drive name, place a small label on the computer to serve as a quick reminder. Remember to change the label when you change the configuration.

The first-come first-assigned rule means that other DEVICE directives for block device drivers (such as VDISK or RAMDRIVE) either affect or are affected by DRIVER.SYS. If these lines appear before DRIVER.SYS, DRIVER.SYS gets higher letters. If these lines appear after DRIVER.SYS, the other devices get higher letters.

This aspect causes problems only when you add or change CONFIG.SYS. Established drive letter assignments are both predictable and stable. When you change the directive, however, you may need to alter batch files, programs, SET commands, or LASTDRIVE directives to accommodate the new logical disk drives.

If your batch files, SET command, or programs depend on a specific letter for a RAM disk or other block device driver, place DRIVER.SYS directives after these DEVICE directives. Only the new logical floppy disk name changes, not the established names. Therefore, you don't have to change batch files and programs that depend on the established drive letters. Using both the ordering techniques discussed earlier and remarks helps smooth any new installations.

If, for example, you use a RAM disk frequently and one of these unusual formatting drives infrequently, you may prefer to place the RAM disk device driver early in CONFIG.SYS so that it is given the next drive letter after the hard disk.

When you add DRIVER.SYS, however, you still must change any batch file, program, or command that uses the SUBST command with the now-occupied drive letters. You need to alter LASTDRIVE to restore the same number of empty logical drive letters. Doing this maintenance work is easier than changing the order of all DEVICE-loaded drives. The SUBST command is run from the DOS prompt, or in a batch file, after CONFIG.SYS has been loaded. Consequently, all the SUBST drives have to be given new letters when you add an additional DRIVER.SYS device in CONFIG.SYS. You can order all the devices within CONFIG.SYS, but SUBST has to occur after CONFIG.SYS.

Exploring Expanded Memory Device Drivers

Most PC users do not have the absolute latest computer and latest version of DOS to go with it. Millions of PCs have been modified since their original purchase. Purchasing a disk cache to speed up a sluggish hard disk is much less expensive than buying a new computer, for example. However, because the PC wasn't originally designed to do all the things that PCs now can do, you may have to make compromises when you enhance an older computer.

Expanded memory, for example, was not an original feature in the PC. In fact, the original IBM PC was supplied with only 16K of memory, expandable to 64K. IBM did not expect the PC to use 640K of memory, never mind the thought of using megabytes of extra memory.

Manufacturers, such as AST and Quadram, provide memory boards that increase the PC's memory. These manufacturers supply a device driver that links the memory board to the main CPU. However, because boards from different manufacturers work in slightly different ways, the boards require different device drivers.

With the advent of 386-based computers, the number of variations has increased. Many 386-based computers are supplied with memory managers that can divide extended memory installed in the computer into extended and expanded memory. These memory managers also are device drivers. Some computers are supplied with two different device drivers, or you can purchase third-party products such as Qualitas' 386-to-the-MAX.

Each expanded memory manager uses its own syntax. Therefore, you need to use the correct expanded memory manager for your hardware and use the correct syntax for that device driver. This section explains the terms used by these expanded memory managers so you can understand the varying syntaxes more easily. Table 8.2 lists the terms used by expanded memory board manufacturers.

Table 8.2
Expanded Memory Terms

Term	Definition
Page	A 16K piece of expanded memory.
Physical page	A page of physical RAM on the EMS board.
	The location in conventional memory in which a specific EMS logical page is mapped (addressed).
Logical page	The number assigned by the EMS manager to a particular physical 16K page on the EMS board.
Page frame	The starting location in conventional memory (less than 1M of memory) where a 16K page of expanded memory is addressed; a synonym for definition 2 of *physical page*. The frame can designate one page or all contiguous pages.
Handle	A process identification number given to a program and used for grouping logical pages.
Ports	The computer's input and output terminals that are used for controlling the EMS hardware.

Although all expanded memory system (EMS) boards provide the same basic functions, almost every one works differently. The specific software instructions (in the device driver software) differ from board to board. Although rare exceptions exist, as a rule you cannot use an EMS manager designed for a board from one manufacturer with a board from another manufacturer.

An EMS memory board's two principal elements, RAM and bank-switching circuitry, shuffle the physical memory in and out of view of the CPU. The bank-switching circuitry uses I/O ports.

A device signals the CPU that it needs attention by using an interrupt. However, the data and controlling information is moved between the device and CPU through ports. *Ports* act like memory and are 8-bit locations that can be written to or read from. Most EMS boards use the same range of ports, starting at either 258H or 268H. Although EMS boards may use the same range of ports, the specific use of each port differs between the boards. For this reason, you cannot mix and match expanded memory managers. The EMS manager must be written specifically for the expanded memory board. If you use PC DOS 4, for example, you cannot use the XMA2EMS driver unless you use IBM memory boards.

The contradiction is that if you use a 386 processor, you can use the XMAEM.SYS and XMA2EMS.SYS combination. Because the 386 can treat all memory (including extended memory) as expanded memory, no special expanded memory board is required. XMAEM makes any extended memory look like expanded memory, making XMA2EMS usable. Chapter 11 discusses the use of XMAEM.SYS.

As Chapter 3 explains, *expanded memory* is a method of mapping small chunks of memory (called *pages*) into the 1M address space of the 8088. These 16K pages are mapped, one at a time, into a page frame located in a known position in the 1M address space. You can have more than one page frame, but each page frame has to have a position in memory not used by anything else. You cannot place a page frame in memory locations being used by the video display, for example.

As you add more devices to the computer, the number of available positions for expanded memory page frames decreases. Each device reserves its own area of memory, leaving less room for page frames. Most device drivers assume that they have a unique position in memory and cannot detect another device, such as an expanded memory manager, which may be using the same area. If you install more than one device in the same memory position, devices "sharing" that memory may not work. This situation is potentially destructive to data. If one of the devices using the same memory location is a hard disk, for example, you may write to the hard disk a file that never gets there—a file that actually is sent to another device.

When EMS memory and another memory board or hardware adapter conflict, items in EMS memory can be corrupted and the hardware adapter can act strangely. The worst cases occur when a disk cache is in expanded memory or when a disk or network adapter conflicts with EMS memory. In these cases, disk files, including files not used in a session, are corrupted.

You can use any area of memory for expanded memory page frames provided that the area is not already in use. This area includes *low memory*, the area below 640K, which is more commonly used as normal user memory. If the computer has less than 640K, you can use some of the memory on an expanded memory board as a page frame located in low memory. This use, however, is not necessarily the best use of RAM.

Although all programs can use low DOS memory when it is used as normal memory, only programs specially written to use expanded memory can use expanded memory. Therefore, you first should fill up the base 640K of memory space with low DOS memory before placing expanded memory page frames in this area. Doing so makes the memory available for all programs, not just those designed for expanded memory. Many expanded memory boards come with software or jumper settings that enable you to assign some of the RAM normally used for expanded memory pages to fill the unused area of low DOS memory instead. This process is called *backfilling*. You backfill the area from the current top of low DOS memory up to 640K. Any remaining memory on the expanded memory board then is used for expanded memory purposes.

When you first install the EMS manager, knowing what memory addresses an adapter RAM or ROM uses is helpful. Table 8.3 lists some locations used by common adapters. Avoid using these locations for the EMS manager.

When you install an EMS manager, be sure to check all devices before assuming that you have chosen a suitable position. This suggestion applies to every new device you install. You may find, for example, that the expanded memory manager works but the network adapter behaves erratically. Some subtle problems may not appear immediately. Keeping all the documentation and a list of current settings (both jumpers on the board and DEVICE directives in CONFIG.SYS) for each device makes fault finding easier. You can draw a memory map for the computer, as Chapter 2 demonstrates. When you add a device, add it to the map. Juggling several devices from different manufacturers is one of the trickiest aspects of configuring a PC. Taking the time to document serves you well for the future.

The most common locations to use for EMS page frames are D000H (if you are not using a networking board) and C000H (if you are not using an EGA card). Try these locations first and then use other locations or temporarily remove other devices if both fail.

**Table 8.3
Locations Used by Common Adapters**

Summary of Memory Usage

Address	Used By
00000-9FFFF	System RAM
A0000-BFFFF	Display adapter space (see the following)
C0000-DFFFF	Adapter ROM/RAM space (see the following)
E0000-EFFFF	System ROM expansion
F0000-FFFFF	System ROM (including ROM BASIC)
100000-FDFFFF	Extended memory (80X86-based systems)
FE9999-FEFFFF	Reserved (80X86-based systems)
FF0000-FFFFFF	Advanced BIOS ROM space (80X86-based systems)

Display Adapter RAM Use

Address	Used By
B0000-B1000	MDA (Monochrome Display and Printer Adapter)
B8000-BCFFF	CGA (Color Graphics Adapter)
B0000-B7FFF	EGA (Enhanced Color Graphics Adapter) with monochrome monitor
B8000-BFFFF	EGA with non-EGA color monitor
A0000-BFFFF	128K to 256K EGA, all enhanced EGA adapters
A0000-BFFFF	VGA (Video Graphics Array)

Adapter Memory Area

Address	Used By
C0000-C3FFF	EGA BIOS
C4000-C5FFF	No common use
C6000-C6FFF	PGC (Professional Graphics Controller) BIOS
C8000-CBFFF	Hard disk BIOS
CC000-CFFFF	No common use
D0000-D7FFF	Network card BIOS

Don't forget that problems can occur when you change the setup (add a new expansion board or replace a board). Any board with ROM can conflict with an established setup. Therefore, almost any expansion board (other than those that exclusively provide additional RAM) can conflict. Most standard serial, parallel, or game ports or combination boards (with or without memory) do not conflict.

Conflicting boards include specialty floppy disk adapters, any hard disk adapters, all video adapters, all network cards, and some I/O boards—usually those that provide unusual interfaces such as IEEE-488 (GPIB) interfaces or data acquisition functions. When you add one of these boards, you may need to revise the arguments for the EMS manager.

Display and Keyboard Enhancements with ANSI.SYS

ANSI.SYS is a special DOS-supplied device driver that works with the display and keyboard. ANSI.SYS provides capabilities beyond those built into DOS. You can use ANSI.SYS to redefine keyboard definitions, for example, or to change the monitor display colors. Although you don't actually change the ANSI.SYS file, you use directives to enable particular parts of the file to accomplish what you want to do. After the file is activated, it always is ready to respond to your special commands.

After CONFIG.SYS loads ANSI.SYS, all input from the keyboard and output to the screen are routed through ANSI.SYS. If you don't load ANSI.SYS, DOS uses simple, adequate I/O routines built into the DOS kernel to control the keyboard and display. You can communicate with ANSI.SYS by modifying the streams of characters it receives and sends with special strings of characters. All ANSI.SYS commands begin with the escape character that alerts ANSI.SYS to look for one of the special ANSI.SYS directives in the string that immediately follows.

ANSI.SYS has a large variety of commands that enable you to change the console (CON) device. However, many alternatives are available from third parties. These alternatives take several forms: enhanced console drivers, keyboard enhancers, or replacement command processors that include an enhanced console driver. Some of these ANSI.SYS replacements, such as FANSI Console from Hersey Computing, can decrease dramatically the time taken to write to the screen. This quick redrawing of text and graphics can improve the computer's performance. Suppose, for example, that your screen takes a few seconds to be redrawn. With the FANSI Console driver, the same redrawing appears to happen instantaneously.

4DOS is a replacement command processor that enhances the ANSI.SYS features. 4DOS is discussed in Chapter 3.

The considerations for placing ANSI.SYS (or its substitute) in CONFIG.SYS are few. The parameters for ANSI.SYS are not part of the CONFIG.SYS directive. Be aware, however, that you have replaced the display and keyboard device driver normally used by DOS. When a new program doesn't display things properly or when the keyboard behaves strangely, remove ANSI.SYS and try again before blaming the new program. Many implementations of DOS and ANSI.SYS are available, and a program cannot be expected to work with every combination. Remember that an enhanced ANSI.SYS is trying to improve on DOS's standard; in so doing, the enhanced ANSI.SYS actually changes the standard.

For example, I used a third-party ANSI.SYS driver for several years; during that time, I upgraded DOS and WordPerfect several times. I didn't upgrade the ANSI.SYS driver, however, and ultimately DOS and WordPerfect went through changes that were incompatible with ANSI.SYS. I observed strange displays. When I switched from document 1 to 2 in WordPerfect, the status line at the bottom of the screen was in the wrong place and my blinking cursor was not on the right line. After I pressed a key, the letter appeared several lines above the cursor position. Removing the ANSI.SYS driver fixed the problem but reduced the speed at which my display was redrawn.

By knowing what device drivers really are installed in the computer and knowing how you have altered them by adding TSRs or other programs, you can help troubleshoot the computer when you use new programs. A software company's technical support department may not have run up against your particular combination of operating system, TSRs, and device drivers. If you call and say everything works fine until you add device X, you get much better service. In most cases, conflict problems can be traced to a particular device.

PS/2 and Other MCA Computers

The expansion bus used in high-end PS/2 computers is different from the IBM PC and IBM Personal Computer AT expansion bus. As Chapter 1 explains, the Micro Channel Architecture (MCA) is physically and electrically different from Industry Standard Architecture (ISA) or Extended Industry Standard Architecture (EISA) expansion buses. Installing a new physical device into a PS/2 involves an additional configuration step not necessary when installing a similar device in an ISA computer.

First, physically put the new device into an expansion slot and replace the cover. Any expansion board, including additional memory boards, counts as a device. With few exceptions, MCA expansion boards do not have any jumpers or switches to be set before installation. Instead, the board is configured through software.

MCA expansion boards have a unique ID that identifies the type of board, such as memory or disk controller, and indicates the port addresses it is built to use. In many cases, a secondary set of addresses also is supplied. This approach allows more than one of each type of board to be installed in a single computer. This technique gives MCA computers an advantage over ISA computers. A PC with ISA rather than MCA, for example, can have only one ST-506 hard disk adapter.

The PS/2 computer comes with a Reference floppy disk. When you add another device, it may come with an additional floppy disk. You use the Reference floppy disk to add any configuration files supplied with the device. These configuration files can include the following items: configuration information, such as the alternate port addresses that can be used; diagnostics that test the installed board; and error messages displayed, when needed, during the POST.

Using the updated Reference floppy disk, you can configure the new expansion board. Most of the details are handled by the installation program, but the process involves each board being interrogated. Any conflicts are resolved, or you are given the choice of disabling the conflicting devices until the conflict is removed.

This installation process is mandatory, but it goes a long way to reducing the problems involved with adding new devices. The various memory locations used by the devices are checked, and each board's position is established. When the device is added to CONFIG.SYS, you can be fairly certain that no potential conflict exists with the other hardware devices.

Incidentally, the ability to disable adapters can ease maintenance by allowing a form of fault tolerance. Some computers, such as those on a production line, must work constantly. The time involved in replacing a failed memory board is expensive. By installing a spare memory board and disabling it, at a later date you can make a temporary fix when the active memory board fails. You simply disable the faulty board, activate the spare, and continue work. Later, when the production line is down for maintenance, you can replace the defective board.

Device Drivers at the Command Prompt

PCs can use a great variety of devices. Whereas most devices are installed from CONFIG.SYS, some devices can be installed after boot time at the command prompt. For example, you can install most mice either as a device driver in CONFIG.SYS or as a program at the DOS prompt. For infrequently used devices, installing after boot time has advantages.

A device driver installed through CONFIG.SYS normally has either a SYS or DRV file extension. The version of the device driver that is run from the command prompt has a different extension—either COM or EXE. These two files are not interchangeable because they have to operate in different ways.

When you install devices, the device driver occupies some of low DOS memory. If you only use a certain device occasionally, you may be limiting yourself when you install that device through CONFIG.SYS. For example, you may only use a mouse every few weeks when running a drawing program. You can make better use of memory by running the mouse driver program from the command prompt rather than from the device driver directive in CONFIG.SYS.

Choosing where to put the mouse driver is relatively easy. If you use the mouse driver all the time, it goes into CONFIG.SYS; if not, run the DOS command prompt program when you need the mouse driver. Mice commonly are supplied with two versions of the device driver—one for CONFIG.SYS use and one for command prompt use. Other device drivers, such as RAM drives, are supplied only with one version. Most of these products are used in CONFIG.SYS, but some third-party vendors supply alternate programs that can be used at the command prompt.

Some of these third-party products provide advanced features. If you want to optimize your computer, consider the advantages of using a different device driver from the one you have been using. Although a new device driver may cost extra, you can achieve higher efficiency and greater productivity with it.

Suppose that you are involved in designing an order entry system in dBASE. You find that the slowest part of the process is when you sort the database. You don't want to use a RAM disk because you don't trust the operator always to copy the files back to the hard disk. One solution is a RAM disk driver installed at the command prompt as part of the dBASE application. The application creates a RAM disk, copies the files to the RAM disk, sorts the database, copies the files back to the hard disk, and removes the RAM disk—faster than sorting the database on a slow disk. The operator doesn't know a RAM disk was used, cannot accidentally leave files behind, and gets fast sorting routines.

At its most basic level, optimizing the computer can improve your productivity with existing software. However, after you understand the PC's true flexibility, you can use this knowledge to tailor your computer for specific purposes. Although having the latest and best in technology is always nice, judicious use of your existing hardware and software and a minor investment can produce gratifying results.

For example, I still have my original PC purchased in early 1983. The PC has some additions, but I don't use it for most of my work because it has only a CGA display and I use a great deal of CAD programs that need a high-resolution display. However, I use that original PC as my communications computer for calling bulletin boards and on-line services. Because most boards accommodate only 2,400-bps modems, I don't need a high-speed computer to communicate. With just the addition of a good disk cache, I have an optimized computer for communications.

Chapter Summary

Some device drivers are necessary for you to operate your computer; however, many device drivers are optional. With careful planning, you can use additional device drivers—expanded memory managers, RAM disks, display enhancers, or disk caches—to improve the computer's performance.

Keeping your configuration information organized is good practice. This practice involves organizing CONFIG.SYS as well as keeping up-to-date information about all your hardware. Because the computer may not boot if you incorrectly change the CONFIG.SYS file, always keep a spare bootable floppy disk and double-check any changes before rebooting.

If you use a PS/2 computer, you have to do two levels of configuration when you install new devices. First, configure the adapter into the MCA expansion slot with the PS/2 configuration floppy disk and, second, alter the CONFIG.SYS file as on other computers.

The next chapter covers your options if the computer has limited memory. Alternatives to purchasing extra memory boards are examined.

Stretching Your Resources

9

Using your computer involves a variety of compromises. Your computer never seems to have enough speed, memory, or hard disk capacity. As you alter your work habits to make more use of the computer's potential, the limitations start to emerge.

This chapter includes some options available for stretching your resources. These solutions may not give your computer the best performance in terms of speed, but they can help you make the best use of your computer's limited resources for your applications. Many of these solutions are appropriate for a floppy-based PC but also may apply to 486-based computers with many megabytes of memory. The options include optimizing your current resources as well as adding new, relatively low-cost items.

Assessing Your Needs

No matter what your computer's current configuration, you always can optimize your existing resources. You can use the techniques discussed in this book to alter DOS's settings for performance. You can add functionality by writing batch files or using device drivers, such as disk caches or ANSI.SYS console drivers. Few users take advantage of all DOS's features. DOS can be tailored in a variety of ways that are not suitable for all users—hence the reason the extra features such as device drivers and batch files are not an integral part of DOS. But, for a specific individual's use of the computer, certain modifications can improve performance dramatically. By examining your current resources and how you use your computer, you can make the best decisions for optimizing.

If you decide that you're interested in a new utility program, for example, don't forget to look at DOS's alternatives before spending your money. In many situations, you must not only determine that you need "something," but you also have to decide how sophisticated the "something" must be and how much money or time you need to spend to get adequate results.

For example, you may decide that you want a menuing program to streamline your loading of applications programs. A fairly simple set of DOS batch files can meet this basic requirement. If you want the menu to look better, you can use ANSI.SYS to produce some elegant screens to accompany the basic list. Most menuing programs use ANSI.SYS types of commands to draw their screens. The time invested in creating a few batch files may well be worth the economy of not purchasing a menu program.

If you want more than a basic list, however, you have to compare the time needed to create elaborate batch files with the relatively minor cost (fewer than $100) of a menuing program. The commercial programs often include many features that you cannot create with DOS. For example, the commercial program may include a hard disk management program that enables you to examine directories and files without having to type numerous DOS commands.

After you decide to purchase this menuing program, don't forget to look at the competition. You may find that a collection of utilities can give you far more value than a single menuing program can. On the other hand, you don't want to have to pay for utilities you don't need just to get a menuing system.

The ability to make this type of decision separates the intermediate or advanced user from the new user. As you learn more about your computer, both the hardware and the software, you can make better assessments of your current and future needs.

A new user, for example, probably thinks that having to create a few batch files for a menuing system is not an acceptable alternative to buying an easy-to-use menuing program. But a more advanced user is more likely to have specific requirements for a menuing program—for example, requiring that it have a disk manager feature. The more advanced user is also more likely to want more than one item and to have to choose among the various collections of programs or buy several individual programs.

To determine the optimum use of your resources, you must step back and look at the big picture. Instead of having the attitude "Give me something to make starting programs easy," you can make more sophisticated decisions, such as "If I assign two-thirds of my extended memory to a disk cache and one-third to expanded memory, I get the best performance from dBASE and 1-2-3."

The best way to approach optimizing your resources involves knowing what you have and use, what you have and don't use, and what you want to do. Chapter 3 covers how to analyze your current computer features and use. Keep the following suggestions in mind:

- You should have a list of the features included in your computer hardware—features such as the hard disk type, memory types and quantities, and video system.

- You need the computer's current configuration—where each device is located in memory and the settings for each element in your CONFIG.SYS file, such as RAM disks, disk caches, and memory managers.

- You need to know the contents of your AUTOEXEC.BAT file and any other batch files you use regularly.

This analysis shows you all the TSRs and device driver programs that occupy your computer's memory. Another thing to know is how you use the computer. Keeping a log of your activity for a week or two can show you which programs you frequently use and which you rarely, if ever, use.

After you know your current status, you can evaluate your needs. Rearranging your current resources may be all that's required for getting satisfactory performance. If, for example, you have been considering a new hard disk because dBASE sorts so slowly on your existing hardware, even with a disk cache, you may find that using a larger disk cache and a smaller amount of expanded memory fixes the performance bottleneck. You may find that a small investment in a math coprocessor improves your computer's video performance in a CAD program to an extent that you can delay upgrading the video. If you are too focused and examine only a specific performance feature rather than the overall computer needs, you may miss the opportunity to reallocate existing resources effectively.

Making Do with the Bare Minimum of Memory

Although you can make do with any PC, two investments are well worth the money: adding low DOS memory and upgrading your DOS version. If you don't have a full 640K of base memory, you should seriously consider upgrading to 640K if you want to make full use of your computer. The later DOS versions provide additional functionality. Many newer, more powerful applications programs require the full complement of RAM and a later DOS version. However, each new version of DOS is larger than the last, so as you upgrade DOS you are reducing available base memory that your programs can use. DOS 5 is the exception, providing methods to actually reduce low DOS memory occupied.

As covered in Chapter 1, you have a variety of choices for this memory upgrade. You usually can add base memory to the system board itself, a specialized memory board, or a normal expansion board that fits in the typical expansion bus. Although purchasing an expansion board that fits in an 8-bit PC expansion bus may seem like the least expensive option, you will have serious performance degradation if you put this board into a 386-based computer.

If you have to spend money to expand your memory, you should spend the funds wisely. If at all possible, add to the memory located on the main system board first. This step may involve just buying some RAM chips and setting a couple of switches. Alternatively, your computer may use SIMMs (single-in-line memory modules). These small circuit boards contain several RAM chips that plug into a socket on the system board, similar to RAM chips. If you are comfortable with taking off the lid of your computer, adding RAM memory yourself is relatively easy. The biggest problem is reaching the sockets into which you plug the extra RAM. Every PC-compatible computer seems to bury the sockets under the disk drives, and disassembly of the whole computer often is necessary. If you get a dealer to upgrade the memory for you, don't be surprised if the cost includes an hour or two of labor. On some systems, the procedure takes a couple of minutes; on others, the procedure is a major exercise.

If you decide to add memory to the system board or to a specialized memory board supplied or available for your particular manufacturer's computer, you need to buy the right type and speed of memory for your situation. For example, the slower the RAM, the less expensive the cost, but slow RAM may not work in your faster computer.

In 8088 through 286 systems, memory speed is simply a matter of using fast-enough RAM. At system clock speeds of 16 MHz or higher, however, major differences come into play. The RAM used in the 8088, 8086, and 286 is not fast enough for the 386.

You can use two types of RAM in a computer: *dynamic* (abbreviated DRAM) and *static* (abbreviated SRAM). The key differences include size, cost, power consumption, and access time. Dynamic memory is not only physically smaller than static memory but also is less expensive and consumes less power. Many computers use only DRAM, but others use a combination of SRAM and DRAM.

The differences between static and dynamic RAM are significant, but the mechanics of retrieving the data are removed from the user and are handled by the computer itself. If the CPU puts an address onto a static RAM chip, the chip accesses the required memory location and outputs the data onto its data pins. On a dynamic RAM chip, the data is not so readily available. The required data is shuffled around the chip until the data is adjacent to the data pins.

As an analogy, consider a dry-cleaning store. Static RAM is like an ordinary clothes rack. Each item on it is immediately available. The assistant walks up to the item and removes it. Dynamic RAM is like the circular conveyer belts in some dry-cleaning stores. Your clothes are on the rack (equivalent to data being in memory) but are not immediately accessible. The rack is rotated until your clothes are where the assistant can reach them.

The data in dynamic RAM is composed of electrical charges stored in cells on the chip. These charges dissipate with time, and consequently the data has to be refreshed hundreds of times a second to preserve its contents. When the CPU places an address on the chip, the DRAM has to be fully recharged before the data can be read with accuracy. Under many conditions, static memory can offer more information than dynamic memory in the same amount of time.

One of the many advantages of static memory over dynamic memory is a faster access time. Dynamic memory requires a precharging time before its contents are ready. A dynamic RAM whose access time is 10 nanoseconds (ns) requires a precharging time of 90 ns. The result is that the effective access time is 190 ns. Dynamic memory is adequate below 16 MHz. The chips are fast enough, but at 16 MHz or higher, the access time of dynamic memory limits the speed of the CPU.

Static memory does not require precharging time; therefore, the access time of static memory is the true access time. The fastest dynamic memory is in the 60 ns range. The fastest static memory is 15 to 25 ns with silicon chips and 6 ns with a different, but more expensive, chip construction.

Memory is priced by its access time. Memory with slow access time is less expensive than memory with faster access time. Buying memory that is too slow, however, causes hardware failures. Either your computer waits for the data to be retrieved, which results in slower performance, or the computer assumes that the information is ready when it isn't and thus takes incorrect data. You can use chips that are faster than required, but you will spend more money than necessary.

Check your computer manuals for the correct speed to use for your system. Most expansion boards require 150-ns or faster DRAM. At 8 MHz, 120- to 150-ns DRAM is required. At 10 to 12 MHz, 100- to 120-ns DRAM is needed, and at 14 to 16 MHz or faster, 80-ns DRAM or 100-ns SRAM is required. Faster speeds require static column memory or static RAM.

Manufacturers balance performance and cost by using a blend of memory in the computer. Some manufacturers (such as COMPAQ in some of its 386 systems) use memory called *static column memory*, a dynamic memory that looks like static memory. Data in the same area as the previously accessed memory is immediately available, as if the memory was static RAM. For data located a long way from the previously accessed data, the CPU has to shuffle the data around to reach the appropriate part, as if the memory was dynamic RAM. Static columns fall somewhere within all the price and performance differences of static and dynamic memory. Static column RAM can move more information than dynamic memory can in the same amount of time.

Some computers, particularly the newer, faster 386- and 486-based systems, use a small amount of static RAM as a cache in association with dynamic RAM. This hardware cache controller enables the computer to improve the time required for most memory accesses. When data is requested, more than the requested amount is placed into static RAM. If the next request is for data in the static RAM, the data is fetched extremely fast. If not, the dynamic RAM is accessed. Depending on the application you are using, this design will improve memory access performance several times over.

The larger the cache, the faster the system. Computers with cache controllers use caches of somewhere between 64K and 256K. The size is determined by the circuit board design, and you usually cannot change it. You often, however, can set a jumper to disable the cache completely. Disabling the cache may be necessary if conflicts exist with a device driver or memory manager.

The implementation of the cache varies, and the computer performance differs depending on the implementation. If the CPU writes to the cache and slower dynamic memory at the same time (called *write-through*), the CPU may have to wait occasionally for the slower dynamic memory to respond. If the cache controller handles the writing to the dynamic RAM from the cache, the CPU has to wait only for the static RAM to respond. This design gives a performance improvement of approximately 10 percent over the write-through system but requires more sophisticated hardware cache controller circuitry, which increases the original cost of the system.

Some computers can accept more than 640K of memory on the system board, but others, particularly PCs, cannot hold a full complement of RAM. Wherever possible, you should add the full complement of system board RAM before using an expansion board for memory to get the best performance. The CPU can transfer data between RAM on the local bus faster than on the expansion bus. Chapter 1 covers the various bus types. You must use the appropriate type and speed of memory regardless of where you place it in the system.

The computers that do not accommodate a full complement of low DOS memory on the system board require you to use an expansion board to make up the full amount of memory. Your alternatives are to buy a board that supplies only the base memory or buy an expanded (or extended) memory board that can backfill the low DOS memory. The memory boards that supply just base DOS memory are inexpensive but are probably not a wise investment for the future; they have no expansion capabilities. You can purchase most expanded memory boards with only a small amount of memory on them. If you choose carefully, you can pick one supplied with a software program that backfills your low DOS memory to 640K and uses any remaining memory as expanded or extended memory. Although probably more expensive, this solution gives you the opportunity to add more memory later without having to throw away a memory board or give up another expansion slot for another memory board.

After you fill the system board with memory, the next best performance bus is any dedicated memory slots. These slots usually are included only on 386-based computers in which the manufacturer has separated the memory bus from the normal AT-compatible bus. This structure supports compatibility with all the AT expansion boards but increases the memory performance. You should put the full complement of RAM into the specialized memory bus before using the expansion bus to get optimum performance. As an example, one of my 386-based computers accepts only 512K of RAM on its system board. (Newer versions of the same computer have the full complement.) I have a 2M extended memory board in the computer in a specialized 32-bit memory expansion slot. I use Qualitas' 386-to-the-MAX to backfill my DOS memory to 640K and supply me with a 1M disk cache in extended memory and about 896K of expanded memory.

Another 386-based computer in my office doesn't have any memory on the system board and uses a dedicated memory slot for both system board memory and extended memory. For optimum performance, all my memory should be on this board. For economic reasons, however, I have 4M of memory on this 32-bit board and a second 4M of memory on a 16-bit expansion board in the normal AT expansion bus. I need to have more than 4M of memory to run certain CAD programs, but because I run these programs only occasionally, I am willing to take the performance penalty so that I can use an AT board from another computer and not pay for a new board. I get a speed degradation only when I use these large CAD programs. The difference when I start using this slower memory, however, is noticeable and would be annoying if I had to use it daily.

After filling the system board and any dedicated memory expansion slots, you add expanded and extended memory boards. Wherever possible, you should use an expansion board that is the full width of the bus, but you can make do with a board that has a smaller bus width. In an AT bus, for example, you should use 16-bit boards even though PC-style 8-bit boards fit and work. If you already own the 8-bit boards, the price of a new 16-bit board may seem steep. If you have to buy a new board, however, the incremental cost for a 16-bit board is probably worthwhile for performance reasons.

Expanding Memory with Little Expense

The expense involved in adding expanded or extended memory boards may seem excessive. Alternatives are available. If you, for example, want expanded memory so that you can create larger spreadsheets in Lotus 1-2-3, you can split your spreadsheet across several files and include a summary spreadsheet.

Not many programs are limited in capacity by the amount of memory in your computer like 1-2-3 is. Other programs, such as WordPerfect, have a minimum RAM requirement and can make use of additional memory, including expanded memory, but they do not require the extra memory. When these programs need more memory, they can swap various parts between RAM and a disk. In a word processor, for example, only the part of your document on which you are working needs to be in RAM, and you don't use all the features at once, so only the commonly used ones need to be in RAM. When you move to another part of your document, the current part is put on the disk in a temporary file, and the new portion is retrieved from disk.

Using Expanded Memory Emulators

Most people get confused with *expanded* and *extended* memory terminology. This confusion is compounded further by many manufacturers and salespeople who interchange the terms in speech and documentation. When memory expansion first was considered on the PC, a variety of standards emerged, and in some cases these standards are not compatible with existing standards.

The situation with new equipment is now much clearer. Certain standards are accepted by the whole industry, and you more easily can find an expanded memory board or an extended memory board that really is an expanded or extended memory board. If you are using older equipment, however, particularly on a PC, the terminology still is confusing and the standards are not as clearcut. Extended memory boards for PCs are correctly named, in that the address of the memory on these boards is not in the 1M addressing capability of the 8088 microprocessor. But they cannot conform to the extended memory specification (XMS) because you need an 80286 to meet this standard for memory addressing.

On PCs, the extended memory boards formerly were used only as RAM disks or disk caches. An expanded memory board included the memory-management features on the board itself, and you couldn't use an extended memory board as expanded memory and vice versa. You can use some PC extended memory boards for expanded memory, however, through a device driver. The driver may be supplied with the board or from a third party, such as Quarterdeck, which supplies the QRAM product.

You need to be conscious of two things. First, know what you have; second, don't double up the use of memory. If you don't have the specifications for the memory boards you're using, you can spend vast amounts of time trying to determine to which specification they conform and for what you can use them.

If you use a device driver to convert extended memory to expanded memory, avoid using a disk cache or a RAM disk on this converted memory. You will have to wait for the memory to be converted from extended to expanded memory before the disk cache or RAM disk device driver can use the expanded memory. You don't have to suffer this performance penalty if you use the extended memory directly as a disk cache or RAM disk. Identifying this doubling of features, however, requires you to know your computer's resources.

Emulating Expanded Memory with Extended Memory

If you have only extended memory on an 80286-based AT-class computer, you can use an expanded memory emulator with most programs that use expanded memory. These programs simulate many of the functions of expanded memory.

Three LIM-ulators (as they often are nicknamed)—Softbytes from Veritech, Turbo EMS from Lantana Technology Inc., and FLASH EMS from Software Masters—offer a combination of device driver and controlling program. Some extended memory board manufacturers provide a device driver called XEMM.SYS or REXX.SYS that performs the emulation. After being loaded into the computer, the device driver and programs use a combination of DOS memory and extended memory to perform the back-switching functions of expanded memory.

Any one of these programs is not a true substitute for expanded memory. They are emulators, not the real thing. Although these programs give you the additional memory, they do not perform as well as expanded memory boards. The translation involved takes time and precious low DOS memory. The device driver itself occupies about 4K of DOS memory—a minor amount. Unfortunately, because the page frame has to be placed in low DOS memory, however, an additional 16K to 64K of DOS memory is used. With a real expanded memory board, the page frame is addressed in high DOS memory, and the expanded memory board supplies the RAM needed for the page frame.

Expanded memory emulators are slower than expanded memory. On an 8-MHz AT, the time difference between real expanded memory and an emulator is a ratio of about 60 to 1. This 60-to-1 time difference occurs each time the applications program requests a different 16K page of expanded memory.

Depending on the application, however, you may not notice a significant difference in performance. If the applications program does not perform large amounts of page switching, you see little difference. With 1-2-3, the size of your spreadsheet determines the depreciation. Most moderately sized spreadsheets take only a few seconds more to recalculate. Large spreadsheets (500K or more) take about 30 seconds or longer to recalculate.

LIM-ulators for the 80286 also cannot emulate perfectly the EMS specification. This specification enables programs to remap the 16K expanded memory pages into any blank area of the first 1M of memory. In other words, the page frame positions can be in any free area of memory. The 80286 hardware cannot provide this remapping, and the page frame is in a fixed location. On expanded memory boards, this remapping is done on the adapter board. For this reason, two major applications, Microsoft Windows/286 and Javelin, cannot use LIM-ulators. Most other programs, however, can use expanded memory emulators.

Emulating Expanded Memory with Magnetic Storage

Even if you don't have an extended memory board, LIM-ulators can approximate expanded memory by using disk storage on an 8088- or 80286-based computer. The data can be as large as disk storage. FLASH EMS, Softbytes, and Turbo EMS use floppy or hard disk storage space and work on 8088-, 8086-, and 80286-based computers.

The same restrictions that apply when you use extended memory to emulate expanded memory also apply when you use disk storage rather than extended memory. The performance is not as good as when you use an expanded memory board. Additional DOS memory is required to house both the device driver and the page frame, and because the disk storage is not a true emulation, some programs do not run. Remember, the access time of RAM is much lower than that of a hard disk, and a hard disk has a much lower access time than a floppy disk. But, if you want to create that large spreadsheet, for example, an emulator is the only alternative to purchasing additional hardware.

The time difference between using real expanded memory and using a hard disk drive on an AT-class computer to emulate expanded memory is 200 to 1. Using a floppy disk as a substitute for expanded memory inflicts a 1,000-to-1 penalty.

LIM-ulating with a disk drive is strictly a matter of cost versus need versus performance. LIM-ulators are inexpensive. If you need to emulate EMS memory for most programs, LIM-ulators provide a software solution to a hardware limitation. If the performance sacrifice is unacceptable, buy an expanded memory board.

Using All Your Resources

Many of the LIM-ulators can cooperate with all the memory you have in your computer. If you have some expanded memory and some extended memory, you can use it all, along with the disk drive, to get the most expanded memory possible. The LIM-ulators handle the particular memory assignment but use real expanded memory first, then extended memory emulating expanded memory, and finally, if you require even more expanded memory, the disk drive as a substitute for RAM storage.

Keeping Purposes Straight

Choosing among memory's different uses and purposes can be confusing. You must make decisions about using extended and expanded memory, giving up base memory for LIM-ulators, and using disk caches, RAM disks, and DOS's BUFFERS and FASTOPEN settings. You may set up your system in its best configuration and then a few months later decide to add something and make the wrong decision. Although changing the smallest amount of your configuration is easiest, doing so may prove to be the worst decision. Consider, for example, a computer that needs to have expanded memory and is using a LIM-ulator to convert extended memory to expanded memory. If you then want to add a disk cache, you have to balance conflicting requirements. You can add the disk cache into the emulated expanded memory. You can give up some or all of the extended memory being used as expanded memory to load the disk cache, but then you may not have sufficient expanded memory. Neither solution is ideal, but the particular application has an optimum solution.

Running a disk cache, or a RAM disk, in emulated expanded memory is a bad solution. The emulator reduces the performance by a factor of several times, degrading the disk cache's performance unnecessarily. If you reassign some of the extended memory to extended memory rather than the emulator program and then load the disk cache into the extended memory, you do not degrade the disk cache's performance with the emulator.

The amount of memory you leave as extended memory rather than use to emulate expanded memory depends on your applications. If you are using a program such as 1-2-3 that limits the size of the spreadsheet you can load based on the amount of memory available, you have to evaluate your maximum and typical spreadsheet size. If you run large spreadsheets only occasionally, you can set up a special CONFIG.SYS and AUTOEXEC.BAT configuration to give you maximum expanded memory and no disk cache. In more normal use, your CONFIG.SYS and AUTOEXEC.BAT can reserve some extended memory for a disk cache. If you must have the expanded memory all the time, you have to suffer with the hard disk's performance or buy some more memory to hold a disk cache or possibly consider buying a faster hard disk.

Being Organized with Your Storage

You can make the best use of your resources by being organized. Even though putting subdirectories on your floppy disks isn't typical, because floppies don't store so much data that they need a hierarchical structure, you can streamline your use of floppies with some forethought. If you use a hard disk, you need to decide on partitioning and directory organization, have good cleanup policies for unused files, and have a filing system that works for you. You can make use of DOS's features, such as the SUBST command, to assist you further.

If you change your system's configuration frequently and keep changing the logical drive letter assignments, you can end up losing your files if you aren't organized. Having an optimized system doesn't always mean speeding up the computer itself. If you can find ways to operate the computer more rapidly, your productivity will increase even if the computer's speed hasn't changed.

Organizing Your Floppy Disks

If you are running from floppy disks only, consider the best way to organize your disks to suit the tasks you perform. While you are creating your log of your computer's use, make a note of tasks that require much disk swapping. Also note when you are using two floppy disk drives to hold a program and are storing data on the same floppy disk as a program. Even if you use a hard disk, you should keep your floppy disks organized.

Labeling Disks

The most obvious organizational aid for floppies is labeling them. Use the paper labels supplied with the disks and mark clearly the contents of each disk. For floppies that are not labeled with their capacity by the manufacturer, mark the capacity on the label when you format the disk so that you don't mistakenly use a low-density disk as a high-density one.

You can use the following informal procedure, for example. Assume that any floppy disk without a label is unformatted. Any floppy disk with a paper label should have HD written on it if it is high density or nothing if it is low density. A blank label (apart from the HD) signifies an empty formatted disk. When you add data to a disk, write on the paper label and use DOS's LABEL command to add an electronic label. Then, in theory, if the paper label falls off the disk, you still know what the disk is for. Never format a floppy disk without doing a DIR command on it first.

You may want to reserve two floppy disks (one high density and one low density) to use for transferring files between computers. Any files on these two disks can be deleted safely if you always make sure to copy the file from the source onto the transfer disk and off the transfer disk onto the destination computer as part of the process. Avoid having files in only one place—particularly on a transfer disk.

Finding the right floppy disk when 12 identical disks have identical labels is almost like not labeling disks at all. Locating the floppy you want is easiest when you use colored labels, use colored disks, and write significant, easily remembered information on each label. For example, you can use a particular color of label or disk for a specific program. You can use yellow labels for all word processing files, blue for all spreadsheet files, and red for all DOS and utility programs. Or you can use colors to classify the types of files, such as blue for data files, red for program files, green for auxiliary programs, and yellow for backup disks.

Because you easily may forget your color-coding scheme, consider the most important trick for labeling floppies: use a standard, meaningful naming pattern. Most disk labels have little space for writing. Therefore, short, standard information is important. For program disks, write the program name and version number, class of program (such as start-up, main, or auxiliary), and DOS version (if the DOS start-up file or COMMAND.COM is included on the disk). Two examples of meaningful label information are *1-2-3 R3.0 Programs, DOS V4.0* and *WordStar R5 Programs, DOS V3.3*. If you use more than one computer, include the system or DOS brand. If you create duplicate floppy disks, label one *original* and one *backup*. You can keep track of your files more safely that way.

Reducing Disk Swapping

With some planning, you can reduce the amount of disk swapping on a floppy disk. Look carefully at your typical computer use and determine which task requires a great deal of disk swapping. Then decide whether you can reduce this swapping by rearranging files.

For example, you may have a floppy disk containing DOS and all the DOS commands, and a separate disk containing utility programs, such as Norton

Utilities. If you find that you are swapping out the DOS disk, replacing it with the utility disk, running a single utility, and swapping back to the DOS disk, consider moving that utility program onto the DOS disk. You don't have to have *all* the Norton Utilities on the DOS disk—just the ones you use all the time. The Directory Sort program, for example, which sorts the files in a directory by a specified criteria, such as name or date, may be a tool you use regularly.

You may be able to reduce the disk swaps necessary for starting a program—a word processor, for example. Consider making your program disk a bootable floppy disk. You need to put CONFIG.SYS and AUTOEXEC.BAT on the floppy, but this approach may enable you to boot from the floppy disk directly into your word processor without having to boot from a DOS disk, swap to a program disk, and then start the word processor.

With this technique, you also can have different configurations for different programs. If your database program works well with a RAM disk for temporary files, but your word processor works better with expanded memory, put the appropriate CONFIG.SYS and AUTOEXEC.BAT files on the same floppy disk as the program. You then don't have to remember which configuration file goes with which program.

If you keep separate floppy disks for different projects but work on several projects in a day, you can rearrange your filing system. Consider using a single working disk for a day rather than several disks organized by project. You can separate the files by project onto backup disks later. The advantage of this method is that you are not swapping disks frequently during a day, but the disadvantage is that you may need to sort out the files later. For example, you can organize your historical backup files by customer but have a working floppy disk (and two backups) for all your current projects, regardless of the customer. As you complete a project for a customer, you can transfer the finished files onto a historical backup and delete all the temporary files from your working disks.

Another possible way to reduce disk swapping is to use a program's start-up options optimally. Your program may use two floppy disks, for example, and you may have to swap the data disk with the program disk just to access the help function. Perhaps you can do without the help feature and thus need to use only one disk.

Other programs may have several modes of operation. InSet, the screen-capture program, for example, has three modes of operation. Although ostensibly designed to use different amounts of DOS memory, the different versions also are handy to have if you're working on a floppy disk system. If you run one of the small models, it uses less memory because it doesn't enable you to print directly to the printer. A side effect of the smaller model is that the program files are smaller, so you may be able to fit the InSet program on the same floppy disk as the program from which you are trying to capture screens. You then don't have to swap disks all the time.

The documentation supplied with each of your programs explains your options for using a floppy drive system with the program. Because many manufacturers target their products to people with hard disks, however, you may have to search through the appendixes and footnotes carefully. For example, using WordPerfect 5.1 on a dual floppy system is possible if you use the /R and /D start-up options. These options enable you to redirect the temporary files and menu overlays to a different disk drive (such as a RAM disk or your other floppy disk). You then can remove the WordPerfect 2 disk and use the disk drive for your data disk. This helpful information, however, is buried in an appendix of the documentation, under start-up options.

Reserving Enough Room

Remember to keep a reasonable amount of free space on working disks. Programs that generate temporary files for your data are ungracious about full disks. You can lose your current work if your program runs out of disk space. Periodically run CHKDSK or DIR on your floppy disk to see how much space is left. If the disk is nearly full, use another floppy or erase unneeded files.

Always keep a formatted floppy disk or two on hand. If you don't have a spare formatted disk on hand, you may be unable to store your data files because you have run out of room on your disk. You may have to abandon your work to format a disk, in the process losing the work done since you last saved the file. You must have formatted disks ready, for example, when you use BACKUP. Unless you use the /F switch (for DOS 3.3) or use DOS 4 or 5, BACKUP expects only formatted disks. When you run out of disks, you must stop BACKUP and format more disks. Another problem occurs when you save a 1-2-3 worksheet on a disk with insufficient room. When you save a worksheet, 1-2-3 deletes the previous version. If the worksheet has grown and 1-2-3 cannot store the new version, you must save the file to another formatted disk or abandon the new version.

WordPerfect requires a surprising amount of room to save your files. WordPerfect does not delete the previous file version until the new version is saved successfully. You should leave about 1 1/2 times your largest document size free on a disk when using WordPerfect. Although the program prompts you when the disk is full, if you don't follow completely the directions supplied, you can corrupt the data disk and all its contents.

Backing Up Your Floppy Disks

All magnetic media "dies." Floppy disks and hard disks are vulnerable to inadvertent operations (such as you erasing the wrong file) and logical damage (from electronic problems). Although backup procedures for hard disks are fairly obvious, you easily can overlook backing up your floppy disks. Floppy disks are more vulnerable to physical damage and wear than hard disks. You must be sure to back up important disks.

The backup schedule you follow depends on the type of system you use and the work you do. If you keep and back up the working files on your hard disks, you must back up only frequently used program disks and data disks. If you use only a floppy-based system, all your data is on floppy disks. In that case, you must back up all data disks and some program disks.

Use the following questions to judge which floppy disks to back up:

- Can you re-create the information on the disk?
- How difficult will re-creating the information on the disk be?
- How long will re-creating the information on the disk take?

The key to backing up floppy disks is assessing the difficulty of re-creating the information located on each disk. If you cannot re-create the information, back up the disk. If you can re-create the information, decide whether re-creating the disk takes longer than backing it up. If the effort and time to re-create the information is greater than the effort and time to back up, back up the disk.

Data disks that change often require frequent backup. If you work with vital files or files that cannot be recovered, back up frequently—daily, or even twice daily. If you can recover your work within a couple of hours, back up the data disk every couple of days to couple of weeks. Every third day, back up information that is difficult to recover; every couple of weeks, back up information that you can recover easily.

Unless you make extensive configuration changes to program disks, those disks do not require frequent backup. In most cases, one backup copy of your operating program disks may be all you need. Generally, you should back up a program disk after you make modifications. Because working program disks don't change that often, your backup of those disks will be infrequent.

A final note on floppy disks is warranted: If you have a hard disk, use it in preference to the floppies. Remember, the access time for floppy disks is several times longer than that for a hard disk. Saving your working files onto the hard disk is usually quicker than using a floppy disk drive as the initial means of storage, even if you save only to a temporary data directory and then copy all the files onto a floppy disk at the end of your work session.

Partitioning Your Hard Disk

Partitions on hard disks are like subdirectories. The best guidelines for establishing and using partitions and subdirectories are determined by the types of programs you use and the way you use them. You should know the answers to the following basic questions about your programs:

- Do your programs load into memory completely, or do they use overlays or other program files extensively?
- What are the size and number of data files your programs use?
- How do you use the programs and the computer?

Planning Partitions with Your Programs in Mind

The first factor refers to whether your programs load into memory completely or whether they use overlays or other program files. For example, Lotus is a menuing program supplied with 1-2-3 and organized into several independent sections that you can load separately. (Many people run only the 1-2-3 portion until they want to print graphs.) The sections include PrintGraph, 1-2-3, and a translation program. When you use the 1-2-3 or PrintGraph section, the entire portion of the program loads into memory; 1-2-3 or PrintGraph returns to the disk for program parts only when you switch between sections.

WordPerfect and dBASE, on the other hand, use overlays; the entire program does not load into memory. When a program piece is needed, these programs load the overlays into memory. WordPerfect uses overlays moderately; the program loads the pieces only on certain infrequent operations. Because most of its applications use many separately loaded command files, dBASE III Plus is an extreme example of a program that uses both overlays and program files. dBASE is almost as disk-intensive in using its program file as it is in using data files—hence the reason that using a RAM disk to store the dbtemp files is such a performance booster.

The second factor refers to the size and number of data files your programs use. The extremes include accounting or database applications on one side and word processing programs on the other. Accounting or database applications usually have only a few data files (a few to several dozen), but the files can be large, from 100K to 10M and more. Word processing applications usually have many small files (scores to hundreds of 2K to 10K files and some files as large as 100K).

The third and final aspect is how you use the program and the computer. This factor concerns convenience. Is working with one partition or several partitions more convenient?

When planning partitions, know that no one scheme is right for everyone and that every partitioning setup has benefits and drawbacks. In some cases, several or smaller partitions work better; in other cases, one or several large partitions work well. Use your programs, the programs' capabilities, and your files as a guide for planning partitions.

Considering Partition Size

The first limitation on partition size is made by DOS. DOS 3.3 and earlier versions do not recognize partitions larger than 32M. DOS 3.31, 4, and 5 do. Even if you have a later version of DOS, however, your applications program also has to be capable of accepting larger partitions if you want to use large partitions. You may have to upgrade both DOS and your applications program if you want to use partitions larger than 32M.

You can plan the size of your partitions based on the file sizes you are most likely to use. If you read Chapter 4, you may remember that DOS's directory scheme sets aside hard disk space in increments of clusters. A *cluster* is a certain number of 512-byte sectors. The number varies depending on the partition size but is typically 4 or 8. If you use too small or too large a partition, a large cluster size is used so that the FAT can store all the directory and file allocation information.

For all DOS versions, partitions of less than 18M use a cluster size of 4K and not the more typical 2K. DOS 3 assigns 2K clusters to partitions between 18M and its maximum, 32M. DOS 4 assigns 2K clusters to partitions between 18M and 128M. COMPAQ DOS 3.31, however, uses 2K clusters for partitions between 18M and 64M, but 4K clusters for other sizes. Your particular DOS implementation may change from 2K to 4K clusters at a slightly different capacity.

DOS allocates space and moves through large files marginally faster when a larger cluster size is used. For accounting or database applications with large data files (in the hundreds of kilobytes or more), the larger cluster sizes are helpful.

Those of you who use COMPAQ DOS 3.31 or DOS 4 or later may be considering increasing the partition size to use the larger cluster sizes (greater than 64M for DOS 3.31 and greater than 128M for DOS 4). But other factors can outweigh the marginal increase in speed gained by working with larger clusters.

For example, Seagate Technologies specifies one of its 40M products as having an average seek time of 40 milliseconds (ms). If the same disk is divided into two 20M partitions, the average seek time is 28 ms. You thus can reduce your hard disk's average seek time by using multiple partitions correctly. When the activity is isolated to one-half of the disk drive, the mathematical average distance is cut by half. Therefore, the seek time is lower.

Organizing Your Files for Optimal Access Time

No matter how many logical disk drives are on the physical disk drive, however, the disk has only one set of recording heads. If your program and the data it is using are in different partitions of the disk, you do not improve the seek time.

If you can organize your files so that only one logical disk drive is used, the disk heads stay within the partition, and you use the faster access time. Also, if the running program does not use another disk drive frequently, using multiple partitions can be faster.

You need to consider, however, the advantages of separating your programs from your data. Because you don't change your programs frequently but do change the data you generate from them, you can improve your overall productivity by placing the programs on one disk and the data on another. You will be using the full average access time of the disk, but you will reduce the time needed for backup and reduce fragmentation. Keeping your data on one disk and your programs on another can reduce significantly the time needed to back up. Each time you back up your data on a disk containing the programs and data, you are copying the same program files that you copied onto the previous backup disk. By separating the data and program files, you more easily can have separate backup sets for your programs and data. You have to create another backup of the programs only when you upgrade or replace a program.

You can create elaborate backup batch files to do partial backups with DOS and keep your data files separate from the programs. You continually have to update these backups, however, as you alter any portion of your directory structure. Other backup programs usually include a means of defining a product set, but just backing up a whole partition is often easier than risking missing a subdirectory.

The other advantage of separating data from the programs relates to fragmentation. Fragmentation occurs when you delete a file from the disk and DOS then stores in that file's place on disk a larger file than the deleted one. Although the file is used in the same way an unfragmented file is used, you see a performance degradation because DOS has to hunt all over the disk for the various parts of the file. By keeping your programs on one disk partition and the data on another, you can isolate fragmentation to the data disk. Then, by using a defragmenter or by reformatting and recopying all your data files onto the disk, you can remove fragmentation periodically.

Don't make the data partition too small. The worst effects of fragmentation can happen sooner on a small logical drive than on a large logical drive. As you delete and add files, less continuous free space at the end of the disk is available. As this space is consumed, empty spaces at the front of the disk are used. When DOS starts recycling the entire partition looking for free room, your files become more scattered and performance slows.

Note that if you use a disk-caching program, you may see little speed improvement when you confine your disk activity to a single partition at a time. If you don't have a disk cache, however, reorganizing your partitions may help you get a performance improvement.

Some operations that affect an entire partition can be faster or more convenient when they use only one partition; other operations can be faster or more convenient when they use more than one partition. The issue depends partially on processing time and the number of times you need to issue a command.

Considering Your Hardware

Other convenience factors related to your particular hardware resources can dictate partition sizes. If, for example, you have a tape backup unit that can back up only a portion of all the data stored on your hard disk, you may want to make the partitions small enough so that each partition can be saved on a single tape. Suppose, for example, that you have an internal tape backup unit that can take 60M tapes in the computer with a 120M hard disk drive. You can use two 60M partitions so that you can back up while you're away from the computer.

Disk defragmenters, which require anywhere from 15 minutes to several hours to finish their work, can fall into the same category. Because the computer is unusable while the program runs, this task demands no attention from the user. Most people run their defragmenters at night. If you can run the defragmenter from a batch file, you don't care how many partitions are defragmented. You place one command for each drive in the batch file.

If the defragmenter requires attention at the beginning or end of its operation, you cannot run it from a batch file. In that case, running the program once on a one-partition drive defragments all files. Two partitions require two runs of the program. Therefore, the one-partition operation is more convenient.

If you use other types of utility programs, you should consider your partitioning. SpinRite, for example, the hard disk analyzer discussed in detail in Chapter 5, takes such a long time to run at its deepest analysis level that on a large disk several partitions are preferable to a single partition.

Note, however, that certain programs require a single partition in order to operate. Novell NetWare, the networking software program, automatically partitions your hard disk as a single partition when you install the program, overriding any partitions you may have established.

Using Subdirectories

If you have a hard disk or even several hard disks, you can improve your productivity by using an organized directory structure. You should separate your programs from their data files wherever possible and use consistent methods of storing your files. Having a fast system doesn't improve your productivity if you have to search for files all the time.

You can find as many ways to organize your hard disk as you can find hard disks. You have to select a method that works for you and your computer use, but a few general suggestions may inspire you.

Consider keeping a directory for files that you know are going to be temporary. If you're trying out a new utility, for example, copy the files into this subdirectory until you decide how you will be using the new program. Keep any temporary text or graphics files in this directory until they have a permanent home. Then, when you find that you are running out of hard disk space, you may have to look only in a single subdirectory to find files you can delete.

When you upgrade a program, remove the old version of the software after you establish that the new one works satisfactorily. Most software license agreements require you to take this step, but forgetting to do so is easy.

After a program is installed and working properly, see whether you can remove any of its files without detriment. For example, many programs include a large number of screen drivers for the different display standards available. If you don't have the particular display, you probably can remove the file. For example, AutoCAD is supplied with drivers for high-resolution displays such as those from Matrox. If you are running on a VGA, you don't need the Matrox drivers. But be careful. You probably don't want to remove the CGA, EGA, or VGA drivers, because even if you are using a VGA display adapter, the program may use the CGA device driver to perform some functions. You can gain a similar savings by deleting unused printer drivers. If you don't have a laser printer, for example, you don't need the laser printer drivers.

Don't use too much structure on your hard disk, or you will be forever typing long path names. DOS restricts the path name length to 63 characters, and each subdirectory name can be 13 characters in length (8 for the root name, 3 for the extension, 1 for the period, and 1 for the backslash). You can use up this space quickly. You have to balance the need for meaningful directory names with the inconvenience of typing numerous long path names. For example, you save time by naming your DOS directory DOS rather than DOS4.01 to signify the DOS version. Because you have only one version of DOS on a system at a time, the version number in the subdirectory name is superfluous. On the other hand, naming your DOS directory D is probably not wise, because you may confuse it with your dBASE directory or your data subdirectory.

If you find that you're often typing long path names, you probably can find a better way to use your computer. Consider starting your programs with batch files that change into the relevant subdirectories for you.

Look carefully at your applications program because it may include tools to assist you. For example, WordPerfect includes a setup feature in which you specify the names of various directories. You can list the location of keyboard and macro files; main and supplementary thesaurus, spell, and hyphenation files; style files; graphic files; backup files; and document files. If you always edit documents filed in the same directory, you can add its path name to the document option of this screen. When you start the program and prepare to retrieve a file for editing, WordPerfect automatically goes to the correct subdirectory.

If several people use the same system, or you use several different subdirectories regularly, you can use the macro facility of many programs to achieve the same result. Again in WordPerfect, for example, you can create a couple of macros that change the current directory to a working directory. You can use this feature, for example, to change from working for one customer to working for another and automatically save each customer's files in different directories.

Using SUBST for Efficiency

DOS itself supplies a tool for avoiding long path names: the SUBST command. With this command, you can assign a logical drive letter to a subdirectory name.

You can assign and unassign these letters at will. If you are using more than five logical disk drives (up to the letter E), however, you need to add a LASTDRIVE directive in the CONFIG.SYS file to accommodate the additional drive letters. DOS then establishes each of the drive letters—up to and including the specified LASTDRIVE—as DOS devices. The alias drive "created" by the SUBST command inherits the directory tree structure of the subdirectory reassigned to the drive letter.

SUBST is commonly used in two different situations. If you are using a program that does not support path names, you can use the SUBST command to assign a drive letter to a directory. The program then refers to the drive letter, and DOS translates the request into a path. If, for example, the data for a program is stored in C:\WORDPROC, you can type the following command:

SUBST E: C:\WORDPROC

This command tells the program that the data is stored in drive E.

The other use for SUBST is to reduce the typing of long path names. Typing long path names can be a tedious process, particularly when the hard drive is used by more than one person. Each user may have a separate section of the hard disk for storing data files but may use common areas of the disk to store the programs. If the paths \USER1\WORDATA and \USER1\SPREDATA exist on drive C, you can reduce the typing needed to reach files in those directories by entering the following command:

SUBST E: C:\USER1

When you request a directory of E, the volume label given is the label from drive C, and the directory itself is the contents of C:\USER1.

As with JOIN and ASSIGN, the choice to use the SUBST command is a compromise. In some situations, using SUBST is beneficial, but you must be aware of the limitations imposed when SUBST is in effect:

- You cannot use SUBST on a networked drive.
- Do not use SUBST with JOIN or ASSIGN.
- Remove any SUBST settings before running DISKCOPY, DISKCOMP, FDISK, PRINT, FORMAT, LABEL, BACKUP, or RESTORE.
- Beware of using CHDIR, MKDIR, RMDIR, APPEND, and PATH with any drives reassigned.

The techniques for improving your productivity require you to be aware of your tasks. If you find that you are doing a repetitive task, you may be able to find a better way. Don't be afraid to go back to manuals for products you know well and see whether those pages offer methods for improving productivity. Many software vendors include this type of information, but you may have missed its significance when the program was new.

Using Alternative Microprocessors

In some cases, you may outgrow your existing hardware. The computer you bought for typing a few memos has become the cornerstone of your administrative office. You spend more time waiting for the computer to process the information than you do typing at the keyboard.

A new computer may seem a large expense, but alternatives are available. The core of your computer is the microprocessor. Adding the fastest peripherals cannot improve your computer's performance beyond that of the microprocessor. But you may consider a replacement or alternative microprocessor as a worthwhile expense.

Using the V20 and V30 Microprocessors

The first option for 8088- and 80286-based computers is to replace the microprocessor. NEC offers replacements for the 8088 and 80286 microprocessors: V20 for the 8088 and V30 for the 80286. The V20 and V30 microprocessors are capable of performing certain instructions faster than their Intel counterparts. Because the faster instructions often are used in software programs, the replacement microprocessor gives a slight performance improvement. One or two instructions, on the other hand, are performed faster on the Intel microprocessor than on the NEC V20 or V30. You can create benchmarks that show dramatic performance improvements with the V20 or V30, but the true test is how much of an improvement you get with a typical PC program mix.

The V20 and V30 are inexpensive (under $15) and have a reputation of being very compatible. All your programs should continue to work. You have to judge whether an average performance improvement of about 5 percent is worth the expense and effort of replacing the microprocessor. As with memory replacement, removing the 8088 or 80286 and replacing it with another chip is a two-minute job on some computers and a two-hour job on others.

Using Math Coprocessors

The next alternative for improving your existing computer is to consider using a math coprocessor. Most computers have a socket that accepts a math coprocessor. This coprocessor works in association with the main microprocessor to perform mathematical functions.

When a microprocessor is designed, it can be optimized for certain types of instructions. The most commonly used instructions are the ones that you want to execute as fast as possible. Rarely used instructions can take longer without being too noticeable. The Intel 80X86 family of microprocessors are general-purpose microprocessors designed so that you can use a wide variety of instructions on them. The Intel 80X87 math coprocessor family is optimized to perform mathematical calculations extremely fast (when compared with the 80X86).

To see a performance improvement with a math coprocessor, you must use programs that can take advantage of it. The instructions for the math coprocessor functions are different from the main microprocessor's equivalent. When you use a math coprocessor, your program uses the main microprocessor for most functions but uses the math coprocessor whenever possible. Most applications that depend on mathematical calculations, such as spreadsheets, CAD, and other engineering software, operate 5 to 20 times faster with a math coprocessor. Software that is not written to take advantage of an installed math coprocessor, however, does not change in performance.

A math coprocessor is not as inexpensive as a V20 or V30, but in the right situation, the performance improvement is well worth the cost. Each Intel 80X88 microprocessor has a companion math coprocessor that you can use. Although an 8087 used with the 8088 costs fewer than $200, a fast 80387 used with the 80386 can cost more than $500.

You don't have to use an Intel math coprocessor. You can buy an alternative from IIT or Cyrix. Although these substitutes can perform certain instructions faster than the Intel equivalents, the IIT and Cyrix products are like the NEC V20 and V30 in that you don't get a large improvement in speed. And these alternatives cost about the same as the Intel equivalents.

The Weitek math coprocessors are another choice. These are true alternative math coprocessors. They use their own instruction sets and can be used only in systems that are designed to use them with software that is designed to use them. In some computers, you can install both a Weitek math coprocessor and an Intel coprocessor and use both at once. The Weitek math coprocessors are found only in 386- and 486-based computers. Typical software programs that can use these alternative coprocessors include sophisticated engineering, CAD, and statistical software. DOS 5 includes support for the Weitek math coprocessor. For these applications, having both math coprocessors gives tremendous performance advantages. Keep in mind, however, that a Weitek math coprocessor is not a low-cost upgrade. The coprocessors cost several hundred dollars apiece.

Using Accelerator Boards

An accelerator board can give an existing PC or AT a new lease on life. An accelerator board consists of a microprocessor, support circuitry, and memory on a typical expansion board. The board fits into the expansion slot of your existing PC or AT. You remove your existing microprocessor and link the expansion board to the microprocessor socket on the system board. Your PC then behaves as if it was an AT or 386-based computer (depending on the accelerator board chosen). Your AT behaves as if it was a 386-based computer.

In either case, the computer is not quite the same as if you had bought a whole new computer, but you do get a good compromise of cost versus performance. Remember, the PC consists of a CPU and support circuitry along with devices. The CPU communicates with the devices through the expansion bus. When you add an accelerator board, you have replaced the CPU and some of the control circuitry, but you haven't replaced the bus. When the CPU communicates with a device, such as the hard disk, the CPU is still going to use the same expansion bus. In a PC, the bus is limited to 8 bits, even when you put in a 386-based accelerator card.

The accelerator boards are supplied with some memory. A 286 accelerator board contains 16-bit memory, and a 386 accelerator board contains 32-bit memory. For data stored on the card, the microprocessor can communicate at its full local bus width. Only when the CPU has to communicate with a device does the performance go down. For this reason, if you upgrade a computer with an accelerator board, you should consider investing additional money in as much memory as possible on the board to get the best performance.

Accelerator boards cost several hundred dollars, and you should be aware of the disadvantages of purchasing an accelerator board rather than a new computer. First, you need to consider the life of the computer.

If you have had your PC for several years, and you add an accelerator board, you are placing a brand new device into an old computer. If the PC portion of the computer was to break—the serial port was to become defective, for example—you would have an unworkable accelerator board. Many PC manufacturers are no longer in business, and repairing an old PC may not be practical. Consider the same situation with the hard disk or the display. If you have to buy a new hard disk, is being limited to a PC-style hard disk worth it? Or would buying a whole new system be a better investment? On the other hand, PCs usually are extremely reliable. If you don't abuse them, PCs work for many years without a problem. Only you can judge the tradeoffs in your situation between buying a new computer or buying an accelerator board.

If your computer is slowing you down significantly, and price is your only criteria, accelerator boards make a great deal of sense. A 386-based accelerator board in a 4.77-MHz PC can show a performance that is close to most 16-MHz 386-based computers.

One caution with buying an accelerator board is to make sure that you can return it if it doesn't work. Thousands of brands of PCs and ATs are on the market, and an accelerator board manufacturer cannot be expected to have tested compatibility with each type. Although your computer may be compatible with the IBM standard when running software, the addition of an accelerator board may reveal hardware differences that prevent the computer from running. The manufacturer usually can tell you with which computers the boards are compatible—and often the ones with which they don't work.

Chapter Summary

This chapter covered ways that you can improve your computer's performance inexpensively. These methods are closely linked to your particular use of the computer. You usually can improve your productivity by examining how you use your computer and changing your work habits. You can reduce typing for repetitive tasks and long path names by using batch files or the features within your applications programs.

Even if you have only floppy disks, you can improve your computer's performance by being organized. If you have a hard disk, your organization makes a significant difference.

You can make a small investment in hardware to get the best use of your computer. Adding more memory to a computer is probably going to give a better price/performance advantage over buying a faster hard disk. On the other hand, adding a hard disk opens new opportunities for floppy disk users.

Depending on your application, adding an alternative microprocessor or accelerator board may give your computer new life. Math coprocessors can improve performance dramatically for mathematically intensive programs but don't change the performance of all programs.

Regaining Base Memory

10

Because DOS is an operating system designed for 8088 microprocessors, current PCs have to live with the limitations imposed by the 8088. If you have a 486-based computer running DOS as the operating system, that computer behaves the same way as an 8088-based PC. It just runs faster.

The 8088 is limited to a 1M address space. The microprocessor addresses up to 1M of memory at one time. As the PC standard has evolved, methods of increasing the actual amount of memory that can be addressed have evolved, but the limit of 1M at one time cannot be changed.

Originally most PCs didn't have much memory. A system with 256K was considered well endowed. However, as the practical uses for a PC increased in number and complexity, the need for a full complement of memory increased. PC users expressed concern about the 640K memory barrier and how to handle its limitations.

Each successive version of DOS (except DOS 5.0), with its associated new features, took more of the low DOS memory. New applications programs had new features that required more memory. Most early word processors, for example, didn't include spell checkers as an integral part of the editor. Now, spell checkers usually are included. The increase in sophistication of programs was possible because more users were willing to upgrade their memory size to take advantage of these features.

PC users hurdled each new development and increased their level of knowledge of PCs. They started using more programs with more features. By using terminate-and-stay-resident programs (TSRs), users were able to make their PCs a complete workstation. At the press of a button, users had access to appointment books, calendars, Rolodexes, and calculators while running their normal applications programs.

Your use of memory can get out of control easily. You can end up with insufficient memory to run the applications if you don't exercise restraint. As your needs become more demanding, the computer's capacity to fit all the utilities and devices into memory along with the applications programs and DOS becomes more important.

This chapter and the following one cover ways to regain base memory. This chapter relates to PCs and ATs and Chapter 11 to 386- and 486-based computers. At the simplest level, regaining low DOS memory involves streamlining the CONFIG.SYS and AUTOEXEC.BAT files. In the same way as you can regain hard disk space by removing no-longer-used programs, you can regain low DOS memory by removing no-longer or rarely used TSRs from the AUTOEXEC.BAT file. This process is independent of the type of microprocessor used in your computer.

The second level of regaining low DOS memory involves making use of the microprocessor's or memory expansion board's capability. For 8088- and 80286-based microprocessors, relatively new products can assist, such as Qualitas' MOVE'EM and Quarterdeck's QRAM. All Computers' ALL CHARGECARD performs a similar function on ATs, and ALL CARD performs a similar function on PCs.

Both approaches to regaining low DOS memory require you to analyze how you use your computer. Remove everything unnecessary from the CONFIG.SYS and AUTOEXEC.BAT files. Add devices and TSRs until you achieve a balance between the amount of low DOS memory remaining for applications programs and the functionality of your computer.

Before you learn more about regaining base memory, examine the history of the 8088, 80286, and DOS memory. Knowing the memory features of 8088 and 80286 microprocessors enables you to understand the role of memory-management programs and their various operating options and features. These programs depend on DOS's memory use and capacity to accept device drivers to give you additional functionality.

Examining 8088 Architecture

Intel's 8088 microprocessor and its sibling 8086 are used in PCs. The 8088 only has one mode of operation: *real mode*. All computers, PCs or others, use the microprocessor in the same way. Programs can access 1M of contiguous memory.

A PC's contiguous memory is split into two areas: memory above and memory below 640K. This division between user memory and memory reserved for devices, made by IBM for the first PC, applies regardless of the operating system running on the computer.

Because DOS was developed to run on PCs, DOS takes advantage of the 1M address space. The lower 640K of memory is considered low DOS memory, and the upper 384K is assigned to various devices that DOS can recognize.

Examining 80286 Architecture

The 80286 microprocessor has two operating modes, unlike the 8088, which has one mode. The 80286's real mode is identical to the 8088's real mode. One megabyte of memory can be addressed at one time. Although expanded memory enables you to appear to access more than 1M, you actually are addressing only 1M at one time.

The other operating mode of the 80286 is *protected mode*. Operating systems such as OS/2 can take advantage of this mode. Although DOS cannot directly take advantage of protected mode, some utility programs running under DOS can. Protected mode includes advanced memory management that allows more than 1M of memory to be accessed. In fact, up to 16M of memory can be controlled while the 80286 is in protected mode.

Memory above 1M is *extended memory*. The utility programs that run with DOS switch the microprocessor in and out of protected mode and manage all the memory. They are, in effect, located between DOS and the hardware. This extended memory feature of the 80286 enables AT owners to do more with their memory than is possible with PCs.

Utility programs switch the microprocessor in and out of protected mode to perform memory mapping. When DOS is actually in control, the microprocessor is in real mode. Switching into protected mode occurs relatively quickly; however, switching back into real mode takes more time.

Examining DOS Memory

Chapter 2 explains in detail the various parts of DOS and their arrangement in memory. Figure 10.1 shows a memory map for a PC running DOS.

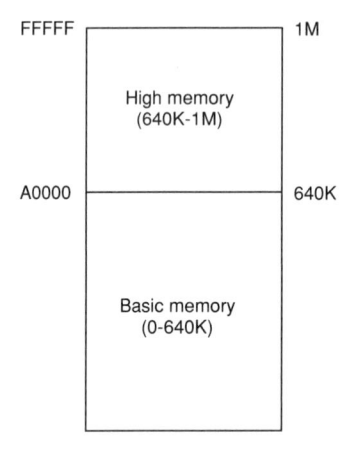

```
FFFFF ┌─────────────┐ 1M
      │             │
      │ High memory │
      │ (640K-1M)   │
      │             │
A0000 ├─────────────┤ 640K
      │             │
      │             │
      │             │
      │ Basic memory│
      │ (0-640K)    │
      │             │
      │             │
      └─────────────┘
```

Fig. 10.1. A memory map for a PC running DOS.

The first 640K of memory address space is known as *low DOS memory,* or *conventional memory.* When you boot your computer, DOS loads its various components into memory starting at the lowest address. After DOS and all the device drivers have been put in CONFIG.SYS and loaded, the AUTOEXEC.BAT file is run. This AUTOEXEC.BAT may include other programs, such as a disk cache, mouse driver, or TSR utility such as Borland International's SideKick.

When AUTOEXEC.BAT file commands have been executed, you are left with a certain amount of conventional memory to run applications programs. You may not have sufficient room to load some applications programs.

The memory between 640K and 1M is also part of the address space that the microprocessor can address. However, various sections of this area are assigned to devices in the computer. Applications programs do not use this memory area as a place to store themselves or their data.

Two methods are available for increasing free base memory: You can reduce the number of items you load into the base memory, or you can put the items in a different place in memory.

You should look carefully at the CONFIG.SYS and AUTOEXEC.BAT files to ensure that you are not loading unnecessary programs. As you alter your computer's configuration, failing to remove unused programs is easy to do. These programs can be found quickly and removed when you are checking to ensure that you are not running unnecessary programs. However, you may be able to make further reductions by analyzing what you use the programs for instead of just whether you use the programs at all.

You may be running a DOS file manager program, such as PC Tools' PC Shell, for example. This program can be run as either a stand-alone or TSR program. If you never use the shell as a TSR program from within another program, you don't need it loaded all the time. You can run it from the DOS command prompt and save the low DOS memory that PC Shell's resident part occupies.

On the other hand, if you run PC Tools' Mirror, which copies the file allocation table (FAT) and root directory to a file on your hard disk, you may want to run the program in memory-resident mode to make use of its delete tracker feature. As a stand-alone program, Mirror copies the FAT and root directory every time you run it at the command prompt. As a TSR program, with the appropriate switches added to the invoking command line, Mirror keeps a file of the files you or your applications programs delete on the hard disk. Obviously, to keep track of these deleted files, Mirror needs to be resident in memory. If you don't run Mirror as a TSR program, you save memory but lose a feature.

DOS recognizes only one contiguous area of memory as user memory. This area is where the DOS commands and applications programs run and store data. On computers with no additional memory managers, this low DOS memory is between 0K and 640K. DOS occupies the lower addresses, but the area between the top of DOS and 640K is available for use.

The area of memory between 640K and 1M is reserved for the basic input-output system (BIOS) and devices, including the video display, hard disks, and any expansion board installed in the computer. Although most of these areas of memory are reserved for particular devices, you cannot put all the devices in the same computer. For example, the CGA and EGA video boards use slightly different addresses, but you wouldn't put an EGA and a CGA in the same computer.

On any given system, "holes" exist in the addressing area somewhere between 640K and 1M. When you add a new device, such as a scanner board, you have to place it in a vacant area of memory. Expanded memory boards put page frames in an empty area of memory. Frequently, the expanded memory page frame is placed at E000H (unless you are using a network board), but it doesn't have to be.

Memory managers can increase in two ways the amount of RAM that DOS sees. The first way is to raise the 640K (A000H) limit up to just below the first device installed in the system—typically the video adapter. The CGA uses addresses B800H to C000H, and the Monochrome Display Adapter (MDA) uses B000H to C000H. The EGA and VGA use A000H to C000H. Consequently, on computers that have only a CGA or an MDA, the area immediately above 640K is vacant. Because DOS can address a single contiguous area of memory, this raising of the 640K limit provides additional memory that all applications programs can use. This alteration is relatively easy, and many programs are available for changing this limit. You probably will find one on a bulletin board or an on-line service. Provided that nothing is using this area of DOS memory, most applications programs run without problems.

The other way, performed by more sophisticated memory managers, is to take advantage of the gaps in memory between your computer's installed devices. By using extended or expanded RAM (depending on the memory manager and the computer), the memory managers fill the gaps in high DOS memory, making high DOS memory available for storing programs and device drivers. These memory managers have to intercept any DOS calls to the programs, move programs between high DOS memory and low DOS memory for use, and return them to high DOS memory after use.

The memory manager you should use depends on your computer's resources. Products suitable for use on 286- or 386-based computers with extended memory, or 8088 computers with expanded memory, are available. The following sections of this chapter introduce some of the available products for the 8088- and 80286-based computers. Next, the memory-managing features of DOS 5.0, which can take advantage of the 80286 microprocessor, are covered. Chapter 11 introduces some of the memory managers specifically for the 386- and 486-based computers.

Using Expanded Memory

Two relatively new products can help you use expanded memory to regain low DOS memory on your computer. MOVE'EM from Qualitas and QRAM from Quarterdeck enable you to load device drivers and TSRs into high memory by using an expanded memory board. On less well-equipped computers, the savings may be small, but for some applications, this memory increase may be sufficient. On other computers, with the appropriate hardware, the savings may be substantial.

If you are using a 386- or 486-based computer, a program that works in association with a 386 memory-management program is the appropriate alternative. Qualitas' 386LOAD, part of 386-to-the-MAX 5.0, and Quarterdeck's LOADHI, part of QEMM, are covered in Chapter 11. The 80386 and 80486 have an operating mode called *virtual 8086 mode,* which requires these load programs to work in a different way with the 386 memory managers.

Expanded Memory Boards

As discussed in Chapter 3, expanded memory boards provide you with a method of accessing more than 1M of memory on a DOS-based system. Only 1M is accessible at any one time, but by swapping memory in and out of a predefined area of this 1M of memory, applications programs can store more information in RAM.

Most expanded memory boards conform to one of two standards: LIM (Lotus-Intel-Microsoft) 3.2 or LIM 4.0. LIM 3.2 has fewer features than 4.0. LIM 3.2 is a single 64K page frame in high DOS memory (between 640K and 1M). This page frame consists of four 16K pages. The applications program swaps 16K blocks of memory in and out of the page frame, giving access to large amounts of RAM. The position of the page frame in high DOS memory can be defined on these boards. Remember, however, that each area of memory can be used by only one device. The expanded memory device must use an area of memory not in use by another device, such as a network board.

LIM 4.0 allows page frames larger than 64K and multiple page frames. To accommodate these additional features, the interface between LIM 4.0 and the applications programs that can use expanded memory has changed from LIM 3.2.

You can buy expanded memory boards that are compatible with the LIM 4.0 standard in a variety of ways. Some boards give you the full capability of the LIM 4.0 standard. You can use all the empty areas of high DOS memory to hold expanded memory page frames. These page frames don't have to be contiguous and don't have to be 64K in size. Examples of this type of board include AST Rampage Plus and Newer Technology Concentration.

The second type of expanded memory board provides more features than the LIM 3.2 standard but not all features. These large frame boards enable you to specify a page frame larger than 64K. You can have only one page frame, however. If the free space in high DOS memory is scattered, you may not be able to fit a large page frame between two devices. An example of this type of expanded memory board is Intel's Above Board Plus.

The third type of expanded memory board is hardware compatible with LIM 3.2 only. The board is supplied with a software device driver that conforms with LIM 4.0, which enables you to use applications programs that use the LIM 4.0 interface. However, the board is not capable of using large or multiple page frames. Everex's Ever for Excellence and RAM 300 Deluxe, Micron's Hands on Excellence, and Quadram's QuadMaster IV fit this category.

The difference between expanded memory boards is performance. If you have only one page frame, the applications program cannot have as many pages of memory available at once and has to do more swapping of data. This swapping slows the performance of the computer; however, the additional swapping is between RAM, which has a fast access time. Although the expanded memory boards with the full functionality should work faster, the speed difference should be small.

If, however, you need to regain low DOS memory and want to use a loader program that places TSRs and device drivers in high DOS memory, the type of board you have affects your ability to free memory.

MOVE'EM

Qualitas' MOVE'EM memory manager works with LIM 4.0 expanded memory, which enables you to load device drivers and TSRs into empty high DOS memory. Use your expanded memory board and its associated expanded memory device driver, followed by MOVE'EM.

Depending on how you configure it, MOVE'EM takes over some or all of the expanded memory page frames and uses them to store device drivers and TSRs. When you want to use one of the device drivers or TSRs, MOVE'EM controls the interface between you and your TSR or device driver. The device driver or TSR thinks it is interfacing directly with DOS, and DOS thinks it is interfacing directly with the device driver or TSR.

If you have a board that allows only a single 64K expanded memory page frame, you have to choose between using MOVE'EM or expanded memory. For boards with a single page frame that can be larger than 64K, MOVE'EM can leave a 64K expanded memory page frame. MOVE'EM uses the rest of the available memory, which would be used for making additional expanded memory page frames if MOVE'EM were not used, to relocate device drivers and TSRs.

Example: Using MOVE'EM To Regain Low DOS Memory

Consider an IBM AT with an EGA board and 1M of expanded memory running DOS 3.3. The third type of expanded memory board discussed earlier is an Everex RAM 3000 Deluxe. This board is LIM 3.2 hardware compatible with a LIM 4.0 software device driver. Only one 64K page frame can be created.

Suppose that your CONFIG.SYS file contains the following:

```
DEVICE=EMM.SYS 258,000
DEVICE=C:\DOS\ANSI.SYS
DEVICE=C:\SYS\NEWPRN.SYS
DEVICE=C:\SYS\BURNDEV.SYS 5000 H+
FILES=30
BUFFERS=30
```

The first line loads the expanded memory device driver. ANSI.SYS, loaded in line 2, enhances your console device driver, and NEWPRN.SYS, a device driver, improves your printing speed. BURNDEV.SYS is a screen-blanking program. The settings for files and buffers are typical.

Suppose that your AUTOEXEC.BAT file contains the following:

```
PROMPT $P$G
PATH=C:\;C:\DOS;C:\PCTOOLS;C:\UTIL;C:\UTIL\ARC;
MIRROR C:
APPEND /E
C:\TSR\CLOCK
C:\TSR\IOLITE
FASTOPEN C:=100
PCSHELL /RT
```

The PROMPT and PATH commands are typical of most AUTOEXEC.BAT files. Mirror runs a PC Tools Deluxe utility that keeps a backup copy of the FAT and the root directory of your disk. If you accidentally reformat or erase your hard disk, this file aids in the reconstruction of the lost data.

Each of the other lines in this AUTOEXEC.BAT file loads a memory-resident program. APPEND /E causes DOS to load the APPEND variables into the environment. APPEND is similar to PATH. DOS uses the directories listed to search for files it cannot find in the current directory. APPEND is for nonexecutable files, and PATH is for executable files. FASTOPEN, also a DOS program, gives you faster access to previously used files on your disk. FASTOPEN keeps track of file locations as you use them. If you use a previously used file, that file is accessed faster than if DOS had to find it from scratch.

The CLOCK program is a memory-resident program that displays the time in a corner of the screen. IOLITE also is memory resident and flashes a character on the screen whenever the disk is being accessed. PCSHELL, another PC Tools Deluxe utility program, is a file manager that enables you to execute many commands that are not available in DOS directly. For example, you can move whole subdirectories, and you can select several files at once and then copy or move them. If you type **PCSHELL/RT**, PC Shell loads into memory as a TSR and the DOS prompt returns.

When the computer is started with these CONFIG.SYS and AUTOEXEC.BAT files, four device drivers and five memory-resident programs are loaded. Running CHKDSK reveals the following:

```
Volume HARD DISK C created Aug 24, 1990 5:00p

21309440 bytes total disk space
   55296 bytes in 4 hidden files
   36864 bytes in 17 directories
 8970240 bytes in 383 user files
12247040 bytes available on disk

  655360 bytes total memory
  553488 bytes free
```

Note that 540K of RAM is available for applications programs and their data to run. With no device drivers or memory-resident programs loaded, 586K of RAM is available. In other words, 46K of memory has been lost because of the contents of CONFIG.SYS and AUTOEXEC.BAT. This 46K is the memory that may be recoverable. You find the value by running CHKDSK after booting the computer with no CONFIG.SYS or AUTOEXEC.BAT.

Measuring Program Size with MOVE'EM

Using a memory manager to load device drivers and TSRs into high memory is a several-step process. First determine what fits into high memory and what is the best order in which to load the drivers and TSRs. Then rearrange the CONFIG.SYS and AUTOEXEC.BAT files to make the best use of memory while maintaining any order-dependent devices, or programs, in the appropriate order. Although MOVE'EM is not capable of determining order dependency, the program does suggest the best way to use available high DOS memory during installation. Chapter 8 covers streamlining the CONFIG.SYS and AUTOEXEC.BAT files and order-dependent devices.

This process of rearranging and streamlining CONFIG.SYS and AUTOEXEC.BAT is relatively easy to achieve; however, understanding the process requires a good grasp of DOS and how memory is assigned. Although following the manual's instructions provides results, understanding the process enables you to make the best decisions.

The first steps in using MOVE'EM are to install the memory manager and determine the size of each device driver and memory-resident program that is a candidate for moving into high memory. MOVE'EM depends on the LIM 4.0 memory manager for its operation. Consequently, the memory manager must be activated prior to MOVE'EM and cannot be moved into high memory.

Using the preceding example, the CONFIG.SYS file is changed as follows:

```
DEVICE=EMM.SYS 258,000
DEVICE=C:\MOVE'EM\MOVE'EM.MGR NOFRAME
DEVICE=C:\MOVE'EM\MOVE'EM.SYS GETSIZE PROG=C:\DOS\ANSI.SYS
DEVICE=C:\MOVE'EM\MOVE'EM.SYS GETSIZE PROG=C:\SYS\NEWPRN.SYS
DEVICE=C:\MOVE'EM\MOVE'EM.SYS GETSIZE PROG=C:\SYS\BURNDEV.SYS 5000 H+
FILES=30
BUFFERS=30
```

The expanded memory manager is loaded as before. The memory manager MOVE'EM.MGR is loaded next. Because the expanded memory board in use is software compatible with LIM 4.0 only, the NOFRAME parameter is needed. If another board were used, you could use other parameters that affect the various page frames MOVE'EM can use for relocation. MOVE'EM takes control of the expanded memory page frame and converts the expanded memory page into high DOS memory that MOVE'EM can use for loading programs and device drivers. If you use MOVE'EM on this type of board, you cannot use the expanded memory as normal expanded memory.

Each device driver line in the original CONFIG.SYS file is altered. The device driver loaded in each case is MOVE'EM.SYS. Two parameters are passed to MOVE'EM.SYS: GETSIZE and PROG=. The GETSIZE parameter is used during installation. MOVE'EM determines the amount of memory used by each device. You then can analyze which programs fit into the available high DOS memory. The PROG= parameter indicates the device driver you want to load into memory.

The AUTOEXEC.BAT file is changed as follows:

```
PROMPT $P$G
PATH=C:\;C:\DOS;C:\PCTOOLS;C:\MOVE'EM;C:\UTIL;C:\UTIL\ARC;
MIRROR C:
MOVE'EM GETSIZE PROG=APPEND /E
MOVE'EM GETSIZE PROG=C:\TSR\CLOCK
MOVE'EM GETSIZE PROG=C:\TSR\IOLITE
MOVE'EM GETSIZE PROG=FASTOPEN C:=100
MOVE'EM GETSIZE PROG=PCSHELL /RT
```

The subdirectory for MOVE'EM is added to the path. Each line that runs a memory-resident program is changed. The MOVE'EM program is run instead. MOVE'EM uses parameters similar to MOVE'EM.SYS. The GETSIZE parameter is used temporarily during the installation process to determine the size of the TSRs being loaded. The various TSRs and their associated parameters are passed to MOVE'EM for processing.

The various elements of MOVE'EM have similar names but are separate entities. MOVE'EM.MGR is the loader device driver used for controlling the entire MOVE'EM program. MOVE'EM.SYS is a device driver used for loading your device drivers and acting as the go-between between DOS and your usual device driver. MOVE'EM is the executable file that performs a comparable function to MOVE'EM.SYS but works for TSRs.

The process of installing MOVE'EM alters the CONFIG.SYS and AUTOEXEC.BAT files. Consequently, you need to reboot your computer every time a change is made. Remember to keep a bootable disk handy so that you can reboot even when you alter a CONFIG.SYS or AUTOEXEC.BAT file that prevents your computer from booting from the hard disk. As you reboot, MOVE'EM analyzes the size of each device driver and program with which you have used the GETSIZE parameter. Instead of loading programs into high memory, MOVE'EM loads each of them into low DOS memory for size determination. You can run MOVE'EM with the SUMMARY parameter to see the results, which are shown in figure 10.2.

```
MOVE'EM -- Version 1.02 -- A Program Loader for PCs
   Copyright (C) 1988-90 Qualitas, Inc.  All rights reserved.
+-----------------------------------------------------------------------+
|                    RESIDENT PROGRAM MEMORY SUMMARY                    |
+---------------+-----------------------+-------------------------------+
|               |    Size Parameters    |                               |
| Device or     +-------+-------+-------+                               |
| Program Name  | Load  |Initial|Resident| Suggested Action             |
+---------------+-------+-------+-------+-------------------------------+
| Dev=MOVE'EM$  | 1,360 | 1,360 | 1,360 | Remove PRGREG=0               |
| Dev=CON       | 1,648 | 1,648 | 1,584 | Remove GETSIZE; no SIZE needed|
| Dev=newprn    |   496 |   496 |   368 | Remove GETSIZE; no SIZE needed|
| Dev=BRNDEV    | 2,592 | 2,592 | 2,368 | Remove GETSIZE; no SIZE needed|
| APPEND.EXE    | 5,552 | 5,552 | 4,400 | Remove GETSIZE; no SIZE needed|
| CLOCK.COM     | 1,536 | 2,048 |   800 | Remove GETSIZE; use SIZE=2048 |
| IOLITE.COM    | 1,024 | 1,536 |   416 | Remove GETSIZE; use SIZE=1536 |
| FASTOPEN.EXE  | 3,888 |70,880 | 5,344 | Remove GETSIZE; use SIZE=70880|
| PCSHELL.EXE   |192,272|218,448|10,544 | Remove GETSIZE; use SIZE=218448|
+---------------+-------+-------+-------+-------------------------------+
| Not all programs/environments fit into high DOS memory in this order  |
+-----------------------------------------------------------------------+
|                    RESIDENT PROGRAM OPTIMIZATION                      |
+------------+---------+---------+------+----------+----------+---------+
|            | Maximum |Resident |      | Best Fit | 2nd Fit  | 3rd Fit |
| Program    | Program |Prg & Env|Group +----------+----------+---------+
| Name       | Size    | Size    |Number|ORD|PRG|ENV|ORD|PRG|ENV|ORD|PRG|ENV|
+------------+---------+---------+------+---+---+--+---+---+--+---+---+--+
|Dev=MOVE'EM$|  1,360  | 1,376   |      | 1 | 1 |  | 1 | 1 |  | 1 | 1 |  |
|Dev=CON     |  1,648  | 1,600   |      | 4 | 1 |  | 3 | 1 |  | 4 | 1 |  |
|Dev=newprn  |    496  |   384   |      | 3 | 1 |  |   |   |  | 3 | 1 |  |
|Dev=BRNDEV  |  2,592  | 2,384   |      | 2 | 1 |  | 2 | 1 |  | 2 | 1 |  |
|APPEND.EXE  |  5,552  | 4,640   |      | 6 | 1 |  | 5 | 1 |  | 6 | 1 |  |
|CLOCK.COM   |  2,048  | 1,040   |      | 5 | 1 |  | 1 | 1 |  | 5 | 1 |  |
|IOLITE.COM  |  1,536  |   656   |      | 7 | 1 |  | 6 | 1 |  |   |   |  |
|FASTOPEN.EXE| 70,880  | 5,584   |      |   |   |  |   |   |  |   |   |  |
|PCSHELL.EXE |218,448  |10,784   |      |   |   |  |   |   |  |   |   |  |
+------------+---------+---------+------+---+---+--+---+---+--+---+---+--+
| Bytes moved into high DOS memory     |  12,080  |  11,696  | 11,424  |
| Bytes available                      |  53,456  |  53,840  | 54,112  |
+--------------------------------------+----------+----------+---------+
| Legend:  ORD = Program loading order (use GROUP= to avoid re-ordering)|
|          PRG = Program region #          blank = load in low DOS memory)|
|          ENV = Environment region # (if different from PRG)           |
+-----------------------------------------------------------------------+
```

Fig. 10.2. The result of running MOVE'EM with the SUMMARY parameter.

Because MOVE'EM is not capable of moving all programs into high memory, MOVE'EM performs an analysis to determine the best loading order. This optimization is shown in the lower portion of figure 10.2.

Because of their nature, TSRs don't require the same amount of memory all the time. A TSR loads itself into memory, initializes itself, and then returns control to DOS, leaving a small portion of itself in memory. To load these programs into high memory, MOVE'EM must have enough high DOS memory to fit the program when loading, initializing, or remaining resident.

All three values are important for fitting programs into high DOS memory. For example, you can load into memory a program that takes a substantial amount of available high DOS memory before you load a program that, although not taking much memory after it has become resident, takes a great deal of memory during loading. Sufficient memory may not be available for loading the second program. If you load the second program first, however, it can temporarily use the memory that the other program uses during loading. In this way, both programs may fit by reordering. Determining the best sequence for program loading is only an exercise in trying every combination; however, many combinations exist. MOVE'EM calculates the best sequence rapidly and gives the summary shown in figure 10.2.

The summary is divided into two parts. The top part shows each program or device name, along with its different sizes during loading, during initializing, and when resident. The right column shows any suggested alterations to the command line in CONFIG.SYS or AUTOEXEC.BAT as appropriate. For example, the screen blanker device requires 2,592 bytes to load and initialize, and 2,368 bytes when resident. The clock program requires 1,536 bytes to load, 2,048 bytes to initialize, and 800 bytes when resident.

None of the device drivers require a size parameter for MOVE'EM; however, the TSRs require a size parameter that gives the maximum size each program requires. In the example shown previously, the TSRs all require the same amount of memory or more to initialize as they do to load. Nevertheless, a different program may need more memory to load than to initialize. The clock program needs a SIZE=2048 parameter to indicate that it needs 2,048 bytes of memory during its loading and initialization process.

The second part of the MOVE'EM summary report, generated only if all the programs do not fit into memory as currently arranged, gives information on the program ordering. The program name, maximum program size, and size of the resident portion and its environment are listed. Three alternative orders are listed for the programs. Each list shows the amount of information moved into high DOS memory and the remaining high DOS memory available for other memory-resident programs.

The column headed ORD is the numerical order in which the devices and programs should be loaded to optimize memory use. The PRG column indicates which area of high DOS memory should hold the moved program. In this example, only one region is available because the expanded memory board can have only one page frame, but on some boards, several different regions are available. MOVE'EM numbers these regions in address order. The region with the lowest address is region 1. Because these regions fill the "holes" in memory between normal devices, these regions vary in size. As a result, program placement into a specific region may make better use of resources. The ENV column listed in the summary gives a region number only when the environment for a program should be loaded into a region different from the program using MOVE'EM parameters.

As shown in the example's summary, FASTOPEN and PCSHELL do not fit into high memory and must be loaded into low DOS memory. FASTOPEN requires 69K during initialization, and PCSHELL requires 213K. Because the page frame is only 64K, the programs do not fit. MOVE'EM also recommends a different order for the program loading. Only one combination allows the seven remaining device drivers and programs to be loaded into memory. The second-best fit involves loading NEWPRN.SYS in low memory, and the third-best fit involves loading IOLITE in low memory.

Note that ANSI.SYS is a replacement console driver. ANSI.SYS gives its name as CON to DOS. Consequently, MOVE'EM detects this device as CON rather than ANSI.SYS.

You need to look at the new order carefully to check for order dependency. In this case, the relocated devices and TSRs can be in any order, but some devices must be loaded in order. For example, the Novell network drivers, IPX and NET3, must be loaded in order (IPX before NET3). Command line parameters are available for grouping devices together. If these devices were the only order-dependent devices, you would add the parameter GROUP=1 to the device driver directive for IPX and NET3. Then, when MOVE'EM performs its analysis, it preserves the sequence. Note, however, that the optimum arrangement may not be to load NET3 immediately after IPX. You specify a different group number for other devices that must be kept in a specific order. Up to nine of these groups can be defined.

Rearranging CONFIG.SYS and AUTOEXEC.BAT for MOVE'EM

Using the same example from the preceding section, the CONFIG.SYS and AUTOEXEC.BAT files can be arranged in the suggested order because no order dependency exists. The changed CONFIG.SYS file is as follows:

```
DEVICE=EMM.SYS 258,000
DEVICE=C:\MOVE'EM\MOVE'EM.MGR NOFRAME PRGREG=1
DEVICE=C:\MOVE'EM\MOVE'EM.SYS PROG=C:\SYS\BURNDEV.SYS 5000 H+
DEVICE=C:\MOVE'EM\MOVE'EM.SYS PROG=C:\SYS\NEWPRN.SYS
DEVICE=C:\MOVE'EM\MOVE'EM.SYS PROG=C:\DOS\ANSI.SYS
FILES=30
BUFFERS=30
```

The AUTOEXEC.BAT file is as follows:

```
PROMPT $P$G
PATH=C:\;C:\DOS;C:\PCTOOLS;C:\MOVE'EM;C:\UTIL;C:\UTIL\ARC;
MIRROR C:
MOVE'EM SIZE=2048 PROG=C:\TSR\CLOCK
MOVE'EM PROG=APPEND /E
MOVE'EM SIZE=1536 PROG=C:\TSR\IOLITE
FASTOPEN C:=100
PCSHELL /RT
```

The GETSIZE statements have been removed from the command lines and SIZE= parameters added as indicated in MOVE'EM's summary. When you run MOVE'EM with the SUMMARY parameter again, you get the results shown in figure 10.3.

```
MOVE'EM  -- Version 1.02 -- A Program Loader for PCs
     Copyright (C) 1988-90 Qualitas, Inc.  All rights reserved.

                    RESIDENT PROGRAM MEMORY SUMMARY
                  Size Parameters
     Device or
     Program Name  Load    Initial  Resident  Suggested Action

     Dev=MOVE'EM$  1,360   1,360    1,360     Remove PRGREG=0
     Dev=BRNDEV    2,592   2,592    2,368     No SIZE parameter needed
     Dev=newprn      496     496      368     No SIZE parameter needed
     Dev=CON       1,648   1,648    1,584     No SIZE parameter needed
     CLOCK.COM     1,536   2,048      800     Continue with SIZE=2048
     APPEND.EXE    5,552   5,552    4,400     No SIZE parameter needed
     IOLITE.COM    1,024   1,536      416     Continue with SIZE=1536

     All programs/environments fit            Prog/env in use    12,080
     into high DOS memory                     Available          53,456
```

Fig. 10.3. The result of running MOVE'EM with the SUMMARY parameter again.

Because all the programs loaded into high memory fit, you are not given a suggested order by the summary screen. Note that the summary still recommends that you alter the MOVE'EM invocation statement. In this example, however, doing so is not possible because you have to use the NOFRAME parameter, causing the `Remove PRGREG=0` message because the expanded memory board is only LIM 3.2 hardware compatible.

Your CONFIG.SYS and AUTOEXEC.BAT now are ready to use. Running CHKDSK shows the following:

```
Volume HARD DISK C created Aug 24, 1990 5:00p

 21309440 bytes total disk space
    55296 bytes in 4 hidden files
    36864 bytes in 17 directories
  8978432 bytes in 386 user files
 12238848 bytes available on disk

   655360 bytes total memory
   562336 bytes free
```

Instead of having 540K of memory available to DOS and applications programs, you have 549K free. In some cases, this amount of available memory may make the difference between being able to run your applications program or not. For example, because of memory limitations, some CAD programs do not run if you have memory-resident programs (including the clock, which takes only 800 bytes of memory). A more typical scenario occurs when a computer is put onto a network. The network device drivers are so large that a previously used applications program does not run. Using a program such as MOVE'EM may make the difference between running that applications program or not.

Making the Best Use of Memory

The advantages gained from using a board that is only software compatible are minimal. You have to sacrifice using expanded memory for high DOS memory. Your particular application affects the best compromise.

Using the computer from the previous example, consider the effect of using a disk cache. PC Tools Deluxe is supplied with a disk cache, called PC-Cache, that can use expanded memory. The following CONFIG.SYS and AUTOEXEC.BAT files are the same as those in the previous example, but PC-Cache is loaded.

The CONFIG.SYS file is as follows:

```
DEVICE=EMM.SYS 258,000
DEVICE=C:\DOS\ANSI.SYS
DEVICE=C:\SYS\NEWPRN.SYS
DEVICE=C:\SYS\BURNDEV.SYS 5000 H+
FILES=30
BUFFERS=30
```

The AUTOEXEC.BAT file is as follows:

```
PROMPT $P$G
PATH=C:\;C:\DOS;C:\PCTOOLS;C:\MOVE'EM;C:\UTIL;C:\UTIL\ARC;
MIRROR C:
PC-CACHE
APPEND /E
C:\TSR\CLOCK
C:\TSR\IOLITE
FASTOPEN C:=100
PCSHELL /RT
```

When you run CHKDSK, you get the following:

```
Volume HARD DISK C created Aug 24, 1990 5:00p

 21309440 bytes total disk space
    55296 bytes in 4 hidden files
    34816 bytes in 16 directories
  8933376 bytes in 367 user files
 12285952 bytes available on disk
   655360 bytes total memory
   541664 bytes free
```

If you load MOVE'EM using GETSIZE and then follow the summary suggestions, the new CONFIG.SYS file is as follows:

```
DEVICE=EMM.SYS 258,000
DEVICE=C:\MOVE'EM\MOVE'EM.MGR NOFRAME PRGREG=1
DEVICE=C:\MOVE'EM\MOVE'EM.SYS PROG=C:\SYS\BURNDEV.SYS 5000 H+
DEVICE=C:\MOVE'EM\MOVE'EM.SYS PROG=C:\SYS\NEWPRN.SYS
DEVICE=C:\MOVE'EM\MOVE'EM.SYS PROG=C:\DOS\ANSI.SYS
FILES=30
BUFFERS=30
```

The new AUTOEXEC.BAT file is as follows:

```
PROMPT $P$G
PATH=C:\;C:\DOS;C:\PCTOOLS;C:\MOVE'EM;C:\UTIL;C:\UTIL\ARC;
MIRROR C:
MOVE'EM SIZE=2048 PROG=C:\TSR\CLOCK
MOVE'EM PROG=APPEND /E
MOVE'EM SIZE=1536 PROG=C:\TSR\IOLITE
PC-CACHE
FASTOPEN C:=100
PCSHELL /RT
```

Then, when you run CHKDSK, you see the following:

```
Volume HARD DISK C created Aug 24, 1990 5:00p

21309440 bytes total disk space
   55296 bytes in 4 hidden files
   34816 bytes in 16 directories
 8943616 bytes in 371 user files
12275712 bytes available on disk

  655360 bytes total memory
  495664 bytes free
```

In this case, the use of MOVE'EM is detrimental. Instead of having 529K of memory free, you have only 484K remaining because PC-Cache, which was using expanded memory for its cache memory, has to use low DOS memory for the cache. You have traded the use of expanded memory for the ability to load device drivers and TSRs into high memory.

On other boards, which allow more than a single 64K expanded memory page frame, you can use both expanded memory and MOVE'EM. You may see a benefit from using MOVE'EM in addition to expanded memory. In some cases, you may have to compromise between the amount of memory you give to MOVE'EM and the amount you reserve for expanded memory.

In previous chapters, the compromises of choosing between expanded and extended memory allocation were discussed. This decision usually involves consideration of performance speed and ability to run large applications programs. Usually the compromise made with MOVE'EM and expanded memory page frames is not a compromise of speed but of functionality.

QRAM

QRAM from Quarterdeck Office Systems offers features similar to those of MOVE'EM. On 8088-, 8086-, and 80286-based computers, a LIM 4.0-compatible expanded memory board can be used in association with QRAM for loading device drivers and TSRs into high DOS memory.

QRAM interfaces with the expanded memory driver. A page frame (or multiple page frames) is used by QRAM as DOS memory above the 640K limit instead of for expanded memory. These regions of high DOS memory can be used for storing device drivers and TSRs, freeing low DOS memory for applications programs.

Expanded memory boards limit QRAM and MOVE'EM in a similar way. If the expanded memory board is software compatible with LIM 4.0 only and is hardware compatible with LIM 3.2 only, you have to give up using expanded memory to use QRAM to create a 64K page frame. If the expanded memory board allows only a single page frame to be created, but it can be larger than 64K, QRAM is capable of using the additional page frames as high DOS memory but not of filling every hole in your high DOS memory area. If the expanded memory board is both hardware and software compatible with LIM 4.0, you can use every area of free address space that holds an expanded memory page frame.

If you remember that QRAM and MOVE'EM work with the expanded memory board device driver, the distinction between the various LIM 4.0 boards is relatively simple. QRAM and MOVE'EM only can create regions of high DOS memory where the expanded memory board has created a page frame. If you have only one 64K page frame, you have to choose between using expanded memory or high DOS memory.

QRAM is the device driver that controls the interface between the expanded memory device driver and the device driver (called LOADHI) loading the device drivers and TSRs into high DOS memory.

Example: Using QRAM To Regain Low DOS Memory

Consider an IBM AT with an EGA board and 1M of expanded memory running DOS 3.3. The expanded memory board is an Everex RAM 3000 Deluxe. This board is LIM 3.2 hardware compatible with a LIM 4.0 software device driver. Only one 64K page frame can be created.

Suppose that your CONFIG.SYS file contains the following:

```
DEVICE=EMM.SYS 258,000
DEVICE=C:\DOS\ANSI.SYS
DEVICE=C:\SYS\NEWPRN.SYS
DEVICE=C:\SYS\BURNDEV.SYS 5000 H+
FILES=30
BUFFERS=30
```

The first line loads the expanded memory device driver. ANSI.SYS, loaded in line 2, enhances your console device driver, and NEWPRN.SYS, a device driver, improves your printing speed. BURNDEV.SYS is a screen-blanking program. The settings for files and buffers are typical.

Suppose that your AUTOEXEC.BAT file contains the following:

```
PROMPT $P$G
PATH=C:\;C:\DOS;C:\PCTOOLS;C:\UTIL;C:\UTIL\ARC;
MIRROR C:
```

```
APPEND /E
C:\TSR\CLOCK
C:\TSR\IOLITE
FASTOPEN C:=100
PCSHELL /RT
```

The PROMPT and PATH commands are typical of most AUTOEXEC.BAT files. Mirror runs a PC Tools Deluxe utility that keeps a backup copy of the FAT and root directory of your disk. If you accidentally reformat or erase your hard disk, this file aids in the reconstruction of the lost data.

Each of the other lines in this AUTOEXEC.BAT file loads a memory-resident program. APPEND /E causes DOS to load the APPEND variables into the environment. APPEND is similar to PATH. DOS uses the directories listed to search for files it cannot find in the current directory, but APPEND is for nonexecutable files. FASTOPEN, also a DOS program, gives you faster access to previously used files on your disk. FASTOPEN keeps track of file locations as you use them. If you use a previously used file, that file is accessed faster than if DOS had to find it from scratch.

The CLOCK program is a memory-resident program that displays time in a corner of the screen. IOLITE also is memory resident and flashes a character on the screen whenever the disk is being accessed. PCSHELL, another PC Tools Deluxe utility program, is a file manager that enables you to execute many commands that are not available in DOS directly. For example, you can move whole subdirectories, and you can select several files at once and then copy or move them. The command line listed loads PCSHELL as a TSR that can be activated by a key combination and returns the DOS prompt.

When the computer is started with the preceding CONFIG.SYS and AUTOEXEC.BAT files, four device drivers and five memory-resident programs are loaded. Running CHKDSK reveals the following:

```
Volume HARD DISK C created Aug 24, 1990 5:00p

21309440 bytes total disk space
   55296 bytes in 4 hidden files
   40960 bytes in 19 directories
 9224192 bytes in 415 user files
11988992 bytes available on disk

  655360 bytes total memory
  553584 bytes free
```

Note that 540K of RAM is available for applications programs and their data to run. With no device drivers or memory-resident programs loaded, 586K of RAM is available.

Using QRAM to Regain Low DOS Memory

The device driver for QRAM must be installed in the CONFIG.SYS file, done automatically by QRAM's installation program. The following line is placed immediately after the expanded memory device driver:

```
DEVICE=C:\QRAM\QRAM.SYS
```

The particular type of expanded memory board used in this example, however, requires a parameter for allowing QRAM to take away the only expanded memory page frame and use it for high DOS memory. The line is modified to the following:

```
DEVICE=C:\QRAM\QRAM.SYS FRAMELENGTH=0
```

After installing QRAM and rebooting the computer to activate it, move your device drivers and TSRs into high DOS memory. The loader program, called LOADHI, is supplied with an automatic program for optimizing the CONFIG.SYS and AUTOEXEC.BAT files. For most installations, this program gives adequate results; however, as this example shows, sometimes the program doesn't give adequate results, so look closely at the manual to see whether you can optimize the arrangement further. Alternatively, you can change the CONFIG.SYS and AUTOEXEC.BAT files manually.

The optimizer, appropriately called OPTIMIZE, works in three stages. First, OPTIMIZE alters the CONFIG.SYS and AUTOEXEC.BAT files. The adjustments add the LOADHI device driver to each device driver and TSR that is a candidate for loading in high DOS memory. An extra parameter is added to the invoking line to allow LOADHI to calculate the size of the invoked program.

The second stage is rebooting the computer to actually use the modified CONFIG.SYS and AUTOEXEC.BAT files. After OPTIMIZE knows the size of each device and TSR, OPTIMIZE calculates how to fit all or some of the programs into high DOS memory. OPTIMIZE alters the CONFIG.SYS and AUTOEXEC.BAT files after establishing the best fit.

Rebooting the computer installs the final LOADHI arrangement. For the example, CONFIG.SYS is altered by OPTIMIZE as follows:

```
DEVICE=EMM.SYS 258,000
DEVICE=C:\QRAM\QRAM.SYS R:1 FRAMELENGTH=0
DEVICE=C:\QRAM\LOADHI.SYS /R:1 C:\DOS\ANSI.SYS
DEVICE=C:\QRAM\LOADHI.SYS /R:1 C:\SYS\NEWPRN.SYS
DEVICE=C:\QRAM\LOADHI.SYS /R:1 C:\SYS\BURNDEV.SYS 5000 H+
FILES=30
BUFFERS=1
```

AUTOEXEC.BAT is changed to the following:

```
C:\QRAM\LOADHI /R:1 C:\QRAM\BUFFERS=30 PROMPT $P$G
PATH=C:\;C:\DOS;C:\PCTOOLS;C:\UTIL;C:\UTIL\ARC;
MIRROR C:
C:\QRAM\LOADHI /R:1 APPEND /E
C:\QRAM\LOADHI /R:1 C:\TSR\CLOCK
C:\QRAM\LOADHI /R:1 C:\TSR\IOLITE
FASTOPEN C:=100
PCSHELL /RT
```

After QRAM is loaded, each device that appears in CONFIG.SYS is loaded into high DOS memory. The device driver LOADHI.SYS interfaces between QRAM and DOS and your applications program. In AUTOEXEC.BAT, only three of the memory-resident programs have been moved into high DOS memory. FASTOPEN and PCSHELL are not moved because they don't fit into 64K. /R:1 specifies the region number into which the program is to be loaded. In this example, only one area of high DOS memory exists; therefore, all the programs are loaded into region 1.

Notice that the BUFFERS setting in CONFIG.SYS has been reduced to 1 and that the AUTOEXEC.BAT file includes a line that sets buffers. QRAM supplies substitute programs for several DOS commands that typically are set in CONFIG.SYS. These substitute programs can be loaded into high DOS memory. Substitutes are supplied for BUFFERS, FILES, FCBS, and LASTDRIVE. (The substitute for BUFFERS does not work with DOS 4.) You can use these programs only on versions of DOS that support these DOS features. For example, FCBS is not a feature of DOS 2.

The optimizing program managed to determine the BUFFERS setting in the example but did not detect the FILES setting. The FILES setting, however, like all settings, can be altered manually.

When you remove the current settings from CONFIG.SYS and place the substitutes into AUTOEXEC.BAT, you still need to include a setting in CONFIG.SYS. DOS's default setting for BUFFERS varies between 2 and 15, depending on the DOS version. After creating a BUFFERS line in AUTOEXEC.BAT, set the CONFIG.SYS BUFFERS value to 1 to use the minimum amount of low DOS memory.

A similar arrangement for the FILES setting is needed so you can use high DOS memory for some of the file handles (names stored by DOS). Because some applications programs don't work correctly when the FILES setting in CONFIG.SYS is too low, the value should be set to 10. The AUTOEXEC.BAT setting increases this number from 10 to the desired number.

Changing the CONFIG.SYS and AUTOEXEC.BAT files manually to give the best results for this example gives a CONFIG.SYS as follows:

```
DEVICE=EMM.SYS 258,000
DEVICE=C:\QRAM\QRAM.SYS R:1 FRAMELENGTH=0
DEVICE=C:\QRAM\LOADHI.SYS /R:1 C:\DOS\ANSI.SYS
DEVICE=C:\QRAM\LOADHI.SYS /R:1 C:\SYS\NEWPRN.SYS
DEVICE=C:\QRAM\LOADHI.SYS /R:1 C:\SYS\BURNDEV.SYS 5000 H+
FILES=10
BUFFERS=1
```

The AUTOEXEC.BAT file is as follows:

```
C:\QRAM\LOADHI /R:1 C:\QRAM\FILES=20
C:\QRAM\LOADHI /R:1 C:\QRAM\BUFFERS=30
PROMPT $P$G
PATH=C:\;C:\DOS;C:\PCTOOLS;C:\UTIL;C:\UTIL\ARC;
MIRROR C:
C:\QRAM\LOADHI /R:1 APPEND /E
C:\QRAM\LOADHI /R:1 C:\TSR\CLOCK
C:\QRAM\LOADHI /R:1 C:\TSR\IOLITE
FASTOPEN C:=100
PCSHELL /RT
```

After the computer is rebooted with these settings, CHKDSK shows the following:

```
Volume HARD DISK C created Aug 24, 1990 5:00p

 21309440 bytes total disk space
    55296 bytes in 4 hidden files
    40960 bytes in 19 directories
  9244672 bytes in 425 user files
 11968512 bytes available on disk

   655360 bytes total memory
   579792 bytes free
```

Note that 566K of low DOS memory now is available for use by DOS or your applications programs, saving 26K of low DOS memory.

ALL CHARGECARD for ATs

With its ALL CHARGECARD for ATs and ALL CARD for PCs, All Computers Inc. has taken a different approach to adding high DOS memory. The principle is similar to that of MOVE'EM and QRAM. You replace vacant areas of high DOS memory with RAM, which can be used for storing device drivers and TSRs.

ALL CHARGECARD and ALL CARD, however, include a circuit board and use hardware rather than software for memory management. The PC circuit board is a typical expansion board in shape; you plug it into an expansion slot. You remove the microprocessor, run a supplied cable from the expansion board to the microprocessor socket, and place the microprocessor onto the expansion board. ALL CHARGECARD makes use of extended memory boards in an AT instead of using a LIM 4.0 expanded memory software device driver. The product consists of two parts: hardware and software. The hardware, a small circuit board, is placed into the socket where the 80286 currently resides. The 80286 then is placed into the circuit board.

After a software driver is installed, any extended memory in the computer can be accessed as expanded memory conforming with LIM 4.0. The extended memory board appears to be LIM 4.0 compatible. You can specify large and multiple page frames and also can backfill your base memory using the software driver. The LIM 4.0 compatibility is supplied by the hardware, and the software driver does not do the memory management portion. ALL CHARGECARD and ALL CARD interface between memory and the microprocessor, unlike software memory managers, which interface between the microprocessor and DOS. Note that the microprocessor always operates in real mode when you use ALL CHARGECARD. The memory mapping features for which the software emulators require protected mode are implemented in hardware on ALL CHARGECARD.

You also can specify areas of high DOS memory for TSRs and device drivers. Trade-offs exist, however. The advantage of ALL CHARGECARD is that you can use any board that can be configured as extended memory and gain full functionality. ALL CHARGECARD accesses the memory under LIM 4.0 much faster because it is doing the memory mapping through hardware rather than software emulation. ALL CHARGECARD enables you to do memory management features that you typically can do only on the 80386—features such as remapping ROM into RAM.

ALL CHARGECARD is more expensive than the software-only products, and you will find that determining whether a program fits into high DOS memory is harder. The software-only products provide a utility that measures the size of the programs during loading and initializing and when memory resident; this utility is not offered with ALL CHARGECARD.

Installing ALL CHARGECARD

The installation of ALL CHARGECARD involves removing the 80286 microprocessor from your computer. Although easy in principle—you just pull the chip out of its socket—removing the microprocessor requires some manual dexterity and mechanical inclination to avoid damaging the pins on the chip, to avoid damaging the chip with static electricity, and to keep the orientation of pin 1 correct. The chip is square but must be inserted into its socket with the correct orientation.

After you remove the 80286 microprocessor, insert it into a small adapter board. Then plug the adapter board, via an adapter cable if necessary, into the now vacant 80286 socket. If you're not comfortable putting expansion boards or disk drives in your computer or flicking the dip switches and changing jumpers, this product is not suitable. If you install it incorrectly, you can damage your computer. The product is shown in figure 10.4.

Fig. 10.4. All Computers Inc.'s ALL CHARGECARD.

After the hardware is installed, install the device driver into CONFIG.SYS so that the new hardware can be used.

Example: Using ALL CHARGECARD To Regain Low DOS Memory

Consider an IBM AT with an EGA board and 1M of extended memory running DOS 3.3. The extended memory board is an Everex RAM 3000 Deluxe. Its dip switches can alter the configuration from a LIM 4.0 board to an extended memory board. Let ALL CHARGECARD do the expanded memory emulation. Also let ALL CHARGECARD do any backfilling of low DOS memory instead of using jumpers on the board for that purpose. ALL CHARGECARD does not have an automatic configuration program, but you can work through the process to configure your computer by reading the manual carefully.

The following CONFIG.SYS file contains the LIM 4.0 expanded memory device driver but has no additional ALL CHARGECARD features:

```
DEVICE=C:\ALL\ALLEMM4.SYS
DEVICE=C:\DOS\ANSI.SYS
DEVICE=C:\SYS\NEWPRN.SYS
DEVICE=C:\SYS\BURNDEV.SYS 5000 H+
FILES=30
BUFFERS=30
```

The first line loads the ALL CHARGECARD device driver. ANSI.SYS, loaded in line 2, enhances your console device driver, and NEWPRN.SYS, a device driver, improves your printing speed. BURNDEV.SYS is a screen-blanking program. The settings for files and buffers are typical.

Suppose that your AUTOEXEC.BAT contains the following:

```
PROMPT $P$G
PATH=C:\;C:\DOS;C:\PCTOOLS;C:\UTIL;C:\UTIL\ARC;
MIRROR C:
APPEND /E
C:\TSR\CLOCK
C:\TSR\IOLITE
FASTOPEN C:=100
PCSHELL /RT
```

The PROMPT and PATH commands are typical of most AUTOEXEC.BAT files. Mirror runs a PC Tools Deluxe utility that keeps a backup copy of the FAT and the root directory of your disk. If you accidentally reformat or erase your hard disk, this file aids in the reconstruction of the lost data.

Each of the other lines in this AUTOEXEC.BAT file loads a memory-resident program. APPEND /E causes DOS to load the APPEND variables into the environment. APPEND is similar to PATH. DOS uses the directories listed to search for files it cannot find in the current directory, but APPEND is for

Chapter 10: Regaining Base Memory

nonexecutable files. FASTOPEN, also a DOS program, gives you faster access to previously used files on your disk. FASTOPEN keeps track of file locations as you use them. If you use a previously used file, that file is accessed faster than if DOS had to find it from scratch.

The CLOCK program is a memory-resident program that displays time in a corner of the screen. IOLITE also is memory resident and flashes a character on the screen whenever the disk is being accessed. PCSHELL, another PC Tools Deluxe utility program, is a file manager that enables you to execute many commands that are not available in DOS directly. For example, you can move whole subdirectories, and you can select several files at once and then copy or move them. The command line listed loads PCSHELL as a TSR that can be activated by a key combination and returns the DOS prompt.

When the computer is started with the preceding CONFIG.SYS and AUTOEXEC.BAT files, four device drivers and five memory-resident programs are loaded. Running CHKDSK reveals the following:

```
Volume HARD DISK C created Aug 24, 1990 5:00p

 21309440 bytes total disk space
    55296 bytes in 4 hidden files
    45056 bytes in 21 directories
  9652224 bytes in 471 user files
 11556864 bytes available on disk

   655360 bytes total memory
   551440 bytes free
```

Note that 539K of RAM is available for applications programs and their data to run.

ALL CHARGECARD is supplied with a program, ALLMENU, that enables you to test various functions and get extensive memory information. The following is an excerpt from ALLMENU, with the previous CONFIG.SYS and AUTOEXEC.BAT files:

```
EMS 4.0 Driver Installed and Is Active.
The Active EMS Driver Is The <ALLEMM4 EXPANDED MEMORY MANAGER>
The Page Frame_Address sits at e000
Raw Page Size In Paragraphs - 1024
Alternate Register Sets    - 8
Context Save Area Size     - 96
DMA Register Sets          - 0
DMA Channel Operation      - 0
The Total Number Of Expanded Memory Pages are 92
The Total Number Of Unallocated Expanded Memory Pages are 52
The Total Number Of Handles available for use is 64
Ax - 0100
```

```
Bx - 0012
Cx - 0100
Dx - 7010
The First 4k Page Of EMS Memory Is 0100
The Number Of 4k Pages Of EMS Memory Is 0100
The Number Of 1st 4k Page Of DMA Buffer In Meg0 Is 0070
The Number Of 4k Pages Of DMA Buffer Is 0010
Conventional Memory Has Not Been Sorted.
Conventional Memory Has Been Filled Up To 640k.
There Is No High RAM.
There Is No Mapped ROM.
Expanded Memory Is Being Used.
Conventional Memory Has Not Been Filled Up To Video Buffer.
                    CONVENTIONAL MEMORY STATUS
        :000 100 200 300 400 500 600 700 800 900 A00 B00 C00 D00 E00 F00
  0000:  US  US  US  US  US  US  US  US  US  US  US  US  US  US  US  US
  1000:  CO  CO  CO  CO  CO  CO  CO  CO  CO  CO  CO  CO  CO  CO  CO  CO
  2000:  CO  CO  CO  CO  CO  CO  CO  CO  CO  CO  CO  CO  CO  CO  CO  CO
  3000:  CO  CO  CO  CO  CO  CO  CO  CO  CO  CO  CO  CO  CO  CO  CO  CO
  4000:  CO  CO  CO  CO  CO  CO  CO  CO  CO  CO  CO  CO  CO  CO  CO  CO
  5000:  CO  CO  CO  CO  CO  CO  CO  CO  CO  CO  CO  CO  CO  CO  CO  CO
  6000:  CO  CO  CO  CO  CO  CO  CO  CO  CO  CO  CO  CO  CO  CO  CO  CO
  7000:  CO  CO  CO  CO  CO  CO  CO  CO  CO  CO  CO  CO  CO  CO  CO  CO
  8000:  CO  CO  CO  CO  CO  CO  CO  CO  CO  CO  CO  CO  CO  CO  CO  CO
  9000:  CO  CO  CO  CO  CO  CO  CO  CO  CO  CO  CO  CO  CO  CO  CO  CO
  a000:  VI  VI  VI  VI  VI  VI  VI  VI  VI  VI  VI  VI  VI  VI  VI  VI
  b000:  MA  MA  MA  MA  MA  MA  MA  VI  VI  VI  VI  VI  VI  VI  VI  VI
  c000:  RO  RO  RO  RO  RO  RO  RO  MA  MA  MA  MA  MA  MA  MA  MA  MA
  d000:  MA  MA  MA  MA  MA  MA  MA  MA  MA  MA  MA  MA  MA  MA  MA  MA
  e000:  PF  PF  PF  PF  PF  PF  PF  PF  PF  PF  PF  PF  PF  PF  PF  PF
  f000:  RO  RO  RO  RO  RO  RO  RO  RO  RO  RO  RO  RO  RO  RO  RO  RO
LEGEND :          / RO - ROM      / CO - DOS Conventional Memory
MA - Mappable / US - Used     / MR - Mapped ROM    / HR - High RAM
EX - Excluded / VI - Video    / PF - Page Frame    / XX - Unknown
CONVENTIONAL MEMORY STATUS
```

The first section shows you all the current settings for the device driver. This computer has been backfilled up to 640K. (The IBM AT has a maximum of 512K on the system board.) The area between 640K and the video board hasn't been filled because the computer contains an EGA, and you cannot use all the graphics modes on an EGA if you fill the area above 640K with RAM. No high DOS memory areas are defined, and the ROM has not been remapped into faster RAM. The expanded memory device driver is installed.

The lower part of this excerpt shows a memory map of DOS's address range. (Appendix B examines hexadecimal addresses.) The segment addresses are listed at the left, and the type of memory in each segment is listed. The area from segment 0000H to 1000H is in use. From 1000H to A000H is conventional DOS memory. The range of addresses from A000H to B000H and B800H to C000H is video memory, and from C000H to C800H and F000H to FFFFH is ROM. The expanded memory page frame is 64K starting at E000H. The other areas of high memory are marked as mappable.

Rearranging CONFIG.SYS and AUTOEXEC.BAT for ALL CHARGECARD

Unlike MOVE'EM and QRAM, ALL CHARGECARD does not supply a method of measuring the various sizes of your device drivers and TSRs. You have to try loading them into high memory. If they work, they have enough space. If they do not work, you have to give them more room or load them in low DOS memory.

Remember that each program has three important sizes: loading size, initializing size, and resident size. You can determine the resident size by running CHKDSK, loading the program into memory, and rerunning CHKDSK. However, this number doesn't include any extra memory (often quite substantial) that the program needs when loading. Consequently, simply ensuring that the high DOS memory area is large enough for the resident portion is not adequate.

If you are conscious about having made changes, however, you will be able to see whether a program doesn't work quickly. Although you may miss some subtle memory space problems, you always can put the program back into low DOS memory temporarily to see whether the problem goes away.

The ALL CHARGECARD method of loading device drivers into high DOS memory is unique. Instead of loading them from the CONFIG.SYS file, you load them from the AUTOEXEC.BAT file. This method enables the loader program to occupy less conventional memory and put more of the device driver program into high DOS memory.

The modified CONFIG.SYS for the example is as follows:

```
DEVICE=C:\ALL\ALLEMM4.SYS RAM
```

Only the expanded memory device driver is loaded from CONFIG.SYS. The RAM option allows all empty areas of high DOS memory to be allocated as high DOS memory. The expanded memory page frame remains unchanged.

The AUTOEXEC.BAT file is as follows:

```
C:\ALL\DEVICE=C:\DOS\ANSI.SYS
C:\ALL\DEVICE=C:\SYS\NEWPRN.SYS
C:\ALL\DEVICE=C:\SYS\BURNDEV.SYS 5000 H+
C:\ALL\FILES=30
C:\ALL\BUFFERS=30
PROMPT $P$G
PATH=C:\;C:\DOS;C:\PCTOOLS;C:\UTIL;C:\UTIL\ARC;
MIRROR C:
C:\ALL\ALLOAD APPEND /E
C:\ALL\ALLOAD C:\TSR\CLOCK
C:\ALL\ALLOAD C:\TSR\IOLITE
FASTOPEN C:=100
PCSHELL /RT
```

Note that, unlike in CONFIG.SYS, in AUTOEXEC.BAT no space is permitted between DEVICE and = and = and the path name.

ALL CHARGECARD is supplied with several programs that are substitutes for DOS commands. The program DEVICE serves a function similar to the DOS CONFIG.SYS directive, but because DEVICE is a program, it runs from AUTOEXEC.BAT. In a similar fashion to QRAM, substitute programs for FILES, BUFFERS, and LASTDRIVE allow some of the memory for these features to be high DOS memory.

The loader program for TSRs, ALLOAD, is equivalent to QRAM's LOADHI and MOVE'EM's MOVE'EM. The loader program name is inserted into the command line for the TSR you want to load in high DOS memory, and the file name for the TSR becomes a parameter for the loader program.

After the computer is rebooted with this new configuration, CHKDSK shows the following:

```
Volume HARD DISK C created Aug 24, 1990 5:00p

21309440 bytes total disk space
   55296 bytes in 4 hidden files
   45056 bytes in 21 directories
 9684992 bytes in 477 user files
11524096 bytes available on disk

  655360 bytes total memory
  573680 bytes free
```

Note that 560K of low DOS memory now is available for applications programs. ALL CHARGECARD saved a total of 21K.

Further refinement of the parameters is possible. You can add the ROM parameter, which causes ALL CHARGECARD to remap the ROM in your computer into RAM. Because RAM has a faster access time than ROM, you will see a performance improvement with this remapping. Note that this feature normally is possible only on computers with a 80836 or 80486 microprocessor. The electronics on the circuit board are responsible for this feature.

ALL CHARGECARD (and its sibling, ALL CARD) also wastes less high DOS memory when loading programs. Both MOVE'EM and QRAM load programs on a page boundary, and each page is 16K in size. If a program doesn't fill completely the last page it uses, the space left in that page is wasted. On ALL CHARGECARD, programs can be loaded onto paragraph boundaries. A paragraph is 4K in size; consequently, you usually waste less space.

Using DOS's HIMEM.SYS Feature

DOS 5.0 includes HIMEM.SYS, a new extended memory manager. HIMEM.SYS, a device driver placed in the CONFIG.SYS file, can increase the amount of free base memory remaining in your computer. (An earlier version of this device driver has been supplied by Microsoft with versions of Windows.)

Note that extended memory is available on only 286-, 386-, and 486-based computers. Consequently, you cannot use HIMEM.SYS on PCs. This device driver can be used in most situations with its default values; however, you can use several optional switches to tailor its action for different computers.

The management of extended memory is closely related to the hardware. Consequently, tailoring may be necessary because not all PC-compatible computers are compatible at this level.

HIMEM.SYS is a new device driver supplied with DOS 5, but it has been supplied before with some versions of Windows. Like all device drivers, HIMEM.SYS is loaded with a DEVICE= directive in CONFIG.SYS. HIMEM.SYS acts as an extended memory manager and allocates the extended memory that programs request. Because this device driver requires extended memory, HIMEM.SYS does not work on 8088- or 8086-based computers.

The standards for programs using extended memory are unclear, and more than one program may try to use the same area of memory. HIMEM.SYS prevents this lack of cooperation among programs by keeping track of which program is using which area of extended memory.

HIMEM.SYS also manages the high memory areas, available between 640K and 1M between your device drivers. HIMEM.SYS makes some of the extended memory in a computer available for programs that can make use of high DOS memory.

You can use HIMEM.SYS in AT types of systems to load DOS into high memory. On 80386- and 80486-based computers, you can use HIMEM.SYS in association with EMM386.EXE, LOADHIGH, and DEVICEHIGH to perform similar functions to other 386 memory managers. EMM386.EXE, LOADHIGH, and DEVICEHIGH are covered in Chapter 11. This section introduces the syntax for HIMEM.SYS and explains how to load part of DOS into high DOS memory on AT types of computers.

Examining the HIMEM.SYS Syntax

The syntax for HIMEM.SYS follows:

DEVICE = *d:\path***HIMEM.SYS** */hmamin=mm* */numhandles=hhh* */int15=iiii* */machine:aa* */a20control:on/off* */shadowram:on/off* */cpuclock:on/off*

The following list explains these parameters:

Parameter	Explanation
d:\path	This parameter is the drive and path of the HIMEM.SYS device driver.
/hmamin=mm	This parameter is the number of kilobytes that a program must use before high memory areas (HMAs) can be used; *mm* is a value from 0 to 63. The default value is 0.
/numhandles=hhh	This parameter is the maximum number of extended memory block handles that can be in use at one time; *hhh* is a value from 1 to 128.
/int15=iiii	*iiii* is the number of kilobytes of extended memory for the INT15 interface; *iiii* is a value from 64 to 65,535. The default value is 0.

/machine:aa	This parameter selects the A20 handler for the type of system being used; *aa* is a Microsoft-designated number for the system type. Alternatively, you can use a Microsoft-designated code name for the computer. The default setting is *at* or 1 (for an IBM AT).
/a20control:on or /a20control:off	HIMEM.SYS controls the A20 address line in all cases if this parameter is set to ON. If this parameter is set to OFF, HIMEM.SYS controls the A20 address line only if the A20 line is set to OFF when HIMEM.SYS is loaded. The default setting is ON.
/shadowram:on or shadowram:off	If this parameter is set to ON, shadow RAM in the computer is unaffected by HIMEM.SYS. If this parameter is set to OFF, HIMEM.SYS tries to disable the shadow RAM and add the RAM to its available memory. For computers with less than 2M of RAM, the default setting is OFF.
/cpuclock:on or /cpuclock:off	If this parameter is set to OFF, the speed of your computer may be affected. If this parameter is set to ON, HIMEM.SYS performs slower, but your computer may work at full speed. The default setting is OFF.

The */hmamin=mm* parameter gives you some control over the programs that are loaded into high memory. You may decide to load only the larger programs rather than small programs that have little effect on the amount of low DOS memory available. If you specify a value for *mm*, only programs requiring more than that number of kilobytes are loaded into high memory.

The */numhandles=hhh* parameter gives you control over the number of different extended-memory-block handles that can be used. The handle identifies which block of memory belongs to which program.

The */int15=iiiii* parameter assigns some extended memory to the interrupt 15H interface. You may have to use this option if an older program doesn't work properly. This interrupt is used by some older programs to access extended memory. If the older program does not use extended memory correctly, it may not be willing to share the memory with HIMEM.SYS. If you reserve some extended memory via this option, you may be able to get the older program and HIMEM.SYS to function together.

The /machine:aa parameter selects the A20 handler for the type of system being used. The computer can access 1M of memory by using the first 20 address pins on the microprocessor (A0 through A19). For your system to access more than 1M of memory—which is necessary for using extended memory—the A20 handler program routine located in your computer's BIOS must be used. On many computers, HIMEM.SYS can detect that an A20 handler is being used, but on other computers, you may have to tell HIMEM.SYS that one is in use. You can specify your computer by a number or a name. Table 10.1 shows some of the names and numbers you can use. The Computer column is the actual name of the BIOS being used in the computer, the Name column is the code name you type after the /machine:, and the Number column is the number you can use instead of the code name.

Table 10.1
A20 Handler Identifiers

Computer	Name	Number
IBM PC/AT	at	1
IBM PS/2	ps2	2
Phoenix Cascade BIOS	pt1cascade	3
HP Vectra (A and A+)	hpvectra	4
AT&T 6300 Plus	att6300plus	5
Acer 1100	acer1100	6
Toshiba 1600 and 1200XE	toshiba	7
Wyse 12.5 MHz 286	wyse	8
Tulip SX	tulip	9
Zenith ZBIOS	zenith	10
IBM PC/AT	at1	11
IBM PC/AT (alternative delay)	at2	12
CSS Labs	css	12
IBM PC/AT (alternative delay)	at3	13
Philips	philips	13
HP Vectra	fasthp	14

If you experience problems using HIMEM.SYS with, for example, an HP Vectra, you can try adding the parameter /machine:fasthp or /machine:14.

Loading Part of DOS into High DOS Memory

Although not as sophisticated as the other memory managers, HIMEM.SYS is supplied as a part of DOS, so it is effectively free. DOS 5 uses less low DOS memory than Version 4 even without the use of HIMEM.SYS, but in some cases, you may be able to reduce this memory even further.

You can use HIMEM.SYS to put part of DOS 5 into high DOS memory. Place two lines in your CONFIG.SYS file: a device driver directive loading HIMEM.SYS, using the syntax just discussed, and a *DOS=HIGH* directive on its own line.

DOS loads part of itself into high DOS memory and gives you even more low DOS memory for your application.

Chapter Summary

This chapter covered the various methods of recovering low DOS memory on PCs and ATs. The first method is to remove any unused device drivers and TSRs from the CONFIG.SYS and AUTOEXEC.BAT files. You should look carefully at the manuals supplied with the applications programs to determine whether you need to run the program as a TSR or from the DOS command prompt.

The second method is to use a loader program. On ATs and PCs with expanded memory boards that conform with LIM 4.0, you can use products such as MOVE'EM and QRAM to convert some of the expanded memory into high DOS memory. The loader program can use this high DOS memory to hold device drivers and TSRs that normally occupy low DOS memory. The benefit of this approach is linked closely to your expanded memory board's functionality. The boards that are software compatible with LIM 4.0 are not necessarily hardware compatible. Although they function with applications programs that use LIM 4.0, the expanded memory boards that are software compatible with LIM 4.0 do not give you full flexibility.

The third method of regaining low DOS memory is to use HIMEM.SYS, supplied as a standard part of DOS 5.0 and some versions of Microsoft Windows. HIMEM.SYS converts extended memory into high DOS memory, into which TSRs and device drivers can be loaded.

Using the Processor's Power   11

All computers that run DOS as an operating system operate similarly. DOS is written for the 8088 microprocessor. When you run DOS on computers with other microprocessors, such as the 80386 or 80486, you actually run them as though they are 8088 microprocessors.

Chapter 10 covers special programs and add-in hardware that work with DOS and your memory boards, enabling you to enhance memory management on PC and AT styles of systems. This chapter covers the memory management programs available for the 80386 and 80486 microprocessors. These programs have two major components. First, you can make the best use of your memory resources for base, expanded, and extended memory, and shadow ROM. Second, the programs offer utilities that enable you to load device drivers and TSRs into high DOS memory.

386 Architecture

The 80386 has two major operating modes: real and protected. When operating in real mode, the 80386 behaves like an 8088. The 80386 has 1M of contiguous address space. When you install DOS, the 1M of memory divides into two regions. DOS and applications programs use the area below 640K, known as *base*, *conventional*, or *low* DOS memory. The area between 640K and 1M is used for devices and ROM BIOS.

To maintain compatibility with the 80286 microprocessor, part of the 80386's protected mode is identical to the 80286's protected mode. Up to 16M of memory can be addressed. Operating systems such as OS/2 use this mode.

The 80386, however, is more advanced than the 8088 and 80286 microprocessors. The 80386's protected mode includes virtual 8086 mode, which enables the microprocessor to run multiple 8086 applications at once. Products using this feature are introduced in Chapter 12.

The 386 memory managers discussed in this chapter take advantage of the virtual 8086 mode to run DOS and a single application. The virtual 8086 mode has many advantages over real mode, particularly relating to memory management. The memory managers can manipulate memory in ways not possible with the single 1M approach of the 8088-compatible real mode.

The 80486 microprocessor follows the same principles as its predecessors—downward compatible with the 8088, 80286, and 80386 microprocessors, yet adding new features. With the 80486, you can run the computer with just DOS as though you are using a fast PC or, more likely, with a 386 memory manager to make the best use of the computer's memory. Intel has stated that each successive microprocessor will be compatible with preceding members of the same family.

386 Memory Managers and Loaders: An Overview

Specialized memory manager programs, such as 386-to-the-MAX and QEMM, take advantage of the additional features found in the 80386 to manage extended and expanded memory. This chapter covers these products in detail.

All Charge 386, 386-to-the-MAX, and QEMM come with loader programs. Loader memory managers work with the 386 memory managers so that you can load device drivers and TSRs into high DOS memory. Loader programs also can load device drivers and TSRs into high DOS memory.

The operation principle of 386 loaders is similar to the operation principles of the AT and PC products, such as MOVE'EM and QRAM. The vacant areas of high DOS memory are assigned to the loader programs, which interface between DOS and the memory managers. Loading and unloading to run programs is transparent to the user but has the advantage of giving you more free low DOS memory to run your applications programs.

Loader programs for ATs and PCs use expanded memory created by a LIM 4.0 device driver supplied with the expanded memory board to fill the vacant memory holes. Loader programs for the 386-based computers use memory available through the 386 memory manager. Because of the close relationship between the memory manager and the loader, you need to use the memory manager from the same company as the loader program.

386-to-the-MAX

Qualitas' 386-to-the-MAX, one of three popular 386 memory managers, uses the protected mode of the 80386 to manage memory. The memory manager interfaces between the hardware and DOS, manages extended and expanded memory, and can provide LIM 4.0-compatible EMS. In a 386-based computer, expansion memory nearly always is extended memory. Because of the 80386's powerful memory manager features, you use a memory manager to emulate LIM 4.0 instead of using an expansion board with expanded memory hardware on it. Doing so gives you full LIM 4.0 compatibility using extended memory and the memory manager. Many new 386-based computers come with an implementation of a 386 memory manager, providing the expanded memory capabilities at no additional cost.

Full implementation of the 386 memory managers, however, can provide far more than just expanded memory management. You can remap ROM with faster RAM, use the loader program to load devices and TSRs into high DOS memory, backfill low DOS memory, and ensure that you are using the fastest memory in the most frequently used areas.

Installing 386-to-the-MAX

An automatic installation program that comes with 386-to-the-MAX modifies CONFIG.SYS and AUTOEXEC.BAT. This section examines how to install the memory manager and its effect on your computer's memory. The following section covers the loader program supplied with 386-to-the-MAX.

Consider a 386-based computer with 4M of extended memory, an EGA, and 512K of base memory running DOS 4. Suppose that the CONFIG.SYS is as follows:

```
BUFFERS = 25
BREAK=ON
FILES=30
LASTDRIVE=M
SHELL=C:\DOS\COMMAND.COM /P /E:256
INSTALL=C:\DOS\FASTOPEN.EXE C:=(50,25)
DEVICE=C:\SYS\NEWPRN.SYS
```

The AUTOEXEC.BAT is as follows:

```
@ECHO OFF
VERIFY ON
SET COMSPEC=C:\DOS\COMMAND.COM
PATH=C:\;C:\DOS;C:\UTIL;C:\BATCH;C:\UTIL\PCTOOLS;D:\HL;C:\WP51;C:\FONTSPAC;
MIRROR C: D: E: /TC
E:\FONTSPAC\FONTRES
E:\MOUSESYS\MSCMOUSE
APPEND=C:\DOS
PROMPT $P$G
HOTLINE
```

The CONFIG.SYS sets BREAK to on and sets a value for FILES, BUFFERS, and LASTDRIVE. The DOS environment is set to 256 bytes with the SHELL directive. A FASTOPEN setting is installed, and a printer device driver is loaded.

AUTOEXEC.BAT includes the typical PATH, APPEND, PROMPT, and COMSPEC settings. The PC Tools Deluxe MIRROR program copies the file allocation table (FAT) and root directory to a file for safekeeping and loads the delete tracker resident, which keeps track of all deleted files. To restore deleted files, you can use PC Tools.

AUTOEXEC.BAT loads three memory-resident programs. FONTRES, the memory-resident portion of Isogon's FONTSPACE and a font utility for LaserJet printers, compresses font files until you print a file, saving substantial amounts of hard disk space. The mouse driver is for a Mouse Systems mouse, and Hotline is an electronic Rolodex program.

After you install 386-to-the-MAX, running CHKDSK gives the following listing:

```
Volume HARD DISK C created 12-26-1989 5:04p
Volume Serial Number is 0C2E-18C9

 23037952 bytes total disk space
   430080 bytes in 7 hidden files
    61440 bytes in 28 directories
 21671936 bytes in 700 user files
     2048 bytes in bad sectors
   872448 bytes available on disk

     2048 bytes in each allocation unit
    11249 total allocation units on disk
      426 available allocation units on disk

   524288 total bytes memory
   286480 bytes free
```

Because this computer is running DOS 4, an alternative is to run MEM; the results follow:

```
524288 bytes total memory
524288 bytes available
286480 largest executable program size

4194304 bytes total extended memory
4194304 bytes available extended memory
```

Because 512K of base memory and several memory-resident programs are available, not much room remains for an applications program to run.

After 386-to-the-MAX is loaded as a device driver in CONFIG.SYS, the new CONFIG.SYS becomes the following:

```
DEVICE=C:\386MAX\386MAX.SYS PRO=C:\386MAX\386MAX.PRO
BUFFERS = 25
BREAK=ON
FILES=30
LASTDRIVE=M
SHELL=C:\DOS\COMMAND.COM /P /E:256
INSTALL=C:\DOS\FASTOPEN.EXE C:=(50,25)
DEVICE=C:\SYS\NEWPRN.SYS
```

The 386 memory manager is loaded early in CONFIG.SYS. The device driver, called 386MAX.SYS, uses the parameters stored in a profile file called 386MAX.PRO.

You have two approaches when using 386MAX.SYS. You can list every option to be used by 386-to-the-MAX on the invoking command line or store the parameters separately in a file. Because the parameters become fairly lengthy on some computers, using a profile file is preferable. In the profile, each parameter is listed separately. You can add comments to each parameter so that you can remember the reasons for the selections. The profile file for the preceding CONFIG.SYS is as follows:

```
USE=B000-B800     ; INSTALL ==> recover RAM in MDA region
USE=F600-F900     ; INSTALL ==> recover fill regions in ROM
USE=FA00-FB00     ; INSTALL ==> recover fill regions in ROM
USE=FC00-FE00     ; INSTALL ==> recover fill regions in ROM
; This profile created automatically by INSTALL
PRGREG=4          ; Load 386MAX.SYS into this program region
```

This profile, created when the program is installed, maps four areas of high memory for use with 386-to-the-MAX. The first region recovers RAM in the area of memory normally used by a monochrome display adapter. The other three areas listed are empty areas of ROM BIOS.

Remember that BIOS is a series of programs installed into ROM. The amount of space in the chip is fixed at a round number, such as 64K or 128K. The BIOS programs, however, don't fill every location in the ROM. By default, 386-to-the-MAX copies the contents of ROM into RAM. Because 386-to-the-MAX can compress the BIOS slightly by, for example, removing the gaps between BIOS routines, the memory manager can recover the vacant space in the ROMs. This regained space is used as a high DOS area.

386-to-the-MAX loads itself into the fourth region of high DOS memory. Region numbering starts sequentially at the first region above 640K.

AUTOEXEC.BAT is unchanged for 386-to-the-MAX to load. After you reboot, 386-to-the-MAX becomes active.

Running MEM on the computer shows the following:

```
 655360 bytes total memory
 655360 bytes available
 537360 largest executable program size

4128768 bytes total EMS memory
3391488 bytes free EMS memory

4194304 bytes total extended memory
  77824 bytes available extended memory
```

386-to-the-MAX backfills the low DOS memory to 640K using some of the extended memory and assigns 4,032K of extended memory as expanded memory.

After installing 386-to-the-MAX, you can look closely at your computer's configuration to determine the adjustments needed to get the best use of your memory. The program 386MAX.COM offers various options that aid with this process. Using the UTIL option with the example computer, you see the listing shown in figure 11.1.

```
386MAX    -- Version 5.00 -- A Memory Manager for 386 Systems
     (C) Copyright 1987-90 Qualitas, Inc.  All rights reserved.
  Serial # 2000201705 - Licensed to Caroline Halliday
 ┌ 386MAX ═══ Version 5.00 ═══════════════════════════ Memory Usage ┐
 │              The First Megabyte of Address Space                  │
 │                                                                   │
 │ ┼──Conventional memory──────────┼Low  ┼EGA┼H┼E┼┼High──┼EMS┼       │
 │                                                                   │
 │   New top of DOS memory    =    640 KB     █ DOS       ≈ Video    │
 │   Added low  DOS memory    =    128 KB     ▓ Low       ■ ROM      │
 │   Added high DOS memory    =    168 KB     ▒ High                 │
 │   Available Extended memory =    76 KB     ♦ Other     # Unused   │
 │   Available EMS    memory  =   3456 KB in segment E000   EMS      │
 └──────────────────────── Copyright (C) 1987-90 Qualitas, Inc. ─────┘
 Extended memory usage...
   Program storage          =    212 KB
   ROM mapping region       =     56 KB, C000-C400, F000-F600, F900-FA00, FB00-FC00,
 FE00-10000
   High DOS memory          =    168 KB, B000-B800, C400-E000, F600-F900, FA00-FB00,
 FC00-FE00
   Low  DOS memory          =    128 KB
   EMS memory               =   3456 KB
   Remaining ext memory     =     76 KB
 Total extended memory      =   4096 KB
   ═> Loading programs in LOW memory...
   ═> 165 KB available in HIGH memory, largest block is 111 KB.
 The current state is ON.
```

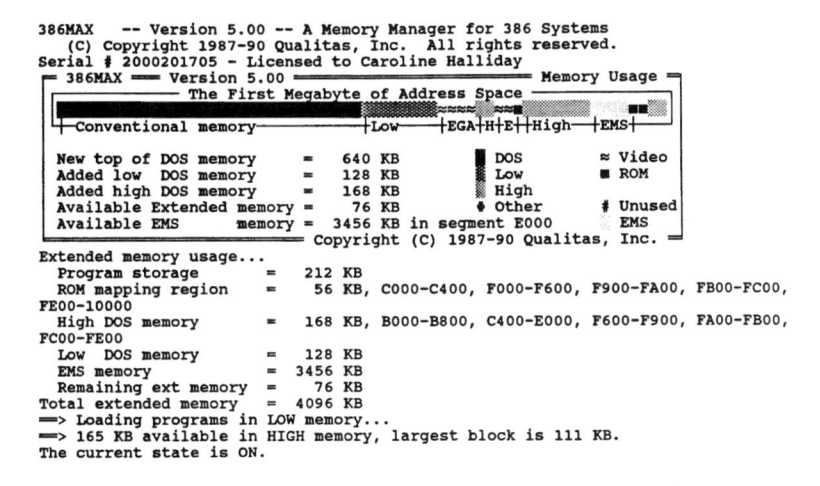

Fig. 11.1. The result of using the UTIL option.

The top portion shows a memory map of DOS's address space, the 128K of backfilled memory, the EGA adapter, ROM locations, and the EMS page frame. You can see that 386-to-the-MAX allocates areas it expects to be unused as high DOS regions. You can use alternative parameters to prevent 386-to-the-MAX from taking all the memory it finds. In this example, however, the idea is to get the most possible from the DOS address area.

The list beneath the address map shows the current use of extended memory, of which 56K is used for remapping ROM into RAM. ROM addresses that have been mapped to RAM are listed. 386-to-the-MAX also assigns 168K of memory as high DOS memory, which you can use to load device drivers and TSRs, increasing the available low DOS memory for your applications. A total of 3,456K of expanded memory now is not in use.

386-to-the-MAX has other explanatory screens that show current computer resources. The MAPMEM option shows the current memory map for resident programs (see fig. 11.2).

```
386MAX   -- Version 5.00 -- A Memory Manager for 386 Systems
  (C) Copyright 1987-90 Qualitas, Inc.  All rights reserved.
Serial # 2000201705 - Licensed to Caroline Halliday
```

	MEMORY MAP for RESIDENT PROGRAMS					
	Low DOS Memory				
Name	Hex Start	Hex End	Hex Owner	Decimal Length	Text or Interrupt Numbers
DOS	0000	0B51		46,352	00 01 03 04 0F 13 1B 29 2A 2B 2C 2D 31 32 34 35 36 37 38 39 3A 3B 3C 3D 3E 3F EF F1 F9 FA FB
Device Drvrs	0B51	1038		20,064	02 09 0A 0C 0D 0E 17 70 72 73 74 76
-Available-	1038	1043		160	
-Available-	1043	1045		16	
FASTOPEN.EXE	1045	12B8	1046	10,016	F0 FE
COMMAND.COM	12B8	141D	12B9	5,696	22 23 24 2E
COMMAND.COM	141D	142E	12B9	256	COMSPEC=c:\dos\command.com|PATH
MIRROR.COM	142E	1439	143A	160	COMSPEC=c:\dos\command.com|PATH
MIRROR.COM	1439	15CB	143A	6,416	19 25 26
MSCMOUSE.COM	15CB	15D6	1710	160	COMSPEC=c:\dos\command.com|PATH
FONTRES	15D6	170F	15D7	4,992	20
MSCMOUSE.COM	170F	1A2C	1710	12,736	0B 10 33 FC
-Available-	1A2C	1A36		144	
APPEND	1A36	1C19	1A37	7,712	21 2F F8
HOTLINE.EXE	1C19	1C24	1C25	160	COMSPEC=c:\dos\command.com|PATH
HOTLINE.EXE	1C24	1CCE	1C25	2,704	08 16 28
-Available-	1CCE	A000		537,360	
	High DOS Memory				
Name	Hex Start	Hex End	Hex Owner	Decimal Length	Text or Interrupt Numbers
-Available-	B000	B7FF		32,736	
= RAM or ROM =	B7FF	C400		49,152	1F 43
-Available-	C400	DFFF		114,656	
= RAM or ROM =	DFFF	F600		90,112	05 06 07 11 12 14 18 1A 1C 1D 41 42 44 45 46 47 48 49 4A 4B 4C 4D 4E 4F 50 51 52 53 54 55 56 57 58 59 5A 5B 5C 5D 5E 5F 68 69 6A 6B 6C 6D 6E 6F 71 75 77
-Available-	F600	F8FF		12,256	
= RAM or ROM =	F8FF	FA00		4,096	
Dev=EMMXXXX0 Dev=386MAX$$	FA00	FADD	FA01	3,520	15 27 40 67
-Available-	FADD	FAFF		528	
= RAM or ROM =	FAFF	FC00		4,096	
-Available-	FC00	FE00		8,176	

Fig. 11.2. The result of using the MAPMEM option.

The memory map lists each device driver and memory-resident program and shows the size of each program and information about the interrupts being used. Chapter 2 explains how device drivers and memory-resident programs install themselves into the interrupt vector table and intercept various interrupt calls.

Now, none of the high DOS areas are being used; consequently, the map shows those areas as available. Equivalent memory maps can be obtained for the device drivers now installed and expanded memory use. You execute 386MAX with the DEV or EMS option.

Installed, 386-to-the-MAX remaps the ROM it has found in RAM, speeding access time. 386MAX's TIM option performs timing tests on all your address space. A typical result is shown in figure 11.3.

```
386MAX   -- Version 5.00 -- A Memory Manager for 386 Systems
         (C) Copyright 1987-90 Qualitas, Inc.  All rights reserved.
Serial # 2000201705 - Licensed to Caroline Halliday
```

Starting Address	Range Start	Range End	Length	Average Time μs	Ratio to Fastest Time (1.0 = fastest)
00000000	0	640	640	553	1.0 ■
000A0000	640	704	64	4292	7.7 ■■■■■■■■■■■■■■■■■■■■■■■
000B0000	704	736	32	553	1.0 ■
000B8000	736	768	32	5760	10.4 ■■■■■■■■■■■■■■■■■■■■■■■■■■■>
000C0000	768	896	128	553	1.0 ■
000E0000	896	960	64		Absent
000F0000	960	4556	3596	553	1.0 ■
00473000	4556	4908	352		Absent
004CB000	4908	5120	212	553	1.0 ■

Timing memory accesses, please wait a moment...
MEMORY ACCESS TIMES

Fig. 11.3. The result of using the TIM option.

On this computer, the only slow areas of memory are the regions used by the video adapter. Video RAM is much slower than normal RAM and cannot be remapped because of the way the video display adapter works.

You can look at this timing chart and determine whether you are using your memory in the best way. You may find an area of ROM not remapped into RAM. You also may find that you are using different types of RAM and want to swap faster RAM for slower RAM. For example, you may use a 16-bit memory board in an expansion slot as the first extended memory board and a 32-bit memory board as further extended memory. Because the 16-bit memory is allocated first, you don't get the best performance possible from your memory. Consider using 386-to-the-MAX to swap the addressees for the 16-bit board with the 32-bit board. Then use 32-bit memory first; use 16-bit memory for the larger applications only.

This inefficient use of memory often happens when you use 386 accelerator boards in PCs or ATs. You can use the 386 memory manager to perform functions that you cannot do ordinarily.

Example: Using 386LOAD To Regain Low DOS Memory

386LOAD, a utility supplied with 386-to-the-MAX, works in a similar way to MOVE'EM but comes with an automatic installation program. You have the opportunity to select the device drivers or TSRs to be loaded high. The installation program does this procedure automatically, however, if you prefer.

386LOAD's installation program alters CONFIG.SYS to include a device driver line to invoke 386-to-the-MAX and analyzes the current CONFIG.SYS and AUTOEXEC.BAT files for candidates that can be moved into high DOS memory. The program also changes invoking command lines, inserting the 386LOAD device driver and a GETSIZE option and rebooting the computer. After 386LOAD knows the size of the programs, the utility adds the required parameters to CONFIG.SYS and AUTOEXEC.BAT and reboots the computer.

Consider a 386-based computer, running DOS 4, with 512K of base memory, 4M of extended memory, and an EGA board. 386MAX.COM gives the summary information shown in figure 11.4.

```
386MAX    -- Version 5.00 -- A Memory Manager for 386 Systems
       (b) Copyright 1987-90 Qualitas, Inc.  All rights reserved.
    Serial # 2000201705 - Licensed to Caroline Halliday
     ┌ 386MAX ──── Version 5.00 ─────────────────── Memory Usage ┐
     │                The First Megabyte of Address Space        │
     │ ████████████████████████████████░░░░░░▒▒▒▒░░░░░░░▓▓▓▓▓▓██ │
     │ ├─Conventional memory─────────┤Low   ├EGA┤H┤E┤┤High┤ ┤EMS┤│
     │                                                           │
     │ New top of DOS memory     =   640 KB      █ DOS    ≈ Video│
     │ Added low   DOS memory    =   128 KB      ▌ Low    ■ ROM  │
     │ Added high DOS memory     =   168 KB      ▓ High          │
     │ Available Extended memory =    76 KB      ♦ Other  # Unused│
     │ Available EMS    memory   =  3456 KB in segment E000  EMS │
     └─────────────────────────── Copyright (b) 1987-90 Qualitas, Inc. ┘
Extended memory usage...
   Program storage       =   212 KB
   ROM mapping region    =    56 KB, C000-C400, F000-F600, F900-FA00, FB00-FC00,
FE00-10000
   High DOS memory       =   168 KB, B000-B800, C400-E000, F600-F900, FA00-FB00,
FC00-FE00
   Low  DOS memory       =   128 KB
   EMS memory            =  3456 KB
   Remaining ext memory  =    76 KB
Total extended memory    =  4096 KB
═> Loading programs in LOW memory...
═> 141 KB available in HIGH memory, largest block is 103 KB.
The current state is ON.
```

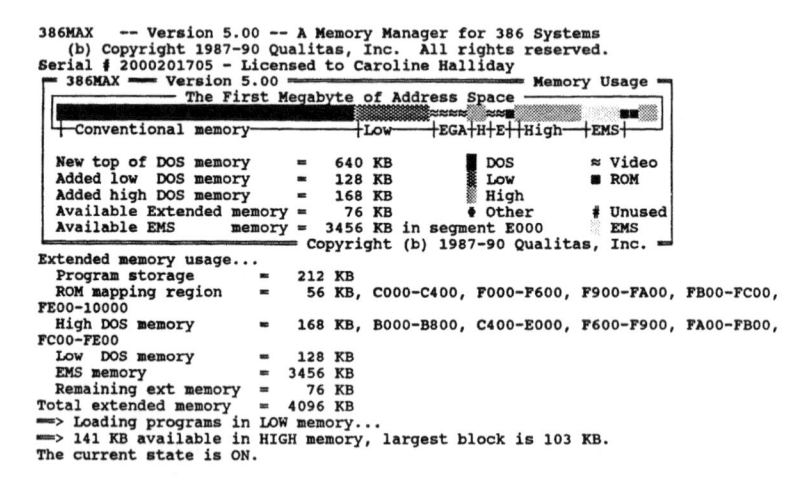

Fig. 11.4. The 386MAX.COM summary information.

386-to-the-MAX uses 128K of the extended memory to backfill the computer so that 640K of low DOS memory exists. An expanded memory page frame starts at segment E000H. 386-to-the-MAX also has found 168K of additional space in which to map high DOS memory. 386LOAD uses this memory area to place device drivers and TSRs.

The CONFIG.SYS for this computer is as follows:

```
DEVICE=C:\386MAX\386MAX.SYS PRO=C:\386MAX\386MAX.PRO
BUFFERS = 25
BREAK=ON
FILES=30
LASTDRIVE=M
SHELL=C:\DOS\COMMAND.COM /P /E:256
INSTALL=C:\DOS\FASTOPEN.EXE C:=(50,25)
DEVICE=C:\SYS\NEWPRN.SYS
```

Chapter 11: Using the Processor's Power

The 386MAX.PRO file referred to in the first line contains the following:

```
USE=B000-B800      ; INSTALL ==> recover RAM in MDA region
USE=F600-F900      ; INSTALL ==> recover fill regions in ROM
USE=FA00-FB00      ; INSTALL ==> recover fill regions in ROM
USE=FC00-FE00      ; INSTALL ==> recover fill regions in ROM
; This profile created automatically by INSTALL
PRGREG=4           ; Load 386MAX.SYS into this program region
```

The first device driver line loads 386-to-the-MAX with the parameters listed in the profile file. (This program was covered in detail earlier in this chapter.) The first four lines define some of the areas of free address space in high DOS memory. The final line loads 386-to-the-MAX into the fourth region of high DOS memory (FA00H to FB00H). The first region is the one closest to the 640K boundary.

The AUTOEXEC.BAT file for this computer follows:

```
@ECHO OFF
VERIFY ON
SET COMSPEC=C:\DOS\COMMAND.COM
PATH=C:\;C:\DOS;C:\UTIL;C:\BATCH;C:\UTIL\PCTOOLS;D:\HL;C:\WP51;C:\FONTSPAC;
MIRROR C: D: E: /TC
E:\FONTSPAC\FONTRES
E:\MOUSESYS\MSCMOUSE
APPEND=C:\DOS
PROMPT $P$G
HOTLINE
```

The CONFIG.SYS and AUTOEXEC.BAT were described earlier in this chapter.

When you run MEM on this computer, you get the following listing:

```
 655360 bytes total memory
 655360 bytes available
 537360 largest executable program size

4128768 bytes total EMS memory
3391488 bytes free EMS memory

4194304 bytes total extended memory
  77824 bytes available extended memory
```

386-to-the-MAX backfills the low DOS memory to 640K using some of the extended memory and assigns 4,032K of extended memory as expanded memory.

This computer has 524K of low DOS memory available. The majority of the 4M of extended memory (less 128K used for backfilling low DOS memory) is assigned to expanded memory.

Running MAXIMIZE To Configure 386LOAD

The installation process for 386LOAD includes an installation program called MAXIMIZE, which you can run to reconfigure your computer when you remove or add another device. Although you are prompted throughout MAXIMIZE's process so that you can alter the settings provided, the procedure is automated. For the previous example, the resulting CONFIG.SYS is as follows:

```
DEVICE=C:\386MAX\386MAX.SYS PRO=C:\386MAX\386MAX.PRO
BUFFERS = 25
BREAK=ON
FILES=30
LASTDRIVE=M
SHELL=C:\DOS\COMMAND.COM /P /E:256
INSTALL=C:\386MAX\386LOAD.COM SIZE=75552 PRGREG=2 FLEXFRAME
PROG=C:\DOS\FASTOPEN.EXE C:=(50,25)
DEVICE=C:\SYS\NEWPRN.SYS
```

The resulting AUTOEXEC.BAT is as follows:

```
@ECHO OFF
VERIFY ON
SET COMSPEC=C:\DOS\COMMAND.COM
PATH=C:\;C:\DOS;C:\UTIL;C:\BATCH;C:\UTIL\PCTOOLS;D:\HL;C:\WP51;C:\FONTSPAC;
C:\386MAX\386LOAD SIZE=58064 PRGREG=2 FLEXFRAME PROG=MIRROR C: D: E: /TC
C:\386MAX\386LOAD SIZE=32736 PRGREG=2 PROG=E:\FONTSPAC\FONTRES
C:\386MAX\386LOAD SIZE=17632 FLEXFRAME PROG=E:\MOUSESYS\MSCMOUSE
APPEND=C:\DOS
PROMPT $P$G
HOTLINE
```

386LOAD places the FASTOPEN directive in high memory, in region number 2. The FLEXFRAME parameter causes the expanded memory page frame to give up some of its memory temporarily to the loading program or device driver. After the program or device driver loads, it returns the memory to the expanded memory page frame.

386LOAD also places each of the TSRs into high DOS memory. Normally, each TSR in turn is loaded into the first available region that can accommodate the program. In this case, MAXIMIZE determines that MIRROR and FONTRES should be in region 2 and MSCMOUSE in region 1, to make the best use of available memory.

The effect of moving these programs and device drivers into high memory can be seen in various ways. CHKDSK shows the following:

```
Volume HARD DISK C created 12-26-1989 5:04p
Volume Serial Number is 0C2E-18C9

 23037952 bytes total disk space
   430080 bytes in 7 hidden files
    63488 bytes in 29 directories
 22048768 bytes in 732 user files
     2048 bytes in bad sectors
   493568 bytes available on disk

     2048 bytes in each allocation unit
    11249 total allocation units on disk
      241 available allocation units on disk

   655360 total bytes memory
   571904 bytes free
```

DOS 4's MEM command shows the following:

```
 655360 bytes total memory
 655360 bytes available
 571904 largest executable program size

4128768 bytes total EMS memory
3391488 bytes free EMS memory

4194304 bytes total extended memory
  77824 bytes available extended memory
```

You now have 559K of low DOS memory available for applications programs, with 35K of memory returned by using 386LOAD.

QEMM

Quarterdeck Office Systems' QEMM-386 includes a 386 memory manager called QEMM and a loader program called LOADHI. LOADHI can load devices and TSRs into high DOS memory. LOADHI is supplied with an installation program that copies the files to a hard disk and places the memory manager into CONFIG.SYS. After it is installed, you run a configuration program that automatically changes your CONFIG.SYS and AUTOEXEC.BAT so that you are using high DOS memory when possible. As with the other 386 memory manager programs, you can perform the whole configuration process manually if you prefer and tune the configuration later.

Installing QEMM

You use the supplied automatic installation program to transfer the programs from the distribution disk to your hard disk. This section covers how a sample computer is modified by the installation program.

Consider a 386-based computer with 4M of extended memory, an EGA, and 512K of base memory running DOS 4. Suppose that the CONFIG.SYS is as follows:

```
BUFFERS = 25
BREAK=ON
FILES=30
LASTDRIVE=M
SHELL=C:\DOS\COMMAND.COM /P /E:256
INSTALL=C:\DOS\FASTOPEN.EXE C:=(50,25)
DEVICE=C:\SYS\NEWPRN.SYS
```

The AUTOEXEC.BAT is as follows:

```
@ECHO OFF
VERIFY ON
SET COMSPEC=C:\DOS\COMMAND.COM
PATH=C:\;C:\DOS;C:\UTIL;C:\BATCH;C:\UTIL\PCTOOLS;D:\HL;C:\WP51;C:\FONTSPAC;
MIRROR C: D: E: /TC
E:\MOUSESYS\MSCMOUSE
APPEND=C:\DOS
PROMPT $P$G
HOTLINE
```

The CONFIG.SYS sets BREAK to on and sets a value for FILES, BUFFERS, and LASTDRIVE. The DOS environment is set to 256 bytes with the SHELL directive. A FASTOPEN setting is installed, and a printer device driver is loaded.

The AUTOEXEC.BAT includes the typical PATH, APPEND, PROMPT, and COMSPEC settings. The PC Tools Deluxe MIRROR program copies the FAT and root directory to a file for safekeeping and loads the delete tracker resident. This utility, as its name implies, keeps track of all files that are deleted. If you want to undelete the files, you can do so by using PC Tools.

Two memory-resident programs are loaded via AUTOEXEC.BAT. The mouse driver is for a Mouse Systems mouse, and Hotline is an electronic Rolodex program.

Running CHKDSK on this computer gives the following information:

```
Volume HARD DISK C created 12-26-1989 5:04p
Volume Serial Number is 0C2E-18C9

23037952 bytes total disk space
  430080 bytes in 7 hidden files
   57344 bytes in 26 directories
21911552 bytes in 747 user files
    2048 bytes in bad sectors
  636928 bytes available on disk

    2048 bytes in each allocation unit
   11249 total allocation units on disk
     311 available allocation units on disk

  524288 total bytes memory
  326288 bytes free
```

An alternative, because this computer is running DOS 4, is to run MEM. The MEM results follow:

```
 524288 bytes total memory
 524288 bytes available
 326288 largest executable program size

4194304 bytes total extended memory
4194304 bytes available extended memory
```

As you can see, with 512K of base memory and memory-resident programs, little room is left for an applications program to run.

After you install QEMM, the CONFIG.SYS file is changed to the following:

```
DEVICE=D:\QEMM\QEMM386.SYS
BUFFERS = 25
BREAK=ON
FILES=30
LASTDRIVE=M
SHELL=C:\DOS\COMMAND.COM /P /E:256
INSTALL=C:\DOS\FASTOPEN.EXE C:=(50,25)
DEVICE=C:\SYS\NEWPRN.SYS
```

Additionally, the path name for QEMM's location is added to the PATH statement in AUTOEXEC.BAT. When you run CHKDSK, you see the following information:

```
Volume HARD DISK C created 12-26-1989 5:04p
Volume Serial Number is 0C2E-18C9

23037952 bytes total disk space

  430080 bytes in 7 hidden files
   57344 bytes in 26 directories
21915648 bytes in 749 user files
    2048 bytes in bad sectors
  632832 bytes available on disk

    2048 bytes in each allocation unit
   11249 total allocation units on disk
     309 available allocation units on disk

  655360 total bytes memory
  539568 bytes free
```

Because this computer is running DOS 4, you can use the MEM command if you prefer. The result follows:

```
 655360 bytes total memory
 655360 bytes available
 539568 largest executable program size

4521984 bytes total EMS memory
3833856 bytes free EMS memory

4194304 bytes total extended memory
      0 bytes available extended memory
```

The memory manager takes control of the extended memory in the computer. The low DOS memory is extended from 512K to a full complement of 640K. QEMM makes some of the extended memory appear to DOS as low DOS memory. The remaining extended memory—4M minus 128K—appears to DOS as expanded memory.

In the example, QEMM is installed without optional parameters, which gives additional low DOS memory, because of the addition of 128K between 512K and 640K. However, you have lost some memory in the process, because the expanded memory manager takes up some RAM space.

You can recover some of this space by loading your device drivers and TSRs into high DOS memory. QEMM-386 is supplied with an automatic configuration program to aid with this process.

After QEMM is installed in your CONFIG.SYS, you can use the OPTIMIZE program to improve your memory use. The following section shows OPTIMIZE results when run on the previously described computer.

Example: Running OPTIMIZE To Configure LOADHI

You start the configuration program by typing **OPTIMIZE** at the DOS prompt. OPTIMIZE starts a three-step process. In the first stage, CONFIG.SYS and AUTOEXEC.BAT change so that OPTIMIZE can analyze potential candidates for moving into high DOS memory. The computer reboots.

During the rebooting, OPTIMIZE assesses the various candidates and decides on a suitable configuration. CONFIG.SYS and AUTOEXEC.BAT are changed again to reflect the new configuration, and the computer is rebooted a second time. If problems arise during the reconfiguration, the original CONFIG.SYS and AUTOEXEC.BAT are replaced.

For the sample computer, OPTIMIZE changes the CONFIG.SYS to the following listing:

```
DEVICE=D:\QEMM\QEMM386.SYS RAM
BUFFERS = 25
BREAK=ON
FILES=30
LASTDRIVE=M
SHELL=C:\DOS\COMMAND.COM /P /E:256
INSTALL=D:\QEMM\LOADHI.COM /TSR /R:2 C:\DOS\FASTOPEN.EXE C:=(50,25)
DEVICE=D:\QEMM\LOADHI.SYS /R:4 C:\SYS\NEWPRN.SYS
```

AUTOEXEC.BAT changes to the following listing:

```
@ECHO OFF
VERIFY ON
SET COMSPEC=C:\DOS\COMMAND.COM
PATH=D:\QEMM;C:\;C:\DOS;C:\UTIL;C:\BATCH;C:\UTIL\PCTOOLS;D:\HL;C:\WP51;C:\FONTSPAC;
D:\QEMM\LOADHI /R:2 MIRROR C: D: E: /TC
D:\QEMM\LOADHI /R:1 E:\MOUSESYS\MSCMOUSE
D:\QEMM\LOADHI /R:3 APPEND=C:\DOS
PROMPT $P$G
HOTLINE
```

In the CONFIG.SYS file, OPTIMIZE changes three lines. The RAM parameter is added to the QEMM device driver, creating regions of high DOS memory between your devices so that you can use the unused space for loading device drivers and TSRs.

The FASTOPEN and NEWPRN lines also are changed. Before OPTIMIZE is used, FASTOPEN is loaded into memory with the INSTALL directive in CONFIG.SYS. Because FASTOPEN is a program, not a device driver, OPTIMIZE replaces the FASTOPEN command with the program loader LOADHI.COM. LOADHI.COM is loaded as a TSR (shown by the /TSR switch). The INSTALL directive installs LOADHI.COM, and LOADHI.COM in turn loads FASTOPEN into high DOS memory region 2 (shown by the /R:2 switch). NEWPRN.SYS is a printer device driver. OPTIMIZE replaces the device driver LOADHI.SYS with NEWPRN.SYS. When you boot the computer, DOS loads the LOADHI.SYS device driver, which loads NEWPRN.SYS into region 4 of high DOS memory.

In AUTOEXEC.BAT, OPTIMIZE makes more changes. MIRROR is loaded into high DOS memory region 2. The mouse driver is loaded into memory region 1, and APPEND is loaded into memory region 3. As with 386-to-the-MAX, the initial arrangement of device driver and TSR loading in CONFIG.SYS is not the best order for loading programs into high DOS memory. By specifying the program region to be used to hold the TSR or device driver, more memory can be saved.

Using MEM again shows the changes in available base memory. MEM gives the following results:

```
 655360 bytes total memory
 655360 bytes available
 576832 largest executable program size

4374528 bytes total EMS memory
3686400 bytes free EMS memory

4194304 bytes total extended memory
      0 bytes available extended memory
```

Instead of having 318K of memory free when using no memory manager, or 527K when using the expanded memory manager alone, you have 563K of free base memory—a savings of 36K.

All Charge 386

All Charge 386 from All Computers Inc. also is a 386 memory manager. Although an automatic configuring program is not included, you can add parameters manually to suit your configuration. Because you probably want to tailor 386-to-the-MAX or QEMM, even after installation, this deficiency probably is insignificant. However, you must understand the principles involved when selecting the parameters.

As with the previous examples, consider a 386-based computer with 4M of extended memory, an EGA, and 512K of base memory running DOS 4. Suppose that the CONFIG.SYS is as follows:

```
BUFFERS = 25
BREAK=ON
FILES=30
LASTDRIVE=M
SHELL=C:\DOS\COMMAND.COM /P /E:256
INSTALL=C:\DOS\FASTOPEN.EXE C:=(50,25)
DEVICE=C:\SYS\NEWPRN.SYS
```

The AUTOEXEC.BAT follows:

```
@ECHO OFF
VERIFY ON
SET COMSPEC=C:\DOS\COMMAND.COM
PATH=C:\;C:\DOS;C:\UTIL;C:\BATCH;C:\UTIL\PCTOOLS;D:\HL;C:\WP51;C:\FONTSPAC;
MIRROR C: D: E: /TC
E:\FONTSPAC\FONTRES
E:\MOUSESYS\MSCMOUSE
APPEND=C:\DOS
PROMPT $P$G
HOTLINE
```

The CONFIG.SYS sets BREAK to on and sets a value for FILES, BUFFERS, and LASTDRIVE. The DOS environment is set to 256 bytes with the SHELL directive. A FASTOPEN setting is installed, and a printer device driver is loaded.

AUTOEXEC.BAT includes the typical PATH, APPEND, PROMPT, and COMSPEC settings. The PC Tools Deluxe MIRROR program copies the FAT and root directory to a file for safekeeping and loads the delete tracker resident.

AUTOEXEC.BAT loads three memory-resident programs. FONTRES, the memory-resident portion of Isogon's FONTSPACE, is a font utility for LaserJet printers that compresses font files until you print a file, saving hard disk space. The mouse driver is for a Mouse Systems mouse, and Hotline serves as an electronic Rolodex program.

Running MEM on this computer gives the following results:

```
 524288 bytes total memory
 524288 bytes available
 286480 largest executable program size

4194304 bytes total extended memory
4194304 bytes available extended memory
```

You have only 280K of memory available for applications.

Adding the All Charge device driver line changes CONFIG.SYS to the following listing:

```
DEVICE = C:\ALL\ALLEMM4.SYS RAM
BUFFERS = 25
BREAK=ON
FILES=30
LASTDRIVE=M
SHELL=C:\DOS\COMMAND.COM /P /E:256
INSTALL=C:\DOS\FASTOPEN.EXE C:=(50,25)
DEVICE=C:\SYS\NEWPRN.SYS
```

The RAM parameter is added for regaining areas of high DOS memory. AUTOEXEC.BAT is unchanged except for the addition of the subdirectory containing All Charge 386 to the path.

Rebooting the computer and running MEM with the new configuration gives the following results:

```
655360 bytes total memory
655360 bytes available
536272 largest executable program size

4374528 bytes total EMS memory
3637248 bytes free EMS memory

4194304 bytes total extended memory
      0 bytes available extended memory
```

All Charge 386 has backfilled low DOS memory from 512K to 640K. You have almost 3.5M of expanded memory available.

All Charge 386 comes with a utility program that shows the current use of your computer's resources. One part of that utility program shows the following memory map:

```
ALLEMM4.SYS 386 version   3.00
Release [mm-dd-yy]                                       : 06-15-90

Status flags_                                            : 0016H
Number of first page of extended memory buffer           : 0100H
Number of 4K pages of extended memory buffer             : 0400
Number of first page of conventional memory buffer       : 10H
Number of 4K pages of conventional memory buffer         : 70H

High RAM  MCB segment address                            : b000H

ALLEMM4   status flags:
Conventional memory has been backfilled up to 640K...
There is High RAM present...
```

```
EMS memory is being used...
ALLEMM4  mode:  0   ( MODE: on   -   V86 mode, EMS enabled )
                       CONVENTIONAL MEMORY STATUS
       : 000 100 200 300 400 500 600 700 800 900 A00 B00 C00 D00 E00 F00
  0000:  CO  CO  CO  CO  CO  CO  CO  CO  CO  CO  CO  CO  CO  CO  CO  CO
  1000:  CO  CO  CO  CO  CO  CO  CO  CO  CO  CO  CO  CO  CO  CO  CO  CO
  2000:  CO  CO  CO  CO  CO  CO  CO  CO  CO  CO  CO  CO  CO  CO  CO  CO
  3000:  CO  CO  CO  CO  CO  CO  CO  CO  CO  CO  CO  CO  CO  CO  CO  CO
  4000:  CO  CO  CO  CO  CO  CO  CO  CO  CO  CO  CO  CO  CO  CO  CO  CO
  5000:  CO  CO  CO  CO  CO  CO  CO  CO  CO  CO  CO  CO  CO  CO  CO  CO
  6000:  CO  CO  CO  CO  CO  CO  CO  CO  CO  CO  CO  CO  CO  CO  CO  CO
  7000:  CO  CO  CO  CO  CO  CO  CO  CO  CO  CO  CO  CO  CO  CO  CO  CO
  8000:  CO  CO  CO  CO  CO  CO  CO  CO  CO  CO  CO  CO  CO  CO  CO  CO
  9000:  CO  CO  CO  CO  CO  CO  CO  CO  CO  CO  CO  CO  CO  CO  CO  CO
  a000:  VI  VI  VI  VI  VI  VI  VI  VI  VI  VI  VI  VI  VI  VI  VI  VI
  b000:  HR  HR  HR  HR  HR  HR  HR  VI  VI  VI  VI  VI  VI  VI  VI  VI
  c000:  RO  RO  RO  RO  HR  HR  HR  HR  HR  HR  HR  HR  HR  HR  HR  HR
  d000:  HR  HR  HR  HR  HR  HR  HR  HR  HR  HR  HR  HR  HR  HR  HR  HR
  e000:  PF  PF  PF  PF  PF  PF  PF  PF  PF  PF  PF  PF  PF  PF  PF  PF
  f000:  BI  BI  BI  BI  BI  BI  BI  BI  BI  BI  BI  BI  BI  BI  BI  SR

CO-DOS conventional memory    BI-BIOS          EX-Excluded      UN-unknown
VI-Video RAM                  SR-Shadow ROM    MA-Mappable
RO-Option ROM                 HR-High RAM      NM-No memory
```

As with ALL CHARGECARD, the 8088 and 80286 equivalent program, the memory map shows the use of each area of addressable memory in the form of a memory map. All areas of memory are in use. All Charge 386 fills the empty areas with an expanded memory page frame and high DOS areas.

Using ALLOAD for 386- and 486-Based Computers

All Charge 386 includes a loader program that compares with 386-to-the-MAX and QEMM. Unlike 386-to-the-MAX but like QEMM, All Charge 386 includes substitute programs for some DOS directives that normally load in CONFIG.SYS.

These programs, for FILES, BUFFERS, and LASTDRIVE, normally reserve low DOS memory for their use. By using the substitute programs, you can reduce the amount of low DOS memory required by using high DOS memory for some of the storage.

All Charge 386 also includes two loader programs that load device drivers and TSRs into high DOS memory. The program DEVICE loads device drivers, and ALLOAD loads TSRs into previously defined high DOS memory areas.

Example: Using ALLOAD To Regain Low DOS Memory

For the same computer in this chapter's example, the new CONFIG.SYS is as follows:

```
DEVICE = C:\ALL\ALLEMM4.SYS RAM
BREAK=ON
SHELL=C:\DOS\COMMAND.COM /P /E:256
INSTALL=C:\DOS\FASTOPEN.EXE C:=(50,25)
```

AUTOEXEC.BAT is as follows:

```
@ECHO OFF
VERIFY ON
C:\ALL\BUFFERS=25
C:\ALL\FILES=30
C:\ALL\LASTDRIV=M
C:\ALL\DEVICE=C:\SYS\NEWPRN.SYS
SET COMSPEC=C:\DOS\COMMAND.COM
PATH=C:\;C:\DOS;C:\UTIL;C:\BATCH;C:\UTIL\PCTOOLS;D:\HL;C:\WP51;C:\FONTSPAC;C:\ALL
ALLOAD MIRROR C: D: E: /TC
ALLOAD E:\FONTSPAC\FONTRES
ALLOAD E:\MOUSESYS\MSCMOUSE
APPEND=C:\DOS
PROMPT $P$G
HOTLINE
```

All Charge 386 moves the BUFFERS, FILES, and LASTDRIVE directives from CONFIG.SYS to AUTOEXEC.BAT. Instead of the DOS-supplied directives being run, the All Charge 386 equivalent programs are run, which enables portions of the memory required for these directives to be in high DOS memory.

The device driver NEWPRN.SYS also is removed from CONFIG.SYS, and a substitute program is supplied. You must list explicitly the program name, such as C:\ALL\DEVICE or C:\ALL\FILES, so that the All Charge 386 version is used and not the DOS version. Note that unlike when the directives and device drivers are located in CONFIG.SYS, you cannot put a space character before or after the equal sign in the command line.

Use the ALLOAD program to load memory-resident programs into high DOS memory. In this example, MIRROR, FONTRES, and MSCMOUSE are loaded high.

Using All Charge 386 to select programs to load high is not as easy as with QEMM and 386-to-the-MAX. All Charge 386 doesn't provide information about loading and initializing sizes for the device drivers or the memory-resident programs. 386-to-the-MAX, however, lists this information with its GETSIZE parameter.

With All Charge 386, you must experiment with the various programs. Remember that the loading or initializing size can be much larger than the resident size for a program. You must run each program to determine whether it works satisfactorily.

When the computer is rebooted with the new configuration, MEM gives the following information:

```
655360 bytes total memory
655360 bytes available
571184 largest executable program size

4374528 bytes total EMS memory
3637248 bytes free EMS memory

4194304 bytes total extended memory
      0 bytes available extended memory
```

You now have 558K of memory available for DOS applications. By loading DOS directives and memory-resident programs into high DOS memory, you have saved 34K of memory.

The utility program supplied with All Charge 386 has a feature that shows how the various programs and DOS directives are located in memory. The following result is for the preceding example:

```
DOS MEMORY BLOCKS INFORMATION

Segment         Type              Size            Name
0x0000          Conventional      46352 bytes     DOS 4.00
0x0B52          Conventional      10752 bytes     CONFIG
0x0DF3          Conventional        176 bytes     ALLMENU
0x0DFF          Conventional          0 bytes     * FREE *
0x0E00          Conventional      10016 bytes     FASTOPEN
0x1073          Conventional       5696 bytes     COMMAND
0x11D8          Conventional        256 bytes     COMMAND
```

```
0x11E9      Conventional        160 bytes      * FREE *
0x11F4      Conventional       7712 bytes      APPEND
0x13D7      Conventional        176 bytes      HOTLINE
0x13E3      Conventional       2704 bytes      HOTLINE
0x148D      Conventional     124240 bytes      ALLMENU
0x32E3      Conventional     446928 bytes      * FREE *
0xA000      Conventional                       _mem_top

0xB001      Reserved          13344 bytes      BUFFERS
0xB344      Reserved           1328 bytes      FILES
0xB398      Reserved           1168 bytes      LASTDRIV
0xB3E2      Reserved            160 bytes      MIRROR
0xB3ED      Reserved            160 bytes      MSCMOUSE
0xB3F8      Reserved          16496 bytes      * FREE *
0xB800      Reserved          49152 bytes      * hole *
0xC401      Reserved            400 bytes      DEVICE
0xC41B      Reserved           6416 bytes      MIRROR
0xC5AD      Reserved           4992 bytes      FONTRES
0xC6E6      Reserved          12736 bytes      MSCMOUSE
0xCA03      Reserved          90064 bytes      * FREE *
0xE000      Reserved                           _mem_top
```

The allocation for programs running in low DOS memory appear first, followed by items in high DOS memory. The utility program ALLMENU in low DOS memory creates this output, which is why ALLMENU appears in the listing.

Improving Performance with All Charge 386

As a default, All Charge 386 does not remap areas of ROM with RAM. You can remap, however, by adding the ROM parameter. You must specify the locations of the ROM in your system; the locations can be found with the utility program. The memory map follows:

```
                       CONVENTIONAL MEMORY STATUS

         : 000 100 200 300 400 500 600 700 800 900 A00 B00 C00 D00 E00 F00
    0000:  CO  CO  CO  CO  CO  CO  CO  CO  CO  CO  CO  CO  CO  CO  CO  CO
    1000:  CO  CO  CO  CO  CO  CO  CO  CO  CO  CO  CO  CO  CO  CO  CO  CO
    2000:  CO  CO  CO  CO  CO  CO  CO  CO  CO  CO  CO  CO  CO  CO  CO  CO
    3000:  CO  CO  CO  CO  CO  CO  CO  CO  CO  CO  CO  CO  CO  CO  CO  CO
    4000:  CO  CO  CO  CO  CO  CO  CO  CO  CO  CO  CO  CO  CO  CO  CO  CO
    5000:  CO  CO  CO  CO  CO  CO  CO  CO  CO  CO  CO  CO  CO  CO  CO  CO
    6000:  CO  CO  CO  CO  CO  CO  CO  CO  CO  CO  CO  CO  CO  CO  CO  CO
    7000:  CO  CO  CO  CO  CO  CO  CO  CO  CO  CO  CO  CO  CO  CO  CO  CO
    8000:  CO  CO  CO  CO  CO  CO  CO  CO  CO  CO  CO  CO  CO  CO  CO  CO
    9000:  CO  CO  CO  CO  CO  CO  CO  CO  CO  CO  CO  CO  CO  CO  CO  CO
    a000:  VI  VI  VI  VI  VI  VI  VI  VI  VI  VI  VI  VI  VI  VI  VI  VI
    b000:  HR  HR  HR  HR  HR  HR  HR  HR  VI  VI  VI  VI  VI  VI  VI  VI
    c000:  RO  RO  RO  RO  HR  HR  HR  HR  HR  HR  HR  HR  HR  HR  HR  HR
    d000:  HR  HR  HR  HR  HR  HR  HR  HR  HR  HR  HR  HR  HR  HR  HR  HR
    e000:  PF  PF  PF  PF  PF  PF  PF  PF  PF  PF  PF  PF  PF  PF  PF  PF
    f000:  BI  BI  BI  BI  BI  BI  BI  BI  BI  BI  BI  BI  BI  BI  BI  SR

    CO-DOS conventional memory   BI-BIOS         EX-Excluded      UN-unknown
    VI-Video RAM                 SR-Shadow ROM   MA-Mappable
    RO-Option ROM                HR-High RAM     NM-No memory
```

ROM exists in address areas C000H to C400H and F000H to 10000H. All Charge 386 requires the first and last ROM address locations as a parameter on the line in CONFIG.SYS that invokes the All Charge 386 device driver.

The CONFIG.SYS for the preceding example changes as follows:

```
DEVICE = C:\ALL\ALLEMM4.SYS RAM ROM=C000-C3FF ROM=F000-FFFF
BREAK=ON
SHELL=C:\DOS\COMMAND.COM /P /E:256
INSTALL=C:\DOS\FASTOPEN.EXE C:=(50,25)
```

The AUTOEXEC.BAT is unchanged. Now when you run MEM, you see the following listing:

```
 655360 bytes total memory
 655360 bytes available
 571184 largest executable program size

4292608 bytes total EMS memory
3555328 bytes free EMS memory

4194304 bytes total extended memory
      0 bytes available extended memory
```

Part III: Managing Memory Resources

The amount of low DOS memory available remains unchanged, but the amount of expanded memory available decreases because the ROM has been remapped with RAM. The computer's performance improves when the command line invoking All Charge 386 is changed.

On the memory map shown by ALLMENU, the utility program changes as follows:

```
ALLEMM4  mode:  0  ( MODE: on  -  V86 mode, EMS enabled )
                    CONVENTIONAL MEMORY STATUS

       : 000 100 200 300 400 500 600 700 800 900 A00 B00 C00 D00 E00 F00
  0000: CO  CO  CO  CO  CO  CO  CO  CO  CO  CO  CO  CO  CO  CO  CO  CO
  1000: CO  CO  CO  CO  CO  CO  CO  CO  CO  CO  CO  CO  CO  CO  CO  CO
  2000: CO  CO  CO  CO  CO  CO  CO  CO  CO  CO  CO  CO  CO  CO  CO  CO
  3000: CO  CO  CO  CO  CO  CO  CO  CO  CO  CO  CO  CO  CO  CO  CO  CO
  4000: CO  CO  CO  CO  CO  CO  CO  CO  CO  CO  CO  CO  CO  CO  CO  CO
  5000: CO  CO  CO  CO  CO  CO  CO  CO  CO  CO  CO  CO  CO  CO  CO  CO
  6000: CO  CO  CO  CO  CO  CO  CO  CO  CO  CO  CO  CO  CO  CO  CO  CO
  7000: CO  CO  CO  CO  CO  CO  CO  CO  CO  CO  CO  CO  CO  CO  CO  CO
  8000: CO  CO  CO  CO  CO  CO  CO  CO  CO  CO  CO  CO  CO  CO  CO  CO
  9000: CO  CO  CO  CO  CO  CO  CO  CO  CO  CO  CO  CO  CO  CO  CO  CO
  a000: VI  VI  VI  VI  VI  VI  VI  VI  VI  VI  VI  VI  VI  VI  VI  VI
  b000: HR  HR  HR  HR  HR  HR  HR  VI  VI  VI  VI  VI  VI  VI  VI  VI
  c000: RO  RO  RO  RO  HR  HR  HR  HR  HR  HR  HR  HR  HR  HR  HR  HR
  d000: HR  HR  HR  HR  HR  HR  HR  HR  HR  HR  HR  HR  HR  HR  HR  HR
  e000: PF  PF  PF  PF  PF  PF  PF  PF  PF  PF  PF  PF  PF  PF  PF  PF
  f000: SR  SR  SR  SR  SR  SR  SR  SR  SR  SR  SR  SR  SR  SR  SR  SR

  CO-DOS conventional memory     BI-BIOS           EX-Excluded    UN-unknown
  VI-Video RAM                   SR-Shadow ROM     MA-Mappable
  RO-Option ROM                  HR-High RAM       NM-No memory
```

Areas previously existing as ROM are replaced with the designation shadow ROM. A RAM area has been set aside for containing the data stored in ROM. Any accesses to ROM by DOS or an applications program are rerouted to RAM rather than ROM. Because RAM has a much faster access time than ROM, your computer's performance improves with this shadow RAM parameter.

> *Note:* Be careful not to remap twice. If your computer already shadows RAM into ROM—and many new computers do—activating this parameter causes ROM to be mapped again. When an applications program or DOS asks for data from the ROM area, two areas of RAM are willing to supply the information. The result can be that your computer behaves strangely or locks up.

EMM386

DOS 5 is supplied with a 386 memory manager that performs some of the functions supplied by the products described previously in this chapter. EMM386 is an expanded memory emulator that can convert your extended memory in a 386- or 486-based computer to expanded memory. This memory manager requires you to use the HIMEM.SYS device driver discussed in Chapter 10. HIMEM.SYS provides access to areas of high DOS memory. EMM386.EXE uses HIMEM.SYS to access these areas and provide expanded memory management. This does not load your devices and TSRs into high DOS memory. To do that procedure, you have to use other directives—LOADHIGH and DEVICEHIGH. LOADHIGH and DEVICEHIGH are discussed later in this chapter.

You add a line to your CONFIG.SYS to load the memory manager. The command syntax is as follows:

DEVICE = *d:\path*__EMM386.EXE__

In most cases, you do not have to use any of the optional parameters. These parameters fall into three categories: memory size, memory options, and Weitek math coprocessor support.

The memory size parameter is a single parameter placed after the file name. You specify the amount of memory you want to use as expanded memory by placing the size in kilobytes as a parameter on the command line. For example, to use 2M of expanded memory, you use the command line

DEVICE=C:\DOS\EMM386.EXE 2048

where EMM386.EXE is located in the DOS subdirectory of drive C. Because this command is invoked via a DEVICE directive, you must include the file name extension.

EMM386 supports the Weitek math coprocessor if you add W=ON to the command line. For example, to use the Weitek coprocessor and 1M of expanded memory, you use the following command line:

DEVICE=C:\DOS\EMM386.EXE 1024 W=ON

As in the previous example, this command line assumes that EMM386.EXE is in the DOS subdirectory of drive C. To disable support, you use W=OFF. As a default, the Weitek coprocessor support is off.

The other options all control the expanded memory emulator. You can set the page frame position, exclude various areas of memory, and specify the amount of memory to be left for extended memory use. The number of alternate register sets and the number of handles that are used also can be selected.

The syntax for the device driver with all the options follows:

DEVICE=*d:\path***EMM386.EXE** *state size weitek framebase pageaddress exclude include banking minextend alteregs handles dmaram ram noems*

An explanation of the options follows:

d:\path	This option is the drive and path where EMM386.EXE is located. If the drive and path are not specified, DOS assumes that EMM386.EXE is located in the root directory of the boot drive.
state	Set this option to ON to activate the EMM386.EXE device driver (default setting). Set this option to OFF to deactivate EMM386.EXE. Set it to AUTO if you want to activate expanded memory support only when a program requests expanded memory.
size	The amount of expanded memory desired is specified in kilobytes. The default size is 256K. The acceptable range is 16K through 32,768K. All values are rounded down to the nearest multiple of 16K.
weitek	**W=ON** enables Weitek support. **W=OFF** disables Weitek support. The default is support off.

framebase Three ways are available for specifying the position of the base page frame: **/P***address* or **FRAME=***address*, where *address* is the segment address for the bottom of the page frame, or **M***x*, where *x* is a code for a particular segment. The *x* can be equal to the following:

Code	Segment
1	C000H
2	C400H
3	C800H
4	CC00H
5	D000H
6	D400H
7	D800H
8	DC00H
9	E000H
10	8000H
11	8400H
12	8800H
13	8C00H
14	9000H

Note that page frame bases numbered 10 through 14 require only 512K of low DOS memory. If you want to to specify a page frame base address of C800H, for example, use **FRAME=C800H**, **/PC800H**, or **M3**.

pageaddress Use this option to specify the page frame for a particular page. Pages are numbered from 0 to 255. Pages 0 through 3 must be contiguous for compatibility with LIM 3.2. If a value for *framebase* is specified, you cannot define pages 0 through 3 via this option. The *pageaddress* has the form **P***n***=***address*, where *n* is the number of the page being specified and *address* is the segment address for the specified pages.

exclude Exclude regions of high DOS memory from being used for placing expanded memory page frames. For each region to be excluded, use **X=***addressrange*. To exclude B000H to B800H, for example, use **X=B000-B800**.

include	Select regions of high DOS memory to be used for placing expanded memory page frames. For each region to be included, use **I**=*addressrange*. To include B000H to B800H, for example, use **I=B000-B800**. If you specify an address range with the *exclude* option and an overlapping address range with the *include* option, the *exclude* option takes precedence.
banking	Specify the lowest address that can be used for expanded memory. Valid addresses range from 1000 through 4000—the value 4000 is the default. Use the form **B**=*address*, where *address* is the segment address required.
minextend	Specify the amount of extended memory not to be converted to expanded memory. Use the form: **L**=*n*, where *n* is the extended memory required in kilobytes.
alteregs	Specify the number of alternate register sets to be allocated. The default value is 7. Use the form **A**=*n*, where *n* is a number between 0 and 254.
handles	Specify the number of handles (file names) that EMM386.EXE can use. The default value is 64. Use the form **H**=*n*, where *n* is a number between 2 and 255.
dmaram	Choose a value for the number of kilobytes of memory reserved for buffering data transferred by DMA (direct memory access). This value should be set to the largest size necessary to accommodate DMA transfers. Use the form **D**=*n*, where *n* is a number between 16 and 256. The value 16 is the default.
ram	Use this switch to permit access to expanded memory and high DOS memory.
noems	Use this switch to gain access to high DOS memory but not expanded memory.

After you have installed EMM386.EXE in CONFIG.SYS after HIMEM.SYS and rebooted your computer, you have access to expanded memory. In most cases, you do not have to use any of the options offered with EMM386.EXE. If you experience any problems with your computer behaving erratically, however, you may have to add parameters to make the parts cooperate.

DEVICEHIGH

DEVICEHIGH is a new DOS 5 feature that enables you to load your device drivers into high DOS memory. You must have HIMEM.SYS in your CONFIG.SYS and include the DOS=UMB command in CONFIG.SYS. Finally, you must have a program that is an upper memory block provider. In most cases, this program is EMM386.EXE, but you can consider third-party alternatives.

A minimum CONFIG.SYS needed to use DEVICEHIGH is

```
DEVICE=C:\DOS\HIMEM.SYS
DOS=UMB
DEVICE=C:\DOS\EMM386.EXE
DEVICEHIGH=device driver name
```

where HIMEM.SYS and EMM386.EXE are located in the \DOS subdirectory of drive C and *device driver name* is the file name for the device driver you want to load into high memory. If your device driver is not in the root directory of the boot drive, you must add the path name.

The full syntax for DEVICEHIGH follows:

DEVICEHIGH=*d:\path\filename parameters*

or

DEVICEHIGH SIZE=*size d:\path\filename parameters*

The first command line loads the device driver named *filename* with any of the device driver's parameters specified; *d:\path* is the drive and path name where the device driver is located.

Use the second line when you want to specify that a particular amount of high DOS memory is available before DEVICEHIGH loads a device driver into high DOS memory. You use this command syntax when you discover that a device driver requires a large amount of memory to load so that DEVICEHIGH attempts to load the device driver into high DOS memory only when sufficient room is available. Remember, most device drivers require more memory to load than when they are resident.

To load NEWPRN.SYS located in the \SYS subdirectory of drive C, for example, use the following command:

DEVICEHIGH=C:\SYS\NEWPRN.SYS

LOADHIGH

You use LOADHIGH to load programs into high DOS memory. These programs are likely to be TSRs, and you often insert the invoking command line into AUTOEXEC.BAT. As with DEVICEHIGH, you need to have included previously three directives in your CONFIG.SYS file so that LOADHIGH has access to a memory manager and high DOS memory. The directives follow:

```
DEVICE=C:\DOS\HIMEM.SYS
DOS=UMB
DEVICE=C:\DOS\EMM386.EXE
```

The syntax of the LOADHIGH command follows:

>   **LOADHIGH** *d:\path\filename parameters*

d:\path is the drive and path name where the program to be loaded is located, *filename* is the name of the program, and *parameters* is the parameters that the program requires.

To load the MIRROR utility program into high DOS memory, for example, use the following command:

>   **LOADHIGH C:\UTIL\MIRROR C: D: E: /TC**

The preceding command assumes that MIRROR is located in the \UTIL directory of drive C.

Chapter Summary

The 386 memory managers can add flexibility and speed to your 386- and 486-based computers. The advanced programs require some technical knowledge to be used to their best efficiency.

You can use memory managers to control expanded and extended memory. Note that with all memory managers, you should run one at a time. Select the manager that includes the options you require.

DOS 5 comes with a 386 memory manager, EMM386.EXE, that can be used for controlling expanded memory on 386- and 486-based computers.

Loader programs work with 386 memory managers to enable you to load device drivers and TSRs into unused portions of high DOS memory.

Improving the Operating System

12

Since the introduction of the PC, the personal computer has evolved substantially. Computers are faster and have more memory, higher resolution graphics with more colors, and a much larger storage capacity. The microprocessors used in the computers have evolved from the 8088 and 8086 to the 80286, 80386, and now 80486. Each microprocessor is more powerful than the last.

Software also has changed since the PC's inception. Applications programs have grown from their infancy into indispensable business tools. Word processors no longer are glorified typewriters but often are sophisticated publishing systems. Database managers that used to be for storing names and addresses now control complete order-entry, invoicing, inventory, and shipping systems. Electronic spreadsheet programs control the financial status of many companies.

Even the home computer user has changed during the life of the PC. Originally, engineers and programmers were the main users. Now most children are taught about PCs at school and do their reports on word processors at home. Although still used for playing electronic games, PCs increasingly are being used for controlling personal finances: tracking investments, balancing checkbooks, and analyzing expenditures.

These advancements all have been made possible by improvements in the software and hardware. The users have demanded more, and the manufacturers have responded. A typical PC now has far more RAM, magnetic storage, and video capabilities and probably a better microprocessor than it had even a couple of years ago.

This evolution, however, is limited. The DOS operating system was written for the 8088 system and has to live with the limitations imposed by that microprocessor. DOS itself, however, has changed with time. DOS now offers more features and has started to include features that are specific to the computer type. DOS 4, for example, includes some commands that can use expanded memory, and DOS 5 includes HIMEM.SYS for use on 80286s and EMM386.SYS for use on 80386s. But DOS also has maintained compatibility with the past. You still can run DOS on a dual floppy PC with a minimum of RAM.

This chapter covers some of the approaches you can take in order to improve your operating system. Some methods enhance DOS features; others replace DOS. All, to varying degrees, preserve compatibility with your existing applications programs. You can get more from your system without replacing everything or learning everything from scratch.

Four classes of products are discussed in this chapter:

- Replacement command interpreters for DOS's COMMAND.COM
- DOS extenders, which make use of the features of the 80286 or 80386 microprocessor to work in cooperation with DOS
- Multitasking operating systems, which enable you to run several applications programs at once on your computer
- Multitasking multiuser operating systems, which enable you to have several people, each with an individual keyboard and display, using the same computer at once

For all these alternatives (except the replacement command interpreters), you need a high-performance PC to make the best use of these products. The DOS extenders, for example, don't work on PCs. Although several multitasking and multitasking multiuser operating systems can be run on PCs, the systems are extremely slow on these systems. If you need the features of these products, purchasing a higher performance computer is well worth the expense.

Examining DOS's Functional Sections

The operating system in a computer is the link between the hardware and the applications software. The operating system provides the recurring services required to run the computer—functions such as disk and file management, memory management, and device management. If you did not use an operating system to provide these functions, each applications program, such as a word processor or database, would have to include the functions. The operating system thus provides an efficient use of the computer resources. The applications program has to provide only the functions not supplied with the operating system.

DOS is the name of the whole operating system typically used on PCs. Several distinct sections, however, make up DOS: the BIOS, system files, command interpreter, and DOS utilities.

The BIOS is contained in ROM on each PC. The contents of ROM vary with the computer model and manufacturer, but in all cases, the BIOS supplies the fundamental communication between the parts of the computer and the next level of DOS, the system files.

The system files, such as IO.SYS and MSDOS.SYS, are not different in every type of computer. They vary only with the version and implementation of DOS. These files are the interface between the BIOS, which is system specific, and the command interpreter (COMMAND.COM) or your applications program.

The COMMAND.COM command interpreter, as its name implies, handles the commands you type at the keyboard. The interpreter displays the command prompt and translates the letters you type into the various internal DOS commands. For example, COMMAND.COM contains the COPY, DEL, and REN commands. COMMAND.COM not only performs these commands but also can give you error messages if it cannot complete the commands.

The final portion of DOS is the utility programs. These programs are the less frequently used external DOS commands. Each command, such as FORMAT.COM and XCOPY.EXE, is a separate program. To the user, if the

DOS subdirectory is on the path, you don't detect any difference between internal and external commands. You type either at the command prompt and press Enter. COMMAND.COM determines whether it has to go to an external file to find the command or whether the command is located within itself.

Replacing Individual DOS Commands

You can enhance DOS's functionality by replacing some of the external commands. The FORMAT command, for example, is potentially dangerous. DOS doesn't check to see whether the disk to be formatted already is formatted, and you easily can overwrite important data. Until DOS 3, formatting a hard disk was just as easy as formatting a floppy disk. If you accidentally typed FORMAT without specifying a drive designator, you could lose all the data on your hard disk. In DOS 3, the warning message `WARNING! ALL DATA ON NONREMOVABLE DISK DRIVE d: WILL BE LOST Proceed with Format (Y/N)?` was added to help, and in DOS 3.2 and later, you are prompted for the current volume label before reformatting can occur.

PC Tools Deluxe, along with other collections of utility programs, includes a replacement formatter. It uses DOS's formatter for the formatting process itself but gives you more protection from overwriting previously formatted disks. When you try to format a disk that is not unformatted, you get a warning message that the disk probably already contains data. You are given the opportunity to abort the command at this point.

You can create your own improved FORMAT command by using batch files. For example, you can create a batch file, using replaceable parameters, that shows a directory on the drive to be formatted prior to activating the FORMAT command. If you get a `General failure` error when you use the FORMAT command, the disk is probably not formatted (or you have forgotten to close the disk drive door). If you see a list of files, you can check that you are not formatting either your hard disk or a floppy disk you want to keep.

You can use these batch-file or third-party techniques to enhance other DOS commands, too. For example, a batch file that automatically backs up your hard disk is in effect enhancing the DOS BACKUP command.

Replacing the Command Interpreter

DOS is designed to enable you to use an alternative command processor, which would be a replacement for COMMAND.COM. Even if you don't want to change the functionality of the internal DOS commands, you may want all the messages and command names in Spanish rather than English, for example. This flexibility in DOS enables third parties to provide alternative command interpreters that greatly enhance DOS's features.

4DOS from J.P. Software is one such product. In addition to including all the standard DOS commands, 4DOS makes extra commands available.

Making Use of Machine Architecture

Although DOS 5 includes features such as HIMEM.SYS and EMM386.EXE that make use of the microprocessor type, most DOS commands are designed for the 8088. With ATs and 386-based systems becoming prevalent in the market, manufacturers have developed ways to take advantage of the more sophisticated features of the microprocessor while maintaining compatibility with all normal DOS applications and commands. Memory managers, such as QRAM and 386-to-the-MAX, for example, use the protected mode of the microprocessor to manipulate memory in ways not previously possible. These products, although giving you flexibility in memory management and improving performance by shadowing ROM in RAM, do not enhance DOS's features.

DOS normally provides all the recurring services required for the computer. An applications program communicates with the computer hardware through DOS services. The applications program has to communicate directly with the hardware only for services that are not supplied as a part of DOS. In some cases, however, in the interests of performance, programs circumvent DOS services. For example, DOS's video functions often are circumvented. The user gets the impression that the program is very fast, because programs can perform the same services as DOS but much faster. For example, if saving a file took four seconds rather than three, you probably wouldn't notice. If redrawing the screen slowed by a second, however, you would notice. The display is the first and often the only feedback you have. Consequently, its performance is important.

A class of products known as *DOS extenders* use the microprocessors' protected modes and improve DOS while retaining compatibility. A DOS extender is a tool programmers use to create applications programs that can use protected mode. The DOS extender provides the equivalent of the DOS services for the applications program but uses the protected mode rather than the real mode of the microprocessor. Thus, along with using typical DOS services, applications programs that incorporate the DOS extender can make full use of the extended memory and other microprocessor-specific functions.

DOS and all the applications programs written to run under DOS are unaffected, but the applications programs written to use the DOS extender have more functionality than is possible with a typical DOS application. In fact, you may be using one of the products and be unaware that it is not a normal DOS application. Applications programs that use a DOS extender include VersaCAD Corporation's VersaCAD/386, Autodesk Inc.'s AutoCAD/386, Borland International's Paradox/386, Oracle Corporation's Professional ORACLE, and IBM's Interleaf Publisher.

Some DOS extenders are for the 80286 and consequently work on ATs, 386-based systems, and 486-based systems. Others are for the 80386 microprocessor and use the features found on the 80386 and 80486. An applications program that requires an AT or 386 to function probably is using some sort of DOS extender. Many programs specify that an AT or 386 is *preferable*, but if the program runs on a PC, even if it is unbearably slow, then it is not using the features found only on the 80286, the 80386, or even the 80486 microprocessor.

The major limitation of DOS, because of its operation on 8088 systems, is that it can address only 1M of memory. Expanded memory is a method of increasing the amount of memory that can be accessed overall, but you still are limited to accessing 1M at a time. Because of this restriction, you cannot store in expanded memory the program instructions you currently are using. Consequently, DOS applications programs are limited in their size. Using expanded memory enables a program to manage large amounts of data and put portions of the program into expanded memory, but this situation is more limiting than being able to access all the memory at once.

The 80286 has an address space of 16M when operating in protected mode. By using memory swapping techniques that are part of the microprocessor hardware, you can address far more than this amount (1 gigabyte, which is 10^9 bytes) but only 16M at once.

The 80386 has an even larger address space, again accessed in protected mode. You can access 4 gigabytes at one time and a total of 64 terabytes (10^{12} bytes), using memory swapping techniques built into the microprocessor.

To understand DOS extenders fully, you need to know the basic steps involved in writing programs. Unless you are writing programs, you wouldn't go out and buy a DOS extender, but you may choose an applications program that uses a DOS extender.

Understanding the Steps to Creating a Program

A *program* is a series of instructions that the computer executes in order to perform a particular task or set of tasks. A programmer creates this program in three steps: coding, compiling, and linking. The program is split in small sections, often called modules, for ease of creation and debugging. The programmer codes (writes) each section by typing expressions into a text editor. The syntax for the expressions varies depending on the computer language chosen. Although BASIC is the language supplied with DOS, most professionally written programs for the PC are written in C, assembler, or Pascal.

The text then is compiled by the language compiler. In this step, the language compiler translates the text into a series of instructions that the computer can understand. Remember that a computer understands only series of 1s and 0s. For example, a particular set of 1s and 0s represents the "add" instruction to the microprocessor. The programmer may have typed an instruction called ADD in the text editor, and the language compiler converts it into the 1s and 0s that the microprocessor understands.

When the compiler finds an instruction that it cannot translate (perhaps because of a typing error), the compiler gives an error message to the programmer. The error can be corrected and the compiling redone until the module can be translated. Note that the completion of this step doesn't mean that the program works correctly. It means only that the compiler can translate each line of the text into instructions.

The third step in creating the program involves linking the compiled modules. The linker program determines the addresses for each section of code and enables them to communicate with each other.

After the compiling and linking are complete, the programmer can test the whole program. Any changes that have to be made are done in the text editor, and the program is recompiled and relinked.

A programmer can use one of many different implementations of compilers. Not only can you choose a C compiler, but you can choose a particular manufacturer's C compiler. These compilers vary in ease of use, specific syntax of commands, and in some cases available commands. For example, Borland International's Turbo Pascal is a popular compiler because it is easy to use and compiles code rapidly. But Turbo Pascal doesn't include every possible Pascal command.

Compilers usually are supplied with collections of standard routines, or miniprograms, that a programmer can incorporate into the program. These collections are called *libraries*. In some cases, a programmer may choose a particular compiler based on its selection of libraries rather than just its ease of use and speed.

The compilers used with DOS are limited to the 8088 microprocessor. They translate the text into instructions that can run on the 8088 regardless of the computer used to compile the instructions. Because the 8088 is an 8-bit device, the compilers use only 8-bit instructions, even though the 80286 can accept 16-bit instructions.

In a similar way, the linker has to understand only 8-bit instructions if the program is going to run under DOS. You can buy compilers and linkers that run under other operating systems, such as UNIX and OS/2. These compilers and linkers are similar to their DOS counterparts in that the compiler translates the text into instructions the microprocessor can understand and the linker links the modules. Because these other operating systems can make use of the 80286 (or the 80386) microprocessor, however, the instructions created are not just 8-bit instructions but take better advantage of the microprocessor's power.

Using DOS Extenders

DOS extenders fall between the DOS compilers and other operating system compilers. By supplying libraries that include the capacity to switch the microprocessor into and out of protected mode, DOS is enhanced. The programmer can use the best features of the DOS extender libraries as well as all the DOS functions and create an extended application that would not be possible with just DOS.

You can think of DOS extenders as being small-scale supplemental kernels for DOS. DOS continues to handle what it can, but the DOS extender gives access to protected mode wherever necessary. Communication between information in protected mode and information in real mode also is handled by the DOS extender. The programmer doesn't use a normal DOS compiler and linker to create the program. Instead, a DOS extender and a compiler and linker that can make use of the DOS extender are used. The programmer links the DOS extender kernel module into the extended application at the linking stage.

Because DOS extenders use protected mode, they do not work on 8088 systems. Some extenders and the compilers and linkers that work with them are for the 80286 microprocessor. Others are specifically for the 80386 microprocessor and can take advantage of the virtual 8086 mode of the 80386.

Remember that if a program works on a particular 80X86 microprocessor, the program works on all the newer siblings, because each new microprocessor introduced in the family is a superset of the previous one. Programs designed to work on the 80386 work on the 80486, for example.

Note that switching between protected mode and real mode is time-consuming on the 80286 microprocessor. The microprocessor must be completely reset. On the 80386, however, switching between modes can be made much faster if a bit is written to a control register on the microprocessor. A DOS extender that takes advantage of this 80386 feature gives a much better performance than one using the 80286 approach to switching in and out of protected mode. Some DOS extenders alleviate this performance bottleneck by operating only in protected mode and not switching between real and protected mode. The disadvantage of this approach, however, is that the DOS extender has to emulate all the DOS functions because they cannot be reached in protected mode. If the implementation is perfect, no problems occur. But compatibility with DOS—and particularly future versions of DOS—is a major concern.

You are not able to choose the DOS extender you want to use with your applications program. The applications program is written using a particular DOS extender. When you understand the differences among the available DOS extenders, however, you can make a more informed choice of your applications program.

A. I. Architects offers a wide range of DOS extenders. OS/286 runs on 80286 systems; OS/386 runs on 80386 systems; and OS/386-HB, which is used with A. I. Architects' 386 accelerator board, the HummingBoard, runs on PCs, ATs, or 386-based compatible computers.

OS/286 enables applications programs to use 16-bit instructions. The program (with its associated data) can be up to 16M in size. OS/386 can use 32-bit instructions and the virtual 8086 mode. You must have a 386-based computer (or better), however, to use the extended application.

The HummingBoard is not a typical accelerator board. It does not replace the existing microprocessor but enables extended applications to use the features of the second microprocessor, which is located on the HummingBoard. Protected-mode applications run on the HummingBoard although normal DOS applications run on the main CPU. Depending on how the specific extended application is written, the HummingBoard can be running some parts of the program at the same time the main microprocessor is running other parts. The parts being run by the main microprocessor are running in real mode, because the main microprocessor may be only an 8088.

Phar Lap Software Inc.'s 386/DOS-Extender is used by such applications programs as AutoCAD/386 and VersaCAD/386, two powerful CAD programs. This DOS extender is popular with programmers because many of the features previously not available with DOS can be accessed by using similar approaches to DOS. 386/DOS-Extender uses the same INT 21H interrupt used by DOS but enhances the features. Programmers do not have to learn a completely new structure.

With 386/DOS-Extender, you can use other 386-based memory management programs, such as 386-to-the-MAX and QEMM, at the same time. Quarterdeck and Phar Lap developed a standard called Virtual Control Program Interface (VCPI) to make this coexistence possible. Other programs that use 386-specific memory management, such as Microsoft Windows /386, do not enable you to use a DOS extender while using the program.

DOS/16M from Rational Systems Inc. is another 16-bit DOS extender designed for the 80286 microprocessor. This extender is particularly suitable for TSRs that operate in protected mode and on computers with limited extended memory.

Increasingly, the most sophisticated applications programs are using DOS extenders. Because of the users' need for speed with these programs, the software developers' demands for an AT or 386-based computer are not unreasonable. Given that the typical user of these more sophisticated applications programs is willing to own an AT or 386-based computer, the software developers wisely decided to take advantage of these DOS extenders to get even more performance and not be limited by the 640K boundary for programs and data.

Instead of using the DOS extender, a software developer can choose to create an applications program to run on a more sophisticated operating system, such as OS/2. This program, however, will require the user not only to have a more powerful computer but also to be willing to give up all the other applications programs currently being used on the user's existing system. When other operating systems have a wide array of business programs that are as popular as the DOS applications such as WordPerfect and 1-2-3, the decision to change operating systems to gain more functionality will not seem to be a step backward for using other products on your PC.

Exploring Multitasking Products

A typical PC running DOS operates one program at a time. Even if you have a TSR loaded, such as a calendar, you stop using your applications program to run the calendar and only restart the applications program when you have finished using the TSR. The reason you can run only one program at a time is that DOS is a nonreentrant operating system. You cannot interrupt DOS when it is executing some instructions. Before a TSR can be serviced, for example, it must wait until DOS has finished a particular function.

The capacity to run more than one program at once on a PC is known as *multitasking*. A variety of multitasking programs are available to enhance DOS. Some of these programs work on all PCs, and others are designed to work on 386-based computers. Multitasking programs take one of two approaches. They either make DOS reentrant, by supplying and modifying the relevant services, or replace DOS completely, supplying the reentrant services and emulating all the other DOS services.

A multitasking program can run more than one program at once. But because you have only one microprocessor in your computer, you are not running all the programs at once at a particular instant in time. The multitasking program shares the microprocessor with all the applications programs running on the computer. Each applications program is given a small amount of time, known as a *time slice*, to perform a few instructions; then the next applications program gets a turn. The division of time affects the performance of the program and in most cases is alterable by the end user.

As covered in Chapter 1, the PC is driven by a clock. All functions in the computer start on a clock tick. Even if an interrupt occurs between clock ticks, it is not serviced until the next clock tick. Multitasking programs use these clock ticks as the basis for assigning time slices to applications programs.

Two forms of multitasking exist: preemptive and cooperative. In a *preemptive* multitasking program, each applications program is assigned a specific number of clock ticks as a time slice. When the time is up, the next program is given control regardless of how much the previous program has achieved in its time slice. Each program receives its time slice in turn. When all the programs have had a turn, the first program is given a time slice and the process continues. The advantage of this method is that every program gets a turn. You usually can adjust the number of clock ticks in a time slice for each program, to make the program as responsive as possible for your particular program mix. In preemptive multitasking, the multitasking program is responsible for switching control among the various programs as well as keeping track of the time slices. DESQview, offered by Quarterdeck Office Systems, is an example of a preemptive multitasking program.

A *cooperative* multitasking program assumes that all the programs are going to "play nicely together." When given control of the microprocessor, a program can, in theory, keep it forever. The cooperative multitasking program doesn't take control away from the applications program. The applications program, however, should be written so that whenever it has completed a small amount of work, it checks to see whether one of the other programs needs the microprocessor. If another program wants control, the first program can complete its current task and then pass control onto the next program. The first program assumes that it will be given another chance to have the microprocessor. The sharing of the microprocessor requires cooperation among the programs. In cooperative multitasking, the multitasking program is responsible for switching among the various programs but exercises less control over the time a particular program has control. Microsoft Windows is an example of a cooperative multitasking system.

In a preemptive multitasking environment, you may end up with wasted time. Consider a situation in which a program is waiting for a printer's print buffer to empty so that the program can send the next part of a document for printing. In a preemptive multitasking environment, this program is given its time slice, regardless of the fact that it doesn't have anything to do until the printer is ready to accept more characters. The program has to be given its time slices just in case the printer is ready. If the printer isn't ready, the time slice is wasted.

In a cooperative environment, the program starts to print, discovers it has to wait for the printer, and gives up control of the microprocessor to another program. When the other programs have had a turn with the microprocessor, the waiting program can look quickly and see whether it can send more information to the printer. If it can, the program performs the next set of instructions; if not, it gives up the microprocessor again. Although all the programs follow the rules and don't keep control for too long, this method is preferable, but the nonassertive programs appear to have a lower performance than the others because they don't get much time with the microprocessor.

In a DOS environment, cooperative multitasking environments involve two negatives. First, most programs were not written to be cooperative, and when they get control they keep it. Second, for a program to be truly cooperative, it needs to be specially written for the particular operating environment. Consequently, the best applications programs for a cooperative multitasking environment are probably not those you are currently using in a stand-alone situation.

The multitasking operating system has to do much more than DOS on its own. Consequently, the performance of a particular computer goes down when you use a multitasking operating system rather than just DOS. With DOS you have to exit an applications program and load the next applications program to change programs. This procedure can take a substantial amount of time. On a multitasking system, you can switch between programs with only a couple of keystrokes. In theory, the degradation in performance when using a multitasking operating system is offset by the speed with which you can change programs.

If you use only a single applications program, multitasking will not be of benefit to you. Many normal business operations, however, require the use of several programs; these operations can be aided by multitasking. For example, if you create in a word processor a report containing spreadsheet information and mail it to customers kept in a database listing, multitasking can simplify the process dramatically.

To enable several programs to run at once on the computer, a multitasking program must make each program think that it has the whole computer to itself. Each program has to accept keyboard input, display information on-screen, and use the disks and other I/O devices. A multitasking program has to fool each program into thinking that it has all the resources it needs yet must keep each program separate. The concept of *virtual devices* makes this situation possible. A device occupies a particular area of memory. The multitasking program gives each program a different area of memory for the same device. For example, each program is assigned an area of memory for the display. Each program thus has what is called a virtual display.

The keyboard is a different problem. Although you, the user, need a key combination to switch between programs, after you have switched, you need to type information into only one program at a time. The multitasking program makes one program the program that can accept keyboard input. Some multitasking programs refer to this program as the *active* program or task; others call it the *foreground* program or task. The other programs on the system are considered *background* tasks. When you switch between programs, the current foreground task becomes a background task, and the new foreground task becomes the task that accepts keystrokes.

In some cases, such as with DESQview, Windows, and VM/386, the multitasking program works in cooperation with DOS. These types of multitasking programs usually are referred to as multitasking environments because they are not complete operating systems. Other products, such as PC-MOS and Concurrent DOS 386, are complete multitasking operating systems that emulate DOS. The following sections discuss the two types of multitasking programs and describe some of the products currently available.

Using Multitasking Environments

In the same way that DOS extenders try to make as much use of DOS as possible yet overcome its shortcomings, multitasking environments make extensive use of DOS. Wherever possible, multitasking environments use the DOS services, but they supply the additional features necessary to run multiple programs.

The multitasking environment cannot exceed the features of the microprocessor. Although you can run DESQview or Windows on 8088-based systems, the programs do not operate as well as their siblings designed specifically for the 80386, because of limitations with the 8088. The 8088 can address only 1M of RAM, so all the programs you are trying to run must fit into the base 640K of memory. If the programs don't fit, you cannot run them simultaneously.

If you have a choice, run a multitasking environment that is tailored to your computer. On a PC, you are limited by the 8088. On a 386-based computer, however, you can use DESQview/386 or Windows 3.0 to take full advantage of the microprocessor.

DESQview

Quarterdeck Office Systems' DESQview has been a popular multitasking program for several years. It runs on all PCs, ATs, 386-based computers, and 486-based computers. You even can run it on a monochrome display. (Because the MDA cannot display graphics, however, you then cannot run any graphics programs.) Although not essential, expanded memory is highly desirable. It gives you more memory for loading several applications programs at once. You can run DESQview from a computer with two floppy drives or a hard disk.

DESQview is a multitasking environment that works in association with DOS to give you the ability to run several applications programs at once. DESQview gives each running program a virtual display device so that the program thinks that it has its own display. You can set aside areas of the screen, called *windows*, to view portions of each applications program running. You can change the size of the windows and have one or many windows visible at once on-screen. You can fit up to nine windows on a single screen.

DESQview itself has its own window, which you use to control the programs you want to run. You use the DESQview control window to start applications programs, close applications programs, and rearrange the windows on-screen. DESQview handles all the memory management necessary to control all the programs. A mouse is supported, but DESQview makes good use of the keyboard for switching programs and altering windows.

Note that because each program is running under DOS, you can have only 640K of base memory assigned to each program. DESQview has to take some overhead from the available space to be capable of controlling the program, and DOS takes its share. Consequently, you are not able to open a window with a full 640K of memory. The only programs that require the absolute limit of memory, however, are those that you would not be using in a multitasking situation anyway.

DESQview saves you memory overall by not copying the DOS services to each program being run. By using memory mapping, each program shares the same DOS area. You need to use memory for only one copy of DOS.

You can transfer data from one window to another by using DESQview's cut and paste features. You can, for example, cut a portion of a spreadsheet and place it into your word processing document. This data-exchange feature is a compelling reason to use a multitasking program. Not only can you operate two programs at once, but you also can swap data between them efficiently.

Using DESQview, however, is not problem-free. Although you can print from any of the applications programs you are running, you cannot print from more than one at once. If you try to do so, the output from the two programs is combined into a single, jumbled mess. Other multitasking programs, such as Windows, can queue your print jobs and wait for the first one to finish before starting the next.

If you are running text-only applications, the DESQview screen is in character mode. If you start a graphics application, all the windows displayed are converted to graphics mode. In some cases, this feature can cause the colors to change and the response time to degrade. When this problem is coupled with the slower performance resulting from a multitasking program's overhead, the performance may be frustrating.

DESQview also suffers with some compatibility problems. These problems are caused not by DESQview but by the applications programs circumventing the DOS routines. DESQview cannot be expected to deal with programs that disobey the DOS rules and do such things as manipulate the serial port without using DOS or BIOS services.

DESQview classifies programs as being DESQview oblivious, DESQview aware, or DESQview specific. The DESQview-specific programs are the utilities supplied with DESQview to help do such things as cut and paste between applications. These programs run only under DESQview.

When DESQview-aware programs are started, they check to see whether DESQview is running. If it is, these programs behave differently than if they are running in a DOS-only system. When DESQview is not present, these programs may, for example, circumvent the DOS functions for writing to the screen and improve their video performance. When they're running under DESQview, however, these same programs don't circumvent so that they can coexist successfully with other programs running at the same time. WordPerfect and Paradox are examples of DESQview-aware programs.

DESQview-oblivious programs don't check for DESQview's presence. Well-behaved programs that use the DOS and BIOS calls run well under DESQview, but programs that write directly to the hardware may cause some compatibility problems. The most common way that programs "ill behave" is by writing directly to video memory instead of using DOS services. Because each program is given its own complete video area, this situation usually is handled properly by DESQview but is the cause of some compatibility problems.

You can buy DESQview in two different versions. DESQview runs on the PC and AT computers. DESQview/386 is a bundled package of DESQview and QEMM, the 386 memory manager, for 386-based and 486-based computers. In this version of the program, DESQview can use the virtual 8086 mode of the 80386. Each program is given its own 1M area of memory, a virtual 8086.

Windows

Microsoft Windows is the best known multitasking operating environment. Windows has a graphical user interface that enables programs specially written to run under Windows to operate in a window on-screen. As with

DESQview, Windows is a supplement to DOS, making use of DOS and BIOS functions wherever possible but supplying the control of multiple programs and memory management.

Windows is designed to be used with a mouse. Although you can use the keyboard, a mouse is much more efficient. All Windows programs have a similar user interface. The windows have common elements that make learning a new program easier than with DOS's stand-alone approach. For example, the main menu for Windows programs is always in a horizontal bar just below the program's title.

Several types of programs run under Windows. The Windows-specific programs use cooperative multitasking and can work with each other at the same time. Instead of each applications program being assigned a time slice, each Windows application is given control of the microprocessor in turn.

Each program is assigned a window on-screen. This window can be in one of three states. As a maximized window, the program is given the whole screen in which to work. The maximized window looks similar to its smaller version, but you cannot see any other windows. As a minimized window, the program is represented by a small icon, usually placed at the bottom of the screen. This icon offers a pictorial representation of the program instead of showing you any of its features. For example, Hewlett Packard's Scan Gallery program, which drives the ScanJet Plus scanner, has a picture of a scanner as its icon. The third window size is a partial-screen window in which the program is given a portion of the screen. You can see the menus and contents of the program within the designated area, but you can see on-screen the windows for other loaded programs, too. You can alter the size and position of this type of window at will by adjusting the window's border position.

Windows can run non-Windows applications, too, such as the typical DOS applications programs. The environment behaves differently and less efficiently, however, when running these other applications. When running applications other than Windows applications, Windows is a preemptive multitasking system. All the Windows applications currently running, known as a *screen group*, are given one slice to share, and each of the other applications programs is given a time slice in turn. Before using a normal DOS application, you first have to create a program information file (PIF) for the program to run under Windows. As a default, Windows assigns the whole screen to a non-Windows application, but many applications will run in a window if you prefer. You simply have to change the PIF configuration.

In some cases, you cannot run an applications program in a window and have to run it as a full-screen application. If you set up the applications program as a full-screen application through its PIF, the program runs, but transferring data between a full-screen application and a windowed application is not as easy as between windowed applications.

Windows is available in many versions. Some are hardware specific; others, including all versions prior to 3.0, work on all PCs. Windows/386 is a special version of Windows designed to work on 386-based systems. Although it uses the memory mapping features available on the 80386, it doesn't use virtual 8086 mode.

Windows 3.0 works on all types of PCs but operates in different ways on the different systems. It has a real mode, a standard mode, and a 386 enhanced mode. You need a hard disk with 8M of free disk space. You use real mode if you are running Windows-specific applications programs that were written for Windows 2.x or have less than 1M of memory. You can use the standard mode on 80286-based computers, but you need at least 1M of memory. 386 enhanced mode uses the virtual 8086 mode of the 80386 microprocessor. You need 2M of memory for this mode.

As with most programs that are specific to the hardware, you can use a particular mode on any computer that has a microprocessor better than the minimum requirements. For example, you can use real, standard, and 386 enhanced mode on 486-based computers because the 80486 can emulate an 8088, an 80286, and an 80386 microprocessor.

Windows 3.0 running in 386 enhanced mode has many more powerful features than standard or real mode. For example, you can alter the size of each time slice and have Windows detect whether the application is idle and waiting for input. The time slice is allocated to the next task instead of being wasted. Although Windows running in 386 enhanced mode uses extended memory, the environment can emulate expanded memory so that the applications programs you run can take advantage of expanded memory.

As with all the multitasking environments, running a program with Windows is not as fast as running it stand-alone. If you regularly use more than one program, however, and want to swap data among programs, you may be prepared to accept the degradation in performance in exchange for the significant advantages in features found with running multiple programs at once. Increasingly, applications programs are being written for Windows. If you run one Windows application, such as PageMaker, you may find that always running with Windows—instead of loading Windows only when you run the application—is worthwhile.

Using Multitasking Multiuser Operating Systems

A multitasking operating system can run more than one program at a time. A multiuser operating system can support more than one user at a time. Using expansion boards, you can add additional displays and keyboards to a single PC. Each user has an individual keyboard and display but shares a single system unit.

Many of the multiuser operating systems can be run without the additional hardware as just multitasking systems. In general, even if the multiuser multitasking operating system works on a PC, you would not want to use it on that type of system for performance reasons. Running several applications programs on a single computer slows the performance substantially. Taking this one step further and having several users running several programs slows the performance even more.

The following paragraphs explore some of the multitasking multiuser environments on the market today.

VM/386

VM/386 from Intelligent Graphics Corporation is also a multitasking multiuser environment. Specifically designed for the 80386, VM/386 makes use of the virtual 8086 mode, which enables you to appear to have multiple 8086s in your computer. Each 8086 has an address space of 1M and can be independent of the other 8086 address spaces.

Using VM/386 as the multitasking environment with DOS, you can create up to 32 virtual machines, although you are in reality much more limited by the amount of memory in your computer. During the configuration process, you assign a certain amount of your memory to each machine. For example, if you have 4M of memory, you may want to assign 1M to one machine and 3M to a second machine. Any given machine appears to you, the user, as if it were an ordinary computer running DOS.

You can switch from machine to machine by pressing a key combination. Each virtual machine has its own area of memory and its own copy of DOS. You run your applications programs as normal. When you want to change programs, you press the appropriate key combination to access the next program. Each program, whether it is in the foreground (accepting keystrokes and displaying data) or in the background, is assigned a time slice in turn. You can configure the program to reassign the length of each time slice or even to detect whether a background task is idle.

Note, however, that a task, according to VM/386, is considered idle if it doesn't use interrupts. If you are doing a recalculation on a spreadsheet in the background, for example, you may find the process suspended. The reason is that a recalculation doesn't require interrupts. Processes such as database sorting, on the other hand, do use interrupts to transfer data on and off the hard disk and so would be given the time slice.

The disadvantage of VM/386 is that you can see only one program at a time on-screen. Also, VM/386 uses only the memory allocated to the particular virtual machine during configuration. If, for example, you usually use a small spreadsheet requiring a small amount of memory and a large word processor, you have to allocate the memory for each machine accordingly. Windows 3.0 running in 386 enhanced mode can assign unused memory to any of the applications programs requesting it.

The other disadvantage becomes apparent when you transfer information between programs. You cannot transfer information displayed on the screen of one program to another program in a different virtual machine. Because you are sharing a hard disk, however, you can save the information to a file and pick up the file from the other program.

VM/386 does, however, have an important advantage: You can reboot each machine separately. When you press Ctrl-Alt-Del, you reboot only the current foreground machine. With DESQview and Windows, you have to reboot the whole computer; if you reach a point where one of the programs has locked up the computer, you lose all the data not previously saved for each of the tasks. With VM/386, you lose unsaved data only on the foreground program.

An additional advantage to VM/386 is that you can run your TSRs with your applications programs. Because each virtual machine is separate, you just start your TSR and load your program. With DESQview and Windows, you have more difficulty. The general approach is to run the TSR in a separate window. Although this method enables you to run appointment calendars and the like, you cannot run a keyboard enhancer in association with your word processor, for example.

As a multiuser multitasking operating system, VM/386 operates similarly to a single-user application. You install a multiport expansion board, such as Arnet Multiport-8, and plug in additional monitors and keyboards. The virtual machines defined are accessible at any of the keyboards through the System Resource Manager.

Concurrent DOS 386

Digital Research's Concurrent DOS 386 is another multiuser multitasking operating system. It is a complete operating system that replaces all the DOS and BIOS routines so that the operating system is reentrant and can run multiple programs.

The advantage over multitasking operating environments is that each task running on the computer requires less memory because the program doesn't have to use the DOS services. The disadvantage is that you have to depend on the compatibility of the substitute DOS commands and services. Although most DOS features are well documented, not all are defined specifically. You may have a program that is using one of the undocumented features not replicated in Concurrent DOS. That program consequently will not work.

If you prefer, you can install Concurrent DOS on the same system as DOS and configure your computer as a dual-boot system. When your computer boots up, you are asked whether you want to boot DOS or Concurrent DOS.

Concurrent DOS 386 uses the virtual 8086 mode of the 80386 to operate. You can run up to four tasks on the main system console (the PC's normal monitor and keyboard), and the additional consoles (monitors and keyboards) each can switch between two different programs.

Concurrent DOS 386 is faster than most of the other multiuser operating systems. Only when the computer is running many programs at once does the performance degrade significantly.

If you are running text-based programs on the system console, you can display the tasks in on-screen windows. You can alter the size and color of each window independently. Because Concurrent DOS 386 doesn't give each task a virtual video device, however, you cannot have windows on-screen when you are running programs that write directly to the video memory.

If you are running a graphics-based program, you cannot have windows on-screen. Each program has to occupy the whole screen. You can, however, switch rapidly between the programs with a keystroke. Transferring information between programs is similar to the process you use with VM/386. You have to save a file, which you then retrieve from the next program. Fortunately, Concurrent DOS is supplied with a utility that saves on-screen information in a file for later retrieval.

You cannot reboot just one of the tasks on the computer. If you press Ctrl-Alt-Del, the computer is rebooted completely, and all the users have to restart their applications. You can, however, lock out the Ctrl-Alt-Del sequence to prevent this rebooting. You can use the REBOOT command, which can be password-protected to prevent unauthorized rebooting.

Concurrent DOS also includes other password protection. You can assign passwords to disks, directories, or individual files. But Concurrent DOS depends on your applications program to do file-locking, which prevents more than one task accessing the same file.

A special program called the Printer Manager controls printing from the multiple tasks. Printed documents are stored as files until the Printer Manager prints them. Up to 254 print files can be queued to one or more printers.

PC-MOS

PC-MOS, a multiuser environment offered by The Software Link, operates on all PCs and ATs. You are unlikely, however, to find the performance acceptable on a PC or AT. 386-based computers now are relatively inexpensive and well worth the investment if you want to run a multiuser system.

Like Concurrent DOS, PC-MOS is a complete replacement for DOS. PC-MOS includes substitute commands—such as DEL, DIR, COPY, and FORMAT—for the DOS equivalents and many additional commands to enable you to have multiple users with multiple tasks. Also included is a print spooler that detects when data is being sent to the printer. If a second program tries to print, its output is spooled into a disk file until the first program has finished printing.

As supplied, PC-MOS gives each task the same-sized time slice in turn. You can alter the priority of each task, and hence its time slice size, however, and activate the option to detect whether a program is idling. If a program is waiting for input, it is not given its time slice.

As with VM/386, you can display only one task on-screen at once, and you have to switch between tasks with a keystroke. You cannot swap data between programs directly, but you can write the information to a file and pick it up in another program. PC-MOS does include various advanced features that enable some applications programs designed to work on a network to work together.

The security system for PC-MOS enables you to set one of 26 security classes (represented by a letter) for every file or directory on the computer. Every user has a particular level of access to these 26 classes. The level of access is determined by a configuration file where a user's name, password, and access level are listed. You can allow one user to read a certain file and others to modify the same file. This feature enables you, for example, to let all the department managers read the accounting spreadsheets but to let only the members of the accounting department change the documents. The same department managers can have full access to personnel records.

One disadvantage is that PC-MOS does not protect against a user pressing Ctrl-Alt-Del. A reboot causes the whole computer to reboot, and unsaved data belonging to each user is lost.

PC-MOS includes many controls that affect the performance and configuration of the operating system. The Software Link recommends that PC-MOS be installed by a supplier, but the end user can make the various adjustments.

386/MultiWare

386/MultiWare from Alloy Computer Products is a multiuser multitasking operating system that takes a slightly different approach to using DOS. Instead of replacing the whole of DOS, 386/MultiWare replaces the BIOS. The BIOS is made reentrant, and each task uses its own copy of DOS.

This design has the disadvantage of requiring more memory to run several programs, because DOS is copied into several different places in memory. The advantage, however, is that the programs are running with the true DOS and not a replacement DOS, and compatibility with DOS—in particular, incompatibility with infrequently used features of DOS—is less of a concern.

386/MultiWare takes better advantage of the 80386 microprocessor than do the other multiuser operating systems mentioned in this chapter. 386/MultiWare can create contiguous areas of virtual memory from memory that may be noncontiguous in the physical address space. The advantage of this capability is that you use the memory more efficiently. The physical memory is assigned to a task only when it is requested. VM/386, for example, requires you to specify during configuration the amount of memory assigned to each task.

386/MultiWare does not support the 80387 math coprocessor, so applications that require a math coprocessor do not run, and products such as 1-2-3 run noticeably slower.

Unlike Concurrent DOS but like the other multiuser systems, 386/MultiWare can display only one task on-screen at a time. You are able, however, to run up to eight tasks on a single workstation.

The product is easy to install. You run an administrative program to configure each workstation after you have added the expansion port that links the other displays and keyboards. You set a privilege level for each workstation and assign user names and passwords. When set to the highest level, a workstation can be used for assigning the user names and passwords. In the next level, called high-level workstations, you can run up to eight tasks and are given a higher proportion of time than the other levels receive. In the low-level workstation, you can run only a single program.

With 386/MultiWare, you swap between tasks by using the Task Swapper, a pop-up utility. You can alter the control of disk drives, COM ports, messages, and users by using the Task Manager. You create the messages that can be transmitted between workstations with the Message Utility program. You also can start a program from one workstation and make the program run on another.

Exploring the Network Alternative

A multiuser operating system shares a single computer among several users. As the number of users increases, the performance of the computer decreases dramatically.

An alternative to a multiuser operating system is a local area network (LAN). A LAN links several PCs, giving each of them access to the hard disks and devices, such as printers, on the other computers. Each workstation, called a *node*, is a separate computer with its own microprocessor.

For a couple of users, a LAN is usually more expensive than a multiuser operating system. But, as the number of users increases, a LAN becomes more cost effective. As the number of users gets higher still, the multiuser system becomes impractical from a performance viewpoint, assuming that the multiuser operating system can accommodate that many users.

On a LAN, your performance is slowed when you are transferring data across the connections between the computers, particularly if several users are transferring information at the same time. As you add more users, the time to transfer increases, but the time required to do the processing is unaffected. On a multiuser system, as you add more users, each task is given a smaller proportion of time in which to run, and the whole computing process goes down in performance.

Chapter Summary

DOS is limited as an operating system by its history. Maintaining compatibility with the original PC limits DOS's capacity to make use of the more advanced microprocessors.

Some applications programs take advantage of DOS extenders to make up for DOS's inadequacies. These programs work only on computers that have the appropriate microprocessor because the programs take advantage of the advanced memory management capabilities of the 80286 or 80386. If a program requires an AT or a 386-based computer to run, the program probably is using a DOS extender. Programs (such as AutoCAD/386) using DOS extenders have two advantages over applications programs using DOS. First, the programs can handle larger amounts of memory because they use extended memory rather than expanded memory. Second, the programs themselves can be larger than is possible when the programs only have access to low DOS memory and expanded memory page frames at one time.

You can improve your computer's capabilities by replacing part or all of DOS. You can replace individual DOS commands by using third-party utilities, or you can replace the whole command processor by using products such as 4DOS.

By using multitasking software, you add to your computer the capacity to run multiple programs. A multitasking environment, such as Windows or DESQview, runs on top of DOS to provide additional features. A multitasking operating system, such as PC-MOS or Concurrent DOS, replaces DOS. Multitasking environments have to live with the limitations imposed by DOS, and multitasking operating systems have to be fully compatible with DOS in order for your applications programs to run.

Some multitasking programs are also multiuser programs. You can share a single computer among several people by adding additional displays and keyboards. For a few users, this approach is economical. When the number of users increases, however, the performance degrades substantially, and the cost effectiveness is reduced. To enable a large number of users to share data on a computer system, you should use a LAN.

Comparing DOS Versions

A

DOS 2 and 3 have several major changes between them. More revisions appear between DOS 3 and 3.3, DOS 3.3 and 4, and DOS 4 and 5. This appendix briefly describes these changes.

Changes between DOS 2.x and DOS 3.0

DOS 3 offers several new commands, changed commands, and changed features.

New CONFIG.SYS Features

With Version 3.0, the following CONFIG.SYS directives are available:

- COUNTRY enables DOS to change date, time, and other characteristics for international use.

- FCBS controls DOS's reactions to a program's use of DOS 1 file handling.
- LASTDRIVE sets the last real or nonreal disk drive that DOS will use.
- VDISK.SYS provides additional RAM (virtual) disk space.

The undocumented SWITCHAR directive is dropped.

New Commands

The following commands have been added to DOS 3:

- ATTRIB enables you to set the read-only attribute of a file.
- GRAFTABL enables you to display some graphics characters legibly if you use the color graphics adapter in medium-resolution graphics mode.
- KEYBxx changes the keyboard layout for different languages.
- LABEL enables you to add, change, or delete a disk's volume label.
- SELECT enables you to customize the start-up disk for use with languages other than English.
- SHARE provides file sharing (file- and record-locking).

Changed Commands

The following commands are changed between DOS 2 and 3:

- BACKUP and RESTORE include the backing up of floppy disks and enable you to put backups on a hard disk.
- DATE and TIME support international date and time formats.
- FORMAT includes the /4 switch to format 360K floppy disks on 1.2M disk drives. The command also warns when a hard disk is to be formatted.
- GRAPHICS includes support for the IBM Personal Computer Compact and Color Printers.

Changed Features

With DOS 3.0, you now can specify a drive and a path name before an external command or program name. You can run programs that do not reside in the current directory or in a directory specified in the PATH command.

Changes between DOS 3.0 and 3.1

This section examines the changes that exist between DOS 3.0 and 3.1.

New Commands

With DOS 3.1, the following commands are available:

- JOIN enables you to connect the directory structures of two different disk drives, thus creating one disk drive.
- SUBST enables you to use a subdirectory as though it is a disk drive.
- The IBM PC Network commands are supported.

Changed Commands

The following commands are different in Version 3.1:

- LABEL prompts you before deleting a volume label.
- SHELL includes the /E:size switch, with size in 16-byte paragraphs.
- TREE displays files in the root directory when the /F switch is used.

Changes between DOS 3.1 and 3.2

This section examines the changes made between DOS 3.1 and 3.2.

New CONFIG.SYS Features

With DOS 3.2, the following new CONFIG.SYS features are available:

- STACKS sets the number and size of the DOS internal stacks.
- The DRIVER.SYS device driver supports various-sized floppy disks—particularly 720K drives of PCs.

New Feature

With DOS 3.2, the IBM Token Ring has support.

New Commands

With DOS 3.2, the following new commands are available:

- REPLACE selectively updates files in one or many directories. The command also adds missing files to a directory.
- XCOPY copies files from one or more directories to another and selectively copies files.

Changed Commands/Directives

With DOS 3.2, the following changes have been made to commands/directives:

- DOS 3.2 now has an ATTRIB+A/–A switch, which controls the archive attribute of files.
- The COMMAND/E switch supports the environment size.
- DISKCOPY/DISKCOMP supports 720K floppy disks.

- FORMAT supports formatting of 720K floppy disks. The command also requests verification before formatting a nonremovable disk that has a volume label. A disk drive name is required.
- SELECT formats the hard disk and copies DOS files.
- The SHELL/E:size switch specifies the environment size in bytes, not in 16-byte paragraphs.

Changes between DOS 3.2 and 3.3

This section examines the changes that exist between DOS 3.2 and 3.3.

New CONFIG.SYS Features

With DOS 3.3, the DEVICE directive now has the following device drivers available:

- DISPLAY.SYS supports code pages (multiple fonts) on EGA, VGA, and PC Convertible displays.
- PRINTER.SYS supports code pages (multiple fonts) on the IBM ProPrinter and Quietwriter III printers.

New Features

With Version 3.3, support is added for 1.44M 3 1/2-inch floppy disks, for COM4: and 19,200 baud rates, and for switchable code pages (international character fonts).

New Commands

DOS 3.3 now has the following commands:

- APPEND is a PATH-like command for data files.
- CHCP provides code page changing.

- FASTOPEN provides a directory-caching program for hard disks.
- NLSFUNC provides support for additional character sets (code pages) and for country-dependent information.

Changed Commands/Directives

With Version 3.3, the following commands and CONFIG.SYS directives have changed:

- ATTRIB has the /S switch to change the attributes of files in subdirectories.
- BACKUP has the /F switch to format floppy disks, the /T switch to back up files based on their time, and the /L switch to produce a log file. The command also places all backed-up files into a single file.
- *batch files* adds support for using the environment variable (%variable%), @ for suppressing display of a line, and the CALL subcommand for running a second batch file and returning control to the first batch file.
- BUFFERS defaults buffers based on RAM in the computer.
- COUNTRY adds support for code pages and a separate country information file (COUNTRY.SYS).
- DATE and TIME set the computer's clock/calendar.
- DISKCOPY/DISKCOMP supports 1.44M floppy disks.
- FDISK supports multiple logical disks on a large hard disk.
- FORMAT adds the /N switch for number of sectors and the /T switch for number of tracks.
- GRAFTABL supports code pages, additional devices, and higher baud rates.
- KEYB replaces the KEYBxx programs and supports additional layouts.
- MODE supports code pages, additional devices and higher baud rates.
- RESTORE adds the /N switch to restore erased or modified files, the /B switch to restore files modified before a given date, and the /L and /E switches to restore files modified after or before a given time.
- SHELL default environment size changes from 128 to 160 bytes.

Changes between DOS 3.3 and 4

This section examines the changes that exist between DOS 3.3 and 4.

New CONFIG.SYS Features

With Version 4, the following CONFIG.SYS features are available:

- With INSTALL, you can load terminate-and-stay-resident programs that earlier are loaded from the DOS command prompt or in the AUTOEXEC.BAT files. The feature includes FASTOPEN.EXE, KEYB.COM, NLSFUNC.EXE, and SHARE.EXE.

- REM enables you to insert remarks in a CONFIG.SYS file, which DOS ignores when the computer boots.

- SWITCHES disables Enhanced Keyboard functions so that software that cannot use those functions remains compatible.

- XMA2EMS.SYS is a new device driver for expanded memory.

- XMAEM.SYS enables emulation of an expanded memory adapter on 80386 systems.

New Features

A new user interface, the DOS Shell, enables the user to run programs and manage files with a graphics- or test-oriented menu system. Many error messages also are changed, and error checking is refined.

New Commands

With Version 4, the following new commands are available:

- MEM provides a report on available conventional, extended, and expanded memory and lists how much of each is unused.

- TRUENAME lists the actual name of a drive or directory affected by a JOIN or SUBST command.

Changed Commands/Directives

The following commands are changed in Version 4:

- ANSI.SYS gains three new parameters: /X, which redefines keys added to Enhanced Keyboards; /L, which tells DOS to override any applications program that resets the number of screen rows to 25; and /K, which turns off extended keyboard functions to comply with noncompatible software.
- APPEND can ignore file operations that already include a drive or path in the original specification.
- BACKUP automatically formats target floppy disks if necessary.
- BUFFERS enables the /X switch, which tells DOS to use expanded memory and to specify up to 10,000 buffers and 1 to 8 look-ahead buffers.
- CHKDSK shows the disk's serial number and tells the size and number of allocation units.
- COUNTRY provides support for Japanese, Korean, and Chinese characters—on special Asian hardware only.
- DEL/ERASE includes /P, which enables you to verify a file name before it is deleted.
- DIR shows the disk's serial number.
- DISPLAY.SYS checks hardware and automatically chooses the most appropriate type of active display if you don't specify an adapter type.
- FASTOPEN and the /X parameter, which tells DOS to use expanded memory, may be loaded from CONFIG.SYS.
- FDISK supports larger disk partitions and has easier-to-use menus and displays.
- FORMAT has a /V:label on the command line as you start to format a disk. FORMAT also has a new /F:size parameter, which enables you to indicate the size of a floppy disk when you want to format the disk for less than its maximum capacity.
- GRAFTABL supports code page 850.
- GRAPHICS supports EGA and VGA adapters and can support more printers.

- KEYB has a /ID:nnn parameter, which can be used for choosing a specific keyboard for countries such as France, Italy, and Great Britain that have more than one Enhanced Keyboard.
- With MODE, you can specify the keyboard rate and number of lines displayed on the screen. The command has parameters for the COM ports.
- PRINTER.SYS has enhanced support for the IBM ProPrinter.
- REPLACE has the /U parameter, which tells DOS to update files that have a date and time more recent than that of a file with the same name on the target disk.
- SELECT is enhanced to install DOS SYS and is changed to enable specification of an optional source drive.
- TIME provides for either a 12-hour or 24-hour clock, depending on the country code in use.
- TREE includes graphics and indentations for showing various subdirectory levels.
- VDISK.SYS has the /X parameter, which tells DOS to use expanded memory, and the /E parameter, which tells DOS to use extended memory.

Changes between DOS 4 and 5

This section examines the changes made between DOS 4 and 5.

New CONFIG.SYS Features

With Version 5, the following CONFIG.SYS directives are available:

- HIMEM.SYS is a memory manager for managing extended memory and high DOS memory.
- DOS=UMB is a directive that causes DOS to load part of itself into high DOS memory, which increases the amount of free low DOS memory for your applications program.

- EMM386.EXE is an expanded memory manager for use on 80386- and 80486-based computers.
- DEVICEHIGH enables you to load device drivers into high DOS memory areas.

New Commands

With Version 5, the following new commands are available:

- DOSKEY is a utility program that enables you to edit command lines, create macros of keystrokes, and recall previously typed commands.
- EXPAND uncompresses a file on the DOS installation or update disk.
- HELP provides on-line information on DOS commands. You also can use the /? switch after a command to get similar information.
- LOADHIGH enables you to load a program into high DOS memory.
- MIRROR copies the contents of the directory and FAT into a file. When you accidentally reformat a disk, you can use UNFORMAT to recover the information stored by MIRROR. Using additional switches makes MIRROR keep track of deleted files so that you can use UNDELETE to recover an accidentally erased file.
- QBASIC is an implementation of the BASIC programming language.
- SETVER is used with programs that do not work with DOS 5 because the programs are looking for a specific DOS version. You can set DOS 5 to lie to these programs about its version number.
- UNDELETE enables you to undelete a file that you accidentally deleted.
- UNFORMAT can restore a disk that has been erased with the FORMAT or RECOVER command.

Changed Commands

With Version 5, the following commands have changed:

- ATTRIB now has -s and -h options that enable you to view and change the system and hidden attributes of files.

- DIR, the directory command, has additional switches that can control the order in which files are displayed. Additionally, you can search for files in more than one subdirectory at a time.

Changed Features

With Version 5, the following features have changed:

- For large hard disks, you can specify partitions up to 2 gigabytes in size without having to use the SHARE directive in CONFIG.SYS.
- You can access more than two physical hard disk drives.
- This version includes support for 2.88M floppy disks.
- A full screen editor, EDIT, has been added.
- The DOS Shell program, DOSSHELL, has changed significantly.

Appendix A

Using Hexadecimal and Memory Addresses

B

The numbers you use in everyday life, such as 146, 300, or 2, have meaning. If you're told that 97 people attended a meeting, for example, you know that means nearly 100. If you talk of millions, you mean a big number, but if you say 1 or 2, you mean a small number. You have a feeling for the size of numbers.

Computers represent numbers differently. A digital computer, such as a PC, can recognize only the presence or absence of electrical signals (often referred to as on or off). To represent numbers on a computer, you use 0s and 1s to indicate the state of the electrical signals. Translating human numbers into forms the computer can understand is difficult for some people because they're not used to seeing numbers in this form.

Binary and Hexadecimal Numbering Systems

The world uses a counting system known as *base 10*, or *decimal*. Ten different symbols represent numbers: 0, 1, 2, 3, 4, 5, 6, 7, 8, and 9. This numbering system probably evolved because humans have 10 fingers. Computers, on the other hand, count in *base 2*, or *binary*, because they have only two symbols, 0 and 1, to represent a number. You can represent all decimal numbers in binary or any other base you choose.

When referring to numbers a computer can use, programmers and users tend to use *base 16*, or *hexadecimal*. Hexadecimal uses 16 different symbols: 0 through 9 (the same as with decimal) and then A, B, C, D, E, and F.

Table B.1 shows the numbers from 1 to 20 decimal in each base.

Table B.1
Binary, Hexadecimal, Decimal Numbers

Decimal	Binary	Hexadecimal
0	0	0
1	1	1
2	10	2
3	11	3
4	100	4
5	101	5
6	110	6
7	111	7
8	1000	8
9	1001	9
10	1010	A
11	1011	B
12	1100	C
13	1101	D
14	1110	E
15	1111	F
16	10000	10
17	10001	11
18	10010	12
19	10011	13
20	10100	14

You represent numbers by using each symbol in turn. When you run out of symbols, you use the first symbol again, except moved one position to the left. In decimal, the number 10 is the first number requiring two digits. In binary, two digits are used much sooner when you're counting because with base 2 fewer symbols are available to represent the numbers. The two digits 10 mean different numbers, depended on the base being used. When converted to decimal, 10 in binary means 2; 10 in hexadecimal means 16.

To reduce confusion, indicate that a number is not in decimal. You can follow the number with the base as a subscript, such as 1101_2, or add a letter after the number—B for binary and H for hexadecimal. For example, you can show the binary number 11101 as 11101_2, or less commonly 11101B, and the hexadecimal number 11101 as 11101_{16}, or more commonly 11101H. You may see the subscript 10 or D added after a number, indicating decimal for clarity. Another convention is to add &H or &B as a prefix to the number.

Binary numbers tend to involve a large number of digits. The decimal number 245, for example, is 11111001 in binary. Programmers use hexadecimal as a base because conversion to binary numbers is easier. If you group binary digits into fours, starting at the binary point, you can translate the group into a hexadecimal digit. For example, split 11111001_2 into 1111 and 1001. The hexadecimal representation for 1111_2 is F and 1001_2 is 9, making the number F9H.

Remember that PCs use bytes of information made up of 8 bits, or digits, at a time. You can use a two-digit hexadecimal number to indicate a byte of binary information. The 8088, an 8-bit microprocessor, reads data 8 bits at a time. The microprocessor has 8 pins that are used for data; 8 bits of binary data can have 256 different values.

Memory Addresses

The 8088's address range, the number of different memory locations the microprocessor can reach, is 1M. A 5-digit hexadecimal number and a 20-digit binary number can represent 1M of memory. FFFFFH is 1,048,575D and 11111111111111111111_2. You can place 1,048,576 different numbers referring to different addresses as electrical signals on the pins of the 8088 chip; 20 pins on the 8088 are used for generating an address used to read data from or write data to memory.

The address range for the 8088 is considered linear because the first address is number 0, the next is 1, and so on, up to 1M. The range of the 1M address space, however, is split into 16 64K segments. The first segment is called segment 0000H, and the next segment is called 1000H, up to F000H. When you see memory maps, you usually see the segment addresses listed at the side. To use memory addresses, programmers indicate a current segment and an offset into that segment instead of giving a single address between 0 and 1M.

DOS and programs use the lower 640K of memory. The programs control the absolute position of programs or data in this area. The devices located above 640K, however, are located in fixed positions. The segment A000H is reserved for the video adapter, for example, and the expanded memory page frame frequently is placed in segment E000H.

The 8088 assumes that all addresses are within the current segment until you say to change segments. The offset is an address relative to the first address of the segment. For example, the program may refer to an offset address of F600H within segment A000H, an absolute address of AF600H. With this method, the microprocessor usually has to deal with only a 16-bit address, which is the offset (in this case, F600H), because the 8088 assumes that the segment is unchanged. Only when you change the current segment does the microprocessor have to consider more bits.

People refer to memory addresses in several ways. The full absolute address may be given in a five-digit hexadecimal number. More commonly, however, because of the way the 8088 is programmed, addresses are referred to as segment and offsets, often written with a colon separating the segment and address. In the previous example, absolute address AF600H turns out as A000:F600.

You may have trouble remembering that 1M isn't exactly a million bytes and 1K isn't exactly a thousand bytes. Programmers—and now users—use these terms to reduce the need to convert numbers between binary or hexadecimal and decimal. As you become familiar with segment addresses, you begin to appreciate that if you refer to a segment of A000H or higher, you are above 640K. Segments lower than A000H are in low DOS memory. Remembering that address number 655,360 is the border between low DOS memory and high DOS memory is not as intuitive as 640K.

Index

386/MultiWare, 399
386 memory managers, 80, 84-85
    using with shadow RAM, 81
    adding parameters, 362-365
386-to-the-MAX, 285, 346-347
    386 LOAD utility, 353-355
    installing, 348-351
386 enhanced mode, 394
386LOAD, 315, 353, 355

APPEND command, 192
arithmetic logic unit, 16
asynchronous, 15
AutoCAD, 301
AutoCAD/386, 18, 382
AUTOEXEC.BAT file, 48
    alterations by 386-to-the-MAX installation, 348-350
    copying to printer, 194
    rearranging, 322-323
    rearranging for ALL CHARGECARD, 337-339
automatic installation program, 348-351
average seek time, 104

A

A. I. Architects, 385
A20 handler identifiers, 342
Above Board Plus, 316
accelerator boards, 305-306, 385-386
active program, 389
Adaptec disk controller, 127
adapter board, 27
adapters, 61
address bus, 24
address lines, 69-70
addressable memory, 70
alignment disks, 105
ALL CARD, 331-332
All Charge 386, 362-365
ALL CHARGECARD, 331-339
ALLOAD, 367-368
analog, 101

B

background program, 389
BACKUP command, 294
bad sectors, 158-159
base 2, 10, and 16, 416
base memory, 20, 346
batch files, 43
    backing up, 298
    including PATH statements, 198-199
    removing fragmentation, 300
    starting applications programs, 198-199

benchmarks, 153-155, 158
Bernoulli box, 208
binary, 416
    values, 20
BIOS (basic input/output
    system), 22, 38, 313
    driver programs, 99
    function, 40-41, 60, 379
    using in DOS, 37
BIU, 16-18
block device drivers, 62-63
boot disk, 47-48
boot sector, 47
booting, 43-44
    loading system files, 47-48
BRIDGE.DRV device driver, 68
buffers, 220-230
BUFFERS directive, 220
BUFFERS settings, 76
bus widths, 27

C

cache controllers, 75, 78-79
caches, 230-232
    changing, 235-237
    improving memory access
        performance, 284-285
CAD programs
    improving with RAM disk, 81
    increasing environment space, 196
CEMM, 80
central processing unit, see CPU
character device drivers, 62-63
CHKDSK command, 139-143
clusters, 121
    allocating, 122-123, 129-131
    contiguous, 123
    definition, 297
    free, 129-130
    linking, 128-130
    logic of, 122
    using with partitions, 297
color graphics adapter (CGA), 28, 61
COMMAND command, 200
command
    interpreters, 379-381
    processors, 196-197, 200
COMMAND.COM
    command interpreter, 38, 379-381

program, 39-42, 48, 51
utility, 88
commands
    APPEND, 192
    BACKUP, 294
    available with
        DOS 3.0, 404
        DOS 3.1, 405
        DOS 3.2, 406
        DOS 3.3, 407
        DOS 4.0, 409
        DOS 5.0, 412
    changes in
        DOS 3.0, 404
        DOS 3.1, 405
        DOS 3.2, 406-407
        DOS 3.3, 408
        DOS 4.0, 410-411
        DOS 5.0, 412
    CHKDSK, 139-143
    COMMAND, 200
    DISKCOPY, 209
    DOS COPY, 50
    DOS MODE, 55
    DOS PRINT, 54
    DOS Shell, 196
    enhancing, 380
    external, 41
        replacing, 380
    FASTOPEN, 226-230
    FDISK, 118-119, 172-174
    FORMAT, 177-178
        improving, 380
    internal, 38
    LABEL, 292
    MEM, 48-49
    MKDIR (Make Directory), 133
    PATH, 192-195
    PROMPT, 192
    RMDIR (Remove Directory), 133
    SET, 192-194
    SUBST, 302-303
        organizing files, 291
COMPAQ, 28, 44
compressing files, 146-151
computer-aided design (CAD), 28
computers
    bus widths for, 27
    getting to know system, 81-82
    improving performance, 303-307
    major elements of system, 81-82
    maximizing resources, 281
    modifying with installation
        program, 358-360
    removing cover, 82-83
    testing various parts, 44

Index

Concurrent DOS 386, 390, 397-398
CONFIG.SYS file, 47, 48, 53, 88
   adding LASTDRIVE directives, 302
   alterations by 386-to-the-MAX
      installation, 348-350
   increasing environment size, 196
   new features with
      DOS 3.0, 403
      DOS 3.2, 406
      DOS 3.3, 407
      DOS 4.0, 409
      DOS 5.0, 411-412
   rearranging, 322-324
      for ALL CHARGECARD, 337-339
   using device drivers, 250
configuration program, 361-362
contiguous memory, 311
control bus, 24
Control Room, 83-89
   versus System Sleuth, 90
controllers, 61
   Adaptec disk, 127
   cache, 75, 78-79
conventional memory, *see also* low DOS
   memory, 70, 346
cooperative multitasking program,
   388-389
CPU, 12
   relation to memory, 20
   servicing outside events, 15
   transferring data from disk to,
      200-201
Cursor Speed feature, 198
cylinder, 103
Cyrix, 305

decimal, 416
defaults, buffers, 221
defragmenting files, 139, 145-153
Dell 310, 63
DESQview, 196, 390-392
device drivers, 48, 53-54, 250
   adding, 53-54
   adjusting, 89
   altering, 82
   block, 62-63
   BRIDGE.DRV, 68
   changing, 53-54
   character, 62-63
   disk, 61-63
   disk cache, 76-78
   display, 67
   function, 61-62
   installable, 53, 64-68
   loading into high DOS memory, 375
   making hardware modular, 63
   moving into high memory, 357
   options, 372-374
   pointing, 68
   RAMDRIVE, 63
   removing, 67
   resident, 53, 64-65
   REXX.SYS, 288
   XEMM.SYS, 288
device handler, 54
DEVICEHIGH, 375
diagnostic programs, 83
directives
   BUFFER, 220
   BUFFER (DOS 4.0), 224
   BUFFER (DOS5.0), 225-230
   changes in
      DOS 3.2, 406-407
      DOS 3.3, 408
      DOS 4.0, 410-411
directories, 127-128
   accomodating large directories,
      131-133
   analyzing sequence, 194
   assigning drive letters, 302
   DOS, 128
   hierarchical, 132
   locating name files, 128
   master, *see also* root, 133
   misspelling directory names, 195
   organizing, 300-301
   ranking, 195
   rearranging, 152
   root, 47-48, 133
   temporary files, 300
disk buffers, 77, 221-230

D

data
   organizing in files, 149-151
   separating from programs, 298-299
   storing digitally, 101
data bus, 24
database programs
   improving with disk caches, 81
   searching for nonexecutable files, 192
dBASE, 296
dBASE III Plus, 296
/DEBUG parameter, 48
DEBUG program, 159-164

disk caches, 76-78
   improving database programs, 81
   look-ahead capabilities, 78
   programs, 230-237, 299
      Control Room, 241-245
      IBMCACHE.SYS file, 232-237
      SmartDrive, 238-239
      Super PC-Kwik, 241-245
   versus cache controller, 79
disk caching software, 75-77
disk drive controller, 22, 61, 201-202
   Adaptec, 127
disk device driver, 63
disk drives, 98
   fixed, *see also* fixed disk, 99
   heads, 101-105
   measuring performance, 104
   understanding, 99
disk maintenance, 199
disk operating system, *see* DOS
disk partition table, 116-119
DISKCOPY command, 209
disks
   adding tracks, 106-107
   alignment, 105
   backing up, 295-296
   boot, 47-48
   cache programs, 230-232
   caches, 231-237
   cylinders, 103
   data transfer rate, 115-116
   defragmenting, 139, 300
   device driver, 61
   double-sided, double-density, 111
   fixed, *see also* hard, 99
   floppy, 100-101
      aligning, 105
      backing up, 295-296
      labeling, 291-292
      organizing, 291-292
      reducing disk swapping, 292-294
      variations between, 106-107
   formatting, 108-109, 294
   hard, 99
      alternative, 205-210
      formats, 113
      limiting structure, 301
      most common, 201
      organizing directory
        structure, 300-301
      partitions, 296
      standard interface, 202-203
      understanding capacity, 113-114

IDE, 203
magnetic medium, 98
managing, 42
movement, 102
obtaining more storage capacity,
   106-107
optimizing use of, 192
performances by type, 204
RAM, 67, 209-216
   adding, 67
   creating, 210
   improving CAD program's
      performance, 81
   versus disk caches, 78
raw capacity, 112
reading data in multiple
   rotations, 115-116
reducing disk swapping, 292-294
removable media, 208-209
removing files from, 123
replicating, 215
reserving disk space, 294
sectors, 108-109
single-sided, double-density, 110
subsections, 117-118
susbtituting RAM, 201
tracks, 102
transferring data to CPU, 200-201
types, 202
typical cluster sizes, 121
usable capacity, 112
using with correct disk
   controller, 202
weakening magnetic imprint, 98
display adapters, 61
   resolution, colors, 29
display screen, 27-28
DOS, 36
   addressing memory, 69
   batch files, 43
   COMMAND.COM, 39-40
   commands, enhancing, 380
   creating partial backup batch
      files, 298
   disk management, 42
   editing keys, 31
   file management, 42-43
   files system, 134-136
   four main components, 38-39
   functional sections, 379
   key combinations, 33
   loading
      device drivers into high
        memory, 375

Index

D (continued)

into memory, 48-51
    part into high DOS memory, 343
    programs into high memory, 376
    using /P switch, 197
memory, 282
moving into high memory, 361-362
quick reference to different versions of, 38
redirecting input/output, 43
regaining, 364-368
rules to improving performance, 80-81
running applications programs, 43
Shell program, 43
using BIOS, 36-38, 41
DOS 3.0, 403-405
DOS 3.1, 197, 405
DOS 3.2, 197, 406-407
DOS 3.3, 297, 407
    beginning environment size, 197
    changed commands/directives, 408
    CONFIG.SYS features available, 407
    FDISK command, 174-177
DOS 3.31, 297-298
DOS 4.0, 297-298, 409
    beginning environment size, 197
    BUFFERS directive, 224
    changed commands/directives, 410-411
    CONFIG.SYS features, 409
    FDISK command, 174-177
DOS 5.0, 297
    beginning environment size, 197
    BUFFERS directive, 225-230
    changes in features, 413
    CONFIG.SYS features, 411-412
    FDISK command, 176
    function keys, 32
    new commands, 412
DOS COPY command, 50
DOS extenders, 382-386
DOS MODE command, 55
DOS PRINT command, 54
DOS Shell command, 196
double-density formats, 110-111
double-sided drives, 101
DRAM (dynamic RAM), 79, 283
driver installation, 64
drives
    disk, 101
    ESDI, 203
    floppy disk, 109, 125-127
    hard disk, 109, 125-127
    logical, 118-119
    physical, 119
    SCSI, 204
    ST-506, 202-203
    virtual, 67
Dynamic RAM, *see* DRAM

E

encoding systems, 202
enhanced expanded memory specification (EEMS), 74
enhanced graphics adapter (EGA), 21, 28, 61
Enhanced Keyboard, 29
environment, 42
    avoiding extending, 198
    default size, 197
    displaying current variables, 192
    increasing size, 196
    regulating size, 196-197
    saving old PATH settings, 200
    string, 42
ESDI (Enhanced Standard Device Interface) drive, 203
Ever for Excellence, 316
expanded memory, 69, 72-74, 85
    accessing, 67
    emulating, 288-289
    managing, 346
    understanding, 71-72
    using RAM disk, 214-216
    versus disk caches, 77
expanded memory boards, 286-287, 315-317
expanded memory emulator, 371-374
expanded memory specification (EMS), 74, 85
expansion bus, 24-26, 200-202
extended memory, 69-71, 85, 235, 311
    accessing with RAMDRIVE, 211
    converting to expanded memory, 287, 371-374
    emulating expanded memory, 288
    making full use of, 382
    manager, 211
    using RAM disk, 214-216
extended memory boards, 286-287

extended memory managers, 339-342
Extended Memory Specification
  (XMS), 287
extended partition, 119
extended-memory addresses, 70
external commands, 41
  replacing, 380

F

/F switch, 141
FASTOPEN command, 226-230
file allocation table (FAT), 120-130, 313
FDISK command, 118-119, 172-177
file allocation table, *see* FAT
file manager, 32
file system, 134-136
files
  accessing, 298-299
  aiding in reduction of disk
    swapping, 292
  AUTOEXEC.BAT, 48
    copying to printer, 194
    rearranging, 322-324, 337-339
  batch, 43
    backing up, 298
    including PATH statements,
      198-199
    removing fragmentation, 300
    starting applications
      programs, 198-199
  compressing, 146-151
  CONFIG.SYS, 47-48, 53
    increasing environment size, 196
    rearranging, 322-324, 337-339
  creating subdirectories, 134
  defragmenting, 105, 146-153
  erasing, 123
  executable, 192-193
  fragmentation, 124, 138-139, 144-153
  IBMCACHE.SYS, 232-237
  improving access time, 298-299
  IO.SYS, 64
  locating name files, 128
  managing, 42
    using FAT, 131
  noncontiguous, 144-145
  nonexecutable, 192
  organizing, 291
    data, 149-151
  repositioning, 152-153
  searching, 193-194
  SMARTDRV.SYS, 238-239
  storing, 123-124
  system, 38, 379
    function, 40
    hidden, 64
    IBMDOS, 50
    loading, 47-48
  temporary, 215
  truncated, 141
FILES settings, 76
firmware, 21
fixed disk, *see also* hard disk, 99
flags, 17
FLASH EMS, 288
floppy disks/drives, 100-101
  aligning, 105
  backing up, 295-296
  formats, 110-112
  labeling, 291-292
  locating clusters of data, 125-127
  organizing, 291-292
  reducing disk swapping, 292-294
  versus hard disks/drives, 109
  variations between, 106-107
flushing buffers, 221-222
FONTRES, 348
FONTSPACE, 68, 195, 363
footprint, definition, 205
foreground program, 389
FORMAT command, 177-178
  improving, 380
formats, 110-114
formatters, low-level, 159-164
formatting, 108-109
  determining disk capacity, 112
  disks, 294
  hard disks, 114, 157-164, 177-178
  low-level, 159-164
    with Disk Manager, 164-172
    with ROM-based formatter,
      159-164
fragmentation
  isolating, 299
  locating with CHKDSK
    command, 144-145
  lost clusters, 139
  reducing, 298
  removing, 138-139
    using batch files, 300
  repairing
    with PC Tool's Compress
      program,
      146-151
    with third-party products, 145-146

free base memory, 313
free cluster, 129-130
function keys (DOS 5 Shell), 32

G-H

Gateway 2000, 40, 44
gigabytes, 70
Hands on Excellence, 316
hard disks, 99
   alternative, 205-210
   bad sectors, 158-159
   drives
      formats, 113-114
         locating clusters of data, 125-127
         versus floppy disks/drives, 109
   formats, 113-114, 157-172, 177-178
   improving performance, 156-159
   interleave, 156-159, 179-188
   limiting structure, 301
   low-level formatting, 114, 159-172
   maintenance, 138-151, 163-176, 189-190
   memory, 225-230
   Microscience 120M, 127
   organizing directory structure, 300-301
   partitioning, 172, 296
   platters, 114-116
   sectors, 114-116
   standard interface, 202-203
   tracks, 114-116
   understanding capacity, 113-114
Hardcard, 205-207
Hardcard II benchmark, 153, 207
hardware, 12
   analyzing, 83
   cache controller, 284-285
   impact on partition sizes, 299-300
   platforms, 116
   requirements, 157
   understanding, 82
heads, 103
   magnetic, 106
   moving from one cylinder to another, 104-105
   read/write, 101
   reversing current, 107
Hercules monographics controller (HGC), 28

hexadecimal, 50, 416
high DOS memory, 20
   loading
      part of DOS into, 343
      programs into, 376
   moving, 357
      DOS into, 361-362
      regaining, 364
HIMEM.SYS extended memory manager, 211, 339-342
Hotline, 195, 348, 363
HummingBoard, 385

I

I/O memory, 21
IBM Personal Computer AT, 18
IBM Personal Computer PS/2 Model 80, 63
IBM Personal System/2 Display Adapter, 28
IBM Token Ring, 406
IBMBIO.COM system, 40
IBMCACHE.SYS file, 76, 232-237
IBMDOS.COM, 40, 60
IDE (intelligent drive electronics) disk, 203
IIT, 305
initializing, 44
input, redirecting, 43
input/output system, 63
INSET.EXE utility, 88
installable device drivers, 53, 64-68
installation program, 358-360
installed expansion boards, 83
installing
   ALL CHARGECARD, 333
   Control Room disk-cache program, 241-245
   IBMCACHE.SYS file, 232-237
   386-to-the-MAX, 348-351
   QEMM, 358-360
   RAMDRIVE, 210
   SMARTDRV.SYS file, 238-239
   Super PC-Kwik, 241-245
instruction queue, 16-17
Intel 80286 microprocessor, 18
Intel 80386 microprocessor, 19
Intel 80386SX microprocessor, 18

Intel 80387 Numeric Data Processor (NDP), 88
Intel 80486 microprocessor, 19
Intel 8086 microprocessor, 17
Intel 8088 microprocessor, 17
Intel microprocessor, 16
Intel systems, 23
interfaces, 202-203
interfacing methods, 202-204
interleave, 115-116, 156-159, 179-188
internal commands, 38
international character set, 67
invalid drives, 195
IO.SYS system file, 40, 64

loading
    part of DOS into high DOS memory, 343
    system files, 47-48
local area network (LAN), 400
local memory, 21
logical disk drive, 118-119
    organizing files under one drive, 298-299
logical sectors, 126
look-ahead buffers, 224
lost clusters, 139
    locating with CHKDSK, 142-143
Lotus 1-2-3, 196
low DOS memory, 312
    regaining, 235, 314, 346, 366-368
        using ALL CHARGECARD, 334-337
        using MOVE'EM, 317-318
        using QRAM, 327-331
    releasing, 354
low-level formatting, 114, 159-172

J-K

J.P. Software, 381
Javelin, 289
kernels, 60-65
keyboards, 29-33
keys
    DOS combinations, 33
    DOS editing, 31
    DOS.5 Shell function keys, 32
    scan codes, 32-33
    special, 30-31

L

LABEL command, 292
language compiler, 383
LaserJet, 195
latency time, 104
libraries, 384
LIM (Lotus-Intel-Microsoft) 3.2, 315-317
LIM (Lotus-Intel-Microsoft) 4.0, 315-317, 326
LIM-ulators, 288-289
link status entry, 128-130
loader programs, 347
    ALLOAD, 365-368
LOADHI, 315, 357, 376

M

machine codes, 14
magnetic energy pulses, 107
magnetic fields
    applying, 98
    increasing in tracks, 107
    material composition, 106
magnetization, 114
main memory, 84
maintenance, 159-190
    disks, 199
    routine, 138-151
master directory, *see* root directory
math coprocessors, 16-17, 19, 88-89, 304-305
Matrox, 301
max parameter, 211
MAXIMIZE installation program, 356
megabytes, 69-70
    addressing, 20
MEM program, 48-49, 51, 83
memory, 220-239
    accessable by microprocessors, 417-418
    accessing more for programs, 69
    adding, 285-286

addressable, 69-70
addresses, 20, 418
allocating, 290
areas, 88
base, 20, 346
boards, 76
conventional, *see also* low
  DOS, 70, 346
dedicated memory slots, 285-286
examining DOS's position during
  loading,
  48-51
expanded, 69, 72-74, 85, 282-286
  accessing, 67
  emulating, 288-289
  managing, 346
  understanding, 71-72
  using RAM disk, 214-216
  versus disk caches, 77
extended, 69-71, 85, 235, 311
  accessing with RAMDRIVE, 211
  converting to expanded
    memory, 287, 371-374
  emulating expanded memory, 288
  making full use of, 382
  manager, 211
  managing, 346
  understanding, 71
  using RAM disk, 214-216
free base, 313
functions, 20-21
high DOS, 20
  loading device drivers into, 375
  loading part of DOS into, 343
  moving device drivers into, 357
  moving DOS into, 361-362
  moving programs into, 357
  regaining, 364
I/O, 21
improving access time using
  caches, 284-285
in relation to programs, 69
local, 21
low DOS, 235, 312, 346
  regaining DOS low memory, 314,
    366-368
  regaining using ALL
    CHARGECARD,
    334-337
  regaining using MOVE'EM, 317-
    318
  regaining using QRAM, 327-331
  releasing, 354
main, 84

mapping, 311
maximizing use, 351-353
pricing various types, 284
RAM, 20-22
  adding, 282-283
  disadvantages, 76
  loading, 44
  setting aside portions, 76-78
range of positions, 20
ROM, 21-22, 76
shadowing ROM with RAM, 79
screens, 86-88
size parameter, 371
static column, 284
status panel, 86-87
storing loaded program values, 42
upgrading DOS memory, 282
user, 20
  recognizing, 313
using expansion boards, 285
using wisely, 324-326
variations in accessing time, 21
video, 88
memory manager programs, 19, 314, 346
  386LOAD, 315
  LOADHI, 315
  MOVE'EM, 310, 314-318
  QRAM, 310, 326-331
memory-resident programs, 54-57
menuing program, 280
menus, 280
MFM (modified frequency
  modulation), 202
microprocessors, 14-15
  80286, 311
  8088, 311
  accessable memory locations,
    417-418
  chip, 12
  function, 22-23
  Intel, 16, 303
  Intel 80286, 18
  Intel 80386, 19
  Intel 80386SX, 18
  Intel 80486, 19
  Intel 8086, 17
  Intel 8088, 17
  Intel systems versus AT systems, 23
  replacing, 303-304
  using in PC, 16-17
  V20, V30, 303
  versus multitasking
    environments, 390
Microscience 120M hard disk, 127

Microsoft Corporation, 36
Microsoft Windows, 392-394
Microsoft Windows/286, 289
Microsoft Windows/386, 386
Mirror (PC Tools), 313, 348
mirroring program, 209
MKDIR (Make Directory) command, 133
modes
    386 enhanced, 394
    operating, 346
    protected, 18-19, 71, 311, 346-347
    real, 18-19, 71, 311, 346
    switching between protected and
        real, 385
    text, 28
    virtual 8086, 19, 315
monochrome display adapter (MDA), 61
Mouse Systems, 348, 363
MOVE'EM, 310, 314-322, 347
MSDOS.SYS system file, 40, 60
multicolor graphics array (MCGA), 28
multitasking
    environments, 390-392
    multiuser environment, 395-399
    programs, 387-394

N-O

node, 400
noncontiguous files, 144-145
nonexecutable files, 192
Norton Utilities, 121, 145-146
    Speed Disk utility program, 151-153
Novell NetWare, 300
numbering system, 416-417
operating modes, 346
operating systems, 35-36, 379
    accessing disk partition table, 117-118
    cylinder control, 117-118
    quick reference to different versions
        of DOS, 38
    written specifically for Intel 80486
        microprocessors, 20
operations (POST), 44-47
OPTIMIZE program, 361-362
output, redirecting, 43
overlays, 296
overwriting, 98

P

Paradox/386, 18, 382
parameters
    /DEBUG, 48
    adding, 362-365
    for using RAMDRIVE.SYS, 210
    max, 211
    memory size, 371
    %PATH%, 199-200
    replaceable, 199
    ROM, 368-371
partitions, 172, 296-300
passwords, 398
PATH
    command, 192-195
    names, 301-303
    parameters, 199-200
    settings, 195-200
    statements, 198-199
PC Tools, 195
PC Tools Deluxe, 145-146
PC Tools Desktop Manager, 55
PC-Cache, 324
PC-MOS, 398-390, 399
peripheral
    definition, 12
    devices, 23
    hardware, 61-62
Phar Lap Software Inc., 386
physical drives, 119
pixels, 61
platters, 99
    multiple, 103, 109
    on hard disks, 114-116
pointing device drivers, 68
POST operation, 44-47
preemptive multitasking program, 387-388
primary partition, 119
Printer Manager program, 398
Professional Oracle, 382
program information file (PIF), 393
programs
    accessing
        math coprocessor, 304
        more memory, 69
    active, 389
    ALLOAD, 367-368
    automatic installation, 348-351
    background, 389

Index 429

CAD
   improving with RAM disk, 81
   increasing environment space, 196
COMMAND.COM, 51
compiling text, 383
Concurrent DOS 386, 397-398
configuration, 361-362
cooperative multitasking, 388-389
creating, 383-384
databases
   improving with disk caches, 81
   searching for nonexecutable files, 192
DEBUG, 159-164
DESQview, 196
DEVICEHIGH, 375
diagnostic, 83
disk-caching, 299
DOS Shell, 43
executing, 41-42
foreground, 389
giving information noninteractively, 192
IBMCACHE.SYS, 76
in relation to memory, 69
installation, 356-360
libraries, 384
linking compiled modules, 383
loader, 347
   ALLOAD, 365-368
LOADHIGH, 376
loading, 41-42
   into high DOS memory, 376
measuring size, 318-322
MEM, 51, 83
memory
   manager, 19, 346
   moving into high memory, 357
   resident, 54-57
menuing, 280
MIRROR, 348
mirroring, 209
multitasking, 387-394
386/MultiWare, 399
OPTIMIZE, 361-362
PC Tools Desktop Manager, 55
PC-MOS (The Software Link), 398-399
planning partition usage, 297
preemptive multitasking, 387-388
Printer Manager, 398
removing unnecessary programs, 313
Rolodex, 363
running multiple, 387-394

Scan Gallery, 393
separating from data, 298-299
Setup, 45
Shell, 32
Sidekick, 56
SMARTDRV.SYS, 76
system IBMBIO, 50
terminate-and-stay-resident (TSR), 54-57, 68
upgrading, 301
using partitions, 296
utilities, 83
   checking interleave factor, 116
   function, 379
   showing current use of computer's resources, 364
   SpinRite, 300
   VM/386, 395-396
   Windows, 196
PROMPT command, 192
protected mode, 18-19, 71, 311, 346-347

Q

QEMM, 19, 80, 346, 357-360
QNX operating system, 118
QRAM, 287, 310, 314, 326-327, 347
quad format, 111
QuadMaster IV, 316
Quarterdeck Office System, 357, 386
QWERTY layout, 29

R

RAM, 20-22, 76
   300 Deluxe (Everex), 316-317
   adding parameters, 364
   avoiding overusage, 198
   buffers, 220
   disk, 67, 209-210
      improving CAD program performance, 81
      memory, 212-216
      versus disk caches, 78

loading, 44
memory, 282-283
remapping, 368-371
setting amount used for environment via /E:size, 197
setting aside portions, 76-78
shadow RAM, 79
types, 283
using as disk substitute, 201
versus disk caches, 231-232
RAMDRIVE, 210-212
device driver, 63
RAMDRIVE.SYS, 210
random-access memory, *see* RAM
Rational Systems Inc., 386
raw capacity, 112
read errors, 98
misaligned heads, 105
read-only memory, *see* ROM
read/write heads, 101
real mode, 18-19, 71, 311, 346
registers, 16-19
removable media disks, 208-209
replaceable parameters, 199
resident device drivers, 53, 64-65
resolution, 28-29
REXX.SYS device driver, 288
RLL (run-length limited), 202
RMDIR (Remove Directory) command, 133
Rolodex program, 363
ROM, 21-22
chip, 44
disadvantages, 76
parameter, 368-371
remapping, 368-371
shadowing with RAM, 79
ROM-based formatters, 159-164
root directory, 47-48, 133
routine maintenance, 138-190

S

saving
hard disk versus floppy disk, 295
PATH settings, 199-200
scan code, 32
Scan Gallery program, 393
ScanJet Plus scanner, 393
SCSI drive, 204
Seagate Technologies, 298
searching files, 193-194
secondary cache, 224
sector translation, 127
sectors, 108-109
allocation log, 120-121
forming clusters, 121
in relation to data density, 109
on hard disks, 114-116
seek time, 104-105
segment register, 18
SET command, 192-194
settings
BUFFERS, 76
FILES, 76
PATH, 195-200
settling time, 104
Setup program, 45
shadow RAM, 79-81
Shell program, 32, 43
SideKick, 56, 312
SIMMs (single in-line memory modules), 282
single-sided, double-density disks, 110
SmartDrive disk-cache program, 238-239
SMARTDRV.SYS, 76, 238-239
Softbytes (Veritech), 288
software, 12
installing, 83
disk caching, 75-77
two main classifications, 35
SpinRite, 105, 300
SpinRite II, 179-188
SRAM (static RAM), 283
ST-412 interface, 203
ST-506 drive, 202-203
stack pointer, 17
standard partition, *see* primary partition
static column memory, 284
strings, 192
subdirectories, 133-134
using in PATH, 193
SUBST command, 302-303
organizing files, 291
summary screen, 86
Super PC-Kwik, 77, 241-245
Sysgen, 68
system
clock, 14-15
files, 38, 379
function, 40
hidden, 64
IBMDOS, 50
loading, 47-48

Index

program (IBMBIO), 50
ROM, 22
System Sleuth, 83, 89-92
system software, 12
systems
  basic input/output, *see* BIOS
  computer, getting to know, 81-82
  encoding, 202
  execution-control, 16
  file, 134-136
  input/output, 63
  numbering, 416-417
  operating, 35-38
    cylinder control, 117-118
    QNX, 118
    UNIX, 53

INSET.EXE, 88
Task Swapper, 400
UnErase, 138
utility programs, 83
  checking interleave factor, 116
  function, 379
  Norton Utilities' Speed Disk, 151-153
  showing current use of computer's resources, 364
  SpinRite, 179-188, 300

V

VersaCAD/386, 382
video
  adapters, 28-29
  memory, 88
  subsystem, 27-28
Video Graphics Array (VGA), 28, 61
virtual 8086 mode, 19, 315
Virtual Control Program Interface (VCPI), 386
virtual disk, *see* RAM disk
virtual drives, 67
VM/386, 390, 395-396

T

Task Swapper utility, 400
temporary files, 215
terminate-and-stay-resident programs, *see* TSR
text mode, 28
third-party programs, 241-245
time slice, 387
tracks, 102-109
  on hard disks, 114-116
TSR programs, 54-57, 68, 222, 310
Turbo EMS, 288
Turbo Pascal, 384

W-Z

Weitek, 305
  3167, 88
  4167, 88
  math coprocessor, 372
windows, 390-394
Windows program, 196
WordPerfect, 32, 195-196, 301
XEMM.SYS device driver, 288

U

UnErase undelete utility, 138
UNIX operating system, 53
usable capacity, 112
user memory, 20, 313
utilities
  386LOAD, 353-355
  COMMAND.COM, 88
  CONFIG.SYS, 88
  DOS, 38, 41
  DOS 3.3, 88

Free Catalog!

Mail us this registration form today, and we'll send you a free catalog featuring Que's complete line of best-selling books.

Name of Book _____

Name _____

Title _____

Phone ( ) _____

Company _____

Address _____

City _____

State _____ ZIP _____

Please check the appropriate answers:

1. Where did you buy your Que book?
   - [ ] Bookstore (name: _____)
   - [ ] Computer store (name: _____)
   - [ ] Catalog (name: _____)
   - [ ] Direct from Que
   - [ ] Other: _____

2. How many computer books do you buy a year?
   - [ ] 1 or less
   - [ ] 2-5
   - [ ] 6-10
   - [ ] More than 10

3. How many Que books do you own?
   - [ ] 1
   - [ ] 2-5
   - [ ] 6-10
   - [ ] More than 10

4. How long have you been using this software?
   - [ ] Less than 6 months
   - [ ] 6 months to 1 year
   - [ ] 1-3 years
   - [ ] More than 3 years

5. What influenced your purchase of this Que book?
   - [ ] Personal recommendation
   - [ ] Advertisement
   - [ ] In-store display
   - [ ] Price
   - [ ] Que catalog
   - [ ] Que mailing
   - [ ] Que's reputation
   - [ ] Other: _____

6. How would you rate the overall content of the book?
   - [ ] Very good
   - [ ] Good
   - [ ] Satisfactory
   - [ ] Poor

7. What do you like *best* about this Que book?
   _____
   _____

8. What do you like *least* about this Que book?
   _____
   _____

9. Did you buy this book with your personal funds?
   - [ ] Yes   - [ ] No

10. Please feel free to list any other comments you may have about this Que book.
    _____
    _____
    _____

— Que —

Order Your Que Books Today!

Name _____

Title _____

Company _____

City _____

State _____ ZIP _____

Phone No. ( ) _____

Method of Payment:

Check [ ]   (Please enclose in envelope.)

Charge My: VISA [ ]   MasterCard [ ]

American Express [ ]

Charge # _____

Expiration Date _____

Order No.	Title	Qty.	Price	Total

You can **FAX** your order to **1-317-573-2583**. Or call **1-800-428-5331**, ext. **ORDR** to order direct.
Please add $2.50 per title for shipping and handling.

Subtotal _____
Shipping & Handling _____
Total _____

— Que —

NO POSTAGE
NECESSARY
IF MAILED
IN THE
UNITED STATES

BUSINESS REPLY MAIL
First Class Permit No. 9918   Indianapolis, IN

Postage will be paid by addressee

que®

11711 N. College
Carmel, IN 46032

NO POSTAGE
NECESSARY
IF MAILED
IN THE
UNITED STATES

BUSINESS REPLY MAIL
First Class Permit No. 9918   Indianapolis, IN

Postage will be paid by addressee

que®

11711 N. College
Carmel, IN 46032